JN
5278
R8

Rubinstein   66-9637
Government of Florence
under the Medici (1434-
1494)

Date Due JUL 2000

OCT 27 '67			
NOV 10 '67			JUN 2004
NOV 24 '67		JUN 09	
		JUL X X 2015	

ⓑⓓ PRINTED IN U.S.A.

OXFORD–WARBURG STUDIES

General Editors

T. S. R. BOASE *and* G. BING

OXFORD–WARBURG STUDIES

———

THE CONFLICT BETWEEN PAGANISM AND
CHRISTIANITY IN THE FOURTH CENTURY
Essays edited by ARNALDO MOMIGLIANO. 1963

JACOPO DELLA QUERCIA'S FONTE GAIA
By ANNE COFFIN HANSON. 1965

THE SISTINE CHAPEL BEFORE MICHELANGELO
By L. D. ETTLINGER. 1965

THE GOVERNMENT
OF FLORENCE
UNDER THE MEDICI
(1434 TO 1494)

BY

NICOLAI RUBINSTEIN

OXFORD
AT THE CLARENDON PRESS
1966

Oxford University Press, Ely House, London W. 1

GLASGOW NEW YORK TORONTO MELBOURNE WELLINGTON
CAPE TOWN SALISBURY IBADAN NAIROBI LUSAKA ADDIS ABABA
BOMBAY CALCUTTA MADRAS KARACHI LAHORE DACCA
KUALA LUMPUR HONG KONG

PRINTED IN GREAT BRITAIN
AT THE UNIVERSITY PRESS, OXFORD
BY VIVIAN RIDLER
PRINTER TO THE UNIVERSITY

PREFACE

THE political régime which was founded by Cosimo de' Medici and perfected by his grandson Lorenzo differed from the despotic states of fifteenth-century Italy in the preservation of republican institutions. Described as a tyranny by its enemies, its critics had to admit that the Medici acted within the framework of the constitution. Whether or not this framework remained a solid structure, and by what means the Medici adapted it to their purposes, are questions that are essential for an understanding of the nature of the position of the Medici in Florence. Yet no contemporary source describes in detail the methods by which they exercised their authority, nor the ways in which they strengthened it; and no modern study exists to give a satisfactory account of either. Historians of the Medici have gathered their information on this subject primarily from Florentine authors who wrote after the fall of the régime in 1494, and especially from Guicciardini's *Storie fiorentine*. But even in the early sixteenth century, Florentines were no longer fully conversant with the way in which the Medicean system had developed after 1434; and their judgements were liable to be biased for or against it. The rich archive materials preserved at Florence have hardly been tapped by modern historians for a study of Medicean government. Even special studies are few and far between: on the early period there is a review article by Pellegrini; on the period of Lorenzo, Ricchioni's valuable book on *La costituzione politica di Firenze ai tempi di Lorenzo il Magnifico*, published in 1913, which however deals primarily with the major constitutional reform of those years, the creation of the council of Seventy. The present work is an attempt to fill this gap.

One of the difficulties facing the student of Florentine politics in the fifteenth century, and one that has affected all works dealing with the Medici régime, is the absence of a constitutional history of Florence during that period. Once again, the sources for such a history are plentiful, but no systematic attempt has ever been made to use them. The Statutes of 1415 provide an ideal starting point; yet they do not give a full picture of Florentine institutions at the time, and are necessarily silent on their working and their subsequent development. It may be hoped that this work, while being primarily concerned with the use made by the Medici régime of Florentine institutions, will also help to explain their nature and functions.

Among the principal sources for this study have been the registers containing the legislation of the statutory councils (*Provvisioni*), of the special councils of the Medici period (*Balìe*), and of the new council of *Cento*, as well as the records of voting results, which also register bills that were not passed by the councils (*Libri Fabarum*). The minutes of the advisory meetings summoned by the government (*Consulte e Pratiche*) allow us a unique insight into everyday politics, and acquaint us with the views of leading citizens on political facts and problems. The electoral records (*Tratte*) afford ample evidence for the mechanism and results of elections; in particular, the registers of the officials entrusted, under the Medici, with electing the government provide much information on the nature and handling of Medicean controls.

Control of elections was one of the chief instruments of Medici policy. The way in which it was established, developed, and handled is therefore the central subject of our study. We shall try to investigate the technical aspects and the development of this system of control, the problems it presented, and the solutions that were adopted for them; and we shall discuss the reactions this policy produced in a city which had a long tradition of republican government. Such a study of the technical organization of Medicean controls necessarily leads to the wider question of the social structure of the régime. Since the constitutional rights of the Medici were not different from those of other citizens of their class, they had to wield their influence through their friends and supporters. The electoral records throw much light on the composition and development of this group. So, in a different field, do the membership lists of the special councils, or *Balìe*, between 1434 and 1480, which are published in the Appendix, and analysed in the text. At the same time this work is not devised as a social history of the Medici period, nor, for that matter, as a biographical history of the Medici and their followers. On the latter subject, much interesting research remains to be done; as to the former, a better knowledge of the nature and development of the Medicean régime will no doubt contribute to a fuller understanding of the men who headed it, and especially of the two greatest of them, Cosimo and Lorenzo.

While the legislative registers and the minutes of the *Pratiche* are

easily accessible, many of the electoral records had to be identified
and dated before being used. Despite the wealth of material preserved in the electoral section of the Florentine State Archives
(*Archivio delle Tratte*), there are many gaps in it, which are due
either to contemporary destruction or to subsequent losses or dis-
persion of records which were meant to be secret, and which often
did not possess any permanent administrative interest. This will
necessarily render some of our results approximate or tentative;
however, our documentation is rich enough for this not to de-
tract from them substantially. Among the writings of contemporary historians and diarists, *Prioristi*, that is lists of Signorie with
marginal accounts of events which took place during their two-
monthly terms of office, have provided valuable information.
Foremost among these are the *Prioristi* of Francesco di Tommaso
Giovanni, Filippo and Alamanno Rinuccini (their so-called *Ricordi
storici*), and Agnolo and Francesco Gaddi. Of sixteenth-century
historians, Francesco Guicciardini's *History of Florence* has been
used occasionally on account of the information its author doubtless derived from his family; however, of greater value to us has
been the remarkable account by his father Piero of the last
electoral scrutiny of the Medici régime, which we publish in the
Appendix. The dispatches of the Milanese orators contain much
information on the political aims and activities of the ruling group
in general, and of the Medici in particular. But while the diarists
take a familiarity with the working of the political system for
granted, the ambassadors do not normally trouble to acquaint their
masters with its intricacies. Italian princes, not unlike later historians, tended to see the Medici as rulers of Florence. Both diarists
and ambassadors do, however, record some of the opposition the
régime encountered; together with the *Consulte e Pratiche* and the
Libri Fabarum, they thus help us to place the development of
the Medici régime into the wider context of Florentine political
traditions and opinions, and to explain why it foundered in 1494.

I should like to express my gratitude to the staff of the Archivio
di Stato and of the Biblioteca Nazionale for their generous co-
operation during the many years I was preparing this book, and
in particular to the Assistant Director of the State Archives,
Dr. Guido Pampaloni. I wish to thank the Central Research Fund
of London University for a travel grant, and Westfield College
for a sabbatical leave which made it possible for me to work in
Florence over a prolonged period. I am deeply grateful to the

Institute for Advanced Study at Princeton for a Temporary
Membership which enabled me to give this work its final shape.
I am indebted to many scholars for advice and help; but I should
like to record my obligation to Professor Felix Gilbert for reading my manuscript and offering valuable suggestions, to Mrs.
Alison Brown for helping me to see the book through the press,
and to my wife for her help and support throughout the prepara-
tion of this work. Finally, I should like to acknowledge my
gratitude to the late Professor Gertrud Bing, whose constant
encouragement and constructive criticism has accompanied the
writing of it until its completion.

N. R.

Westfield College, London
March, 1965

CONTENTS

SELECT BIBLIOGRAPHY

GIOVANNI ANTONELLI, 'La magistratura degli Otto di Guardia a Firenze', *Archivio Storico Italiano*, CXII (1954), pp. 3–39.

ST. ANTONINUS, *Chronica*, Lyons, 1586.

VESPASIANO DA BISTICCI, *Vite di uomini illustri del secolo XV*, ed. Paolo d'Ancona and Erhard Aeschlimann, Milan, 1951.

ALISON M. BROWN, 'The humanist portrait of Cosimo de' Medici, Pater Patriae', *Journal of the Warburg and Courtauld Institutes*, XXIV (1961), pp. 186–221.

DOMENICO BUONINSEGNI, *Storie della città di Firenze dall'anno 1410 al 1460*, Florence, 1637.

BENJAMIN BUSER, *Die Beziehungen der Mediceer zu Frankreich während der Jahre 1434–1494* . . ., Leipzig, 1879.

GIOVANNI CAMBI, *Istorie*, in *Delizie degli eruditi toscani*, ed. Ildefonso di San Luigi, XX–XXIII, Florence, 1785–6.

GIUSEPPE CANESTRINI, *La scienza e l'arte di Stato* . . ., Florence, 1862.

GIOVANNI CAVALCANTI, *Istorie fiorentine*, Florence, 1838–9.

ANGELO FABRONI, *Magni Cosmi Medicei vita*, Pisa, 1789.

—— *Laurentii Medicis Magnifici vita*, Pisa, 1784.

FRANCESCO GUICCIARDINI, *Memorie di famiglia*, in *Scritti autobiografici e rari*, ed. Roberto Palmarocchi, Bari, 1936.

—— *Storie fiorentine dal 1378 al 1509*, ed. Roberto Palmarocchi, Bari, 1931.

CURT S. GUTKIND, *Cosimo de' Medici, Pater Patriae, 1389–1464*, Oxford, 1938.

LUCA LANDUCCI, *Diario fiorentino* . . ., ed. Iodoco del Badia, Florence, 1883.

LOUIS F. MARKS, 'The financial oligarchy in Florence under Lorenzo', in *Italian Renaissance Studies : A tribute to the late Cecilia M. Ady*, ed. Ernest F. Jacob, London, 1960, pp. 123–47.

DOMENICO MARZI, *La cancelleria della repubblica fiorentina*, Rocca S. Casciano, 1910.

ALFREDO MUNICCHI, *La fazione antimedicea detta del Poggio*, Florence, 1911.

ROBERTO PALMAROCCHI, *La politica italiana di Lorenzo de' Medici*, Florence, 1933.

GUIDO PAMPALONI, 'Fermenti di riforme democratiche nella Firenze medicea del Quattrocento', *Archivio Storico Italiano*, CXIX (1961), pp. 11–62. The relevant sections of the *Consulte e Pratiche* ed. ibid., pp. 241–81, and CXX (1962), pp. 521–81.

FRANCESCO CARLO PELLEGRINI, *Sulla repubblica fiorentina al tempo di Cosimo il Vecchio*, Pisa, 1880.

ALFRED VON REUMONT, *Lorenzo de' Medici il Magnifico*, 2nd ed., Leipzig, 1883.

VINCENZO RICCHIONI, *La costituzione politica di Firenze ai tempi di Lorenzo il Magnifico*, Siena, 1913.

ALAMANNO RINUCCINI, *Dialogus de libertate*, ed. Francesco Adorno, *Atti e Memorie dell'Accademia toscana di scienze e lettere La Colombaria*, XXII (1957), pp. 270–303.

FILIPPO DI CINO RINUCCINI, *Ricordi storici dal 1282 al 1460, con la continuazione di Alamanno e Neri suoi figli fino al 1506*, ed. G. Aiazzi, Florence, 1840.

RAYMOND DE ROOVER, *The Rise and Decline of the Medici Bank, 1397–1494*, Cambridge, Massachusetts, 1963.

NICOLAI RUBINSTEIN, 'Politics and constitution in Florence at the end of the fifteenth century', in *Italian Renaissance Studies*, cit., pp. 148–83.

GIOVANNI SORANZO, 'Lorenzo il Magnifico alla morte del padre e il suo primo balzo verso la Signoria', *Archivio Storico Italiano*, CXI (1953), pp. 42–77.

Statuta Populi et Communis Florentiae, 'Friburgi', 1778–83.

ALESSANDRA MACINGHI NEGLI STROZZI, *Lettere di una gentildonna fiorentina del secolo XV ai figliuoli esuli*, ed. Cesare Guasti, Florence, 1877.

Reference has also been made, among other unpublished narrative sources, to the following:

AGNOLO and FRANCESCO GADDI, *Priorista*, Florence, Archivio di Stato, Tratte, 132 *bis*; British Museum, MS. Egerton 3764.

FRANCESCO DI TOMMASO GIOVANNI, *Priorista*, Florence, Biblioteca Nazionale, Magl. XXV. 379.

—— *Ricordanze*, Florence, Archivio di Stato, Carte Strozziane, 2ª serie, XVI *bis*.

Paolo di Matteo Pietrobuoni, *Priorista*, Florence, Biblioteca Nazionale, Conventi soppressi, C.4.895.

ABBREVIATIONS

(Unless otherwise indicated, references to unpublished sources relate to
material preserved in the Archivio di Stato of Florence)

ASM, Pot. est.	Archivio di Stato, Milan, Potenze estere
ASMo	Archivio di Stato, Modena
Bibl. Ambros.	Biblioteca Ambrosiana, Milan
Bibl. Nat., MS. ital.	Bibliothèque Nationale, Paris, Manuscrit italien
Bibl. Naz.	Biblioteca Nazionale, Florence
Carte Strozz.	Carte Strozziane
Cons. e Prat.	Consulte e Pratiche
Med. av. Pr.	Mediceo avanti il Principato
Provv.	Provvisioni, Registri

PART I

Cosimo de' Medici and the Foundations of the Medici Régime

I

THE BEGINNINGS OF ELECTORAL CONTROLS

In September 1433 the conflict between Rinaldo degli Albizzi and Cosimo de' Medici culminated in Cosimo's arrest and banishment. Cosimo having been exiled for ten years,[1] Rinaldo's ascendancy may have seemed firmly restored, but only a year later Cosimo was recalled to Florence, and it was Rinaldo's turn to be exiled from his city. This reversal of the political situation had been made possible by the appointment by lot, as was the custom in Florence, of the Signoria which entered office on 1 September 1434. This Signoria turned out to be in favour of recalling Cosimo; and Rinaldo's unsuccessful attempt to forestall a decision to this effect by seizing its palace only helped to precipitate events. On 28 September the Signoria summoned a general assembly of the citizens (*Parlamento*), and sought and obtained the creation of a special council with full powers (*Balìa*), which lasted until 31 December.[2] It was this council which, on 29 September, recalled Cosimo and his friends from exile,[3] and,

[1] He had been banished, on 11 Sept. 1433, for five years to Padua; on 29 Sept. this sentence had been raised to ten years: Balìe, 24, fols. 10ᵛ–11ʳ, 22ʳ–23ᵛ. On 11 Sept. Cosimo and his family had been deprived of all political rights for ten years, and on the 29th had been declared magnates.

[2] Balìe, 25, fols. 1ʳ–2ʳ. It was to last until 31 Oct., but was given powers to extend its term of office until 31 Dec., which it actually did. On *Balìe*, see below, Chapter 3.

[3] Ibid., fols. 18ᵛ–19ᵛ. All the sentences against Cosimo and his family were quashed, 'inspicientes quod . . . deliberata per illos de balia [of 1433] apparent facta nulla causa preexistente, ut ex eorum lectione constat'.

three days later, banished Rinaldo degli Albizzi and his son Ormanno.[1]

During the weeks following Cosimo's return on the 6th of October, many citizens of the Albizzi party shared the fate of Rinaldo in being exiled from Florence. In November a number of families were deprived by the *Balìa* of political rights. These measures were, in the first place, a reply to those adopted against the Medici a year earlier. However, they soon assumed proportions which were far in excess of any of the political persecutions under the Albizzi régime, including those of 1433. While in September and November of that year eight Medici and two Pucci had been exiled, to be followed, in February 1434, by Agnolo Acciaiuoli,[2] the total number of citizens banished in October and November 1434 was seventy-three.[3] Moreover, while in 1433 only the Medici, and not even all of them, and the family of Antonio Pucci, had been deprived of all political rights, in 1434 a large number of citizens, including the family of Rinaldo degli Albizzi, the Guasconi, and nearly all the Peruzzi, were disqualified for a number of years or permanently.

The contrast reflects a difference in political aim: in 1433 the consolidation of the existing régime; in 1434 the establishment of a new one. Significantly, the disfranchisements of families were decided only after an entirely pro-Medicean Signoria had entered office on 1 November: its predecessors, who had been instrumental in recalling Cosimo, may still have had qualms about so radical an action.

However, there were limits to the utility of repressive measures. On a smaller scale, they had proved of little use to the Albizzi, and there was the danger that too violent a persecution might undermine the popularity of the Medici and their followers. That they were aware of this danger is shown by the advice of the *Pratica*, or advisory commission, summoned by the Signoria on 2 November. 'Lo errore è chiaro che cominciò nel 1433 del

---

[1] Balìe, 25, fol. 21[v] (2 Oct. 1434). They were banished for eight years. On the same day, Ridolfo di Bonifazio Peruzzi was exiled for three years, his sons and his brother Donato being disqualified from civic office for the same period (fol. 22[r–v]).

[2] Balìe, 24, fols. 10[v]–11[r], 22[r]–23[r], 54[v]–55[r] (partly ed. by A. Fabroni, *Magni Cosmi Medicei vita* (Pisa, 1789), ii, pp. 79 ff.). See F. C. Pellegrini, *Sulla repubblica fiorentina al tempo di Cosimo il Vecchio* (Pisa, 1880), pp. 92 ff., and C. S. Gutkind, *Cosimo de' Medici, Pater Patriae, 1389–1464* (Oxford, 1938), pp. 86 ff. For Agnolo, Balìe, 25, fol. 31[r–v].

[3] Otto di Guardia e Balìa, periodo repubblicano, 224, fols. 21[r]–68[r]. This includes twelve citizens *confinati* outside the city. See also Balìe, 25, fols. 21[v]–23[r], 55[r]–56[r], 57[r]–58[v], 60[v]–61[r], 63[v]–65[v]. The list in G. Cavalcanti, *Istorie fiorentine* (Florence, 1838–9), i, pp. 600–3, is not always correct.

mese di septembre', and which had culminated in Rinaldo's conspiracy against the government; since those who took part in it, directly or indirectly, were many, it would be wiser that 'non si vada dietro alla multitudine, che sarebbe troppo lungo, ma puniscasi e capi'.[1] On 3 November the special committee of the *Pratica*, appointed on that day to advise the Signoria on this matter, proposed the disqualification of a number of families and individual citizens, and the *Balìa* passed the proposal on the same day.[2] This, however, appeared insufficient to some exponents of the new régime. In the *Pratica* of 4 November, Lorenzo Ridolfi asked the special committee to examine 'si satis est factum pro firmamento status et tollendis suspicionibus'.[3] Additional proposals, of 5 and 9 November, for disqualifications and banishments were passed by the *Balìa* on the 6th and the 9th,[4] and were followed by further measures of this kind on the 17th.[5] After this date, the *Balìa* passed only one more punitive decree for political offences, when on 26 December it increased Palla Strozzi's term of exile by five years.[6] The *Balìa* ended its session on 31 December, after having delegated further condemnations *pro negotiis status* to the *Capitano di Balìa*,[7] Jacopo de' Lavagnoli. He made use of these powers only in relatively few cases for new banishments; most of his sentences for political reasons concerned citizens who, having violated their conditions of exile, were now declared rebels, among them Rinaldo and Ormanno degli Albizzi.[8] Giovanni degli Ufredini, his successor, was reappointed, with these special powers, until the end of 1437;[9] but for all practical purposes, the political persecutions

---

[1] Consulte e Pratiche, 50, fol. 204ʳ. One of the four spokesmen was Cosimo de' Medici.

[2] Ibid., fol. 204ᵛ: the sons and descendants of Rinaldo Gianfigliazzi, Ridolfo Peruzzi and his sons, Bardo, Simone, and Bernardino de' Bardi and his brothers, and Piero Cavalcanti and his sons and descendants were to be declared magnates, and nearly all the Peruzzi, the Guasconi, the family of Veri Rondinelli, Rinaldo and Ormanno degli Albizzi, and all but two of the Signori of Sept.–Oct. 1433 and their sons were to be deprived of political rights (i.e. *posti a sedere* or *privati degli uffici*). Cf. Balìe, 25, fols. 55ʳ–56ʳ.

[3] Cons. e Prat. cit., fols. 205ʳ–206ʳ.

[4] Ibid., fol. 207ʳ⁻ᵛ. Balìe, 25, fols. 57ʳ–58ᵛ, 60ᵛ–61ʳ, with a few slight alterations; thus Piero Ardinghelli was exiled for three instead of four years.

[5] Balìe, 25, fols. 63ᵛ–65ᵛ.

[6] Ibid., fol. 111ʳ.

[7] Ibid., fol. 127ᵛ (30 Dec.): 'quod condemnationes tam facte quam faciende de cetero per capitaneum balie presentem pro negotiis status valeant et observari debeant tanquam essent facte per baliam presentem'. The Captain of the People had been granted by the *Balìa*, on 29 Sept., special powers (*balìa*) to carry out punitive measures, to last until 31 Dec., which had been extended by five months on 25 Oct. (ibid., fols. 18ʳ⁻ᵛ, 45ʳ).

[8] Otto, 224, fols. 68ᵛ ff.

[9] Atti del Capitano, 3215–81.

were concluded with the decrees of November 1434. Although these persecutions may have gone beyond the original intentions of some members of the new régime, they were evidently meant to be kept within bounds. While a number of families suffered wholesale, in most cases only branches of families, or individual citizens, were victimized. The most striking example of this discrimination between different branches of the same family is presented by the Albizzi. Rinaldo's fate was shared only by his sons and descendants. The rest of the family was not affected by it; indeed, the branch of Luca di Maso degli Albizzi was to occupy an important position in government and administration under the new régime.

The persecution of members of the enemy party was not the only measure in which the new régime followed, and went beyond, the pattern set by the Albizzi in 1433. The Albizzi party had hoped to strengthen their position through electoral reforms, and here too the Medici régime followed suit.

The electoral system, which by that time had been in existence for over 100 years,[1] consisted of successive qualification of candidates and sortition. The *squittino*, or scrutiny, which qualified citizens for specific offices, was to take place, according to the Statutes of 1415, every five years;[2] the final *tratta*, or sortition, from the purses or bags in which the names of the qualified citizens had been placed, occurred whenever an office had to be filled. There were a number of mostly minor officials who were appointed by simple election; but these were the exception to the rule.[3] The candidate whose name had been drawn was appointed to the post in question, unless he was temporarily barred from assuming it by age, tax debts, or disqualification (*divieto*) arising from his having held it recently, from family connexions with office-holders, or from similar causes.[4] By this strict distinction

---

[1] Definitively from 1328 onwards. See Giovanni Villani, *Cronica*, x, 108, ed. I. Moutier (Florence, 1823), v, pp. 145–8; D. Marzi, *La cancelleria della repubblica fiorentina* (Rocca S. Casciano, 1910), pp. 107–9; R. Davidsohn, *Geschichte von Florenz*, iii (Berlin, 1912), p. 863. The law of 8 Dec. 1328 is in *Delizie degli eruditi toscani*, ed. Ildefonso di San Luigi (Florence, 1770–89), xii, pp. 288–305.

[2] *Statuta populi et communis Florentiae . . .*, ii ('Friburgi', 1778), p. 481.

[3] See e.g. ibid. ii, pp. 559–60 ('quod domini cum collegiis possint eligere rationerium sive scribam regulatorum'), 571 ('. . . possunt eligere castellanum in roccha ubi deficit aliquis extrahendus'), 586–7 ('Balia dominorum et collegiorum eligendi offitiales balistariorum'), 649 ('Scribani, provisores seu rationerii cuiuscumque gabellae . . . qui ad dicta offitia per viam electionis deputantur . . .'). The 'foreign' *Podestà* and Captain of the People were, of course, elected, and so were the ambassadors and other diplomatic personnel.

[4] Ibid., pp. 732 ff.; see also pp. 831–4.

and chronological separation of the two electoral stages, the impact of political and economic interests on the actual appointment to office was necessarily reduced, as had been originally the intention, and was limited to the periodical scrutinies. The scrutinies therefore assumed the central position in the electoral process, the function of the *tratta* being purely technical and executory, and consequently played an important role in the political life of Florence. If this was the case in normal circumstances, it was so even more in revolutionary situations. Thus, in 1378 and 1382 scrutinies were used as instruments of the political and social struggle.[1]

Owing to the large number of offices of varying importance for which the scrutinies had to provide, they were in their turn subdivided: the scrutiny of the *Tre Maggiori*, the three highest offices, qualified citizens for the Signoria and the Colleges, that is the *Sedici Gonfalonieri* and the *Dodici Buonuomini*; the scrutiny of the *uffici intrinseci ed estrinseci* qualified for other internal offices, and especially for the offices of the territorial administration, and frequently took place at different times from that of the *Tre Maggiori*.[2] This distinction and separation reflects the different character of the two scrutinies, the former being, broadly speaking, concerned primarily with government, the latter with administration.[3]

A few days after banishing Cosimo to Padua for five years, the *Balìa* of September 1433 decreed the holding of a new general scrutiny,[4] although the next scrutiny of the *Tre Maggiori* was not due until 1436, the last one having been held in 1431.[5] This decision was caused by the desire to strengthen the Albizzi

[1] On the scrutiny of 1378: *Cronaca prima d'Anonimo*, ed. G. Scaramella, in Muratori, *Rerum Italicarum Scriptores*, new ed., xviii. iii (Bologna, 1917), pp. 77–78; *Aggiunte anonime . . .* ibid., p. 36; *Diario d'Anonimo fiorentino*, ed. A. Gherardi, in *Documenti di storia italiana*, vi (Florence, 1876), pp. 371, 372; on that of 1382: Marchionne Stefani, *Cronaca fiorentina*, rubr. 906, ed. N. Rodolico, in Muratori, *Rer. Ital. Script.*, new ed., xxx. i (Città di Castello, 1903–55), p. 398; *Diario d'Anonimo*, p. 435. See also A. Rado, *Maso degli Albizi . . .* (Florence, s.d. [1927]), pp. 60–62; N. Rodolico, *I Ciompi* (Florence, 1945), pp. 137–8.

[2] A list of the internal offices that were filled by sortition is in *Statuta* 1415, ii, pp. 725–7. There were periodical scrutinies for the officials of the Guelph Party and the commercial tribunal, the *Mercanzia*. Also the consuls of the guilds were appointed by sortition preceded by scrutinies; see A. Doren, *Le arti fiorentine*, tr. G. B. Klein (Florence, 1940), i, pp. 282 ff. By the Statutes of 1415, the Signoria had special powers to carry out, together with the XVI, the XII, and usually with the Captains of the Guelph Party, and the VI *di Mercanzia*, scrutinies for a number of offices, if they so wished: op. cit., ii, pp. 656 ff. For a fuller discussion of the scrutinies, see below, Chapter 3.

[3] See below, pp. 57 ff.

[4] Balìe, 24, fols. 14ᵛ, 18ᵛ (20 and 24 Sept. 1433).

[5] Provv., 122, fols. 27ᵛ–29ʳ (20 April 1431).

régime in a moment of crisis by revising the distribution of electoral qualifications for the government. Moreover, by entrusting the scrutiny to the *Balìa*, instead of having it carried out, according to the statutory regulations, by a specially created council including many official members, the leaders of the régime may have hoped to achieve their objective more easily. Similar action had been taken in 1382 to bolster up the victory of the 'oligarchy' after the Ciompi revolt,[1] and in 1393, when Maso degli Albizzi and his followers had the Alberti disfranchised.[2] In fact, the measures adopted in 1393 seem to provide the pattern for the policy pursued by Rinaldo degli Albizzi forty years later.[3] He may have hoped that the methods by which his father had so successfully consolidated the régime in 1393 would save it in 1433.

But a premature revision of the eligibility lists was not the only way in which the Albizzi intervened, in autumn 1433, in the normal functioning of the electoral process. In this process, the qualification of candidates for office formed only the first stage. Once a scrutiny was completed, the names of the successful candidates had to be inserted in the purses from which the drawing by lot would take place whenever an office had to be filled. To carry out this *imborsazione*, as it was called, special officials were elected before the scrutiny: *Accoppiatori* for the three highest offices, and *Secretari* for the remaining ones. In so far as they carried out the decisions of the scrutiny council on the eligibility of citizens, their office was strictly executive, although the *Accoppiatori* had, as we shall see later, important discretionary powers concerning the distribution of the names among the various purses for the Signoria.[4] Limited as their function was to the scrutiny, they did not participate at all in the final stage of the electoral process, the drawing by lot; indeed, their office came to an end as soon as they had filled the purses that served for this purpose. It was therefore a drastic departure from constitutional law and practice when, in October 1433, the *Accoppiatori* of the new scrutiny were, jointly with the Signoria, put in charge of electing the latter's successor for November–December, sortition

---

[1] Balìe, 18, fol. 21ʳ (23–24 Jan. 1382; ed. G. Capponi, *Storia della repubblica fiorentina* (Florence, 1875), i, pp. 617–20), and fols. 28ᵛ–29ʳ (27 Jan.). Of the ninety-six non-official members of the scrutiny council, fifty-two were to be members of the *Balìa*.

[2] Balìe, 19, fols. 36ᵛ–38ᵛ (27 Oct. 1393). The scrutiny was to be carried out by the *Balìa* and twenty-one additional members.

[3] See also below, p. 7.

[4] See below, pp. 45–46.

having been temporarily suspended.[1] In this respect too, Rinaldo and his friends followed the precedent of October 1393 when the *Accoppiatori* had functioned as extraordinary electors of the next Signoria.[2]

However, as in 1393, no attempt appears to have been made in 1433 to extend the exceptional powers that had been granted to the *Accoppiatori*: from December 1433 onwards, the Signoria was once more chosen by lot.[3] By then, the new *borse* were ready, and were in fact used for the drawing of the Signoria which entered office on 1 January.[4] But contrary to what had happened in 1393, when the scrutiny of 1385 had been annulled,[5] in 1433 the old *borse*, dating from the scrutinies from 1391 onwards, were combined, to be used together with those based on the new scrutiny.[6] Cavalcanti states that 'accecati gl'intelletti de' governatori della repubblica, lasciarono le vecchie borse, senz'avere riguardo che le rimanessero tramischiate con le nuove', with the result that 'cavatasi la Signoria più volte, quasi mai ne' tratti alcuna differenza non avea da quelli di prima'.[7] Despite his usual tendency to exaggerate, Cavalcanti was doubtless right in thinking that had it not been for the failure of the Albizzi to press the advantages they had won by their electoral policy in autumn 1433, Cosimo de' Medici would probably not have been recalled, a year later, by the initiative of a Signoria whose names had been drawn a few weeks before from the ballot bags which had been prepared in 1433.

The Medici had the advantage of being able to learn from both the successes and the mistakes of the Albizzi. Following the precedent of 1433, the *Balìa* of 1434 decided, on 4 and 6 October, to carry out a new general scrutiny, again long before

[1] Balìe, 24, fol. 27ʳ (1 Oct. 1433). See also Domenico Buoninsegni, *Storie della città di Firenze dall'anno 1410 al 1460* (Florence, 1637), p. 48.

[2] Balìe, 19, fols. 29ᵛ–30ʳ (25 Oct. 1393): the next Signoria to be elected by the eight *Accoppiatori* of the new scrutiny and the Gonfalonier of Justice, Maso degli Albizzi; the *Accoppiatori* to be chosen by the *Balìa* from among its members. See also Buoninsegni, *Historia fiorentina* (Florence, 1579), p. 727.

[3] Tratte, 198.

[4] Ibid.

[5] Balìe, 19, fol. 17ᵛ (21 Oct. 1393; Capponi, i, pp. 634–5).

[6] Balìe, 24, fols. 14ᵛ–15ᵛ (20 Sept. 1433). The combined *borse* were called 'la nuova imborsazione del 1391, 93, et 98 cum additionibus suis'. On 29 Dec. it was used for the drawing from the *borsa generale*, while the new *borse* were used for that from the *borsellino*, and for the balloting of the Gonfalonier of Justice and the notary of the Signoria (Tratte, 198). On the meaning of these terms, see below, p. 45. In the next sortition, of February, the procedure was reversed. This method was in force until Sept. 1434; it was similarly used for the sortition of the XVI and XII (ibid.).

[7] *Istorie fiorentine*, i, p. 558.

the statutory quinquennium was over;[1] on the 25th, the day
after the scrutiny of the *Tre Maggiori* was completed, it decided
that the *Accoppiatori* and Secretaries for the scrutiny should elect,
jointly with the Signoria in office, the Signoria of November–
December, whose *tratta* was due at the end of October.[2] At the
same time, the new *Balìa* went beyond its predecessor, by
altogether revoking the scrutiny of 1433 and ordering its electoral
lists to be burnt.[3] We shall presently discuss the results of this
electoral revision. The *Balìa* made it quite clear that its timing
was exceptional by decreeing that the next scrutiny was to be
held in January–February 1440, *secundum ordinamenta* in force
before September 1433; after that date, scrutinies were to take
place at five-yearly intervals, as laid down by the Statutes.[4] In
accordance with this decree, the next scrutiny of the *Tre Maggiori*
actually took place in January–February 1440 and that of the
external and internal offices between February of that year and
January 1441.[5]

There was, then, evidently a desire to restore normal conditions speedily, at least as far as the periodicity of scrutinies was
concerned. It remains to be seen whether this policy was made
possible by a thoroughgoing 'expurgation' of the electoral lists.
Unfortunately, we do not possess the scrutiny registers for 1434;
but we have the register for the *Quartiere*, or district, of San
Giovanni, with the results of the scrutiny of the three highest
offices which took place in 1440.[6] An analysis of the names
entered in it shows, firstly, much the same concentration of
political influence in a relatively small number of families, which
had been characteristic of the 'oligarchical' régime after 1382: of
the 411 citizens whose names are entered as belonging to the
Greater Guilds, that is to the largest and wealthiest group on the
electoral lists, 240 belong to 25 families only.[7] It shows, secondly,

---

[1] Balìe, 25, fol. 25^{r-v} (4 Oct. 1434), for the scrutiny of the *Tre Maggiori*; for that of the
external offices, fols. 25^v–26^r (6 Oct.).

[2] Ibid., fols. 44^v–45^r. See below, p. 11.

[3] Ibid., fol. 25^r (4 Oct. 1434) 'che s'intenda essere rivocato in tutto lo squittino del
priorato e notariato de' priori fatto del mese d'ottobre . . . [1433] con ogni poliza dove si
fusse messa'. The register of that scrutiny was to be burnt, under penalty of 1,000 florins.
Similarly, two days later, the 'squittini degli ufici di fuori fatti per diliberatione della balìa'
of 1433 were abolished (fol. 26^r).

[4] Ibid., fol. 87^r (15 Dec.): 'et sic procedatur postea de quinquennio in quinquennium'.

[5] See below, p. 15.

[6] Tratte, 1150.

[7] These familes score even more if we consider the number of *polizze*, or name tickets,
with which they are entered (citizens could accumulate *polizze* from successive scrutinies, if
they had not used them up by being appointed to the office, or for some other reason). They

a substantial continuity in the names of the families represented on the scrutiny registers of 1433 and 1440—a continuity which is the more remarkable as both scrutinies contained strong elements of political discrimination.[1] In fact, the differences between the two scrutiny registers are partly reflected in the lists of citizens who had been banished or deprived of political rights in 1433 and 1434 respectively. Thus the Guasconi, who had been represented in 1433 by 24 members, are absent from the 1440 register, while the Rondinelli, who had had no less than 32 members qualified in 1433, are left with one member only in 1440. Similarly, in the *Quartiere* of S. Croce, the Peruzzi, who had been one of the most heavily represented families in the scrutiny of 1433, with 20 members, are absent from the scrutiny register of 1444, the earliest we possess for the Medici period of that *quartiere*.[2] Conversely, the Medici, who have one member only in the 1433 register—Nicola di Vieri—have no less than 19 members in the 1440 register; while the Pucci, who are absent from the 1433 register, are entered in that of 1440 with 14 names. Yet apart from such changes in the class of the citizens qualified for the highest offices which were brought about by political persecution, the differences between the personnel of the scrutiny registers of 1433 and 1440 are less drastic than might be expected. Some families which were not hit by those persecutions were more strongly represented after 1434, others less so;[3] but this was not necessarily always due to political reasons. In a number of cases, families whose members were largely unsuccessful in the scrutiny of 1433 benefit from the new régime: the Masi, of whose ten candidates of 1433 only one was qualified, appear with seventeen names in the scrutiny register of 1440. However, despite all these changes, the extant eligibility lists show a considerable similarity in the composition of the

possess 702 out of a total of 1,074 *polizze* for the Signoria, i.e. *c.* 65 per cent., while their share in the *polizze* reserved for the Gonfalonierate of Justice amounts to 87 out of 109, i.e. to nearly 80 per cent. The Lesser Guilds provided two of the nine members of the Signoria, with the exclusion of the Gonfalonier of Justice, and normally a quarter of the members of the other offices. See also below, pp. 64–65.

[1] For the scrutiny of 1433, see Tratte, 46 and 47, and Manoscritti, 555. The continuity would no doubt be even more pronounced if we could also take into account the names of the citizens who, in 1433, retained *polizze* from scrutinies that had taken place before 1433: see above, p. 7.

[2] Tratte, 15. They had nearly all been disfranchised in 1434: see above, p. 2.

[3] Thus the Martelli, who were represented by 5 members in 1433, had 11 in 1440; the Alessandri and Pandolfini, represented by 6 and 7 respectively in 1433, had 11 each in 1440; while the Cerretani and Bartolini Scodellari, who had 7 and 8 members respectively in 1433, had 5 each in 1440.

class qualified to hold the highest offices before and after 1434.[1] There remained, therefore, the problem of how to secure and increase political ascendancy within this oligarchical structure of government. This had also been the chief problem for the Albizzi, who had, in the end, failed to solve it. The events of 1433 and 1434 had given it a fresh and pressing significance. The solution adopted by the new régime was, first of all, to try to acquire control of the appointment of the Signoria.

For despite manifold checks on its authority, the Florentine constitution gave the Signoria very considerable powers. Foremost among these were the exclusive right, with the approval of the Colleges, to initiate legislation, and the right to issue ordinances by its sole authority, as well as to proceed in criminal cases involving the safety of the state. Moreover, the Signori played a leading role in the shaping and carrying out of foreign policy.[2] Their power, says a fifteenth-century survey of Florentine institutions, 'is great beyond measure', although they do not use it fully unless rarely and in extreme cases, 'but rather follow the written statutes of the Commune'.[3] To control their appointment could consequently provide ample opportunities for influencing government and legislation, and the statutory election by lot, which had been in force since 1328, was precisely designed to prevent this from happening.[4]

In his *Ricordi*, Cosimo de' Medici states that after 1434, 'the purses of the Signoria remained for five years in the hands of the *Accoppiatori*',[5] and Guicciardini said later that in Cosimo's time,

---

[1] In many cases, families were represented by the same members in 1433 and 1440: thus of the 7 Dietisalvi entered in 1433, 6 are also registered in 1440; of the 12 Della Stufa, 9 (their total representation in 1440 being 8 and 11 respectively); of the 17 Carnesecchi entered in 1440, 10 had been qualified in 1433.

[2] See *Statuta* 1415, ii, pp. 518 ff. On legislative initiative, ibid., pp. 664–71. On the right of the Signoria and Colleges to fill a number of (usually minor) offices by election, and, together with other magistracies, to carry out scrutinies for certain offices, see above, p. 4.

[3] Gregorio Dati, *Istoria di Firenze*, ed. L. Pratesi (Florence, 1904), p. 148: 'L'uficio e balìa e autorità e potenzia di detti Signori è grande sanza misura; ciò che volessono potrebbono mentre che dura il loro uficio; ma non adoperano questa potenzia se non in certi casi necessari estremi di rado; anzi seguitano secondo gli ordini scritti del Comune. . . .' According to H. Baron, *Humanistic and Political Literature of Florence and Venice at the Beginning of the Quattrocento* (Cambridge, Mass., 1955), pp. 62–68, book ix, which presents a survey of Florentine institutions, was written by 1410, but contains many subsequent additions.

[4] See above, p. 4, n. 1. Villani, *Cronica*, x, 108 : the reform was made 'acciocchè si levassono le sette tra' cittadini . . . le sette de' malvagi cittadini, che al tutto voleano reggere sopra gli altri . . .'.

[5] '. . . rimasero le borse per 5 anni in mano degli Accoppiatori, cioè le borse del priorato' (Fabroni, *Cosmi vita*, ii, p. 103).

the Signoria was nearly always elected by *Accoppiatori*.[1] Modern historians have generally accepted these statements.[2] In contrast to them, Pellegrini argued, in a review of a book on Cosimo, in 1899, that only the Signoria of November–December 1434 and its successor of January–February 1435 were elected by *Accoppiatori*; that in 1435, the normal method of appointing the government by lot was restored; and that it was not until 1443 that the election of part of the Signoria was once more, temporarily, entrusted to *Accoppiatori*.[3] In fact, the decree of 25 October 1434 only concerned the election of the next Signoria;[4] and the registers in which the chancery entered the names of successive governments already show the Signoria of January–February 1435, as well as its successors, as having again been appointed by lot, from the purses based on the scrutiny of 1434.[5] Did, then, the departure from the constitutional appointment by lot of the government remain limited, as in 1433, to one election only, or did it immediately become the normal method of appointing the government? And if so, how is this to be reconciled with the evidence of the official records? The answer to these questions will reveal the gradual manner in which the Mediceans established what was to become one of the cornerstones of their system of government. It is supplied by examining the laws of the *Balìa* and of the statutory councils, and the ordinances of the Signoria, for the years following Cosimo's return from exile.

The first piece of legislation which concerns us is a decree of the *Balìa* of 15 December 1434, extending, until 22 April 1435, the term during which the *Accoppiatori* of the scrutiny 'that had been held in October' had to fill the purses with the results of that scrutiny.[6] This meant that the new purses would not be ready for the sortition of the next Signoria, which was due on 28 December, and possibly not even for that which was due at

---

[1] '. . . e' signori quasi sempre a suo tempo non si trassono a sorte, ma si eleggevano dagli accoppiatori a modo suo . . .' (*Storie fiorentine*, ed. R. Palmarocchi (Bari, 1931), pp. 4–5).

[2] See e.g. Gutkind, *Cosimo de' Medici*, p. 109.

[3] Review of K. D. Ewart, *Cosimo de' Medici*, in *Arch. Stor. Ital.*, 5ª ser., xxiv (1899), pp. 127–8. The review has been summarized by K. D. Vernon [*née* Ewart], in *Engl. Hist. Rev.*, xv (1900), pp. 519–23.

[4] Balìe, 25, fols. 44ᵛ–45ʳ (25 Oct. 1434): 'quod priores artium et vexillifer iustitie populi et communis Florentie et eorum notarius, quorum officium incipere debebit die primo mensis novembris proxime futuri, eligi . . . debeant die vigesimonono presentis mensis octobris per presentes dominos priores artium et vexilliferum iustitie una cum aliis copulatoribus et secretariis eorum consociis proximis diebus electis . . .'.

[5] Tratte, 93.

[6] Balìe 25, fol. 87ᵛ. The *imborsazioni* for the XVI *Gonfalonieri* and XII *Buonuomini* were to be completed by the original date, i.e. by 28 Dec.

the end of February; while the old ones had, as we have seen, been ordered to be destroyed. To meet this difficulty, the *Balìa* laid down that *infra tempus eis concessum*, that is up to 22 April, the bags for the Priors be filled by the *Accoppiatori* with at least ten names of eligible citizens each, that for the Gonfalonier of Justice with at least four; *et sic*, the decree continues, *observetur postea*.[1] It is these four words which provide the clue to the development of electoral controls during the first years of the Medici régime. The obscurity of the phrase may have been intentional: what it really meant was that until the *imborsazione* of the new scrutiny was completed, the *Accoppiatori* should continue to elect the Signoria by way of filling special purses for the two-monthly sortition.[2] Since seven purses were required for the election of the eight Priors, the two Priors recruited from the Lesser Guilds being drawn from the same purse, the *Accoppiatori* could place as few as 70 names into the special purses of the Priorate, and four into that of the Gonfalonier of Justice, while normally the purses that were filled on the basis of the scrutiny would contain about 2,000 names.[3] We shall presently discuss the full meaning of this development.

In April 1435 the *Accoppiatori* had not yet completed the *imborsazione* of the scrutiny; but already in February they had received, from the councils of the People and Commune, an extension until the end of June, 'ad faciendum imbursationes et alia sibi commissa'[4]—an apparently innocent phrase, which covered, as we have seen, a drastic suspension of constitutional law. Further short extensions by the councils followed: in April to the end of October, in October to the end of November, and in November to the end of March 1436.[5] These two last extensions are of particular importance for the continuation of

[1] '... quod presentibus copulatoribus scructinei prioratus celebrati de mense octobris ... intelligatur esse et sit prorogatum tempus eis assignatum ad perficiendum imbursationes usque ad per totum diem vigesimum secundum mensis aprilis proxime futuri ... salvo quod pro extractione officii prioratus et vexilliferi iustitie infra tempus eis concessum, bursellini et generales et burse artificum, de quibus fieri deberent extractiones secundum ordinamenta, ad minus habeant quelibet earum decem habiles ad officium prioratus, et bursa vexilliferi habeat ad minus quatuor habiles ad dictum officium, et sic observetur postea ...'. The apparently arbitrary date of the 22nd may indicate that the *borse* were intended to be available for the sortition of the Signoria of May–June, due to take place on the 28th. In the minute of this decree, the date is originally the 30th, which is corrected to the 22nd (Provv., Protocolli, 10, fol. 236ʳ).

[2] See below, pp. 34 ff.   [3] See below, p. 62.

[4] Provv., 125, fol. 235ʳ⁻ᵛ (26–28 Feb. 1435).

[5] Provv., 126, fols. 37ᵛ–38ʳ (29–30 April 1435), 237ʳ⁻ᵛ (6–7 Oct. 1435), and 310ʳ–311ʳ (18–19 Nov. 1435).

electoral controls. As we have seen, the election of the Signoria by the *Accoppiatori* had at first been explained as being necessitated by the fact that the *Accoppiatori* had not yet completed filling the purses with the results of the new scrutiny. Accordingly, the first extensions granted to them concerned both the *imborsazione* and the election of the Signoria by way of special purses. The October decree abandons this approach. The main business connected with the former is now to be completed by the end of November; but the authority of the *Accoppiatori* 'to create the Priors and the Gonfalonier of Justice . . . as . . . they do now', *prout . . . faciunt ad presens*, is extended until October 1436. Moreover, the Signoria is empowered to grant, with the approval of its Colleges, but without the consent of the councils, further extensions to the *Accoppiatori* by way of simple ordinance, as long as these do not exceed one year, *quoquo modo*.[1] But already in November the final date for the filling of the bags for the three highest offices is once more postponed until the end of March 1436, and the Signoria with its Colleges is authorized, *ultra auctoritatem alias concessam*, to extend the powers of the *Accoppiatori* to elect the Signoria for further periods of up to one year *in totum*; a decision to this effect having to be passed by at least twenty-eight out of thirty-seven votes.[2] While the ballot bags of the *Tre Maggiori* appear to have been finally completed by June 1436,[3] the *Accoppiatori* thus continued in office in their new capacity of electors of the Signoria, which in its turn had authority to renew the powers of the *Accoppiatori*. Accordingly, on 3 April 1436, the Signoria and the Colleges 'prorogaverunt copulatoribus scructinei prioratus' of October 1434, 'tempus sibi concessum ad faciendum priores et vexilliferum modo et forma et prout tunc poterant et faciebant', until the end of October 1437,[4] and in May 1437 they extended it for a further

---

[1] Provv. cit.

[2] Provv., 126, fols. 310r–311r (18–19 Nov. 1435): '. . . semel et pluries prorogare dictis copulatoribus tempus concessum ad imbursandum [on the meaning of this term in this context, see below, p. 34] vexilliferos iustitie et priores artium, prout possunt et imbursant ad presens, usque in unum annum in totum . . . et non ultra . . .'.

[3] On 27–30 June the *Accoppiatori* were given additional time, until the end of Aug., to transfer names from the old to the new bags of the other internal and of the external offices (Provv., 127, fols. 107v–108r), and on 30–31 Aug., they get another extension for this job until 15 Sept. (ibid., fol. 182r–v). After this date, there are no further renewals in the registers of *provvisioni* concerning the filling of the bags from the 1434 scrutiny. See also below, pp. 41 ff.

[4] Deliberazioni dei Signori e Collegi, speciale autorità, 25, fol. 152r: 'vigore auctoritatis . . . eisdem concesse . . . de mense octobris proxime preteriti'.

year until the end of October 1438.[1] By that time, the election of
the Signoria had been for four years in the hands of the *Accoppiatori*. Having been introduced in a revolutionary situation as an
exceptional measure, this method of electoral control was well
on the way to becoming a permanent feature of the new régime.

What is particularly striking in this development is its gradual
and almost experimental character, in contrast to the view that
the new system was fully established on Cosimo's return to
Florence, or that it was abandoned, for the time being, shortly
afterwards.[2] The first measures could still be justified on the
purely technical grounds of the completion of the scrutiny
business. The *Balìa* having dissolved at the end of 1434, they had
to be passed by the statutory councils of the People and the
Commune, which were elected, every four months, by names
being drawn from bags that had been prepared by the Signoria
and the Colleges.[3] Since from October 1434 onwards the Signoria was in its turn elected by the *Accoppiatori*, it might well be
expected to have influenced the composition of the councils in
favour of the new régime. Even so, the voting returns of the
council of the People reveal considerable opposition to the renewals granted to the *Accoppiatori*, which were passed only with
narrow majorities in February, April, and October 1435.[4] It
was doubtless this conciliar opposition which explains the attempt
to delegate to the Signoria the authority to grant the *Accoppiatori*
further extensions. The bill of 6 October 1435 was something of
a *ballon d'essai*, the delegation of authority being limited to one
year only. On 18 November new legislation was thereupon introduced to grant the Signoria this authority for a further year. This
second bill was won by the government with a majority of one.[5]
Although the passage of the bill secured for the time being the
appointment of the Signoria by the *Accoppiatori*, it also revealed

---

[1] Ibid., 26, fols. 10ᵛ–11ʳ (15 May 1437): 'obtento partito per vigintiocto fabas nigras
vigore auctoritatis . . . eis concesse . . . et maxime per provisionem' of 19 Nov. 1435 (the
text has 1436, which is evidently a slip for 1435; there is no *provvisione* of that date in 1436).

[2] See above, pp. 10–11.

[3] See *Statuta* 1415, ii, p. 660. The council of the People began its sessions at the beginning
of Feb., June, and Oct., that of the Commune at the beginning of Jan., May, and Sept. The
drawing of the names of the members was to take place a month or more before the beginning of these sessions (Provv., 108, fols. 179ᵛ–180ʳ; 22 Dec. 1418). The scrutiny by the
Signoria and the Colleges had been abolished by the *Balìa* of 1433 (Balìe, 24, fol. 17ᵛ; 28
Sept. 1433), and restored by that of 1434 (Balìe, 25, fol. 24ʳ; 4 Oct. 1434).

[4] With 157 against 70 votes in Feb., 141 against 58 votes in April, and 155 against 60 in
Oct. (see above, p. 12). A two-thirds majority was required.

[5] 139 votes to 68. Also in the council of the Commune, the opposition was stronger than
before, 48 against 98. Loc. cit.

the strength of the opposition to the suspension of the constitutional system of electing the government, and rendered it questionable whether the councils could be persuaded to grant further delegations of their powers to the Signoria.

The more so as the new scrutiny, which was to be held at the beginning of 1440,[1] was rapidly approaching. It necessitated, according to the Statutes, the election of new *Accoppiatori*.[2] Would it be possible to carry on with the new method of electing the Signoria, considering that all the renewals between 1434 and 1437 had been granted to the *Accoppiatori* of the scrutiny of 1434? In May 1438, exactly one year after the last renewal of their powers by the Signoria, legislation was sought and obtained from the councils to create a *Balìa*, or *Consiglio Maggiore*, for three years,[3] which was not only to hold the scrutiny, but also to decide whether in the meantime the Signoria should be elected in 'quel modo si fa al presente o in qualche altro modo'.[4] The new council decreed, on 11 June 1438, after the Signoria had sought legal advice, 'che il tempo che anno gli accoppiatori' of the scrutiny of 1434 be extended until the end of 1439.[5] That the Signoria should have felt it necessary to ask for professional advice on the legality of this measure, can only be due to the absence, in the legislation of the *Balìa* of 1434, of any provision that would warrant the renewal of the powers of the *Accoppiatori* to elect *a mano*.[6] The *Consiglio Maggiore* also decided to carry out the scrutiny of the three highest offices in January and February 1400;[7] and, on 11 January of that year, to elect new *Accoppiatori* for the scrutiny, who were to have prepared the new bags by 31 January 1441.[8] Until that date, the election of the Signoria was to be carried out in the present manner, but by the newly-appointed *Accoppiatori*—'nel modo presente che s'è facto per li achopiatori passati dello squittino dell'anno MCCCCXXXIIII'.[9] In what manner

---

[1] See above, p. 8.   [2] See above, p. 6.

[3] See below, p. 71.

[4] Provv., 129, fols. 34ᵛ–35ʳ.

[5] Fragments of the register of the *Consiglio Maggiore*, in Tratte, 60, fols. 225ʳ–226ʳ.

[6] The three lawyers, Giovanni Girolami, Guglielmo Tanaglia, and Domenico Martelli, advise the Signoria, on 2 June 1438, that the *Consiglio Maggiore* may grant the *Accoppiatori* in office authority to continue to elect the Signoria *a mano* until 31 Dec. 1439, 'non obstantibus dispositis . . . in dicta balìa del 34' (fol. 224ʳ).

[7] Ibid., fol. 225ᵛ. At the same time, it decided to hold a scrutiny of the other offices. For this scrutiny, *Secretari* (corresponding to the *Accoppiatori* for the scrutiny of the *Tre Maggiori Uffici*) were, as usual, to be elected.

[8] Ibid., fol. 228ᵛ: 'debbano infra uno anno [as from 1 Feb.] . . . avere formate le borse del decto scrutineo del priorato . . .'. The new *Accoppiatori* were elected on 12 Jan. 1440.

[9] Ibid., fol. 228ʳ.

it was to be carried out *after* the new ballot bags had been completed, was left to the subsequent decision of the *Consiglio Maggiore*.[1] Accordingly, before it dissolved,[2] that council decided, on 8 January 1441, firstly, that the *Accoppiatori* must have completed, by 12 February 1441, the ballot bags for the Signoria, and, secondly, that with the completion of this task their office, and hence their powers to elect *a mano*, were to come to an end.[3]

The decree of the *Consiglio Maggiore* does not give any reason for this momentous decision to end the new system of appointing the Signoria, which had so painstakingly been established after 1434, and no records of debates are extant that could help to explain it.[4] It may have been, at least partly, due to the financial situation. The new council had been created in the second year of the renewed war with Filippo Maria Visconti of Milan, and had been given special powers to decide on taxes and military policy.[5] The Florentines were suffering under the heavy taxation resulting from the war,[6] and while the presence of the *uomini del reggimento*, the citizens of the régime, might be expected to facilitate the passage of tax bills,[7] concessions to public opinion could become necessary. This was particularly the case after the military situation had greatly improved in consequence of the Florentine victory at Anghiari, on 29 June 1440.[8] Moreover, this victory had dashed the hopes of Rinaldo degli Albizzi to return to Florence in the wake of Niccolò Piccinino, and with the help of the citizens who were dissatisfied with the régime.[9] The Mediceans may have felt that it was now safe to relax controls and abandon elections *a mano* of the Signoria.

The restoration of the traditional system of electing the

---

[1] '. . . rimanga liberamente nella dispositione di decto Consiglio Maggiore' (ibid.).

[2] The last entry in the extant minutes of its register is for 23 Feb. See also below, p. 74.

[3] '. . . sia finita ogni auctorità et balìa de' decti accopiatori' (fol. 246ʳ). They could, however, still elect *a mano* the Gonfalonier of Justice for March–April 1441 (ibid.).

[4] The records of the debates in the *Pratiche* (Consulte e Pratiche) show a gap for the years 1437–46.

[5] See below, p. 73.

[6] Buoninsegni, *Storie*, p. 67: 'parendoci non poter supplire alla spesa che bisogniava, per essere stracchi dalla gran quantità delle gravezze pagate.'

[7] Provv., 129, fol. 35ʳ: 'acciò che 'l trattare di racconciare o fare nuova graveza di prestanza . . . si fusse generalmente a' vostri cittadini come al tempo si cognosce essere necessario si muova e faccia unitamente cogli uomini del reggimento . . .'.

[8] Leonardo Bruni, *Rerum suo tempore gestarum commentarius*, ed. C. di Pierro, in Muratori, *Rer. Ital. Script.*, new ed., XIX. iii (Città di Castello, 1914; Bologna, 1926), p. 458: 'maxima fuit victoria, finem bello impositura, si nostri sequi eam voluissent.'

[9] Cavalcanti, *Istorie fiorentine*, ii, pp. 51–54, 72–73. See C. C. Bayley, *War and Society in Renaissance Florence* (Toronto, 1961), pp. 163–4, 171–3.

Signoria lasted less than three years, and when it was again suspended, there was no war which could provide an argument in favour of elections *a mano*. The circumstances in which this took place in 1443 reflect again the tentative and experimental character of the constitutional policy of the Medici régime during its formative period.

In October 1443 the councils decided that a new scrutiny of all the offices except the *Tre Maggiori* (which was not due until January 1445) was to take place, although the last scrutiny of the external offices had been held only three years earlier, between February 1440 and January 1441.[1] As usual, *Secretari* were to be elected for this scrutiny. This would normally have completed the legislation necessary for the purpose. However, the law also laid down that ten *Accoppiatori* were to be elected to carry out the election *a mano* of part of the Signoria,[2] the last *Accoppiatori* having ended their term of office in February 1441.[3] The new *Accoppiatori* were to elect *a mano* from the bags of the Gonfalonier of Justice and from the *borsellino*, the more select of the two principal purses of the Priorate, while the *borsa generale* was still to be used in the statutory manner. The same doubtless applied also to the bags of the Lesser Guilds, which provided two members of the Priorate.[4] In this way the *Accoppiatori* were to control the election of four out of nine members of the Signoria.[5] On the other hand, these powers were no longer granted for a renewable term of one year, as after 1434, but straightway for a period of three years. While it was clearly advisable to proceed cautiously, this lengthening of the period for which elections *a mano* were granted was a significant step in the direction of greater permanency of the new electoral system. The first phase of its development had ended, in 1441, with the restoration of the traditional election by lot; it may well have been hoped that by granting the *Accoppiatori* a longer term, a more lasting success might be obtained.

---

[1] Provv., 134, fols. 131ʳ–134ʳ (1–2 Oct. 1443). For the previous scrutiny of the external offices, Tratte 60, fols. 237ʳ–243ʳ. See above, p. 15, n. 7.

[2] Ibid., fol. 133ʳ⁻ᵛ. They were to be elected by the Signoria, the Colleges, and the previous *Accoppiatori* and Secretaries.   [3] See above, p. 16.

[4] The bags from which the *Accoppiatori* were to elect *a mano* were those which had been closed, i.e. made ready for elections by lot, after the scrutiny of 1440, in 1441. Signori, Deliberazioni, Bastardelli di sbozzi, 7, fol. 113ᵛ (11 Oct. 1443): 'elegerunt infrascriptos decem, ut teneant bursas prioratus del 1439 [Florentine style] in manibus pro tempore et prout in reformatione continetur'.

[5] See also *Priorista* of Francesco di Tommaso Giovanni, Bibl. Naz., XXV. 379, fol. 151ʳ: 'ripresono le borse a mano, cioè la borsa del gonfaloniere de justitia e del borsellino'. See below, p. 31.

In 1444, ten years had passed since the return of Cosimo de' Medici. By the end of that year, the sentences of a large number of citizens who in 1434 had been banished or deprived of political rights, were due to expire.[1] However successful the Mediceans had been in consolidating their régime, there remained the danger that the vanquished faction might one day attempt to overthrow it, as Rinaldo degli Albizzi had tried to do in 1440.[2] In 1434, the measures against the Albizzi faction had been initiated by the *Balìa*, and it was evidently safest to let a *Balìa* deal with the problem arising from their expiry. This was doubtless one of the reasons for the creation of a new *Balìa* in May 1444;[3] and it was a measure of Medicean ascendancy that a term of no less than five years could be obtained for it from the councils. One of its first decisions concerned, in fact, the citizens who had been condemned, from 29 September 1434 onwards, *pro occasione status*: their sentences were extended by another ten years.[4] In June, a number of citizens, among them those who had served as *Accoppiatori* in 1433, were newly deprived of political rights, equally for ten years,[5] while some others had their prison sentences commuted into exile.

A further reason for the creation of the new *Balìa* is to be sought in the dissatisfaction with the results of the scrutiny of the external offices, which had been held at the end of 1443.[6] According to Cavalcanti, it had qualified many suspects and relatives of exiles.[7] The *Balìa* was accordingly granted authority to hold not only the scrutiny of the *Tre Maggiori*, which was due in 1445, but also that of the other offices, the recent scrutiny of these having been annulled.[8] That of the *Tre Maggiori* was already completed in June 1444, in which month the *Accoppiatori* began

---

[1] See above, p. 2.

[2] Above, p. 16.

[3] Balìe, 26, fols. 7ʳ–10ᵛ (20–23 May 1444). See also below, pp. 74 ff.

[4] Ibid., fol. 24ᵛ (29 May 1444): all those who had been banished, or deprived of political rights, from the day of the *Parlamento* of 1434 onwards, had their sentences extended by ten years as from the following June.

[5] Otto di Guardia e Balìa, 224, fol. 78ʳ: sentence of the Captain of the People of 2 June. They were the Serragli, with the exception of Giorgio di Piero and his sons and brothers, Bernardo di Francesco Canigiani and his sons and brothers, Jacopo di Piero Baroncelli and sons and brothers, Francesco di Matteo Castellani and sons, Bartolomeo di Ser Benedetto Fortini, the sons of Ser Paolo di Ser Lando and their sons, Piero di Jacopo Ardinghelli and sons, and Neri di Ser Viviano and sons, and the *Accoppiatori* of 1433 and their sons and brothers. Cf. Cavalcanti, *Istorie fiorentine*, ii, p. 192; Buoninsegni, *Storie*, p. 79.

[6] See below, pp. 54–55.

[7] Op. cit., ii, pp. 191–2; see below, p. 54.

[8] Balìe cit., fol. 9ᵛ.

to use the new purses for the election of the Signoria.[1] By virtue
of the law of October 1443 their powers should have expired in
1446. In fact, we find them in charge as long as the *Balìa* lasted,
that is until 1449. Although no renewal of their powers to elect
a mano is registered among the legislation of either the statutory
councils or the *Balìa*, some such extension was probably decreed
in 1444 by the *Balìa* for its duration,[2] thus bringing the electoral
policy into line with the situation that had existed until 1441,
when the dissolution of the *Balìa* coincided with the termination
of elections *a mano* and of the office of the *Accoppiatori*.[3]

A bill proposing to close the bags by the end of August, which
also contained the proposal to dissolve the *Balìa* before its time
was up but to hold the new scrutiny in 1449, was not passed by
the council of the People in April 1448.[4] Subsequent attempts to
prolong the session of the *Balìa* were, on the other hand, equally
unsuccessful;[5] and in March 1449, a bill proposing the extension
by one year of the powers of the *Accoppiatori* to elect *a mano* was
defeated by the *Balìa* itself.[6] In the debates of the *Pratica* of that
month, war, plague, and financial difficulties appear once more
as arguments in favour of elections *a mano*. In the words of the
special committee appointed to advise on this matter, 'if ever
there was a time when the bags of the Signoria should be a *mano*,
it is now'.[7] The war of the Milanese succession forms, in fact, the

[1] Tratte, 200, to 28 June 1444, with marginal note: 'Prima extractio de scrutineo del
1444.' The extant registers of this scrutiny (Tratte, 15, 49; see below, p. 61, n. 4) refer to
it as having taken place in June 1444. Cf. also the register of the *Accoppiatori* of 1443
(Tratte, 1148, pt. 2, fol. 5ʳ): 'in scrutineo trium maiorum celebrato de dicto mense junii'
1444, and the *Priorista* of Paolo di Girolamo di Ser Paolo, Tratte, 448, *ad annum*: 'feciono
adì XII uno squittino del priorato'. On the new *Accoppiatori*, see below, p. 31.

[2] Possibly in connexion with its decision concerning the scrutiny, which is likewise not
registered (see below, p. 54, n. 2). The extension may have been decreed on the strength of
the *Balìa* having been granted the same powers as that of 1438 (below, p. 75, and above,
p. 15).

[3] In the *Pratica* of 6 Dec. 1446, a speaker suggests that 'tempus quinquennii esse
expectandum' before the ballot bags were closed (Cons. e Prat., 52, fol. 1ᵛ).

[4] Libri Fabarum, 61, fols. 108ʳ⁻ᵛ, 109ᵛ, 110ʳ⁻ᵛ (8, 9, 10, 11, and 12 April 1448). The bill
of 8 April also contained a proposal on the election of the members of the council of the
People, and that of 12 April on the election to the councils of the People and Commune
('quod pro consilio populi et communis fiant burse'. See below, p. 118, n. 2), which may
have been one of the reasons why it was defeated.

[5] See below, pp. 76–77.

[6] The bill was to the effect that the *Accoppiatori* should be empowered to prepare the
election *a mano* of the next six Signorie before closing the bags, i.e. to control the election
of the Signoria for a period of one year after the end of their office. It was defeated in the
Balìa on 26, 27, and 31 March (Libri Fabarum, 60, fols. 93ᵛ, 94ʳ). See also below, p. 86.

[7] Cons. e Prat., 52, fol. 75ʳ (27 March 1449). The spokesmen are Agnolo Acciaiuoli,
Giovannozzo Pitti, Otto Niccolini, Neri Capponi, and Cosimo de' Medici. The first meeting
on the subject was on 16 March (ibid., fol. 74ʳ).

background to these debates. After the death of Filippo Maria
Visconti on 13 August 1447, the principal aim of Florence's foreign
policy was to prevent King Alfonso of Naples from advancing further into Tuscany, on the pretext that Venice was seeking to acquire
Milanese territory.[1] In April 1448 Florence accepted Alfonso's
peace overtures, the city being, as Cosimo writes to the Florentine
orators in Venice, 'in a bad state, owing to the war and to lack
of money'.[2] The negotiations broke down in the same month,
Alfonso refusing to evacuate Tuscany; and Florence continued to
press Venice for effective military help. But by March 1449 the
military situation had improved: at the end of 1448 Alfonso had
raised the siege of Piombino, and the war was now confined to
Lombardy, where Francesco Sforza, since October in alliance
with Venice, was advancing on Milan.[3] There was certainly less
of a case for justifying the continuation of electoral controls
on grounds of military necessity in 1449 than in the preceding
year.[4]

The *Balìa* ended its five-year session, as laid down, in May
1449; and in the same month, the *Accoppiatori* closed the bags.
The traditional system of electing the Signoria by lot was once
more restored.[5] Not, however, for long. If the argument that the
war necessitated electoral controls carried little weight in spring
1449, it could be pressed home with greater strength in 1452.
On 21 February 1452 a league was signed between Florence, the
King of France, and the Duke of Milan, Venice having allied
with the King of Naples early in 1451; and war began in May, in

---

[1] É. Jordan, 'Florence et la succession lombarde', *Mélanges d'archéologie et d'histoire de
l'École française de Rome*, ix (1889), pp. 93 ff.; M. F. Sacchi, 'Cosimo de' Medici e Firenze
nell'acquisto di Milano allo Sforza', *Rivista di scienze storiche*, ii (1905), pp. 282–3.

[2] '. . . in malo ordine, avendo a stare in guerra e per mancamento del denaro, et per le
tristi gente abbiamo et in poca concordia insieme' (15 April 1448; Sacchi, op. cit., p. 406);
cf. Jordan, op. cit., pp. 103–4.

[3] Jordan, pp. 110–12; Sacchi, pp. 284–5. See also *Storia di Milano*, vi (Milan, 1955),
pp. 423 ff. Cf. Buoninsegni, *Storie*, pp. 87–88, and Neri di Gino Capponi, *Commentari*, in
Muratori, *Rer. Ital. Script.*, xviii (Milan, 1731), cols. 1206–7.

[4] See also below, p. 26.

[5] The last entry in the register of the *Balìa* of 1444 is of 20 May 1449; see below, p. 77.
That the bags were effectively closed in May 1449 appears from the titles of the extant
registers of the *imborsazione* of 1449 for the *Quartieri* S. Maria Novella and S. Giovanni:
'Campione . . . di quelli che furono imborsati . . . a' tre maggiori di maggio 1449 nel serrare
delle borse' (Tratte, 49), as well as from the register of the *Accoppiatori*, where the last
entry referring to an election of the Signoria is of 25 April 1449 (Tratte, 1148). See also
Priorista of Paolo di Girolamo di Ser Paolo, Tratte, 448, *ad annum*: 'si finì la balìa adì
XX di maggio . . . e le borse del prioratico si serrorno adì 30 di maggio', and the *tratte*
register, Tratte, 200, to 28 June 1449: 'Prima extractio dominorum post . . . clausuram
bursarum.'

Lombardy, and in June, in Tuscany.[1] On 14 July 1452, in view of the 'imminentia pericula et casus occurrentes presertim ad hostiles incursus regis Aragonum', a new *Balìa* was created, to last for the duration of the war and six months after its conclusion, provided that the total period did not exceed two years.[2] By the same law it was decreed that the *Accoppiatori* who in May 1449 had closed the purses should once more elect *a mano*, but this time the Gonfalonier of Justice only.[3] This limitation went further than that adopted in 1443; it was, however, abandoned as early as August, when the *Balìa* extended elections *a mano* also to the Priors.[4] This meant the full restoration to the *Accoppiatori* of the powers they had possessed between 1434 and 1441.[5] On 5 November 1453, the *Balìa* prolonged these powers by no less than five years beyond their original term.[6] It was by far the longest period for which the election of the Signoria had been placed under their control. Since the war could evidently not be used to justify an extension which was to come into force after it had ended, the law merely refers, in general terms, to the 'conditioni de' tempi che corrono, et veduta l'utilità che è seguita per avere avuto le borse a mano'. In the following month, the councils of the People and Commune similarly extended the term of office of the *Balìa* by five years.[7] The constitutional foundations of the régime had never before appeared so strong.

The last two measures were taken under the Gonfalonier Luca Pitti, at a time when, on papal initiative, peace negotiations were taking place in Rome.[8] In Florence, it was widely believed

[1] L. Rossi, 'Lega tra il duca di Milano, i Fiorentini e Carlo VII re di Francia (21 febbraio 1452)', *Arch. Stor. Lombardo*, xxxiii (1906), pp. 246–98. The league was proclaimed in Florence on 9 April, and Alfonso declared war on Florence on 2 June. Cf. Buoninsegni, *Storie*, p. 98.

[2] Provv. 143, fols. 196ᵛ–201ʳ (10–14 July 1452); see below, p. 77.

[3] Ibid., fol. 199ᵛ: 'solum et dumtaxat quoad officium vexilliferi iustitie habendi pro dicto tempore et non aliud'. Substitutes were to be elected in the place of *Accoppiatori* who had died in the meantime.

[4] See above, p. 17. Balìe, 27, fols. 26ᵛ–27ʳ (9 Aug. 1452): 'quod dictis copulatoribus . . . sit concessa eadem auctoritas . . . quoad ceteros de numero priorum artium ultra vexilliferum iustitie habendos et eligendos'. This measure was, in its turn, defended in terms of military emergency: 'deinde [i.e. since July 1452] augescentibus negotiis non minime importantie circa conservationem libertatis et defensionem status et nascentibus per consequens etiam suspictionibus plurimis, inspecta condictione temporis et imminentibus periculis guerre, expediens et utillimum esse videtur providere quod pro quolibet prioratu durante dicto tempore habeantur viri electi et probi ac fidi et zelatores dicti status . . .'.

[5] See above, pp. 10–16.   [6] Balìe, 27, fol. 158ᵛ (5 Nov. 1453).

[7] Provv., 144, fols. 47ᵛ–50ᵛ (18–22 Dec. 1453). The *Balìa* had been holding a new scrutiny in Nov. and Dec. (see Balìe, 27, fol. 199ʳ), which the *Accoppiatori* used from Feb. 1454 onwards (Tratte, 200, *ad* 26 Feb. 1454).

[8] G. Soranzo, *La Lega italica (1454-1455)* (Milan, 1924), p. 12.

that peace was close at hand.[1] According to the law of July 1452 this would have meant the early end of the *Balìa* and of elections *a mano*.[2] In these circumstances, Luca Pitti and other leading members of the régime may have felt that the time had come to extend, while the war was still on and the *Balìa* in office, controls that had been introduced on account of the military situation. If so, their action proved ultimately unsuccessful. For the peace of Lodi had hardly been concluded, and ratified by Florence (23 April 1454), when the councils of the People and Commune decided, on 22 and 23 May, to dissolve the *Balìa*, notwithstanding the law of December 1453 extending its term by five years;[3] and in February 1455, a month after the ratification of the peace by King Alfonso of Naples, and his adhesion to the Italian League,[4] they decreed, ostensibly on the suggestion of the *Accoppiatori*, that the bags of the Signoria be closed by the end of June, with the office of the *Accoppiatori* coming to an end by that date.[5]

Never before had there been so abrupt a reversal of the electoral policy of the Medici régime; on both the previous occasions when the bags were closed, the *Accoppiatori* had been allowed to complete their term of office. Coming as it did close on the premature dissolution of the *Balìa*, the abolition of elections *a mano* forms part of a general reaction against the attempt, which seemed to have been so successful after the outbreak of the last war, to give the Medici régime institutional security by providing *Balìe* and *Accoppiatori* with unprecedentedly long terms of office. The leading citizens of the régime were clearly unable, in 1454 and 1455, to persuade the Florentines to continue to accept measures which they had time and again defended in

---

[1] See Neri di Gino Capponi, op. cit., col. 1214: 'si mandò [to Rome] pe' Dieci di Balìa Messer Otto di Lapo Niccolini, e quasi per tutto il popolo si tenne che egli andasse per isconciarla; in modo che pubblicamente e da' fanciulli . . . si cantava per le vie . . .: "La pace è fatta, se Messer Otto non la guasta", benchè gli fu levato a torto questa boce . . .'. On Cosimo's desire for peace, see Francesco Sforza's instruction for Nicodemo Tranchedini da Pontremoli, 'ituri Romam pro facto pacis', of 24 Jan. 1454 (ed. C. Canetta, in *Arch. Stor. Lomb.*, ix (1882), p. 130): 'parendo alluy [Cosimo] che pace debbia essere che siamo contenti de fare quanto alluy pare'.

[2] See above, p. 21.

[3] Provv., 145, fols. 60ʳ–61ᵛ (22–23 May 1454). The peace treaty was concluded on 9 April between Milan and Venice, and ratified by Florence on the 23rd (J. C. Lünig, *Codex Italiae diplomaticus* (Frankfurt, 1735), IV, ii, no. 93).

[4] 26 Jan. 1455. See Soranzo, op. cit., pp. 112 ff.

[5] Provv., 145, fols. 330ᵛ–331ᵛ (23–24 Feb. 1455). Cf. Alamanno Rinuccini, *Ricordi storici*, ed. G. Aiazzi (Florence, 1840), p. lxxxv (read 'giugno' for 'gennaio'). The *Accoppiatori* still elected the Signoria for July–Aug. 1455 *a mano*, the first election by lot after the closing of the *borse* taking place in August (Tratte, 201).

terms of military necessity. Their failure to do so, and the consequent return to the traditional electoral system, forms a landmark in the development of the Medici régime. The challenge this restoration implied for the Mediceans was taken up in 1458, when the régime was given a stronger constitutional fabric than it had ever possessed. In the meantime, the conclusion of what was hoped to be a lasting peace, after the long series of wars since 1423, may well have seemed to promise a permanent return to the traditional Florentine system of government, and thus a final abandonment of the measures that had been developed during, and time and again justified by, those wars.

·   ·   ·   ·   ·   ·

If the events of 1454–5 reflect the reaction against the new electoral methods, opposition to them was, as we have seen, certainly not a new development. Unfortunately the extant minutes of discussions in the *Pratiche* are all but silent on this matter until 1446, but the narrow majorities with which continuation of elections *a mano* was obtained in 1435[1] bear eloquent witness to the strength of the opposition in the council of the People—a fact which is the more significant as the council had changed membership twice between the first and last electoral bill of that year.[2] The return to the traditional method of electing the Signoria at the beginning of 1441 was probably a concession to public opinion, and so doubtless was the limitation of the powers of the *Accoppiatori* when elections *a mano* were restored in 1443.[3] In December 1446, when the question arose whether these powers were to continue, we find the first full-scale discussion on the new electoral policy in the *Pratiche*.

On 6 December 1446 the Signoria asked the advice of a *Pratica* as to whether the bags of the Signoria should be closed, or kept open.[4] One of the Signoria was Niccolò Soderini and the first speaker was Agnolo Acciaiuoli; we shall find both as leaders of the opposition in 1465–6.[5] As he was to do more successfully in 1465, Agnolo Acciaiuoli demanded that the bags should be closed. He was not alone in this: of the 29 speakers,

[1] Above, p. 14.
[2] On 1 June and on 1 Oct. The councils of the People and of the Commune were appointed for four-monthly periods.
[3] Above, pp. 16, 17.
[4] Cons. e Prat., 52, fols. 1ʳ–2ʳ: 'utrum marsupia honorum claudi an aperta teneri debeant'. *Honorum* doubtless refers to the Signoria only.
[5] See below, Part II.

6 were definitely,[1] and 5 with some reservations,[2] of his view; 7 were opposed to the closing of the bags ('via presens est tutior'),[3] 6 did not know, or did not want to commit themselves,[4] while 5 others took the attitude that though it would be preferable not to close the bags, public opinion necessitated it.[5] The principal figure of this group was Cosimo de' Medici. His speech is the first full statement of the arguments with which the leading citizens of the régime justified the new electoral system. While revealing the difficulties they had to face, it shows Cosimo's own cautious attitude. The speakers who were opposed to a restoration of elections by lot pointed, above all, to the security the new electoral method provided,[6] and also to its usefulness in times of war and for the imposition of taxes.[7] Cosimo, on the other hand, takes it for granted that all citizens wish, *cum tempus postularet*, that the bags be closed. Elections *a mano*, he says, had been introduced to help defend Florence's independence (*libertas*), so that 'sine aliqua sevitia status civitatis servetur'. The present time was, because of the war and the need for new taxation, no less fraught with dangers; and provided the leading citizens, the *principes civitatis*, agreed, he would consequently be of the opinion that no changes be made, were it not for the fact that the rumour had been spread in the city that the bags were to be closed. He therefore feels that it is now necessary that this should be done, *obsequens votis civium*. He does not know how it can best be put into practice; and he asks that the technicalities be discussed fully, so that, 'summa cum pace et securitate libertatis', and, last but not least, 'status presentis, ea de re agatur'.[8] In the

---

[1] Agnolo Acciaiuoli, Domenico Martelli, Nerone di Nigi Dietisalvi, Otto Altoviti, Andrea di Salvestro Nardi, Alessandro d'Ugone Alessandri.

[2] Sandro di Giovanni Biliotti ('claudenda si in eo status sit securitas'), Giovanni di Domenico Bartoli, Neri di Domenico Bartolini (in 4 to 6 months), Franco di Nicol Sacchetti ('si periculum absit'), Antonio di Marsilio Vecchietti.

[3] Bernardo di Bartolomeo Gherardi, Nero di Filippo del Nero, Matteo di Marco Bartoli, Giovanni d'Antonio Canigiani, Bernardo di Lorenzo Ridolfi, Otto Niccolini (unless 'quid periculi aut necessitatis appareret'), Carlo Federighi.

[4] Lorenzo d'Andrea della Stufa, Alamanno Salviati, Puccio d'Antonio Pucci, Francesco di Jacopo Ventura, Lodovico di Cece da Verrazzano, Domenico Tani.

[5] Cosimo de' Medici, Piero di Cardinale Rucellai, Francesco di Niccolò del Benino, Antonio di Giuliano Ginori, Giovannozzo Pitti.

[6] Bernardo di Bartolomeo Gherardi: 'via presens est tutior'. Similarly Nero del Nero and Bernardo Ridolfi.

[7] Matteo Bartoli: 'propter tributa imponenda et bellum'.

[8] Loc. cit., fol. 1ᵛ: '. . . omnes cives desiderare, cum tempus postularet, marsupia clausa existere. Sed ob libertatem tuendam fuisse inductum, ut eo timore sine aliqua sevitia status civitatis servetur. Deinde dixit quod presens tempus cum propter tributa imponenda, tum propter bellum quod geritur, non esse minus periculosum quam quando secretariis marsupia

Pratica held four days later, it emerged that nearly all the speakers had come round to Cosimo's view: as Neri di Gino Capponi puts it, the bags are to be closed in such a way that 'status et libertas cum honore secretariorum [i.e. of the *Accoppiatori*] servetur'.[1] Even Giovannozzo Pitti, who six years later took the initiative in restoring elections *a mano*, insists that the bags be closed before the end of the year. As usual, a smaller committee was put in charge of discussing the proposal; and on 14 December it reported its conclusions to the *Pratica*.[2] These were very different from what might have been expected after the earlier meetings. The two spokesmen, Otto Niccolini and Cosimo de' Medici, state that, 'since the open bags appear essential for the preservation and security of the present régime, and since it is most useful both with regard to present conditions and the needs of the city, as well as for avoiding danger and discord', the committee unanimously advises that the bags should on no condition whatsoever be closed: 'nec de hac re amplius disputandum.'[3] There is, then, no more talk of war, plague, or taxes, to justify control of elections; the chief argument is, in plain terms, the security of the régime. The committee's advice, after having been accepted by the *Pratica*, was approved, on 15 December, by the *Sedici Gonfalonieri* and the *Dodici Buonuomini*;[4] after which nothing more is heard on this subject until 4 April 1448. On that day, Cosimo de' Medici reports the advice of a *Pratica* to the effect that, if it could be done in such a way as not to jeopardize the security and preservation of the régime, the bags should be closed, 'per pace et concordia del populo'—an argument that had been used for exactly the opposite purpose in December 1446.[5]

---

data fuerunt: et propterea si principes civitatis in hoc concordes essent, sue sententie esse ut marsupia eo modo manerent. Sed cum per non mediocres civitatis iam rumor divulgatus sit, opus esse ut marsupia claudantur, iccirco obsequens votis civium concludebat ut clauderentur; de modo vero se nescire quid sit dicendum. Sed de hoc iterum atque iterum consulendum, ut summa cum pace et securitate libertatis et status presentis ea de re agatur.'

[1] Ibid., fols. 2ᵛ–3ʳ (10 Dec. 1446). Matteo de' Bartoli is still against it, but 'maiori parti assentiebatur'.

[2] Ibid., fol. 3ᵛ.

[3] Ibid., fol. 3ᵛ (14 Dec.): 'Cum marsupia aperta ad conservationem et securitatem presentis status rei publice pertinere videantur, cumque id et ad presentia tempora et ad ea que sunt necessaria civitati, et demum ad pericula discordiasque vitandas utilissimum esse videatur, omnes hi cives, qui inferius scribentur, concordi sententia retulerunt, nullo modo esse claudenda. Nec de hac re amplius disputandum, sed potius consulendum esse rei publice tum in ceteris rebus, tum maxime in comparanda pecunia et novis tributis statuendis.'

[4] Ibid., fol. 4ʳ⁻ᵛ.

[5] Ibid., fol. 38ʳ: 'Et che par loro per pace et concordia del populo che le borse si debbino serrare, sì veramente con quella forma et modo dove s'intenda essere la sicurtà et conservatione del presente et buono stato.' The other spokesman was Bernardo de' Giugni.

The discussions in the *Pratica* of March 1449 on the advisability of asking the councils to prolong the powers of the
Accoppiatori show a similar division of opinions.[1] This final
extension, limited to six Signorie, was proposed by the committee elected on this matter, which included Cosimo de' Medici,
as well as Otto Niccolini, Giovannozzo Pitti, Neri Capponi,
and Agnolo Acciaiuoli, the arguments in favour being once
more the war, the financial difficulties, and the danger of
plague.[2] Since the *Balìa* itself was unwilling to pass this extension,
the committee suggested, on 27 March, the summoning of
a *Pratica* of 40 citizens, 'fuori di noi de' più principali del reggimento', to examine the matter. These members of the inner circle
of the régime proved more critical of the proposal to continue
elections *a mano* than might have been expected. True, there was
a large majority, including such men as Agnolo Acciaiuoli, in
favour of what was after all only a short-term measure. However,
the committee exaggerates when, the day after the meeting of
the *Pratica*, it declares that nearly all, *quasi tucti*, supported this
measure in principle.[3] In fact, about one in five of the *Pratica* had,
in varying degrees, been opposed to a further continuation of
electoral controls, both on account of their unpopularity and
because there was no real danger of war or plague. 'The Signoria
must not be advised to act against the wishes of the council . . .
there is no sign of plague'; 'the will of the majority must prevail;
there is no enemy at the gates, nor does any great danger
threaten us'[4]—if such views could be held among the leading
citizens of the régime, it is not hard to imagine how sceptical the
opposition in the statutory councils must have been about the
arguments put forward in favour of continued controls. To
what degree concessions to public opinion were necessary was,
on the other hand, one of the principal problems of the régime,
and Matteo Palmieri put into a nutshell what was doubtless the
view of many of its adherents: 'Nec dubium esse securius fore
marsupia esse aperta quam clausa. Et quamvis videatur magis
populare ut claudantur, tandem illi popularitati securitatem

---

[1] See above, p. 19.

[2] Cons. e Prat., 52, fols. 74ʳ (16 March 1449), 74ᵛ (21 March), 75ʳ (27 March). See also
above, p. 19, n. 6.

[3] Ibid., fol. 77ᵛ (29 March): 'Hora inteso i consigli di circa 50 electi citadini quasi tucti
aprobare questo medesimo, ma essere diversi solamente nel tempo . . . .'

[4] Ibid., fols. 75ᵛ–77ʳ (28 March): Sandro Biliotti, Francesco del Benino (fol. 75ᵛ). Mariotto
Lippi says that 'populum desiderare morem antiquum et libertatem pristinam recuperare . . .'.

anteponendam.'[1] But there were limits to the extent to which such an attitude was practical politics. The failure to have the extension law passed by the *Balìa*, after it had been approved by the *più principali del reggimento* in the *Pratica*, spotlights the difficult position of a régime which depended on conciliar assent for the continuation of safeguards that were considered essential for its security, and which could not even always rely upon a council recruited from its supporters. It was, accordingly, in an atmosphere of impending crisis that the *Balìa* came to an end and the bags were closed by the *Accoppiatori*.[2] A number of supporters of the régime concluded a pact to help, with all their power, preserve and strengthen the *presente stato et reggimento* and all its *fautori, amici et seguaci*, and to persecute its enemies.[3] Among the first 63 citizens who signed the pact we find 16 members of the *Pratica* of March, including Otto Niccolini, Giovannozzo Pitti, and Matteo Palmieri, and 9 out of the 20 *Accoppiatori* who were just engaged in closing the bags:[4] over one-half belonged to the *Balìa* which ten days later ended its session.[5] The list is headed by Giovannozzo Pitti and Otto Niccolini, who a few weeks earlier had reported, together with Cosimo, the committee's decision in favour of a continuation of electoral controls.[6] It was on the initiative of Giovannozzo Pitti that a new *Balìa* was created in 1452 and elections *a mano* of the Gonfalonier of Justice restored.[7] When, less than a month later, in August 1452, the Signoria presented to the *Balìa* a bill extending the powers of the *Accoppiatori* once more to the entire Signoria, it met with considerable opposition (as a similar bill had done in the *Balìa* of 1449[8]), and was passed with a majority of one vote only; so did the extension by

---

[1] Fol. 76[r].   [2] See above, pp. 19–20.

[3] They justify this action by affirming 'che non solamente in publico et ordinario [i.e. by constitutional channels], ma etiandio extraordinariamente et con consigli, opere et adiutorii secreti et particulari si debba continuamente et con ogni affetione attendere alla conservatione et accrescimento della nostra republica ...'. This 'sottoscrizione' has been published by A. Sapori, *Una pagina di storia fiorentina. Il patto giurato del 10 maggio 1449* (Milan, s.d., [1946]), from the document in the Niccolini archives, and has been erroneously interpreted by him as emanating from the opposition to Cosimo. Both the text and the signatures of this document show without a shadow of doubt that its purpose was the security of the Medici régime.

[4] See above, p. 20. Of the *Accoppiatori* who had held the bags *a mano* since 1444, Tommaso Soderini, Luca Pitti, Francesco Orlandi, Manno Temperani, and Dietisalvi Neroni; of the *Accoppiatori* of the scrutiny of 1448, Luigi Ridolfi, Bartolomeo Michelozzi, Bernardo Gherardi, and Matteo Morelli.

[5] See below, p. 77.

[6] See above, p. 26. Otto Niccolini had acted in the same capacity in 1446; above, p. 25.

[7] See above, p. 21.

[8] See above, pp. 19, 21.

five years of the term of office of the *Accoppiatori* in November 1453.[1] In fact, these bills were passed only because it had been decided that an absolute majority was sufficient for the passage of laws in the *Balìa* instead of the statutory two-thirds majority—a decision which was doubtless prompted by the fear that the latter might not always be obtainable, and which was severely criticized as a *chattiva et dolorosa provigione*.[2] These fears were, in the event, fully justified. The voting results are the more remarkable as the *Balìa* was largely composed of picked members; one may easily imagine what the opposition would have been in the statutory councils, had their consent to the *Balìa*'s legislation been required.[3]

The events preceding the closing of the bags in June 1455, show once more the unpopularity of the electoral controls, as well as of the *Accoppiatori* who had to carry them out. In January 1455 the Signoria failed to get a new tax passed by the council of 200, a tax law of November 1454 having already been passed with much difficulty.[4] The predicament of the Signoria was discussed in the *Pratica* on 17 and 24 January and on 20 February; on that day, it was finally suggested that since the government had done everything in its power and *non plus potuit*, the only way out was to yield to popular demands and to close the bags.[5] 'In discussing taxation', states Manno Temperani, 'one should consider ways and means of satisfying the people. Consequently the bags should be closed and the ancient popular system restored. Once the people have obtained this, they will agree to everything that is necessary.'[6] This view was supported by the

[1] Cf. Libri Fabarum, 63, fol. 4ʳ (9 Aug. 1452): 102 votes against 100; fol. 29ʳ (5 Nov. 1453): 113 votes against 102. An absolute majority was required for the passage of the bills.

[2] According to Francesco di Tommaso Giovanni, this was contained in the *provvisione* creating the *Balìa*, without the councils realizing it: 'e non acorgendosene e consigli contenere la provisione per modo che posson per la metà e lᵃ più, essendo ragunata almeno 2/3 della balìa, ottener qualunche deliberatione' (*Ricordanze*, in Carte Strozz., 2ᵃ ser., XVI *bis*, fol. 15ᵛ). But there is no such regulation in the *provvisione*, and Pietrobuoni was probably right in saying that it was the *Balìa* itself which decreed it (*Priorista*, Bibl. Naz., Conv. soppr., C. 4. 895, fol. 160ʳ): 'La prima volta si raghunò la balya vinsono molti partiti; fra gli altri fu uno che detta balya raunati in sufficiente numero, cioè pello meno duo terzi di detta balya, che quello che ssi vincessi per loro partito per la metà delle fave e una più avessi luogho chome se lla fussi vinta pe' duo terzi come si soleva fare prima. Fu tenuta una chattiva et dolorosa provigione da tutto 'l popolo . . . Et però n'o voluto fare un pocho di nota.'

[3] On the superseding of legislation by the ancient councils during sessions of *Balìe*, see below, pp. 75 ff.

[4] Libri Fabarum, 64, fols. 4ᵛ–11ʳ (14–24 Nov): 'Impositio sex onerum super presenti distributione cinquine'; fols. 23ʳ–25ʳ (15–24 Jan.): 'Quod eligantur x cives qui imponant fi. 100,000.'

[5] Cons. e Prat, 53, fols. 149ʳ–155ᵛ.

[6] Ibid., fol. 154ʳ⁻ᵛ: '. . . Conata est dominatio providere, sed non plus potuit. Sicut de

rest of the *Pratica*, including Giovannozzo Pitti himself; and two days later, Agnolo Acciaiuoli and Neri di Gino Capponi, in the name of the *copulatores sortitionum*, presented the Signoria with a draft bill—a kind of self-denying ordinance that had been passed by them unanimously, to the effect that their office should come to an end and the bags be closed.[1] The electoral controls had been introduced in 1452, 'trovandosi questo popolo in grave et pericolosa guerra'; they had borne *optimo fructo*; and now the war was over, 'et hora trovandosi questo popolo in tal pace', it was time to return to the 'uso consueto di questo popolo'.[2] Significantly the *Accoppiatori* fail to mention the extension for five years granted them in 1453, which had nothing to do with the war, and which now might prove somewhat of an embarrassment to them. It is only in their preceding report to the Signoria that they point out their decision to disregard it, 'benchè il tempo duri anchora più anni'; and perhaps in order to protect themselves against future criticism, they specially ask for their report to be put on paper.[3] The vast majorities which this law obtained in the councils were a measure of the opposition to continued electoral controls; in the council of the People, it was passed by 218 votes against 22, in that of the Commune by 169 against 7.[4]

---

tributis consultatur, ita cogitetur de consolatione populi, ut marsupia claudantur, et veniatur ad ad [*sic*] antiquum vivendi modum popularem. Et cum populus hoc habebit, tunc omnibus concurret que oportuna erunt. . . .'

[1] See above, p. 22. Cons. e Prat., 53, fol. 157^r: 'Nomina copulatorum qui supradicta fecerunt et unanimiter retulerunt sunt . . .'.

[2] Ibid., fols. 156^r–157^r. The bill, which was presented to, and passed by, the councils on 23 and 24 Feb. (Provv., 145, fols. 330^v–331^v), follows this draft.

[3] Fol. 155^v: 'et hec verba scribi voluerunt'.

[4] Libri Fabarum, 64, fol. 27^{r-v}.

2

THE *ACCOPPIATORI*

THE *Accoppiatori* had some reason for being apprehensive. Before they had closed the bags for the last time, in 1449, it had been pointed out in the *Pratica* that the bags were being 'kept open' *maximo odio copulatorum*.[1] Not only were the functions and the duration of the office itself, as they had developed since 1434, contrary to the letter and the spirit of the Florentine constitution; but also the length of the terms of office of its personnel constituted a radical departure from normal constitutional practice.

Rapid rotation of office was a fundamental feature of Florentine government and administration. The length of appointments ranged from two months to one year, office-holders being normally allowed to be reappointed only after intervals of up to three years.[2] Even the members of an extraordinary magistracy like the *Dieci di Balìa*, created with special powers (*balìa*) in times of war, had their terms normally limited to six months, and were not re-eligible for three years,[3] although in exceptional cases this could be waived.[4] However, between 1434 and 1455, the *Dieci* in office were re-elected only on two occasions, once for two and the other time for six months.[5] The extensions granted to the *Accoppiatori* between 1434 and 1438 radically broke with that practice, concerning as they did not only the office, but also its personnel. It will be remembered that at first these extensions were justified on the grounds that the *Accoppiatori* had not yet completed the filling of the bags; it was evident that for this purpose the same officials would have to be allowed to finish the job. But this argument was no longer applicable after September 1436 when the bags had at last been filled.[6] Fortunately, the authority to extend the term of office of the *Accoppiatori* had, in the meantime, been delegated to the Signoria, and in 1438 the

---

[1] Cons. e Prat., 52, fol. 77ʳ (27 March 1449; Mariotto Lippi).

[2] On such *divieti*, see, e.g., *Statuta* 1415, ii, p. 831.

[3] Cf. G. Pampaloni, 'Gli organi della Repubblica fiorentina per le relazioni con l'estero', *Rivista di studi politici internazionali* xx (1953), pp. 261–96; *Statuta* 1415, ii, p. 831.

[4] Ibid.

[5] In 1438 and 1451; cf. Tratte, 80, fols. 441ʳ⁻ᵛ, 454ʳ⁻ᵛ.   [6] See above, p. 13, n. 3.

new *Balìa* used its powers to grant them yet another extension.[1]
By the end of 1439, when the *Accoppiatori* finally retired, they
had been in office for over five years.[2] Their successors, who were
appointed in January 1440, ended their office after they had filled
the bags in February 1441.[3] But if this marked a return to constitutional practice, the development that had taken place
between 1434 and 1439 had created a precedent of far-reaching
importance. It had shown that by their *de facto* permanency, as
well as by their powers, the *Accoppiatori* could become the pivot
of the Medici régime.

We have seen that when electoral controls were reintroduced
in 1443, this was done with some caution, in the manner of
a compromise: of the nine members of the Signoria, four only
were to be elected *a mano*.[4] Furthermore, the *Accoppiatori* of
1434-9 and those of 1440-1, although they participated in the
election of their successors, were barred from re-election.[5] In
May or June 1444 the new *Balìa*, after deciding to hold a scrutiny
of the *Tre Maggiori*, elected for it new *Accoppiatori* who, following
the precedent of 1440, took over also elections *a mano* from their
predecessors; these were, consequently, in office for less than one
year.[6]

The next scrutiny of the *Tre Maggiori* took place in 1448, and
again the statutes were observed, new *Accoppiatori* being elected
for the scrutiny.[7] This time, however, they were not also put in
charge of elections *a mano*, as had happened in 1440 and 1444.

---

[1] Above, pp. 13, 15.

[2] Above, p. 15. In the place of Niccolò di Cocco Donati, who had died in office, the
Consiglio Maggiore of 1438 had elected, on 11 June 1438, the then Gonfalonier of Justice,
Bartolomeo di Giovanni Orlandini. This entry is, however, cancelled in the extant minutes
of that council (Tratte, 60, fol. 225^{r-v}).

[3] Above, p. 16.   [4] See above, p. 17.

[5] Provv., 134, fol. 133^{r-v} (1–2 Oct. 1443). The election took place on 11 Oct.: Tratte,
1148, part 1, fol. 1^v. The other electors were the Signoria, the Colleges, the Captains of the
Guelph Party, the *Sei di Mercanzia*, the Secretaries of the scrutinies of the external offices of
1434 and 1440, and the 21 consuls of the guilds who had been chosen for the scrutiny (see
below, p. 54). Substitutes had been elected for the *Accoppiatori* and Secretaries who had died.
The total number of electors was consequently 108.

[6] At its creation on 20–23 May the new *Balìa* was given powers to carry out the scrutiny,
which actually took place in June, as emerges from the extant scrutiny lists (Tratte, 49). But
the decree ordering the scrutiny to take place, which the *Balìa* must have passed, is not
entered in its register (Balìe, 26). This decree must have contained the customary regulations
concerning the election of the new *Accoppiatori*. That they were elected in May or June
emerges from Tratte, 1148, part 1, fol. 25^v, which gives the names of the 'Accoppiatori dello
squittino del 1444'; that they took over elections *a mano*, is shown by their register (Tratte,
1148, part 2, fols. 2^v ff.). See also below, p. 54, n. 2.

[7] Balìe, 26, fol. 190^{r-v} (16 July 1448). It was to take place in the second half of August.
The *Accoppiatori* were once more elected by the *Balìa*.

The *Accoppiatori* of 1444 continued in charge until the bags were closed in spring 1449[1] and, as the results of the scrutiny of 1448 were to be combined with those of the preceding one, they collaborated with their colleagues in this job.[2] This proved to be a new departure: for when in 1452 elections *a mano* were once more restored, they were entrusted not, as in 1443, to newly appointed *Accoppiatori*, but to those who *clauserunt bursas ultima vice*, i.e. to the *Accoppiatori* of 1444 and 1448. Their term of office, having been extended by five years in 1453, was brought to an abrupt end in 1455.[3] In 1452 their number had been increased to twenty, substitutes having been elected for the four members who had died.[4] Of these twenty, eight had been in office since 1445 with the exception of the three years between May 1449 and July 1452 when the bags were closed; Luca Pitti had been *Accoppiatore* also between 1434 and 1439.[5]

These periods of office would have been considerably longer, had the extension of elections *a mano* by five years, passed in 1453, been observed. It is, then, clear that the electoral legislation of 1452–3 followed the precedent set after 1434 not only in its effort to institutionalize the office and its powers, but also in preserving the continuity of its personnel. The same trend is also reflected by the family connexions between members of this office at different periods. We find the Pitti represented between 1434 and 1439 by Luca di Bonaccorso, between 1440 and 1441 by Giovannozzo di Francesco, and between 1444 and 1449, and 1452 and 1455, once more by Luca; the Medici, between 1440 and 1441 at first by Lorenzo and then by Cosimo di Giovanni, and between 1448 and 1449, and 1452 and 1455, by Piero di Cosimo; the Dietisalvi by Nerone di Nigi between 1434 and 1439, and by his son Dietisalvi between 1444 and 1449, and 1452 and 1455; the Martelli by Domenico di Niccolò between 1443 and 1444, and by his brother Ugolino between 1445 and 1449, and 1452 and 1455. The office of *Accoppiatore* had not only become one of the cornerstones of the new régime, but was also well on the way to being monopolized by a small

---

[1] This emerges from the register of the *Accoppiatori*, Tratte, 1148.

[2] Balìe, cit.: 'fiat simul immixtio per copulatores qui ad presens sunt una cum copulatoribus qui de novo eligentur pro presenti scructinio.'

[3] Above, pp. 21–22.

[4] Agnolo Acciaiuoli, Antonio Lenzoni, Lionardo Bartolini, and Lorenzo della Stufa, for Domenico di Matteo Pescioni, Guarente Guarenti, Carlo Federighi, and Bernardo Carnesecchi (Tratte, 1148, fol. 25ᵛ). See below, Appendix, no. I.

[5] See Appendix, no. I. Ugolino Martelli had succeeded Giuliano Martini in 1445.

group of citizens and families. What did the powers of the *Accoppiatori* precisely consist of? We have hitherto referred to elections *a mano* in a general way; it is now time to clarify what they entailed and how they were conducted.

The Statutes of 1415 are naturally silent on this matter, for the simple reason that elections *a mano* of the Signoria were unconstitutional, and contemporary chroniclers take a familiarity with technicalities for granted. These have therefore to be discovered from a variety of sources, and primarily from the electoral records preserved in the Florentine State archives.

A first, somewhat startling, result of this inquiry is the absence of any substantial difference in the formula used, before and after 1434, in the electoral registers of the chancery to record the two-monthly elections of the Signoria. There are two such registers: firstly, that which contained *all* the names drawn on the occasion of these elections, as well as of those of the Colleges, whether or not their owners were appointed to the office (henceforth called *tratte* registers), and, secondly, the register of the chancery which recorded only the names of the citizens who were actually appointed as Signori or *Collegi*. Now both registers continue, after 1434, to refer to the election of the Signoria as being still carried out by lot, just as that of the *Sedici Gonfalonieri* and *Dodici Buonuomini*, with the *Podestà* drawing the names from the purses;[1] and just as before 1434, the dates are entered of the scrutinies which had served for the filling of these purses. In contrast to this, the Signoria of November–December 1434 appears in the second register as 'elected by the Signoria, the *Accoppiatori*, and the *Secretari* by virtue [of the decree] of the *Balìa*',[2] and is not recorded in the *tratte* register; instead we find a note to the effect that 'here a Signoria is missing'.[3] To judge from this evidence, sortition of the Signoria was restored at the end of 1434, and

---

[1] Cf., e.g., Tratte, 199, for Signoria of May–June 1435 : '... In consilio populi Florentie et in eiusdem palatio ad sonum campane et voce preconis coadunato Magnificus miles ... D. Jacobus Angelide Messina, potestas civitatis Florentie, sorte et fortuna secundum ordinamenta Communis Florentie extrassit infrascriptos ... ad officium prioratus artium et vexilliferatus Justitie', &c. In exceptional cases, the place of the *Podestà* could be taken, by ordinance of the Signoria, by other high magistrates, such as the Captain of the People.

[2] '... electi vigore balie per dominos et accopulatores et secretarios intus et extra' (Tratte, 93, fol. 14ᵛ).

[3] 'Hic deficit unus prioratus' (Tratte, 198, fol. 166ᵛ). The same note occurs in connexion with the Signoria of Nov.–Dec. 1433 which was equally elected *a mano* (ibid., fol. 142ᵛ), while the second register has 'electi per vigorem balie per dominos et accopiatores' (Tratte, 93, fol. 14ᵛ).

remained in force during the following years. How can this be reconciled with the fact that, until 1441, the Signoria was continually elected *a mano* by the *Accoppiatori*?

The *tratte* registers show three things: firstly, that the *Accoppiatori* continued using the scrutinies for the election of the Signoria,[1] secondly, that a form of sortition remained in force,[2] and, thirdly, that it was not the *Accoppiatori* who carried out the drawing by lot. What they did was to prepare it on the basis of the existing eligibility lists. As we have seen, when the *Accoppiatori* had their powers renewed for the first time, in December 1434, they were ordered not only to fill the purses with the results of the scrutiny that had been held in October, but also to see to it that in the meantime the bags from which the names of the Signoria were to be drawn, according to the Statutes, by lot, contained a minimum number of names.[3] In the following renewals of these powers to the *Accoppiatori*, the term *imborsare* acquires a dual meaning: on the one hand, it refers to the traditional procedure of filling the bags which were to be used until the next scrutiny; on the other, it describes the new method of filling special purses to be used for each of the two-monthly elections of the government only. Accordingly, when the Signoria renewed the *Accoppiatori's* powers in 1436 and 1437, they could use the expressions 'to make' and *imborsare* the Signoria synonymously.[4] At the same time, they indicated the innovation in electoral method by adding that these terms referred to the way in which the Signoria was now elected.

While *imborsazione* and sortition thus remained part of the electoral process, they did so in a manner that differed sharply from constitutional law and practice. The Statutes prescribed that every two months the bags which contained the names of the citizens who were eligible for the Signoria, and which had been filled by the *Accoppiatori* with the results of the quinquennial scrutinies, were to be taken from the sacristy of S. Croce, where they were kept, to the Palace of the Signoria. Here the

---

[1] In the *tratte* registers, the dates from which new scrutinies are used are recorded, e.g. to 27 Feb. 1440 (Tratte, 199): 'Hic incipit prima extractio de scrutineo anni 1439.'

[2] There is no reason to doubt the accuracy of the *tratte* registers, which were destined for the internal use of the chancery only.

[3] See above, p. 12.

[4] '. . . ad faciendum priores et vexilliferum modo et forma et prout tunc poterant et faciebant'; 'ad imbursandum vexilliferos iustitie et priores artium eo modo et forma et prout consuevit usque in presens' (Deliberazioni dei Signori e Collegi, speciale autorità, 25, fol. 152^v; 26, fols. 10^v–11^r). See above, pp. 13–14.

Podestà would, in the presence of the highest magistracies and of anyone else who wished to attend the ceremony, draw, one by one, the names of eligible citizens from the purses of the Signoria, until candidates were found who were not barred by temporary disqualifications from accepting office.[1] Under the new system the public drawing by lot continued, *secundum ordinamenta*; but the purses from which the *Podestà* drew the names of the future Signoria were no longer identical with those that had been filled after the scrutinies, but had been specially prepared by the *Accoppiatori* for that election only. As the law of October 1443, restoring elections *a mano*, put it: the *Accoppiatori* were to *tenere bursas ad manus* in such a way as to place a minimum number of names in the purses of the Signoria, 'as often as one proceeded to the drawing by lot of the Signoria'.[2]

This, however, did not mean that the *Accoppiatori* could choose for this purpose any names they wished. Their choice was restricted to those citizens who were eligible by virtue of the scrutiny which was in force at the time of the election. This was already made clear when the *Accoppiatori* were first given, shortly after Cosimo's return, powers to elect the government: it was expressly stated that they were not allowed 'to elect anyone who had not been qualified in the scrutiny for the Signoria that had been held during this month'.[3] Subsequent renewals of these powers emphasized that the men whose names the *Accoppiatori* placed in their purses must be *habiles* for the Priorate, or the Gonfaloniership of Justice as the case might be.[4] Thus, instead of the statutory two stages in the election of the Signoria, i.e. scrutiny and sortition, there were now three, the *imborsazioni* by the *Accoppiatori* having been inserted between the scrutiny and the final sortition. While the scrutiny thus still remained the basis for their choice, and while the last decision was still left to the lot, they could now not only choose from among the eligible citizens whomsoever they wished to present for sortition, but also determine the chances of their candidates by deciding how many

[1] Statuta 1415, ii, pp. 495–8. See above, p. 4.

[2] '. . . tenere bursas ad manus et facere vexilliferum iustitie' and three of the Priors, 'ita tamen quod quotiens ad extractionem dominorum devenietur, imbursari debeant pro qualibet tali vice', etc. (Provv., 134, fol. 133^{r-v} (1–2 Oct. 1443)).

[3] '. . . nec aliquem possint eligere, qui non obtinuerit in scructineo prioratus celebrato de presenti mense' (Balìe, 25, fol. 45^r).

[4] Ibid., fol. 87^v. Tratte, 60, fol. 225^r (11 June 1438). Provv., 134, fol. 133^{r-v} (1–2 Oct. 1443): 'imbursari debeant pro qualibet vice . . . habiles ad dictum officium', etc.; 143, fol. 99^v (10–14 July 1452), and Balìe, 27, fol. 26^v (9 Aug. 1452). See also above, pp. 11, 15, 17, 21.

names of *tunc habiles ad officium* to place in the purses, over and
above the minimum laid down by the law.

The minimum number of names which the *Accoppiatori* were
obliged to place in their special bags for the two-monthly
tratta of the Signoria was, between December 1434 and April
1438, ten for each of the seven bags of the Priorate, and four for
that of the Gonfaloniership of Justice.[1] In 1438 the minimum
was reduced to five for the Priorate and three for the Gonfaloniership of Justice,[2] and this ratio was maintained when elections
a mano were restored first in 1443 and then in 1452.[3] After this
reduction, the *Accoppiatori* would, accordingly, short-list at least
thirty-five names for the Priorate and three for the Gonfaloniership—the final decision remaining, as before, with the lot.
Sortition was, consequently, not simply a façade for an election
by the *Accoppiatori*; its constitutional function survived, although
deprived of most of its original meaning.

For the new system drastically curtailed the chances of eligible
citizens of being elected to office. The extent to which this was
the case may be illustrated by the following example. In 1440,
that is at a time when the *Accoppiatori* were not required to
select more than five names per *quartiere* for the election of the
Priors, and not more than three for that of the Gonfalonier of
Justice, the new scrutiny qualified, in the *Quartiere* of San Giovanni, 411 members of the Greater, and 95 members of the
Lesser Guilds for the Signoria, 65 of the former being declared
eligible for the Gonfaloniership of Justice.[4] Normally, all these
citizens would have had their names placed in the purses for the
two-monthly elections of the government. In the course of the
five years until the next scrutiny, the *Accoppiatori* would necessarily have to select a considerable proportion of the citizens who
had been qualified.[5] But not only could they do so when they
wished, and thus determine the composition of the single

---

[1] In the sortition of the Signoria, a total of eight bags was used: one for the Gonfalonier
of Justice, the office rotating among the four *quartieri*; one for the two artisan members,
for the *quartiere* which happened to provide the Gonfalonier; and six for the remaining
three *quartieri*, that is three from each of the two kinds of bag from which the Priors'
names were drawn, the *borsellino* and the *borsa generale* (on the meaning of this distinction,
see below, p. 45). Cf. Balìe, 25, fol. 87ᵛ (15 Dec. 1434), for the minima.

[2] Tratte, 60, fol. 225ʳ (11 June 1438).

[3] Provv., 134, fol. 133ʳ⁻ᵛ (1–2 Oct. 1443); Balìe, 27, fol. 26ᵛ (9 Aug. 1452).

[4] Tratte, 1150.

[5] Over a period of four years and eight months, each *quartiere* supplied 42 Priors
belonging to the Greater Guilds, 14 belonging to the Lesser Guilds, and 7 Gonfaloniers
of Justice.

governments, but they were also able to exclude altogether a large number of eligible citizens from the final ballot.

As the entries in the *tratte* registers for all offices show abundantly, several, and often many, names had usually to be drawn until one was found whose owner was not temporarily disqualified from accepting the office in question. Thus the average number of *polizze* drawn at the two-monthly elections of the Signoria between 1430 and 1433 was 52, and in the first four elections of 1434, 79·5.[1] After the introduction of elections *a mano*, numbers drop sharply: on 29 December 1434 only 13 names were drawn, and this remains roughly the average until the closing of the bags in February 1441 when the number suddenly jumps to 88.[2]

The new system reduced the chances of eligible citizens not only of being elected, but also of having their names drawn at the two-monthly elections of the Signoria. Under the 'oligarchical' régime before 1434, the citizens whose names had been 'seen' (*veduti*), that is, had been drawn at the elections to the three highest offices but who had been temporarily disqualified from accepting the office, and thus from being *seduti*, had begun to form, together with their families, a privileged group.[3] Since the scrutiny registers were secret, to have been *veduto* was, in fact, the only official evidence, short of actually assuming the office, that a citizen had his name in the ballot bags, and had consequently been successful in the scrutiny. The sharp reduction in the number of names drawn at the elections *a mano* of the Signoria after 1434 thus presented a serious problem.

In particular, it was bound to affect the chances of the younger members of the upper-class families who, while having been qualified for the *Tre Maggiori* in a previous scrutiny, had not yet had their names drawn; between 1434 and 1440, their chances were, for all practical purposes, limited to the offices of the Sixteen *Gonfalonieri* and the Twelve *Buonuomini*, who continued to be appointed in the traditional manner. Not more than three citizens were, during the entire period, 'seen' for the highest and most sought-after office, the Gonfaloniership of Justice; while after the closing of the ballot bags, in the year 1441 alone,

[1] Tratte, 198.
[2] Tratte of 29 Dec. 1434: ibid., fol. 169^{r-v}. The figures for the years 1435–40 are: 1435: 14, 13, 20, 13, 10, 14; 1436: 13, 12, 12, 11, 16, 17; 1437: 19, 9, 16, 10, 11, 14; 1438: 10, 10, 13, 11, 11, 12; 1439: 14, 11, 12, 12, 12, 19; 1440: 10, 15, 15, 14, 11, 15 (Tratte, 199).
[3] See below, pp. 116 ff.

twenty-nine citizens were 'seen' for it.[1] Restrictions of this kind were evidently liable to make the *Accoppiatori* unpopular with many people. Consequently, when elections *a mano* were partly restored in October 1443, there appears to have been a change of policy: in the following sortitions of the Signoria, the number of *veduti ai Tre Maggiori* roughly averaged that of normal conditions.[2] Possibly the *Accoppiatori* of 1443 went too far; for as soon as their successors were elected in May or June 1444,[3] the number of *veduti* dropped again, although not as drastically as after 1434, to rise once more just before the closing of the bags in 1449.[4] Simultaneously, there was a sharp drop in the number of *veduti* for the Gonfaloniership of Justice: between June 1444 and February 1446 there were no such *veduti* at all, in 1446 there were nine, in 1447 three, and in 1448 none; so that the chief difference in the number of *veduti* under the two electoral systems now concerned the Gonfaloniership of Justice.[5] After elections *a mano* were once more restored in 1452, the total of *veduti* for the Signoria remained, for the time being, roughly on the same level as during the preceding period, when the bags were closed, and in 1454 even rose considerably above it.[6]

These changes in the numbers of *veduti* were clearly the result not of chance but of policy. After the first period of *a mano* elections, when the *Accoppiatori* all but eliminated *veduti*, they compromised with Florentine tradition by increasing the number of names of citizens who were temporarily disqualified and would therefore, if drawn, be *veduti* and not *seduti*. In other words, they selected names specially *per far vedere*, as this procedure came to

---

[1] Tratte, 198 and 199. The names of the three *veduti* for the *Gonfalonierato* were drawn in the last election prepared by the *Accoppiatori* of 1434, of 29 Dec. 1439 (Tratte, 198). See above, p. 15.

[2] No less than 169 *polizze* were drawn in the first sortition after the partial restoration of elections *a mano* in Oct. 1443, as against 68 in Aug. of that year. In the following *tratta*, of Dec. 1443, the total is again down to 86; but this roughly corresponds to the average for the years 1441–3, when the bags were closed (Tratte, 199).

[3] See above, p. 31.

[4] The approximate average figures for the *polizze* drawn in the elections of the Signoria between June 1444 and Dec. 1448 are: 1444 (4 elections): 32; 1445: 30; 1446: 23; 1447: 17; 1448: 19 (Tratte, 200). In Feb. and April 1449: 34 and 36 (ibid.).

[5] Tratte, 200.

[6] The approximate average figures for the *polizze* drawn in *tratte* of the Signoria between June 1449 and June 1452 are: 1449 (4 *tratte*): 52; 1450: 46; 1451: 40; 1452 (3 *tratte*): 47. Between Aug. 1452 and June 1455: 1452 (3 *tratte*): 25; 1453: 48; 1454: 102; 1455 (3 *tratte*): 54 (Tratte, 200, 201). On the other hand, the total of *veduti* for the Gonfaloniership, which had risen after the closing of the bags in 1449 to 6 in Aug., 10 in Oct., and to as many as 28 in 1451, dropped to 2 in Aug. 1452, after the restoration of elections *a mano*, after which date only 5 citizens were *veduti* until the restoration of elections by lot in 1455 (ibid.).

be called. In doing so, they brought, after 1443, the total of *veduti* in the single elections roughly up to the level which in normal conditions would have been the accidental result of the lot, exceptional treatment being reserved for the Gonfaloniership of Justice, for which the number of *veduti* remained very low.[1] This development thus constitutes yet another of the concessions to Florentine constitutional practice which were characteristic of the early period of the Medici régime. It was not without its dangers. As we shall see, when organized in groups, the *veduti* and their families were liable to be regarded as security risks, to the extent of being forbidden, in 1444 and again in 1455, to meet in religious confraternities.[2] Evidently, the *imborsare per far vedere* placed an additional responsibility on the shoulders of the *Accoppiatori*.

This, then, was the extent of the powers of the *Accoppiatori* in 'electing' the Signoria *a mano*. There is no evidence that they went beyond them either by eliminating names from the scrutiny registers once these had been completed, or by introducing into their bags others which were not on those registers. The former was hardly necessary in view of their opportunities for selecting names; the latter would have been difficult enough to conceal. The absence of complaints on this count adds additional weight to the fact that not one case could be found in which a citizen was elected to the Signoria under the *a mano* method who had not been previously qualified in a scrutiny.[3] At the same time, the *Accoppiatori* could influence the distribution of the scrutiny results by exercising their statutory duties.

It will be remembered that the *Accoppiatori* who in October 1434 were put in charge of elections *a mano* had originally been appointed for the scrutiny which was to be held in that month, and that until November 1435 the successive renewals of their powers also concerned the filling of the bags with the results of that scrutiny. This operation appears to have been completed by June 1436.[4] Their successors, who were elected in January 1440, were appointed for the next scrutiny, although they also took over elections *a mano* from their predecessors. They closed the new bags in February 1441.[5] Similarly, the *Accoppiatori* of 1444 were appointed both for the new scrutiny and for the election

---

[1] See below, pp. 119-21.　　　　　　　　　　　[2] See below, p. 118.
[3] In a few isolated cases, *Accoppiatori* may have increased the number of *polizze* which a citizen had acquired by means of the scrutiny.
[4] See above, p. 13.　　　　　　　　　　　[5] See above, p. 16.

of the Signoria; and again in 1448, new *Accoppiatori* were elected
for the scrutiny of that year, and collaborated with those of 1444,
who had remained in charge of electing the Signoria, in the closing of the bags in 1449.[1] Finally, the *Accoppiatori* of 1444 and
1448, who had jointly been put in charge of elections *a mano*
when these had been restored in 1452, were also entrusted with
the *imborsazione* of the new scrutiny, which they completed in
1455.[2] In fact, the scrutiny bags for the *Tre Maggiori* were still
required for the sortition of the XVI *Gonfalonieri* and XII
Buonuomini, and were used by the *Accoppiatori* in preparing the
special purses for the drawing of the Signoria,[3] which is also
indicated by the technical term *tenere le borse a mano*. While the
Accoppiatori could evidently begin using the scrutiny bags for
such elections *a mano* before they were entirely filled, they had to
have them completed before closing them, as they did in 1441,
1449, and 1455.[4]

One of the major problems of the periodical scrutinies was the
fate of the name tickets, or *polizze*, from previous scrutinies,
which remained unused in the bags. To disregard them amounted
to a kind of partial disfranchisement, and was considered to be
unfair to the citizens who had been unlucky in the ballots.[5]
Hence in 1378, 1404, and 1407, legislation was introduced prohibiting the holding of scrutinies as long as there were still names
in the bags.[6] But such prohibitions were difficult to put into
practice, conflicting as they did with the principle of periodicity
of scrutinies, and were in fact time and again suspended.[7] The
Statutes of 1415 prescribed the use of the old bags together with

---

[1] See above, pp. 31–32.

[2] See above, pp. 21–22, 32. On the scrutiny, see below, p. 55.

[3] Moreover, they were also required for the *tratta* of part of the Signoria in and after 1444.

[4] This emerges from the register of the *Accoppiatori* of 1452–5. While they begin to use
the scrutiny of 1453 for the election of the Signoria of March–April 1454 (Tratte, 201),
they carry out the distribution of the new *polizze* among the *borse* of the Priorate and of the
Gonfalonierato only in June 1455, that is, after it had been decided to close the bags (Tratte,
16, fols. 15ʳ, 16ᵛ–31ʳ; 19–20 June).

[5] Especially so if, although their names had been drawn, they had been temporarily
disqualified from accepting office.

[6] Provv., 65, fols. 278ʳ–279ʳ (23–25 Feb. 1378); 93, fols. 126ᵛ–127ʳ (28–29 Oct. 1404); 96,
fols. 136ᵛ–138ʳ (1–2 Oct. 1407). According to the laws of 1404 and 1407, bills to hold a new
scrutiny could, however, be proposed, if they were first passed unanimously by the Signoria
and its Colleges.

[7] Provv., 104, fols. 32ʳ–35ʳ (12–14 Nov. 1414), for a scrutiny of the external offices: 106,
fols. 32ʳ–36ʳ (19–20 June 1416), for a scrutiny of the three highest magistracies. Another
way of dealing with this problem was to prohibit the *use* of the new *borse* as long as the old
ones still contained names: see Provv., 74, fols. 51ʳ–53ʳ (13–15 May 1385): '. . . nulla extractio fieri possit . . . nisi vacuis bursis ad presens pro dictis offitiis vigentibus'.

the new ones;[1] similarly, it was also possible to combine the contents of the old and new bags, or alternatively to keep both in use, but increase the contents of the former by adding name tickets for the citizens who had been successful in the new scrutiny (*immixtio, rimbotto*). This last method was used in 1433, alternate drawings being ordered from the two *imborsazioni*.[2] In these cases the *Accoppiatori* were put in charge, under regulations issued at the time, of the technical business connected with the filling of the purses, their functions being of a purely executive order.

The *Balìa* of 1434 did not follow the traditional procedure. Instead, it ordered, as we have seen, that the scrutiny of 1433 should be destroyed, 'con ogni polizza dove si fusse messa', and that a new one should take its place.[3] There remained, however, the problem of what to do with the *polizze* that remained from the pre-1433 scrutinies. To destroy these as well would have penalized the citizens who had been qualified before the Albizzi *coup* in 1433, possibly as far back as 1391. Such a penalization would have been considered entirely unfair and out of step with Florentine electoral practice. On the other hand, the bags based on the earlier scrutinies contained many names of citizens who had been closely associated with the past régime; a wholesale preservation of such *polizze*, to be used together with those based on the new scrutiny, would evidently have been dangerous. Accordingly the *Accoppiatori* were given powers to transfer names from the bags of the *Tre Maggiori*, which had been filled in 1433 with the name tickets that had remained from the scrutinies held before 1433, into the new bags, even in the case of citizens who had not been successful in the scrutiny of 1434.[4]

---

[1] *Statuta*, 1415, ii, p. 498.

[2] Balìe, 24, fols. 14ᵛ–15ᵛ (20 Sept. 1433). The remaining *polizze* from the scrutinies of 1391, 1393, and 1398, together with their subsequent additions, were combined with *polizze* from that of 1433. See above, p. 7.   [3] See above, p. 8.

[4] See above, p. 7. *Balìe*, 25, fol. 25ʳ (4 Oct. 1434): 'Alla prima imborsatione [i.e. of 1434] si possa agiugnere insino in due polize intere, cioè de' Signori e Collegi, chiunche fusse deliberato pegli accopiatori . . . intendendo solo di quelli che avessono vinto il partito del priorato nello squittino del'anno millequattrocentotrentuno o da indi adrieto per insino allo squittino del'anno milletrecentonovantotto inclusive.' A *polizza intera* for the *Tre Maggiori* consisted really of three *polizze*, one for each of these magistracies. Cf. *Priorista* of Francesco di Tommaso Giovanni, Bibl. Naz., XXV. 379, fol. 138ʳ. 'A' sopradetti acopiatori fu data molta altorità fra le quali fu di potere imborsare in detto squittino qualunche citadino avese ottenuto alchuno degli squittini fatti l'anno 1393 al 1431 per 2 polize, non ostante non avese ottenuto questo nuovo . . .'; *Priorista* of Paolo di Girolamo di Ser Paolo, Tratte, 448, fol. 98ᵛ: '. . . dierono balìa [*scil.* to the *Accoppiatori*] . . . che di tutte l'altre borsse vechie potessino che [!] per ciaschuno che vi fussino dentro arane [!] 1ᵃ poliza o 2 di choloro che a loro proprio parese, e detto [!] una o dua polize che a loro paressi, mettere in sul detto [*scil.* scrutiny of] 1434. . . .' Buoninsegni, *Istorie fiorentine*, p. 55 : 'annullaronsi tutti

This amounted to a revision of past electoral qualifications supplementary to that achieved by this scrutiny. Evidently a concession to public opinion, in so far as the *Accoppiatori* could in this way mitigate the effects of the destruction of the old *borse*, and, indeed, those of the scrutiny itself, it created a precedent. Also after the following scrutinies, the *Accoppiatori* were given powers to correct their results by the addition, within specified limits, of names of unsuccessful candidates—a procedure which was called *reducere*. The term itself implies that they were confined, in their choice, to citizens who had had their names in old ballot bags; and after 1434, that year served as the deadline for such *reductiones*.[1] A large-scale operation of this kind was carried out before the *Accoppiatori* closed the bags in May 1449, when they added over 300 names to those of the 2,000-odd citizens who had been successful in the scrutiny of 1444, which may have been considered particularly severe.[2] Similarly, they carried out *reductiones* after the scrutiny of 1453, before closing the bags in 1455.[3] But this time they were allowed to go even further in correcting the results of the last scrutiny of the *Tre Maggiori*. 'To remedy whatever disorder or neglect may have taken place' in it, they could add to the names of those who had been qualified in the scrutiny the names of unsuccessful members of the scrutiny council, as well as those of up to twenty other citizens, as long as these names had been drawn in the sortitions from 1440 onwards;[4] an innovation which went beyond the right to transfer names from the old purses to new ones, and which was considered important enough by a contemporary diarist to deserve special mention.[5]

gli squittini fatti pel passato con certa autorità negl'Accoppiatori di poter mettervi alcuni delle borse vecchie innanzi al 1433. . . .'

[1] In 1440, they were given authority to *reducere*, with not more than one *polizza*, citizens who, although they were 'aliqualiter imbursati super scrutineo del 1434', had failed to get a majority in that of 1440 (Tratte, 60, fol. 235ᵛ; 13 Feb. 1440). They could also transfer *polizze* of citizens who in 1434 had been placed in the Lesser Guilds bags into those of the Greater Guilds, if they had been successful in this category (ibid.). Only one *reductio* seems to have been made by the *Accoppiatori* in 1444, although they had powers to act (register of *Accoppiatori* of 1444 in Tratte, 1148, fol. 5ʳ).

[2] These figures are based on the lists of *reducti* between 27 and 30 April 1449, Tratte, 1148, fols. 5ᵛ ff., and on the extant scrutiny registers of 1444, see below, p. 61, n. 4.

[3] Register of the *Accoppiatori* of 1452, Tratte, 16, fols. 8ᵛ–9ᵛ (3 June), 10ʳ–11ᵛ (6–7 June), and 12ʳ–ᵛ (14 June 1455). See also below, pp. 60–61.

[4] Balìe, 27, fol. 199ʳ–ᵛ (26 December 1453): 'per supplire a qualunche disordine et manchamento fusse acchaduto'. The majority required for this purpose was 12 out of 20 votes.

[5] Rinuccini, *Ricordi storici*, p. lxxxi: '. . . feciono che gli accopiatori potessono imborsare 20 uomini che fussono veduti dal 1439 in qua, che paresse loro, non ostante che non avessono ottenuto il detto priorato', i.e. in the scrutiny. The *Accoppiatori* used these powers

Powers to eliminate, *extrahere*, names from, as against adding them to, the purses, had first been given to the *Accoppiatori* in 1434.[1] The maximum was then fixed at twenty, evidently because a measure of this kind was bound to be extremely unpopular, apart from being unconstitutional. Accordingly, when in 1448 the *Accoppiatori* were ordered to have the bags prepared, to be closed by May 1449, they were granted the same powers as their predecessors of 1434, provided that they did not eliminate anyone who had been successful in the recent scrutiny.[2] The *Accoppiatori* of 1452, having been granted the powers of their predecessors, but without any reservations,[3] took this to mean that they were allowed to take out up to twenty names, and proceeded to do so before closing the bags in June 1455.[4] Yet it was a measure of the legality of their proceedings that they did not exceed this figure, which probably constituted less than one per cent. of the number of citizens who had been qualified in the scrutiny of 1453.[5]

Although the *Accoppiatori* did not regain the vast powers with regard to the scrutiny which they had been given in the revolutionary situation of 1434, by 1453 they had acquired, in this respect too, a much stronger position than they had possessed before 1434. However, their powers to correct electoral scrutinies by adding or 'extracting' names were subject to precise and detailed regulations; and there is no evidence that they did not observe these limitations of their authority.

If one expected sensational revelations from the additions they made to the bags after 1434, one would be disappointed. Socially and politically, they did not substantially alter the composition of the main electoral lists. Thus, in the *reductiones* of 1449, the vast majority of names belong to families[6] which are

on 7 June 1455, after stating, perhaps by an oversight, that the maximum was fifteen. They only chose fourteen, and added the proviso that these citizens 'imbursati fuerint in scrutineo trium maiorum del 44 et 48, seu in altero eorum', so that in the end they treated them not differently from the *reducti*.

[1] Balìe, 25, fol. 25ᵛ (4 Oct.). These powers referred to the principal *imborsazione* of 1434 only, not to the supplementary one (to be used in case not enough name tickets remained in the principal purses).

[2] Balìe, 26, fol. 190ᵛ (16 July 1448).   [3] Balìe, 27, fol. 199ᵛ.

[4] Register of the *Accoppiatori* of 1452 cit., fols. 15ᵛ–16ʳ (21 June 1455). In fact, they only eliminated nineteen names. Each *Accoppiatore* could nominate one citizen for this purpose, and one of them, Bartolomeo Michelozzi, had recently died.

[5] See below, p. 62, n. 3.

[6] In the *Quartiere* of S. Spirito, of the 81 *reducti* belonging to the Greater Guilds, 65, i.e. over 70 per cent., belonged to such families. Of these 65, 25 were sons of citizens who had been qualified in the scrutiny of 1444. The ratio is lower for the members of the Lesser Guilds: of 13 *reducti*, only 4 belonged to such families (Tratte, 1148, cit., and Tratte, 49).

already represented in the extant scrutiny lists of 1444, many of them by sons or brothers of *reducti*. Moreover, the lists of newly-added names present much the same cross-section of Florentine society. The most significant changes concern a few individual families, mostly of lower-class origin, which are given more than the average number of additional names. Two of these, the Corsellini and the Del Nero, still belonged partly to the Lesser Guilds.[1] Of the latter, three are the sons of Nero di Filippo; one of these, Bernardo, was to play a prominent role under Lorenzo de' Medici.

The picture is similar in 1455, when 197 citizens are *reducti* into the bags of the *Tre Maggiori*, although the general tendency seems to be more democratic: relatively more citizens belonging to the Lesser Guilds are qualified than in 1449.[2] There is one evident attempt to promote an entire family: the Petrucci, who, like the Del Nero and the Corsellini in 1449, still belonged partly to the Lesser Guilds.[3] But we also find many upper-class families among the *reducti*, like the Pitti, Albizzi, Davanzati, Gianfigliazzi, and the Medici themselves. It is difficult to detect any definite political criteria in this selection, although it is doubtless significant that of the fourteen who were given the benefit of the 1453 scrutiny,[4] nearly all had been members of *Balìe* since 1434 or had had relatives in them, and must consequently have been considered especially reliable.[5] From one of the lists it is possible to discover the names of unsuccessful candidates.[6] In some cases, the reason for their failure was doubtless personal, in others, political, as in that of Giannozzo Manetti and his brother Filippo.[7]

---

[1] The Corsellini are represented by 5 names, the Del Nero by 6. The other two families of the *Quartiere* of S. Spirito who receive more than the average number of names are the Biliotti with 5, and the Dietifeci with 4 names.

[2] Fifty-five members of the Lesser Guilds as against 142 of the Greater Guilds. The respective figures in 1449 were 62 and 336. In other words, in 1449, the 'artisans' provided about one-fifth of the *reducti*, in 1455 over one-third.

[3] They are *reducti* with no less than 10 names.   [4] See above, p. 42.

[5] To the former category belong Benedetto Galilei (*Balìa* 1452), Giannotto Ottavanti (*Balìa* 1438), Giovanni Cappelli (*Balìe* 1434, 1438, and 1444), and Tommaso Martini (*Balìa* 1444); to the latter the two sons of Domenico Petrucci (*Balìa* 1452), who had been *Accoppiatore* in 1440, Carlo Gondi, whose brother Simone had been in the *Balìa* of 1434, Paolo Benvenuti, with a brother in that of 1452, Priore Ottavanti, with a brother in that of 1438, and Gherardo Guardi, with a brother in the *Balìa* of 1452.

[6] The list is in Tratte, 61, fols. 145ʳ–148ᵛ. It includes subsequently cancelled names with the marginal note: 'Non fuit reductus in 1453.'

[7] Giannozzo had had six *polizze* in the *borse* of 1449, of which three were for the Gonfaloniership of Justice: this was the highest number of qualifications in his *gonfalone* (Tratte, 61, fol. 78ᵛ).

On the other hand, the reasons which, on 21 June 1455, the *Accoppiatori* gave for taking the names of nineteen citizens out of the ballot bags, are frankly political: 'admodum quod utile futurum pro rei publice florentine quiete ac pace'.[1] Among the victims we find Giovanni di Paolo Rucellai, who, as he says later in his *Zibaldone*, was at that time still 'non accetto ma sospetto allo stato'.[2] Mariotto di Dinozzo Lippi had been a member of all the *Balìe* since 1434, which indicates that in the eyes of the *Accoppiatori*, there could be exceptions to the reliability of *Balìa* members; but they may have been unfair to Mariotto, for we find him three years later once more in a *Balìa*.[3] Most of the *extracti* were, however, citizens without an outstanding record in civic life.[4]

·   ·   ·   ·

Considering the limitations to which the *Accoppiatori* were subjected in the matter of additions or eliminations of names, the distribution of the *polizze* between the various bags of the Signoria still remained, after 1434, the most important way in which they could influence the results of the scrutinies, as distinct from electing the Signoria *a mano*. Since the scrutinies qualified indiscriminately for the Signoria as such, it had always been one of the principal functions of the *Accoppiatori* to decide into which of the purses of the Signoria the *polizze* of successful candidates were to be placed. From 1387 onwards, there were, for the members of the Greater Guilds, two purses for the Priorate, the *borsellino*, which contained specially selected names, and the general purse, the *borsa generale*; and there was the purse

[1] Tratte, 16, fols. 15ᵛ–16ʳ. The names are, for S. Spirito: Bardo di Jacopo Bardi, Filippo di Piero di Bernardo Magli, Mariotto di Dinozzo di Stefano Lippi, Luigi di Giovanni di Niccolò Soderini, and Tommaso di Giorgio di Piero Serragli; for S. Croce: Jacopo di Tommaso Sacchetti, Cristofano di Rinieri di Cristofano del Pace, Tommaso di Niccolò del Buon Busini, Jacopo di Bellaccino Bellacci, and Giovanni di Domenico Giugni; for S. Maria Novella: Piero di Jacopo di Francesco Neretti, Giovanni di Paolo di M. Paolo Rucellai, Giovanni di Bartolomeo di Bartolomeo Federighi, and Simone di M. Piero di Lionardo Beccanugi; for S. Giovanni: Francesco del Maestro Antonio da Scarperia, Domenico d'Antonio di Bartolomeo di Ser Santi Bruni, Marco di Parente di Giovanni Parenti, Giuseido d'Antonio di Migliore Guidotti, and Agnolo di Chimenti Stefani.

[2] *Giovanni Rucellai ed il suo Zibaldone*, i, ed. A. Perosa (London, 1960), p. 122. See also below, p. 124, n. 1.

[3] See Appendix, no. VI.

[4] From the extant scrutiny registers of 1449 and 1453, it emerges that the majority of the *extracti* had possessed one or two *polizze* only, nearly always in the *borsa generale* of the Priorate. The one exception to this rule is Simone Beccanugi, who in 1449 was *imborsato* with five *polizze* in the *borsellino* and with one in the *borsa* of the Gonfaloniership of Justice. For the terms see below.

for the Gonfalonier of Justice.[1] While the *Accoppiatori* could thus increase or reduce the chances of being appointed one of the eight Priors by placing name tickets in one or the other of the two purses for that office, it depended altogether on them whether a citizen was eligible for the Gonfaloniership of Justice. In view of the growing importance of the *seduti* and *veduti* Gonfaloniers of Justice in political life, qualification for the Gonfaloniership was a matter of even greater responsibility than it had been before 1434.

San Giovanni is the one *quartiere* in which the extant records allow us to follow the distribution of *polizze* between that office and the Priorate from 1440 to 1455.[2] Of the 67 names which are entered for the *Gonfalonierato* in 1440, we find 47 again in 1449, together with 28 new entries, the total having risen to 75. In 1455, the total is reduced to 56, of which 26 are new entries. A large proportion of the citizens who are newly qualified for the Gonfaloniership of Justice belong, however, to families which are already represented in the bags of the highest magistracy, and many of them owe their qualification no doubt to the death of relatives whom they are now chosen to replace. Of the 28 newcomers of 1449, 10 only belong to families who are not represented in the lists for the Gonfaloniership of 1440; of the 16 qualified in 1455, 6 have no relatives on the lists of 1440 and 1449.[3] Moreover, these 16 belong to no less than 15 different families, so that, with one exception, each of the 'new' families is represented by one member only.[4] In contrast to this, 15 'established' families provide, in 1449, a total of 49, and in 1455, of 41 names.

Apart from thus making new citizens eligible for the Gonfaloniership of Justice, the *Accoppiatori* could increase the chances of those who were already qualified for that office, and who had acquired a new *polizza* for the Signoria in a scrutiny of the *Tre Maggiori*, by placing this *polizza* not in one of the bags of the Priorate, but in that of the Gonfalonier of Justice.

---

[1] On the *borsellino*, see *Cronica volgare di Anonimo fiorentino*, ed. E. Bellondi, in Muratori, *Rer. Ital. Script.*, new ed., xxvii, ii (Città di Castello, 1915–18), pp. 34–35; Buoninsegni, *Historia fiorentina*, p. 681. Each *borsa* consisted, strictly speaking, of four purses, one for each of the city's four districts; moreover, there were separate purses for the members of the Lesser Guilds, but for the Priorate only, since artisans were not eligible for the Gonfaloniership of Justice.

[2] 1440: Tratte, 1150, part 2; 1449: Tratte, 49, part 5; 1455: Tratte, 16, fols. 19ᵛ–20ʳ, 28ᵛ–31ʳ.

[3] Based on Tratte, 1150, 49, and 16, fols. 19ᵛ–29ʳ.

[4] The Benci are the only family with two members. They were business associates of the Medici; see R. de Roover, *The Rise and Decline of the Medici Bank* . . . (Cambridge, Mass., 1963), pp. 57–58 *et passim*.

Similarly, by placing a name ticket in the select bag, the *borsellino*, of the Priorate, instead of the *borsa generale*, the *Accoppiatori* could give its owner a better chance of having it drawn.[1] Thus, single families could raise their total qualifications for the Gonfaloniership of Justice not only through additional members being qualified for that office, but also through already qualified members acquiring additional name tickets. Alternatively, their total qualifications could be reduced; this could, for instance, happen when the newly-acquired *polizze* did not offset those lost through appointment to office.[2] In this way, to give a few examples, between 1440 and 1455 the Martelli increased the total number of their *polizze* for the Gonfaloniership of Justice from 3 to 10 and 16,[3] the Dietisalvi from 6 to 11 and 19, the Della Stufa from 6 to 10 and 19, and the Medici from 11 to 18 and 25. On the other hand, the number of *polizze* of the Aldobrandini del Nero declined, in the same period, from 5 to 2; while the Ginori, who have 4 *polizze* in 1440 and as many as 11 in 1449, have only 5 in 1455.

That the accumulation of *polizze* for the Gonfaloniership had oligarchical implications is evident. In June 1455 the *Accoppiatori* reacted against this trend by deciding not to place the *polizze* of more than three citizens per family or *consorteria* in the bags of that office, which they were about to fill prior to the restoration of election by lot.[4] This decision was in keeping with their relatively liberal attitude towards new qualifications, which we have already noticed.[5] A fortnight later, however, they raised the maximum to five members per family for six families, in view of 'the differences between families, since in some there are more, in others fewer who are suitable for such a dignity',[6] but probably because of pressure from leading citizens. The Medici would have been among those who would have suffered most from this regulation; and it is thus not surprising to find them among the privileged families, together with the Capponi, the Dietisalvi,

[1] Even during the periods when elections were *a mano*, since the *Accoppiatori* were bound to select three *polizze* from the *borsellino*.

[2] Once a name ticket had been used up in consequence of its owner having been actually appointed to the office, it lost its validity. Similarly, *polizze* would be torn up on being drawn when it was discovered that their owners had tax debts.

[3] On the Martelli, see L. Martines, 'La famiglia Martelli e un documento sulla vigilia del ritorno dall'esilio di Cosimo de' Medici', *Arch. Stor. Ital.* cxvii (1959), pp. 29–43.

[4] Tratte, 16, fol. 9^{r-v} (6 June 1455).

[5] See above, p. 44.

[6] Ibid., fol. 13^r (19 June 1455): 'considerantes disparitatem familiarum, quia in aliqua sunt plures, in aliqua pauciores ad talem dignitatem idonei'.

the Pitti, the Ridolfi, and the Rucellai.[1] They, as well as the Pitti and the Capponi, are, in fact, represented by six names, and by more names than any other family, on the Gonfaloniership list of 1455; however, they have not increased their 'representation' since 1440, nor can they boast of a much higher total of *polizze* than the Pitti and the Ridolfi. In fact, the qualifications for the higher office that were made in June 1455 show little change among the great families of the régime, if compared with those of 1440. Most of those which had been represented by more than one member in 1440 were still in that position fifteen years later.

While one may detect certain general trends in the distribution of electoral qualifications between the various bags of the Signoria, it is impossible to assess the influence of personal favouritism. In order to be qualified for the Gonfaloniership of Justice or the special bag (*borsellino*) of the Priorate, a citizen had, in 1455, to obtain the votes of at least twelve of the nineteen *Accoppiatori*; and there is no way of discovering the motives which prompted the single *Accoppiatori* to vote one way or the other, or, indeed, how they voted at all. We know, however, that they gave preferential treatment to themselves and their families.[2]

This raises a question which has not yet been discussed. The *Accoppiatori* had become the most powerful instrument of the Medici régime. Was it Cosimo who determined the use it was put to? In his *Ricordi*, he writes that while elections of the Signoria were *a mano*, the *Accoppiatori* could appoint whomsoever they wished, 'quelli vorranno fare a loro piacimento'.[3] He himself was *Accoppiatore* for a few months only, from October 1440[4] to

---

[1] Tratte, 16, fols. 13ʳ, 15ʳ. The *Accoppiatori* nominated up to eight families per *quartiere*; those families which obtained at least twelve votes were granted the special maximum. The privileged Ridolfi were those of the *Gonfalone* Ferza.

[2] They decided that each of them should be *imborsato* for the Gonfaloniership, with as many as he wished of the *polizze* he had for the Signoria; that Tommaso Ridolfi was to be *imborsato* for the Gonfaloniership with as many *polizze* 'quot dixit Loysius pater eius', who was one of them; that Giovannozzo Pitti, the relative of another *Accoppiatore*, 'quodcumque partitum de vexilliferis capiat'; and that Cosimo de' Medici and Nerone Dietisalvi, whose sons were *Accoppiatori*, might be similarly *imborsati* with all their *polizze* for the Signoria. Two other *Accoppiatori*, Neri Capponi and Agnolo Acciaiuoli, were left to decide how many such *polizze* Neri's son Gino and Michele di Zanobi Acciaiuoli respectively were to receive. Finally, the *Accoppiatori* were allowed to nominate members of their *consorteria* for qualification for the Gonfaloniership. Neri Capponi was given permission to nominate five members of his family, including himself, and was granted, for this purpose, the special maximum. The same permission was given to Piero de' Medici, who nominated, besides himself, his brother Giovanni, Orlando di Guccio, Bernardo di Antonio, and Carlo di Nicola de' Medici, although the Medici had not yet received the special maximum. He evidently took the result for granted. Ibid., fols. 13ᵛ–14ᵛ, 16ᵛ.   [3] Fabroni, *Cosmi vita*, ii, p. 103. See above, p. 10.

[4] Tratte, 60, fol. 241ᵛ (7 Oct. 1440).

February 1441, in place of his brother Lorenzo who had died; and also his son Piero had served, by 1455, for shorter periods than some of his colleagues.[1] In fact, between 1434 and 1440 and between 1443 and 1448, the Medici were not represented in that office at all. Nor can it be argued that the *Accoppiatori* were all clients of Cosimo, who accordingly could dispose of them freely. He was later criticized for having raised men of humble origin to positions of political influence at the expense of the *ottimati*.[2] We find such men among the *Accoppiatori*;[3] however, most of them belong to established families, some of considerable wealth, such as the Acciaiuoli, the Capponi, the Guicciardini, and the Ridolfi.[4] The Medici are only one of the families which profited from the special treatment afforded by the *Accoppiatori* to their relatives. As a rule, the *Accoppiatori* probably sought Cosimo's advice on the candidates they chose in electing the Signoria *a mano*. But without more evidence to go on, they appear as 'representatives' of the inner circle of the régime rather than as tools used by Cosimo.[5] Like the members of other magistracies, they meet at regular intervals, take decisions by majority vote, and keep registers. Minutes of their discussions would be invaluable to us; but that they do not exist is not particularly surprising, since the same also applies to other offices.

. . . . .

It was a measure of the restraint exercised by the Medici régime that, as far as the *Tre Maggiori* went, elections *a mano* were confined to the Signoria. The Colleges, that is the *Sedici Gonfalonieri* and the *Dodici Buonuomini*, continued to be appointed by lot, and so did nearly all magistracies which had previously been appointed in this way. The most notable exception were the *Otto di Guardia*, who were in charge of security. They had played a prominent role in the political persecutions of 1434–5,[6] and might at any moment be called upon to defend the régime;

---

[1] See Appendix, no. I.

[2] Guicciardini, *Storie fiorentine*, pp. 3–4.

[3] e.g. Nero di Filippo del Nero, whose son Bernardo was to play a leading role under Lorenzo de' Medici.

[4] The large number of *polizze* which the families of *Accoppiatori* had in the purses of the *Tre Maggiori* previous to their appointment bears out their political and social status. In the *imborsazione* of 1449, the average number of such *polizze* was twelve per family (based on Tratte, 49, and 61, fols. 66^r–80^v).

[5] See also below, pp. 133–4.

[6] See above, p. 2, n. 3.

conversely, even a temporary loss of control of this office might
be full of dangers. To leave it in the hands of citizens loyal to the
régime may well have been considered second in importance only
to the electoral controls of the government. In this respect too,
the Albizzi faction had, in September 1433, created a precedent
by having the *Otto* elected by the Signoria and the Colleges.[1]
Nor is it surprising that the *Accoppiatori* should also have been
used for electing the Eight. While the Eight who entered their
six-monthly office on 1 October 1434 were once more elected by
the Signoria, this time without the Colleges,[2] their successors
were, by decree of the *Balìa* of 20 December, elected jointly by
the Signoria and the *Accoppiatori* and Secretaries of the new
scrutiny.[3] For the appointment of the next Eight, a mixture of
election and sortition was adopted. Such combined electoral
procedure was not unfamiliar in Florence; it had, for instance,
been used, between 1427 and 1433, for the appointment of the
Ufficiali del Monte.[4] In the circumstances, it clearly represented
a compromise which would be more palatable than simple
election.[5] The *Balìa* had, in fact, taken precautions for the time
when sortition was restored for the Eight, by ordering, on 31
October 1434, that the new *borse* of this office were to be filled
by the Signoria of November and December and the *Accoppiatori* and Secretaries.[6] However, in March 1436 the Eight were
once more elected, this time by the Signoria, the Colleges, and
the *Accoppiatori* and Secretaries of the scrutinies.[7] This followed
the advice of the *Pratica* of 6 and 7 March to elect the next Eight
once more *a mano*, and for eight months,[8] Cosimo having

---

[1] Balìe, 24, fol. 11ᵛ (13 Sept. 1433): the next Eight of Ward to be elected, within three
days, by the Signoria and the Colleges, and to function until the 15th of March 1435. (The
normal term of office of the Eight was two months.)   After this, appointment by *tratta*
was restored with half the office-holders being appointed at one time (Tratte, 80, fol. 14ʳ).

[2] Balìe, 25, fols. 19ᵛ–20ʳ (29 Sept. 1434). For the rest of the term of their predecessors,
they were to function jointly with them—i.e. until 14 and 30 Nov. respectively.

[3] Ibid., fol. 90ᵛ. The election was to take place, for six months, in Feb. 1435. The time lag
between the *Balìa*'s decision and the actual election was due to the fact that the session of
the *Balìa* came to an end on 31 Dec., and that it evidently wished to settle this important
matter before dissolving.   [4] Tratte, 80, fol. 393ʳ.

[5] Provv., 26, fols. 174ᵛ–175ʳ (19–20 Aug. 1435). Six names per *quartiere* to be drawn from
the *borse* of the Eight, and to be voted on by the Signori and *Accoppiatori*, the candidates
who received most votes being appointed.

[6] Balìe, 25, fols. 53ᵛ–54ʳ: 'bursa officii octo reficiatur per novos dominos una cum
copulatoribus et secretariis.' At that time, it was expected that election by lot would be
restored presently, for the decree lays down that 'pro tribus annis fiant extractiones pro
sex mensibus pro vice'.

[7] Provv., 126, fols. 423ʳ–434ᵛ (9–10 March 1436); for eight months.

[8] Cons. e Prat., 51, fol. 17ᵛ (7 March).

proposed this longer period in view of the danger of plague.[1] Although the *Pratica* had advised to elect *a mano* only on this one occasion, the same procedure was followed for the next Eight.[2] After this, the combined election and *tratta* was revived, but with the balance shifted to the former;[3] and this method apparently continued to be used until 1440.[4] In 1440 there was a short-lived return to simple election;[5] but in December the normal election by lot was restored—that is, a few weeks before the *Consiglio Maggiore* decided to abolish elections *a mano* of the Signoria.[6]

But as early as June 1442 the combined procedure was re-introduced,[7] and after the creation of the new *Balìa* in May 1444 controls were further tightened by the *Balìa* taking over the election of the Eight.[8] In October 1447, however, the *Balìa*, having appointed the Eight who were then in office to the magistracy of the *Dieci di Balìa*, decided to restore the lot for the appointment of the Eight.[9] Finally, in December 1448, it again adopted an intermediate method by voting on names that had previously been drawn from the *borse*.[10] Shortly afterwards,

[1] Ibid., fol. 16ʳ (6 March).

[2] Provv., 127, fols. 197ᵛ–198ʳ (19–20 Oct. 1436).

[3] Provv., 128, fols. 29ᵛ–30ᵛ (16–17 May 1437). Six names per *quartiere* were to be drawn from the *borse* of the Eight; to these, the Signoria and Colleges could add up to ten names per *quartiere* by way of nomination. All the names were then voted upon by a commission consisting of the Signoria, the Colleges, the Captains of the Guelph Party, the Eight, the VI *di Mercanzia*, and the *Accoppiatori* and Secretaries.

[4] Provv., 128, fol. 167ʳ⁻ᵛ (12–17 Oct. 1437); 129, fols. 28ʳ–29ʳ (29–30 April 1438); fols. 166ʳ–167ʳ (21–24 Oct. 1438). There are no entries in the registers of *provvisioni* concerning the appointment of the Eight between Nov. 1438 and April 1440 (Provv., 130).

[5] This time, by the Signoria, the Colleges, the Captains of the Guelph Party, the Eight, and the Six *di Mercanzia*—the *Accoppiatori* of 1434 having retired by the beginning of the year (see above, p. 15). Provv., 131, fols. 9ᵛ–10ʳ (8–9 April 1440); 140ᵛ–141ᵛ (11–12 Aug. 1440); 205ᵛ–206ᵛ (12–13 Oct. 1440).

[6] See above, pp. 15–16. Tratte, 80, fol. 15ᵛ. No *provvisione* restoring sortition is entered in the register of *provvisioni* (Provv., 131), presumably because, in the absence of legislation to appoint the Eight by election, the normal procedure was automatically restored.

[7] Provv., 133, fols. 30ʳ–31ᵛ (4–5 June 1442).

[8] Balìe, 26, fol. 56ʳ (30 July 1444). Each of the XVI *Gonfalonieri* nominated twelve candidates; in addition, each member of the *Balìa* could nominate one. On 8 Jan. 1445, the *Balìa* reduced the term of the Eight in office, and decreed that their immediate successors were to be elected by the Signoria, the XVI, the XII, the Captains of the Guelph Party, the VIII, and the VI *di Mercanzia* (ibid., fol. 87ʳ⁻ᵛ). After this, the *Balìa* periodically passed legislation authorizing itself to elect the Eight: ibid., fols. 87ᵛ–88ʳ (26 Jan. 1445); 107ᵛ (30 July 1445); 127ᵛ–128ʳ (3 Feb. 1446), 143ʳ⁻ᵛ (11 Aug. 1446), 157ʳ⁻ᵛ (2 March 1447), and 162ᵛ–163ʳ (13 Sept. 1447).

[9] Ibid., fol. 165ᵛ (23 Oct. 1447): as from 1 Nov. See also Tratte, 80, fol. 18ʳ.

[10] Balìe, 26, fols. 202ᵛ–203ᵛ (7 Dec. 1448). For each post to be filled, ten names were to be drawn from the *borse* of the Eight, and the candidates who had received most, as well as two-thirds of the votes, were to be appointed. Previously, on 27 Sept. 1448, the *Balìa* had once more dismissed the Eight in office, and had ordered that their substitutes be elected by the Signoria, the Colleges, the Captains of the Guelph Party, and the VI (ibid., fol. 198ʳ). Their successors were once more appointed by lot (Tratte, 80, fol. 18ᵛ).

it dissolved;[1] and from May 1449 onwards, the Eight were once more appointed by *tratta*, until the new *Balìa* of 1452 reintroduced election.[2] Except for two occasions in 1453, when the Eight were again appointed by lot,[3] this remained the procedure during the lifetime of the *Balìa*.[4] The day before the council of the People passed the bill dissolving the *Balìa*, on 21 May 1454, the new Eight entered office; they had once more been elected by lot.[5] Nine months later, elections *a mano* were abolished also for the Signoria.[6]

Election by the *Balìa* provided a solution, however temporary, for controlling not only the composition of the *Otto di Guardia*, but also that of the *Dieci di Balìa* and the *Ufficiali del Monte*. Both of these were offices of great importance, the one in charge of military affairs and diplomatic relations in times of war, the other of the funded debt (*Monte*), and hence of the central machinery of Florentine finance. Owing to the vast responsibilities that attached to them, these magistracies had already before 1434 been filled by election, or by combined election and sortition. Thus the *Dieci* created for the war against Lucca in 1429 were elected by the council of 145;[7] while the *Ufficiali del Monte* were appointed, between 1427 and 1433, by election and sortition.[8] In these circumstances, it was probably not too difficult to transfer their election to the *Balìa*. In 1447 and 1448, and again in 1452 and 1453, the Ten were elected in this way;[9] and equally between 1445 and 1448, and in 1452 and 1453, the *Ufficiali del Monte*.[10] After the Peace of Lodi, the Ten were no longer required and resigned on 14 May 1454; and for the *Ufficiali del Monte*, as for the Signoria and the Eight, the years 1454 and 1455 brought a return to sortition,[11] which remained in force until the Medicean restoration of 1458.

---

[1] See above, p. 20.

[2] Tratte, 225 *bis*, fols. 92v–94v; Balìe, 27, fols. 13v–14r (27 July): by the Signoria, the Colleges, *Dieci di Balìa*, and *Accoppiatori*.

[3] i.e. the Eight for July to Sept., and for Sept. to Nov.

[4] Tratte, 225 *bis*, fols. 94v–95r.   [5] Ibid., fol. 95r. See above, p. 22.

[6] See above, p. 22.

[7] Provv., 120, fol. 394v (12–13 Dec. 1429); see below, p. 68, n. 4.   [8] Tratte, 80, fol. 393r.

[9] Tratte, 80, fol. 454r–v. On 23 Oct. 1447 the *Balìa* appointed the Eight in office to be members of the newly-created *Dieci* (against the King of Naples), electing the two additional members (Balìe, 26, fol. 165r–v). Their successors were elected by the *Balìa* (ibid., fols. 183v–184r, 15 March 1448).

[10] Tratte, 80, fols. 393v–394r. The *Ufficiali* were elected by the *Balìa* in 1452, and were confirmed in their office in Sept. 1453, for another year as from 1 March 1454. Cf. also Balìe, 26, fols. 105r–106v (24 July 1445); 146v–147v (22 Oct. 1446: extension of term of office); 169r–170r (7 Dec. 1447: *idem*); 202r–v (2 Dec. 1448: to serve from 1 March 1449). In 1445 the candidates were nominated by the XVI *Gonfalonieri*; in 1449, their names were drawn.   [11] Tratte, 225 *bis*, fol. 156r; 81, fol. 65r.

3

ELECTORAL SCRUTINIES

It might be argued that the development of the office and functions of the *Accoppiatori* during the twenty years following on Cosimo's return was bound to undermine the position of the scrutinies in the Florentine electoral system. The foregoing observations should suffice to show that this is not borne out by the facts. However long the *Accoppiatori* actually remained in power, their office was not a permanent one; nor could it always be safely expected that their term would be extended, or that, once abolished, elections *a mano* would be restored. Moreover, their powers to hold the *borse a mano* only concerned the Signoria;[1] the vast majority of the magistracies inside and outside the city were still filled by the normal method of sortition. As we have seen, the *a mano* system itself did not entirely dispense with the latter, and presupposed the existence of scrutiny qualifications; indeed, from a purely technical point of view, all it did was to insert an additional stage into the electoral process, between the scrutiny and the drawing by lot. Finally, if the *Accoppiatori* had acquired certain discretionary powers to modify the results of the scrutinies before filling the bags, these powers were almost exclusively limited to the addition of names of citizens who, in their turn, had been qualified in previous scrutinies.

Indeed, after Cosimo's return from exile, scrutinies of the *Tre Maggiori*, and of the other internal and external offices (*uffici intrinseci ed estrinseci*, or briefly *uffici*), continued to be held at regular intervals of about four to five years, with the exception of that of the *uffici* of 1445, which will be discussed presently. As for the scrutinies of the three highest offices, the *Tre Maggiori*, the first Medicean scrutiny, of 1434,[2] was followed by scrutinies in 1440,[3] 1444,[4] 1448,[5] 1453,[6] and 1458.[7] The intervals were

[1] And their notary.   [2] See above, pp. 7–8.   [3] Above, p. 15.   [4] Above, p. 19, n. 1.
[5] Above, p. 31. Balìe, 26, fol. 190ʳ (6 July 1448): the scrutiny is to be held during the second half of Aug. See also fol. 197ʳ (27 Sept.): the scrutiny of the *Tre Maggiori* has been carried out *de proximo*.   [6] Above, p. 21, n. 7.
[7] The *Balìa* of 1458 decreed that the scrutiny was to start at the beginning of Nov. (Balìe, 29, fols. 26ʳ–27ʳ, 26 Aug. 1458). A year later, it is referred to as having been 'celebratum novembris et decembris' 1458 (Tratte, 17).

slightly shorter than the quinquennial ones prescribed by the Statutes, between 1440 and 1444, and between 1444 and 1448; on the latter occasion, it was admitted that the scrutiny should really have taken place in the following year: it was now to be held earlier 'because of the danger of plague'.[1]

As to the decision to hold a scrutiny in June 1444 instead of about six months later,[2] it may be connected with that to revise the scrutiny of the *uffici intrinseci ed estrinseci* of 1443, in which case it was probably designed to sweeten the pill.

This revision was, in fact, the only substantial deviation, in our period, from the statutory quinquennium. The scrutiny of the *Tre Maggiori* was, as we have seen,[3] quite distinct from that of the other offices, which had its *Secretari* in the place of the *Accoppiatori*, although both scrutinies were sometimes held by the same council. This had been the case in 1433,[4] 1434,[5] and 1440,[6] the scrutiny of the *uffici* being held after that of the *Tre Maggiori* and, because of the much larger number of offices concerned, naturally lasting much longer. In October 1443, on the other hand, it was decided to hold a scrutiny of the *uffici intrinseci ed estrinseci* only, and indeed over one year before it was due;[7] and since no *Balìa* was then in office,[8] a special scrutiny council was, in the statutory manner, elected, which began its business on 13 October and concluded it on 27 December.[9] According to Cavalcanti, the results of this scrutiny caused much dissatisfaction among the supporters of the régime, because of the many opponents of it who had been qualified, 'ch'erano entrati dentro alle borse'. This had happened because the 'popolo', incensed against the aristocrats, voted in favour of the relatives of the exiles, and even of some political suspects.[10] The scrutiny was therefore

---

[1] Balìe, 26, fol. 190ʳ (16 July 1448): 'imminente suspictione pestis'. The real reason was, no doubt, that had it been held in 1449, the *Balìa* would no longer have been in charge of it.

[2] The relevant decree of the *Balìa* is not entered in its register; that the *Balìa* had to pass legislation to this effect is obvious, and that it did so is confirmed by its *provvisione* of 5 June (ibid., fol. 34), which refers to the scrutiny as having been *nuper* decreed by it. This is yet another case of a law passed by this *Balìa* not being entered in its register: see above, p. 19, and below, p. 58, n. 3.   [3] Above, p. 5.

[4] Balìe, 24, fols. 14ᵛ, 18ᵛ (20 and 24 Sept. 1433).

[5] Balìe, 25, fols. 25ʳ–26ʳ (4 and 6 Oct. 1434). The latter had not yet been completed by 26 Dec. (ibid., fol. 111ᵛ).

[6] The proceedings (*partiti*) of this scrutiny are entered in the fragmentary register of the *Consiglio Maggiore* of 1438, Tratte, 60, fols. 240ʳ–245ʳ. It began on 16 Feb. and was to be completed by 15 Jan. 1441.   [7] Provv., 134, fols. 131ʳ–137ʳ (1–2 Oct. 1443).

[8] That of 1438 had ended its session early in 1441; see above, p. 16, and below, pp. 73–74.

[9] Its register is in Tratte, 1148.

[10] *Istorie fiorentine*, ii, pp. 191–2: 'disperatamente irato contro a' patrizii, renderono le fave a ciascuno parente degli usciti, ed ancora ad alquanti sospetti.'

called 'lo squittino del fiore d'aliso', for the lily is beautiful to be-
hold, but has an evil smell.[1] When a few months later, in May 1444,
a new *Balìa* was established, it was accordingly put in charge of
the scrutiny not only of the *Tre Maggiori* but also of the other
offices, 'et etiam de quibuscumque scructineis hactenus factis'.[2]
This meant that the scrutiny of the preceding year was to be considered annulled.[3] In fact, the *Balìa* began the new scrutiny of the
uffici intrinseci ed estrinseci on 19 January 1445, after having carried
out that of the *Tre Maggiori* in June 1444.[4] In this way, a *Balìa* was
once more put in charge of both scrutinies, and this procedure
was also observed in 1448 and 1453, when scrutinies of the
uffici followed on those of the *Tre Maggiori*,[5] although the scrutiny
of the *uffici* of 1453 was suspended at the end of that year for the
duration of the war against Venice and Naples, and for four
months after the conclusion of peace.[6] Work on the scrutiny
began again, in fact, at the end of 1454, the peace of Lodi having
been proclaimed in April.[7] Since the *Balìa* of 1452 had been
dissolved in May, a special scrutiny council was appointed for
this purpose, in the statutory manner, as in 1443.[8] Finally, in
August 1458, the new *Balìa* decided to hold a scrutiny of all
offices, including the *Tre Maggiori*, to be completed by the end of
January, 1459.[9]

Is it possible to discover any electoral policy in the procedure
or results of the scrutinies, which in their periodical occurrence

[1] Ibid., p. 192.

[2] Balìe, 26, fol. 9ᵛ (20–23 May 1444).

[3] Cavalcanti, ii, p. 191: 'lo squittino del fiore d'aliso posero che sedesse.'

[4] It lasted until 7 March 1445. The registers of its proceedings are in Tratte, 60, fols.
291ʳ–332ʳ, and Tratte, 18. On the scrutiny of 1444, see above, p. 19, n. 1.

[5] Balìe, 26, fols. 197ʳ–198ʳ (27 Sept. 1448); 27, fols. 169ʳ–170ʳ (19 Nov. 1453); cf.
Provv., 143, fol. 200ʳ (10–14 July 1452), empowering the *Balìa* to hold a general scrutiny
either when it was due, or at an earlier date. On 26 Aug. 1453 the *Balìa* had decided not to
hold the scrutiny before the end of that year (Balìe, 27, fol. 33ᵛ), but it revoked this decision on 19 November.

[6] Balìe, 27, fol. 204ᵛ (26 Dec. 1453). A *Pratica* of 24 Dec. had given advice to this effect
(Cons. e Prat., 53, fol. 49ʳ); Neri di Gino Capponi had, on that occasion, pointed out that
'negocia ardua communis vocant dominationem ut alia curet quam scrutinea', and Bernardo
de' Gherardi had concluded that it would therefore be 'commodius vacare scrutineis'.

[7] An attempt to postpone it once more failed in Aug. 1454: see below, p. 123.

[8] Cf. Rinuccini, p. lxxxiv: 'Questi Signori [i.e. of Nov.–Dec. 1454] feciono lo squittino di
fuori e drento, eccetto che il priorato ch'era fatto di novembre 1453.' The names of the
members of the scrutiny council are in Bibl. Naz. II. IV. 346, fols. 146ʳ–148ᵛ ('per squittinare
solo di fuori sono gl'infrascripti'). The lists of the successful candidates for the *Quartieri*
of S. Croce and S. Maria Novella are in Tratte, 119. Provv., 145, fols. 228ʳ–230ᵛ (22–25 Nov.
1454).

[9] Balìe, 29, fols. 26ʳ–27ʳ (26 Aug. 1458); see below, pp. 107–8.

follow, by and large, the long-established quinquennial pattern? The answer is fairly simple for the first scrutiny of the *Tre Maggiori*: a general revision of electoral qualifications for the highest offices was evidently considered essential for the security and the continued existence of the régime. It is less so for the subsequent scrutinies. Our evidence on the manner in which these were carried out is mainly limited to the regulations, issued at the time, governing technical procedure, which do not allow us more than occasional glimpses of general policies. As for the results of the scrutinies, they have to be analysed on the basis of incomplete sets of scrutiny registers, which in no case comprise all the four *quartieri* of the city.[1] Even so, they may enable us to arrive at fairly accurate, if approximate, general conclusions.

It is clear from this evidence that electoral procedure in the scrutinies of the *Tre Maggiori* after 1434 did not differ substantially from that in force before that date. According to a *provvisione* of 1415, nominations of candidates for qualification were made separately for each of the sixteen *gonfaloni* by their *Gonfalonieri*, candidates being divided into two groups to be voted on successively: the first consisted of citizens who, from 1382 onwards, had been *veduti* or *seduti*, i.e. had had their names drawn, for the *Tre Maggiori* or the Captainship of the Guelph Party; the second, of those who did not have this advantage.[2] Much the same procedure was adopted in the scrutiny of 1440;[3] only that the first group was also to include the fathers, brothers, uncles, sons, and grandsons by male descent of the *veduti* and *seduti*, while the second was limited to 125 names per *gonfalone*.[4] There was then clearly a tendency to favour 'established' families, which can also be discovered in later scrutinies: thus in that of 1458, the maximum of *non veduti* was reduced to eighty per *gonfalone*.[5] In fact, the procedure of voting in two stages was also adopted in 1443, 1445, and 1448, and doubtless also in 1453.[6] As was customary, the members of the Signoria, of the Colleges, and of a number of

---

[1] See below, pp. 61 ff.

[2] According to the Statutes of 1415 (ii, p. 485), the Captains of the Guelph Party and the consuls of the guilds also had the right to make nominations; however, the *provvisione* of 16 Oct. 1415 which deals with this matter only mentions the XVI *Gonfalonieri* (Provv. 105, fols. 152ᵛ–153ᵛ).

[3] Tratte, 60, fol. 229ʳ (13 Jan. 1440).   [4] See also below, pp. 116 ff.

[5] Tratte, 60, fol. 336ʳ (29 Nov. 1458): 60 of the Greater and 20 of the Lesser Guilds.

[6] Tratte, 1148 and 18 (scrutinies of 1443 and 1445); Balìe, 26, fol. 193ʳ (6 Aug. 1448; also with reference to the scrutiny of 1444).

other high magistracies (the so-called *cerchio*), as well as the knights and doctors, were not included in these two groups, being voted on before anyone else. In 1440, the *Accoppiatori* and the members of the *Balìa*, which was carrying out the scrutiny, were also granted precedence.[1] However, if the tendency to favour established families was present both in the scrutinies of the *Tre Maggiori* and in those of the other offices, it was less pronounced in the latter. This applies particularly to the offices of minor importance: for the top offices, such as those of the Captain of Pisa or the *Podestà* of Arezzo, much the same criteria were doubtless operative as for the three highest magistracies.

For the Florentine citizens in general, the scrutinies of the 'internal and external offices' were in some ways just as, or even more important than those of the *Tre Maggiori*. While the latter gave access to the *onori*, the former provided *onori* as well as *utile*, honour as well as emoluments. The highest magistracies did not carry any, or only nominal, salaries with them; but the vast majority of the other offices were salaried, including all those belonging to the administration of the territory (*uffici estrinseci*). Salaries ranged from small sums for minor offices to very substantial ones for posts of great responsibility, such as those of the Captain and *Podestà* of towns like Pisa and Arezzo. How desirable such posts in the administration could be to Florentine citizens for purely economic reasons, is shown by the many petitions to the councils by citizens requesting election, even though the office was normally filled by *tratta*, which would thus have to be temporarily suspended. In these petitions, the applicants would usually state they were 'sine aliquo exercitio lucrativo', and this might be embellished by such particulars as 'habet uxorem et novem filios', 'habet aliquas filias indotatas', 'habet multum debitum, unde ut possit suis creditoribus satis-facere et se, uxorem et suam familiam honeste substentare'.[2]

---

[1] 'Sed tamen reserventur extra bursam domini, milites, doctores, gonfalonerii, XII, capitanei partis, X Balie, Octo custodie, officiales montis, accoppiatores et secretarii [subsequent addition], Sex mercantie, et omnes scrutinatores' (Tratte, 60, fol. 229ʳ).

[2] Provv., 156, fols. 55ᵛ–57ʳ, 95ᵛ–96ᵛ (8 June, 16 July 1465); 96ᵛ–97ʳ (16 July); 142ʳ (28 Aug.); 162ʳ⁻ᵛ (26 Sept.). The story told by Alderotto di Luigi di Neri Pitti is particularly moving (8 June 1465): he had been Captain of Livorno since Nov. 1463, having been re-appointed to that office. 'Et cum ibi stetisset per plures menses, supervenit sibi et eius uxori una ex illis febribus liburnensibus, que tenuit eos circa sex menses ita gravatos, quod pro maiori parte illius temporis non potuerunt exire de lecto, et consumpsit in dicta infirmitate plus quam centum florenos largos, et ultra hoc amisit in istis fallimentis proxime preteritis florenos mille vel citra, quorum maior pars erant de dote uxoris sue'; and thus, 'cum videat se et dotem uxoris et quicquid lucri fecerat amisisse seque ea de causa ad tantam inopiam

Owing to the large number of these offices,—the annual vacancies occurring for them by far exceeded the 150 for the *Tre Maggiori*[1] —and since many of them were only of minor importance, for which the criteria for qualification were bound to be less strict, a larger social group was directly interested in the scrutinies of the *uffici estrinseci* than in those of the *Tre Maggiori*.

According to Cavalcanti,[2] the scrutiny for the 'offices' of 1443 was, as we have seen, criticized, and then suspended, because it had qualified many opponents of the régime or their relatives. It is therefore somewhat surprising to find that on 24 February 1445 the *Balìa*, which had been put in charge of the new scrutiny, decided that 'si dia pienamente perfectione alla imborsatione dello squittino del 43'.[3] The *polizze* from it were to be combined with those of the 1440[4] scrutiny in new bags, and alternate sortition was to take place from these combined bags and from those of the new scrutiny of 1445. Some of the 1443 *polizze* may have been cancelled previously; however, the extant registers for the 1445 scrutiny show that a very large proportion of those who were successful in 1445 had also been so in 1443:[5] in the *Quartiere* of S. Maria Novella, 440 out of 718.[6] It thus looks as if in the end the main difference between the scrutiny of 1445 and that of 1443 lay in the addition rather than in the elimination of qualifications for office; and possibly the dissatisfaction with the former was in its turn due not only to political motives, but also to disappointment that not more citizens had succeeded in being qualified. Of the total of 718 citizens whose names are entered in the register of the scrutiny of the *uffici* of 1445 for the *Quartiere* of S. Maria Novella, 183, that is about a quarter, are described as not having been qualified previously. This is a large proportion,

---

deductum quod nisi se aliter exerceret, presto cogeretur mendicare; ne ad id devenire habeat, cupiens aliquod officium habere quo suis huius modi calamitatibus aliqua ex parte supplere queat,' he petitions for his term of office to be extended; which in fact was granted. Legislation was passed on 22–23 Aug. 1459 and on 19 Aug. 1466 to make such petitions for offices that were to be filled by lot more difficult (Provv., 150, fols. 86ᵛ–87ᵛ; 157, fols. 119ʳ–120ʳ). See also below, p. 156.

[1] 6 times 9 for the Signoria, 3 times 16 for the *Sedici*, and 4 times 12 for the *Dodici*.

[2] See above, pp. 54–55.

[3] This deliberation of the *Balìa* is contained in the register of the scrutiny (Tratte, 18). It is not entered in the register of the *Balìa* (Balìe, 26). For such non-registration see above, pp. 19, 54, n. 2.

[4] In the case of the *Ufficiali*, the *Provveditore* and the *Cassiere* of the *Monte*, with those from the scrutiny of these offices of 1442.

[5] Citizens who had been successful, for the same offices or groups of offices, in 1445 as well as in 1440, 1442, or 1443, were to gain one *polizza* in addition to that due to them in 1445.

[6] Tratte, 49. The entries have marginal notes: 'obtinuit in 43' 'obtinuit in 39' (Florentine style), 'non obtinuit in aliis'.

considering that only one year had passed since the last scrutiny. In contrast to this, in the scrutiny of the *Tre Maggiori* for the same *quartiere*, which was held in June 1444, only about one-fifth of the successful citizens were newly qualified, although over four years had passed since the last scrutiny for these offices.[1] While the scrutiny which served to fill the three highest magistracies was, by definition, more exclusive than that of the *uffici*, the scrutiny of the *Tre Maggiori* was notably less liberal in 1444 than in 1440 in the matter of new qualifications.[2] This may have been one of the reasons why that of the *uffici* of 1445 was relatively generous. A more liberal distribution of qualifications for the internal and external offices could indeed help to offset the sense of frustration among the citizens who had failed to qualify for the three highest magistracies. In this way some compromise might be achieved between the political needs of the régime and the ambitions of the Florentine citizens.

We have already briefly discussed the problems presented by the name tickets remaining from preceding scrutinies of the *Tre Maggiori*.[3] Scrutinies could act as a revision of previous qualifications for office if it was decided that these should be automatically invalidated unless reconfirmed by fresh qualification. This procedure was followed in 1440, when the *Balìa* decreed that citizens who had been successful in the scrutiny were to receive, over and above the normal one *polizza*, one or three additional *polizze*, if they had also been successful in the scrutiny of 1434, or if their names had been added subsequently by the *Accoppiatori* from the old purses.[4] In this way, citizens who did not obtain a majority in the new scrutiny would automatically lose their earlier qualifications. A check of this kind was evidently felt to be necessary in view of the imminent restoration of election by lot. Among the citizens who as a result of it lost their eligibility to the three highest offices, were no doubt several who were considered security risks, such as Giorgio di Piero Serragli and his sons,[5] and seven members of the Ridolfi family (a Ridolfi, Bartolomeo di Jacopo, had been *Accoppiatore* after the Albizzi

---

[1] Tratte, 15. Of the 496 successful citizens, 114 had not been qualified in the preceding scrutiny. Of these, 19 had been qualified in 1434.

[2] See also below, p. 62.

[3] See above, pp. 41 ff.

[4] Tratte, 60, fol. 235^r (13 Feb. 1440). 'Three' is corrected from 'two' in the extant draft of the decree. See also above, p. 41.

[5] See above, p. 18, n. 5.

coup in September 1433[1]). Similarly, in 1444, only the citizens
who had been successful in the new scrutiny of the *Tre Maggiori*
retained the *polizze* which they still had in the purses; these were
added to the one new *polizza* they received on account of the
scrutiny.[2] In 1448, on the other hand, the check element was
abandoned, the results from the new scrutiny being simply added
to all the *polizze* that were left from the preceding scrutinies.[3]
As a result, a citizen who had been successful in the scrutiny of
1444, but had not obtained a majority in that of 1448, would
keep such *polizze*. The scrutiny of 1448 was, therefore, comple-
mentary to that of 1444; we find, accordingly, references to it as
to the scrutiny of 1444 'cum additionibus 1434, 1439 [Florentine
style], 1448',[4] or simply as to the scrutiny of 1444.[5] The reason
for this procedure may have been that the 1444 scrutiny was considered too severe, and that what was wanted were additions to
its results.[6] That of 1453 certainly did cause dissatisfaction, for on
26 December additional regulations for it were passed by the
Balìa, 'per pace et quiete et più unione de' cittadini et per supplire
a qualunche disordine et manchamento fusse acchaduto nello
isquittino del priorato facto de proximo nel mese di novembre
proxime passato et di dicembre presente'.[7] Of what kind this
dissatisfaction was can be gathered from the contents of the regulations. While all citizens who had been successful in this scrutiny
of 1453 were to gain one new *polizza*, which was to be added
to whatever previous qualifications they possessed through the
imborsazione of 1449, those of them who had been *veduti* for the
Tre Maggiori[8] since 1440, or who had a close relative in that position, were given preferential treatment: they were to gain two

---

[1] He was deprived of political rights in 1444; see above, p. 18.

[2] The legislation of the *Balìa* concerning this scrutiny is not extant (see above, p. 54, n. 1);
however, the scrutiny lists show that this was the case. See also the brief account of proce-
dures followed in the matter of old *polizze*, which is appended to the minutes of the *Accoppiatori* of 1472 (see below, p. 187, n. 6): 'Nel 1444 chi ottenne il priorato [fu imborsato per]
1ª poliza, e tutte l'altre avessi nelle borse del 1434 o 1439 [Florentine style] si riducessino
nel [squittino del] 1444 e di quelle borsse si traessi . . .' (fol. 335ʳ). 'Priorato' stands here, as
it often does in technical terminology, for 'Tre Maggiori'.

[3] Balìe, 26, fol. 190ᵛ (16 July 1448): 'quod dictum scructinium novum prioratus . . .
uniatur et coniungatur simul cum presenti scructinio . . . et fiat simul immixtio per copulatores qui ad presens sunt, una cum copulatoribus qui de novo eligentur pro presenti
scructinio'.

[4] e.g. in the register of *veduti* in Tratte, 352.

[5] Tratte, 1151.

[6] See above, p. 59.

[7] Balìe, 27, fol. 199ʳ (26 Dec. 1453).

[8] See above, pp. 37 ff.

polizze, instead of the customary one *polizza*.[1] Since this gave an advantage to the established families over the *gente nuova*, it may have been an attempt to counter criticisms of the scrutiny of 1448, to the effect that 'entrò allora nelle borse molta gente nuova e mai usata al regimento, con grande infamia del governo e con displicenzia de' buoni popolani usi al regimento'.[2] In fact, only a fraction of the successful candidates did not qualify, in 1453, for this premium: in the *Quartiere* of S. Maria Novella, only nineteen out of 660.[3]

The results of the scrutinies convey a similar picture. While conclusions from these returns can only be tentative, owing to the incomplete nature of the extant records,[4] we possess enough material for a fairly reliable estimate of the developments in the distribution of electoral qualifications for the *Tre Maggiori*.

The outstanding impression one gains from an analysis of these records is one of normalcy. The electoral machinery continues to function, as far as the scrutinies are concerned, in the traditional fashion; what is new is that they are now nearly always entrusted to *Balìe*.[5] As before, successful candidates gain, as a rule, one *polizza* or name ticket, which is duly entered in the scrutiny registers for each of the three highest magistracies. There are no all-round changes: a few families rise, others decline, new citizens are qualified, while others, who had been successful on previous occasions, are no longer so; but this had also happened before 1434.[6]

---

[1] Balìe, 27, fol. 199ʳ: 'Che chi arà vinto lo isquittino del priorato facto del mese sopradetto di novembre et di dicembre MCCCCLIII et abbia beneficio d'essere stato tracto o veduto insino questo dì dal anno millequattrocentotrentanove o da indi qua ad alcuno de' tre maggiori uffici, o padre, avolo, zio o fratello carnale o nipote carnale di padre, debba essere imborsato pe' presenti venti accopiatori e per due polize in su detto squittino del MCCCCLIII; et chi a vinto il sopradetto squittino et non avessi detto beneficio, sia imborsato in su detto squittino per una poliza.'

[2] *Priorista* of Francesco di Tommaso Giovanni, cit., fol. 156ʳ.   [3] Tratte, 1151.

[4] Of the scrutinies and *imborsazioni* for the *Tre Maggiori* registers are extant, for 1440, for the *Quartiere* of S. Giovanni (Tratte, 1150); for 1444, for S. Spirito (Tratte, 49), S. Croce (ibid.), and S. Maria Novella (Tratte, 15); for 1448–9, for S. Spirito (Tratte, 61, fols. 66ʳ–80ᵛ), S. Maria Novella (Tratte, 49), and S. Giovanni (Tratte, 49); for 1453–5, for S. Croce (Tratte, 1151, fols. 387ʳ–399ᵛ, and 61, fols. 136ʳ–142ᵛ) and S. Maria Novella (Tratte, 1151, fols. 408ʳ–420ᵛ, and 61, fols. 66ʳ–86ᵛ).   [5] See below, p. 67.

[6] We take the newly-qualified citizens to be those who are entered with one *polizza* only against their name for the three highest offices, except in 1453, when most of them obtained two *polizze* (see above, pp. 60–61). This assumption contains a margin of error, for theoretically it could happen that a citizen who is entered with one *polizza* had actually been qualified in the preceding scrutiny, but had since lost all his *polizze* (i.e. for the Signoria, the *Sedici Gonfalonieri*, and the *Dodici Buonuomini*) through being appointed to all three of these offices, or for other reasons. In practice, this was unlikely to happen except on rare occasions, and may therefore be ignored for the purpose of this inquiry.

The Medici were sometimes criticized by Florentine *ottimati* for raising men of humble origin to positions of political and social influence. One may ask whether this is borne out by the evidence of the newly-qualified citizens.

In 1440 they constituted over a quarter of the total of the successful candidates whose names are entered in the only extant register of the scrutiny of that year, for the *Quartiere* of S. Giovanni.[1] So large a proportion was, however, exceptional, and, being probably due to the dissatisfaction the electoral situation was causing at the time,[2] reflects the desire to widen the group of eligible citizens.

Compared with the scrutiny of 1440, those of 1444, 1448, and 1453 were less liberal, the proportion of newly-qualified citizens oscillating around one-fifth of the total.[3] Since in many cases new qualifications were offset by the deaths of previously qualified citizens, or by the failure of citizens to qualify once again, they did not necessarily imply an increase in the total of eligible citizens. Such an increase did, however, take place over the years: between 1440 and 1449 the total number of citizens who were eligible for the three highest offices in the *Quartiere* of S. Giovanni rose from 508 to 721; between 1444 and 1453 the corresponding numbers in the *Quartieri* of S. Croce and S. Maria Novella rose from 458 to 623 and from 496 to 660 respectively.

The social status of the citizens who were newly qualified is obviously of considerable interest for an appreciation of the electoral policy of the régime. One would expect many of them to be sons or brothers of citizens who were already eligible for the *Tre Maggiori*; but it comes as a surprise to find just how many of them fall into this category. Thus, in 1448, of the 131 citizens who were newly qualified in the district of S. Spirito, 95 were sons, and 15 brothers, of citizens who had been successful in the

---

[1] Out of a total of 508 citizens, 142 are entered with one *polizza* only for each of the *Tre Maggiori*. Some of these could, of course, have been *imborsati* before 1434 and not re-qualified after the return of the Medici (Tratte, 1150).

[2] See above, pp. 59–60.

[3] Scrutiny of 1444: in S. Spirito, 100 out of 541; in S. Croce, 76 out of 458; in S. Maria Novella, 95 out of 496 (Tratte, 49 and 15). *Imborsazione* of 1449 (after the scrutiny of 1448): in S. Spirito, 131 out of 772; in S. Maria Novella, 157 out of 695; in S. Giovanni, 172 out of 721 (Tratte, 61 and 49). Scrutiny of 1453: in S. Croce, 152 out of 623; in S. Maria Novella, 159 out of 660 (Tratte, 1151). Among the newly-qualified of 1444 I have not included the citizens who had been qualified in 1434, and not in 1440, and who were consequently entered in the scrutiny lists of 1444 with the one *polizza* only which they had acquired in that year. The figures for the newly-qualified of 1453 are based on the names that are entered in the scrutiny lists of 1453 as not having been included in the lists of '1444', which in fact also contained qualifications made in 1434, 1440, and 1448 (see above, p. 60).

scrutiny of 1444. In 1453, out of the 159 newcomers in S. Maria Novella, 135 were sons, 8 brothers, and 2 grandsons of men whose names were in the purses of 1449.[1] Contemporary criticism of the scrutiny of 1448 as having been too democratic[2] has therefore to be taken with a grain of salt: in S. Spirito, only 9 out of the 131 citizens who were newly qualified in 1448[3] belonged to families which were not represented in the preceding scrutiny of 1444, or about one per cent. of the total of *imborsati* when the bags were closed in 1449.

'Elections' which were to such an extent based on close family relationships greatly narrowed the area of effectual choice of eligible citizens. There was nothing new in this: electoral continuity based on the family had a long tradition in Florence; and before 1434, as after, it would be natural for scrutiny councils to tend to favour relatives of previously qualified citizens. In these circumstances the qualification of *gente nuova* could be the result of personal favouritism, of pressure from the humbler elements in the scrutiny councils, particularly from among the Lesser Guilds, or of deliberate policy.[4] However, the leading families always scored over the rest, so much so that changes among the eligible citizens in our period concern the 'representation' of single established families rather than the introduction of new families or the elimination of previously 'qualified' ones.

The first impression provided by a study of the scrutiny lists is the predominant position, in the single *quartieri*, of a small number of families which share among them very much more than the average number of qualifications. This had been the situation under the so-called oligarchy, and the Medici régime did not substantially change it. The earliest of these lists after 1434 is that of 1440 for the *Quartiere* of San Giovanni. We have already discussed the continuity it shows, in the composition and social structure of the 'electorate', with that of 1433.[5] Of the 411 *imborsati* of the Greater Guilds, 240, i.e. *c.* 58 per cent. belong to the 25 families which shared among them *c.* 65 per cent. of the *polizze* for the Signoria and nearly 80 per cent. for the Gonfalonier of Justice. In the *Gonfalone* of Lion d'oro, for instance, the 7 families with the largest number of members provide 86 out of 123 citizens, with altogether 249 out of 329

---

[1] This analysis is based on the lists in Tratte, 49 and 61.   [2] See above, p. 61.
[3] That is, those entered with one *polizza* only in the scrutiny register.
[4] See below, p. 215, on the scrutiny of 1484.   [5] See above, pp. 8–10.

polizze. This was the *gonfalone* of the Medici, and of the Masi, Della Stufa, Aldobrandini del Nero, &c. The ratio is similar in the *Gonfalone* Chiavi, where the Albizzi, the Alessandri, the Da Filicaia, and the Pandolfini lived (75:111; 206:260); it is somewhat less favourable to the leading families in the *Gonfaloni* Drago (46:96; 121:260) and Vaio (44:81; 122:197).[1] Much the same picture is provided by the other *quartieri* in subsequent scrutinies; thus, in 1444, in the *Gonfalone* Scala of S. Spirito, 5 families provide 41 out of 63 entries, with 117 out of 167 *polizze.*[2] While there were differences between the single *gonfaloni*, which reflect differences in the social topography of the city, the general picture is one of decisive numerical preponderance, in each *quartiere*, of a relatively small number of families; a preponderance which is even more pronounced when we consider, not the citizens who were eligible for the three highest offices, but the *polizze* they had in the purses for those offices.

For in analysing the social implications of the scrutinies, one has to take into account not only the 'representation' of single families, but also the number of *polizze* with which they were 'represented'. Once qualified by a scrutiny, a citizen would normally stand an excellent chance of being also successful in subsequent scrutinies, especially if he belonged to an influential family.[3] Since the odds against having one's *polizza* used up were fairly heavy,[4] it was comparatively easy to accumulate *polizze* through successive scrutinies. Thus older citizens had often five or six or even more *polizze* in the bags of the three highest offices, with the result that their chances of being drawn, while sortition was in force, would be much greater than those of younger men: a premium on age in keeping with the responsibilities attached to the offices. When it was decided, in October 1434, to burn the old ballot bags and reduce the maximum of *polizze* that could be retained from them to two, this amounted to a temporary levelling down of electoral

---

[1] In each case, this refers to the seven families with the largest representation.

[2] Based on the scrutiny register in Tratte, 49.

[3] See above, p. 62.

[4] The number of name tickets which were used up over a period of five years by citizens being appointed to the Signoria was 270. To this have to be added the *polizze* which were taken out of the purses after having been drawn and not replaced, as was normally the case when it was found that their owners were temporarily disqualified by a *divieto*. *Polizze* whose owners were *a specchio*, i.e. had tax debts, were torn up, while those which belonged to citizens who did not meet the age regulations for the office, were, until 1451, replaced in the purses when their owners reached the required age; from 1451 onwards they were replaced immediately (Provv., 141, fols. 272ᵛ–273ʳ; 11–16 Feb. 1451).

qualifications to a maximum of three *polizze,* including the one acquired by the new scrutiny.[1] While this 'equalization' of the franchise had its democratic aspects which might appeal to public opinion, it also meant that the new régime was beginning its electoral policy with a relatively clean slate. However, the social effect of this measure was more apparent than real. For a single citizen, the loss of previous qualifications could seriously reduce his chances of being appointed, provided the office was filled by lot; for a strongly 'represented' family, the effect of such individual losses might be less serious, since it would still command a substantial proportion of all the *polizze.* Thus, after the scrutiny of 1440, a quarter of the 'qualified' families of the Greater Guilds in San Giovanni shared among them about 65 per cent. of the *polizze* contained in the purses of that group. Among the members of the Lesser Guilds, 6 out of 46 families commanded no less than 93 out of 231 *polizze,* or over 40 per cent. of the total.[2]

Were there any significant changes in the social structure of the section of the population which was eligible for the three highest offices during the period between the scrutiny of 1434 and that of 1453? While the extant electoral lists show a small number of such families to be as predominant in 1453 as they had been in 1440, they suggest that the total gains in 'representation' and *polizze* were relatively larger among the citizens of lower social rank.[3] This does not come as a surprise; for while the principal families had to rely largely on the qualification for office of the younger generation, and hence on a high birthrate, in order to retain or increase their share, 'new' families were clearly more flexible. A family which was represented by one member only in 1434 would treble its 'representation' if two more of its members were subsequently qualified. It was probably this kind of development, rather than any spectacular shift in the social distribution of eligibility, which caused complaints about too many *gente nuova* being qualified for the highest magistracies. While the social criteria of eligibility remained substantially unchanged, there was some broadening at the base, which might give the régime a more democratic appearance, and hence contribute to its popularity.

[1] See above, pp. 8, 41. [2] Cf. Tratte, 1150, and above, p. 8, n. 7.
[3] The fact that only one of the four scrutiny lists for 1440 is extant, i.e. that for the *Quartiere* of S. Giovanni, makes it impossible to arrive at more than tentative conclusions in this matter.

So much for the over-all picture. If we turn to single families, we find changes at the top as well as at the bottom of the social scale. Now, as before 1434, some families would advance and others decline; but after the revolutionary measures of 1434, such changes were, as a rule, moderate and gradual. The *Gonfalone* of Lion d'oro, in which the Medici lived, may serve to illustrate this pattern. If we compare the number of names and of *polizze* which the more heavily represented families had in the purses of the Signoria after the scrutiny of 1440 and the *imborsazione* of 1449, we arrive at the following results.

	Scrutiny of 1440			Imborsazione of 1449	
	Names	Polizze		Names	Polizze
		Greater Guilds			
Masi	17	35	Medici	19	58
Medici	16	35	Masi	18	60
Aldobrandini del Nero	12	37	Aldobrandini del Nero	17	65
Ginori	12	36	Ginori	17	60
Della Stufa	11	43	Martelli	17	58
Martelli	11	35	Dietisalvi	13	48
Dietisalvi	8	30	Della Stufa	11	61
Cambini*	6	15	Ciai	7	20
Bruni	5	5	Bruni	7	18
Ciai	4	11	Cambini*	6	24
Inghirami	3	7	Inghirami	6	15
Di Piero	2	2	Bonvanni*	5	20
Bonvanni*	1	4	Di Piero	4	6
			Pucci (di Lionardo)*	1	1
		Lesser Guilds			
Bonvanni*	6	13	Pucci (di Lionardo)*	9	21
Di Monte	6	12			
Pucci (di Lionardo)	6	10	Del Troscia	6	16
			Bucherelli	5	18
Cambini*	4	16	Di Monte	5	17
Bucherelli	4	9	Del Giocondo	5	7
Panuzzi	4	4	Cambini*	4	18
Del Troscia	2	8	Panuzzi	4	11
Del Giocondo	1	1			

* See also under Greater and Lesser Guilds respectively.

This comparison shows that nearly all the most heavily represented families of 1440 remain so in 1449; what changes is their order of precedence. But these changes are moderate, and more pronounced among the Lesser than the Greater Guilds.

The impression we gain from an analysis of the social character of the early Medicean scrutinies accords broadly with that conveyed by the policy of the *Accoppiatori*.[1] While single

[1] See above, pp. 43 ff.

families or individuals are subjected to discrimination on political grounds, and while new men and families are admitted, the scrutinies remain firmly rooted in the oligarchical foundations of Florentine government.

By what means could the régime determine the results of the scrutinies? According to the Statutes of 1415, specially appointed councils had to be convened for each scrutiny. The Signoria, the Colleges, the nine Captains of the Guelph Party, the *Sei di Mercanzia*, and the proconsul of the guild of Judges and Notaries were members *ex officio*, and were joined by one consul from each of the twenty-one guilds and by eighty elected members, chosen by the Signoria and the Colleges.[1] The government thus played a leading role in choosing the elective members of the council, which could be turned to the advantage of the régime when the Signoria was elected *a mano*. However, the twenty-eight members of the Colleges, that is of the *Sedici Gonfalonieri* and *Dodici Buonuomini*, continued to be appointed by lot, and hence provided an element of chance. In these circumstances, it was no doubt preferable to delegate the scrutinies to *Balìe*; for the methods by which these special councils were appointed presented far greater safeguards for the régime than the statutory scrutiny councils.[2] There were precedents for such a procedure. In 1382 and 1393 scrutinies had been entrusted, entirely or partly, to *Balìe*, and in 1433 the *Balìa* created after the Albizzi coup had been put in charge of the new scrutiny.[3] It was this precedent which was followed in October 1434.[4] In all these cases the background was a revolutionary situation in which a faction tried to secure or consolidate its ascendancy by controlling eligibility to the highest offices in the state. Between 1434 and 1453 all the scrutinies of the *Tre Maggiori*, and all those of the other internal and external offices, with the exception of that of 1443, were carried out by *Balìe*. Indeed, the criticism to which the scrutiny of 1443 was subjected at the time, and which resulted in its suspension,[5] may have served to underline the advantages of the new system. Moreover, *Balìe* constituted, between 1434 and 1454, one of the cornerstones of the Medici régime, and it was only natural that they should also be expected to fulfil a function that was essential for its security and consolidation.

[1] *Statuta* 1415, ii, pp. 481–4. See also above, pp. 6, 54.
[2] See below, pp. 80 ff.   [3] See above, pp. 5–6.
[4] See above, p. 7.   [5] See above, pp. 18, 54–55.

MEDICEAN COUNCILS

I T was customary in Florence to grant special powers (*balìa*) to magistracies or councils for limited periods and specific purposes. The most important of such magistracies with special powers was, at the time of the establishment of the Medici régime, that of the *Dieci di Balìa*; from 1394 onwards it was appointed in times of war, or danger of war, to conduct military operations and diplomatic business.[1] In internal affairs, the Captain of the People could be granted special judicial powers or *balìa* for reasons of security, as happened in 1433 and 1434.[2] Less extensive were the powers granted from time to time, or normally, to the Signoria to dispatch some specific business.[3] Finally, the councils could delegate authority to impose taxes to special councils, and they often granted *balìa* for this purpose to a council which consisted of eighty-one official and sixty-four specially appointed members.[4]

What these delegations of powers had in common was their specific and limited purposes. In contrast to this, full powers were, on rare occasions, granted to *ad hoc* councils, to carry out reforms, and generally to effect legislation which was likely to be thrown out by the statutory councils. These *Balìe*, as they were called by the generic term, consequently superseded, while

[1] Its members were normally elected for six months, while the office itself would last until after the conclusion of peace. See the comprehensive study by Pampaloni, 'Gli organi della Repubblica fiorentina per le relazioni con l'estero' (see above, p. 30, n. 3).

[2] Balìe, 24, fols. 12ᵛ–13ʳ (16 Sept. 1433); 25, fol. 18ʳ⁻ᵛ (29 Sept. 1434). See also above, p. 3.

[3] See Davidsohn, *Geschichte von Florenz*, iv, 1, pp. 102–3. A number of such limited *balìe* are contained in *Tract.* I of book V of the Statutes of 1415 (ii, pp. 479 ff.).

[4] Cf. Provv., 116, fols. 46ᵛ–47ᵛ (27–28 May 1426): *balìa* is granted to the Signoria, Colleges, Captains of the Guelph Party, Eight of Ward, *Sei di Mercanzia*, twenty-one consuls of the guilds, and sixty-four *arroti* (in all 145), for 'imponendi onera super nova distributione prestanzionis'. The 145, as this special council came to be called, were again appointed, for the purpose of imposing taxes, in Feb. 1427 (ibid., fols. 265ᵛ–267ᵛ; for eight months), and Dec. 1429 (Provv., 120, fols. 398ᵛ–400ʳ; for one year). This did not mean that during these periods the ancient councils entirely abdicated financial legislation to the 145; in 1430, for instance, the usual procedure was for tax laws to be passed first by the council of 200 (see below, p. 69), and then by the councils of the People and Commune. In 1429 the 145 were also entrusted with the election of the *Dieci di Balìa*, for the war against Lucca; see above, p. 52.

they lasted, the councils of the People and Commune. Since normally the latter could hardly be expected to vote their own temporary suspension, the ancient popular assembly (*Parlamento*) was, as a rule, used for this purpose. The *Parlamento*, although it had long ceased to exercise any legislative function, could come again into its own in times of crisis.[1] Summoned by the Signoria to the square in front of their palace, it would be presented with the proposal to create a *Balìa* invested with full powers[2] for a period of a few weeks or months. The results of such a plebiscite were a foregone conclusion in conditions where a revolutionary situation allowed the dominant faction to apply all kinds of pressure to the popular assembly.

The *Balìe* drastically interfered with the normal channels of legislation, which had been recently perfected by the creation of the councils of 200 and of 131. According to Florentine constitutional law, all bills, whether public or private, had to be initiated by the Signoria. Having received the consent of the Colleges, they were then sent to the council of the People, and if passed by it, to that of the Commune; only if passed by the latter did they obtain force of law.[3] In 1411 two new councils, the 200 and 131, were placed above the councils of the People and the Commune for legislation concerning military affairs, alliances, and related matters;[4] the former being recruited by drawing from purses containing the names of all the citizens who, from 1382 onwards, had been *veduti* for the three highest magistracies, the latter consisting of 83 official and 48 specially elected members.[5] Bills on military and related matters had now first to be passed by the 200 and then the 131, before being presented to the councils of the People and Commune. Yet there was no question of a delegation of authority by the ancient councils: the decisions of the 200 and 131 had no force of law without their assent. But it was precisely this consent—as well as that of the 200 and 131—which was temporarily suspended by the *Balìe*.

---

[1] See Davidsohn, *Geschichte*, iv, 1, pp. 58–59.

[2] The formula for these powers was 'habentes generalem auctoritatem potestatem et baliam quam habet totus populus florentinus' (*Balìa* of 1382; Balìe, 18, fol. 2ʳ).

[3] *Statuta* 1415, ii, pp. 664 ff.

[4] Provv., 99, fols. 168ʳ–169ʳ (4–5 Feb. 1411); ed. Pellegrini, op. cit., Appendix, no. 3.

[5] Provv. cit., fol. 168ᵛ. From 1381 onwards according to Florentine style: but the *terminus post quem* is, no doubt, the scrutiny of Jan. 1382 (Florentine style: 1381); see above, p. 5). The ancient councils, on the other hand, were appointed every four months by drawing names from purses that had been previously prepared by the Signoria and the Colleges (*Statuta* 1415, ii, p. 660).

The opposition of the Florentines to such temporary suspensions of the normal legislative machinery would allow these to be used at times of internal crisis only, when circumstances might be taken to justify the recourse to plebiscitarian methods. Thus the *Balìe* of 1378 and of 1382 marked the beginning and the end of the Ciompi revolt, that of 1393 sealed the victory of the Albizzi over the Alberti, while those of 1433 and 1434 brought about the defeat of Cosimo de' Medici and of Rinaldo degli Albizzi.[1] All except the first of these *Balìe* owed their existence to a *Parlamento*. It was significant of the internal stability of the Albizzi régime that between 1393 and 1433 only one *Balìa* was created, and not by a popular assembly; nor did this *Balìa*, of June 1412, possess full powers, having been appointed by the councils for the specific purpose of dealing with an alleged conspiracy of the Alberti.[2]

This reluctance to resort to *Balìe* is reflected in their short duration. Their terms of office never exceeded, in the first place, that of the Signoria at whose request they were established, and subsequent extensions never that of its successor. The *Balìa* of 1378 lasted from 23 to 30 June, that of 1382 from 21 January to 28 February, and that of 1393 from 19 to 31 October.[3] The *Balìa* of 1433 was created on 9 September to last until 31 October, but with authority to extend its session until the end of the year;[4] and similarly, the *Balìa* established by the *Parlamento* of 28 September 1434 was to dissolve on 31 October, unless it decided to continue in office until 31 December.[5] They both made use of this authority.[6]

The *Balìa* of 1434 thus belongs to the traditional short-term *Balìe* with full powers, i.e. with 'totalis, integra, libera et absoluta potestas et balia nullis . . . legibus limitata, et quam et prout habet totus populus et communis Florentie'.[7] It duly dissolved on 31 December; but it left a legacy of special powers which, although temporary, went far towards establishing the constitutional foundations of the new régime.

---

[1] The *provvisione* of the councils creating a *Balìa*, on 22–23 June 1378, Provv., 66, fols. 51r–52v, is ed. by C. Falletti-Fossati, *Il tumulto dei Ciompi* . . . (Rome, 1882), pp. 331–2. A summary of its decisions, Capitoli, 11, fols. 124r–158r, is ed. ibid., pp. 333–45. The legislation of the *Balìe* of 1382 and 1393 is in Balìe, 18 and 19 (some of it is ed. by Capponi, *Storia*, i, pp. 609–38); that of the *Balìe* of 1433 and 1434 in Balìe, 24 and 25. See also above, pp. 1–2.

[2] Provv., 101, fols. 121r–123v (17–18 June 1412). The *Balìa* was to end its session by 30 June. Its register is in Balìe, 20.

[3] See above, n. 1.   [4] Balìe, 24, fol. 1v.   [5] See above, p. 1, n. 2.
[6] Balìe, 24, fols. 43v and 55v; 25, fol. 43r.   [7] Balìe, 25, fol. 1v.

On 15 December the *Balìa* extended the term of office of the *Accoppiatori*, and with it their powers to elect the Signoria *a mano*, until April 1435; and we have seen how this first extension was followed by others; with the result that electoral controls continued uninterrupted until 1441.[1] Similarly, on 25 October, the *Balìa* extended the special judicial powers granted to the Captain of the People until 31 December by another five months.[2] It also delegated, on 26 December, to the council of 145, powers to impose taxes during the following year;[3] and the 145 made repeated use of these during 1435.[4] This delegation of authority by the *Balìa* terminated in December of that year; but on 14 May 1436 we find the 145 again passing a tax bill, this time by virtue of powers they had received from the councils two days earlier.[5] This procedure was also followed in 1437 and in 1438, when, on 13 February, the 145 were put in charge of imposing up to 12 *ventine*.[6] On this occasion, the delegation of powers met with strong opposition in the council of the People, which rejected the bill twice, and then passed it with a majority of three.[7] If financial legislation was, even occasionally, to be taken out of the hands of the statutory councils, a more efficient system had clearly to be devised. It is against this background that the creation, on 18 May 1438, of a new council, for three years, has to be viewed, which, although technically a *Balìa*, differed in several important respects from its predecessors.[8]

Like these, it had its non-official members appointed by election, and not by lot, as was normal for the appointment of councillors; and, like the *Balìe* of 1433 and 1434, it was put in charge of the next scrutiny, which meant that, once again, the

---

[1] See above, pp. 11 ff.

[2] Balìe, 25, fol. 45^r. See above, p. 3, n. 7.

[3] Balìe, 25, fol. 111^v: 'possint semel et pluries . . . infra unum annum proxime futurum . . . imponere et indicere civibus florentinis quecumque onera secundum quamcumque distribu-tionem onerum pro florentinis civibus ordinatam videlicet catasti ordinarii et novinarum ad presens vigentium . . .' &c. Tax bills had, however, to be passed first by the Signoria and the Colleges, with at least 28 out of 37 votes.

[4] Signori e Collegi, Deliberazioni, speciale autorità, 25, fols. 89^v–93^r (20 Jan.), 110^v–112^v (31 May), 123^r–126^r (30 Sept.), 127^v–129^v (24 Oct.), and 137^r–140^r (9 Dec.).

[5] Ibid., fols. 159^v–163^r. Provv., 127, fol. 52^{r-v} (11–12 May 1436).

[6] Libri Fabarum, 57, fols. 127^v–130^r (8–12 March 1437); 173^r–175^r (8–13 Feb. 1438). Provv., 127, fols. 348^r–349^r; 128, fols. 238^v–239^v.

[7] With 146 out of 215 votes. See also above, p. 68, n. 4.

[8] Provv., 129, fols. 34^r–37^v. Its title was council of 200 'vel plures' (Tratte, 60, fol. 225^r); but it was called *consilium maius* (cf., e.g., Libri Fabarum, 58, fol. 71^v: 'in consilio novo quod dicitur maius'), or also *Balìa* (ibid., fol. 15^v: 'in balìa'). This latter usage is followed by 15th-century *Prioristi*: see Tratte, 132 *bis*, fol. 163^v; Bibl. Naz. XXV, 379, fol. 143^r.

statutory regulations on the election of *ad hoc* scrutiny councils were suspended.[1] On the other hand, it was not granted full legislative powers. Its further business was confined to taxation, the *Monte*, and military affairs, and what was more, its decisions required the consent of the statutory councils to become law. As far as military matters were concerned, the new council took the place of the 200 and 131: no new military enterprise could be started without having first been approved by it. It is this drastic limitation of its powers which explains why the law creating it could be presented to the councils, instead of being proposed to a *Parlamento*—and to summon a *Parlamento* at so short a distance from that of 1434 might have been dangerous to the régime. That the law nevertheless met with considerable opposition in the council of the People, which passed it in its first reading with a majority of seven only,[2] was probably due, to no small extent, to the exceptionally long term of its elected personnel.

The new *Balìa* or *Consiglio Maggiore* was to consist of an unusually large number of official members, including the officials in charge of finance and scrutinies, and of at least 200 additional members, *amatori del presente reggimento,* who were to be co-opted by the former.[3] To appoint councillors for three years was an innovation which contrasts with the short terms of the earlier *Balìe,* as well as with the four-monthly sessions of the councils of the People and the Commune (as for the 200, their names were drawn whenever they were to be summoned),[4] and is in keeping with the tendency we have already observed in the case of the *Accoppiatori,* who by 1438 were well on the way to becoming a quasi-permanent institution. The new council was also put in charge of deciding, during the next three years, whether the Signoria was to be elected *a mano* ('in quel modo si fa al presente') or by lot.[5] The time of the new scrutiny was

---

[1] See above, pp. 15–16.   [2] Libri Fabarum, 58, fol. 4ᵛ.

[3] The Signoria, the XVI, the XII, the Captains of the Guelph Party, the next Eight of Ward and their predecessors, the Ten, the *Accoppiatori,* the Secretaries of the external scrutinies, the *Ufficiali del Monte,* the *Ufficiali del Banco,* the *Sei di Mercanzia,* and twenty-one consuls of the guilds chosen by the other official members. When it began its session, the new council consisted of 124 official members and *c.* 224 *arroti*; see Appendix, no. III. It was given permission to co-opt up to 100 additional members in Jan. 1440 for the holding of the scrutiny.

[4] Provv., 99, fol. 168ᵛ (4–5 Feb. 1411).

[5] See above, p. 15. Pellegrini, in his review of K. D. Ewart's book on Cosimo de' Medici (see above, p. 11, n. 3), pp. 126 ff., has already disposed of the erroneous view, based on Guicciardini, *Storie,* p. 5, that Cosimo ruled Florence through quinquennial *Balìe.* However, Pellegrini's brief account does not do full justice to the slow and complicated process by which *Balìe* became one of the cornerstones of the Medici régime under Cosimo.

approaching, and with it the appointment of new *Accoppiatori*, which would put an end to the annual re-election of the *Accoppiatori* of 1434.[1] By delegating decisions on the method of electing the Signoria to the new council, the continuation of elections *a mano* could at least be secured until it had completed the scrutiny, that is for another three years.

No attempt was made to justify the creation of the new council on account of the military situation, which indeed was not too bad in the spring of 1438, despite Niccolò Piccinino's campaign in the Romagna; on 28 March peace had been arranged with the Duke of Milan.[2] But the war had produced a difficult financial situation,[3] and accordingly the preamble of the law states that tax legislation would be facilitated if carried out *unitamente* together with the 'men of the régime', the *uomini del reggimento*.[4] In this respect, the new council was clearly planned to replace the council of 145 which, as we have seen, had recently run into difficulties.[5] Its record in this field was, however, not spectacular. The first time we find it legislating on new taxes is on 23 October 1439, that is well over a year after its creation; and the fact that it threw out, three times running, the bill proposed on that occasion, shows that the traditional Florentine opposition to such legislation could be just as vocal in the new council as in the long-established ones.[6] In the following months tax bills were first presented to the council of 200, instead of to the *Consiglio Maggiore*;[7] and the attempt, in November and December 1439, to delegate to that council temporary control of the payments to the *Monte Comune* met with unusually sharp resistance in the council of the People, which rejected the bill seven times, and finally passed it with a majority of one.[8]

The term of office of the *Consiglio Maggiore* ended in May 1441; but having completed the scrutiny in January, it does not seem

---

[1] See above, p. 15.

[2] *Storia di Milano*, vi, p. 327. Cf. Buoninsegni, *Storie*, pp. 67–68.

[3] Buoninsegni, p. 67: '. . . parendoci non poter supplire alla spesa che bisognava, per essere stracchi dalla gran quantità delle gravezze pagate . . .'.

[4] Provv. cit. above, p. 16, n. 7.

[5] See above, p. 71.

[6] Libri Fabarum, 58, fol. 71ᵛ (23 Oct. 1439): 'Modum et formam nove distributionis onerum per viam quinquine.' Rejected on 23 and 24 Oct. The same, 'per viam septine', rejected on 26 Oct., and passed on 6 Nov. It was passed, on 7 and 9 Nov., by the councils of the People and Commune (ibid., fols. 72ʳ⁻ᵛ, 77ʳ⁻78ʳ). *Quinquinae* and *septinae* were taxes imposed by committees of five and seven respectively.

[7] Ibid., fols. 78ᵛ⁻81ᵛ (13–19 Nov. 1439), 91ᵛ⁻93ʳ (6–11 Jan. 1440), 99ʳ⁻100ʳ (8–9 March 1440), &c.   [8] Ibid., fols. 82ʳ⁻86ᵛ (20 Nov.–8 Dec.).

to have met after February 1441,[1] and no attempts seem to have
been made to extend its term. In January 1441 it decreed that,
with the new scrutiny in force, elections *a mano* were to cease, and
the *Accoppiatori* to resign.[2] By spring 1441 none of the institutional innovations of the new régime survived.

Two years later, another new council was created, primarily to
carry out financial legislation. Ostensibly a successor of earlier
councils concerned with finance, the council of 121 had also a
political twist: no decisions regarding rebels or political exiles
could be taken without having first been approved by it. While
its term was longer than that of the *Consiglio Maggiore* of 1438,
namely five instead of three years, its personnel was to change
every year.[3] However, it had not much opportunity of proving
its value, for already in May 1444 yet another conciliar reform
bill was presented to the councils. The expiry of many sentences
against political enemies was approaching, and the safeguards
that had been introduced a year before could not prevent the
statutory councils from refusing to extend their sentences.
Moreover, the recent scrutiny had caused dissatisfaction among
the Mediceans on grounds of security.[4] To delegate decisions on
the exiles, as well as the next scrutiny, to a *Balìa* was the obvious
solution, which could not be welcome to the councils; and their
opposition was no doubt greatly sharpened by the proposal that
the *Balìa* should last for no less than five years. Accordingly, the
law creating the *Balìa* was passed, in its first reading on 20–21 May,
with majorities of two only in the councils of the People and the
Commune,[5] that is with the same kind of extremely narrow
majority with which nine years earlier the legislation on the
Accoppiatori had been passed.

[1] The *Consiglio Maggiore* held the scrutiny of the *Tre Maggiori* in Jan.–Feb., that of the
other offices from Feb. 1440 to Jan. 1441: Tratte, 60, fols. 229r–245r. The last entry in
this (fragmentary) register of the council is for 23 Feb. 1441 (fols. 249r–250r).

[2] See above, p. 16.

[3] Provv., 134, fols. 25r–26v (16–20 May 1443). Their competence extended to the *Monte*
and to taxes, their decisions on new taxes requiring the assent of the ancient councils. They
were not allowed to concern themselves with the next scrutiny, which was due to take place
in the following year. One hundred members were to be appointed by drawing from bags
filled with names selected by the Signoria, the Colleges, the Eight, the *Ufficiali del Monte*,
the Six, and the *Accoppiatori* and Secretaries, from among citizens who had been *veduti ai
Tre Maggiori*, or to the Captainship or College of the Guelph Party; to these were added the
names of 128 citizens who did not possess these qualifications. The remaining twenty-one
members were provided by twenty-one consuls of the guilds, chosen by the Signoria and the
Colleges.   [4] See above, p. 54.

[5] Libri Fabarum, 59, fols. 139r–140v: 175 to 85, and 134 to 65. The law (Balìe, 26, fols.
7r–10v) was passed, in the final reading, with 166 votes to 40 and 129 to 56 respectively on
22 and 23 May.   [6] See above, p. 14.

The powers of the new *Balìa*—the term is used concurrently with *Consiglio Maggiore*[1]—resembled those of the *Balìa* of 1438, in so far as it had full authority to determine the next scrutinies, including the revision of that of 1443,[2] and could pass tax bills, which had then to receive the assent of the councils of the People and Commune. It could also, whenever it wished to do so, carry out the election of the *Otto di Guardia*; and it could 'deliberare ultra iam dicta omnia et singula que fuerant permissa', in 1438, 'illis qui vulgariter dicebantur il consiglio maggiore', and, in 1443, 'illis qui dicuntur i centoventuno'. But while the *Consiglio Maggiore* of 1438 had been appointed for three years, that of 1444 was created for five; and while the council of 121 was to be annually elected during five years, the personnel of the *Balìa* of 1444 was to remain in office throughout the five years of its existence.[3] It thus constitutes the highest achievement so far of the conciliar policy of the Medici régime, and concludes its formative and experimental period.

During the five years of its existence, the problem of the relationship between this new type of long-term *Balìa* and the ancient councils, which was already inherent in the *Consiglio Maggiore* of 1438, was thrown into sharp relief. The short-term *Balìe* until 1434 had operated on an altogether different level from the statutory councils. This was changed as soon as *Balìe*, created for much longer periods, were expected to collaborate with those councils in a number of fields, while in others they had full powers to act alone. The danger to such a lasting *modus vivendi* between the new and old councils lay precisely in these dual functions of the Medicean *Balìe*. Would they not attempt to extend their full powers also to fields in which their competence was limited, and thus try to approximate to the pre-Medicean type of *Balìa*?

The history of the *Balìa* of 1444 shows how this problem was now coming to a head. The records of this *Balìa* afford ample evidence of independent legislation in cases in which the assent of the ancient councils was required, especially in financial matters.[4] The question was whether the councils could be induced to accept this loss of power. That there was considerable

---

[1] Balìe, 26, fol. 24ʳ (29 May 1444): 'consiglio maggiore'.
[2] See above, p. 58.   [3] Ibid., fol. 9ᵛ (20–22 May 1444).
[4] A comparison between the voting registers of the *Balìa* and those of the councils of the People and Commune (Libri Fabarum, 60 and 61) shows that the *Balìa* did not, as a rule, send tax bills for approval to the councils of the People and Commune, as it should have done. The latter continued to transact some financial business, but this was mainly of minor importance.

dissatisfaction with it is shown by a law passed by them on 26 and 27 August 1446.[1] The authority granted to the *Balìa* having allegedly been misused by individual citizens, the law sets out to define that authority. It is to be limited 'pro futuris contingentibus ad conservationem libertatis et status solum', and, specifically, to military business, to elections of the *Otto di Guardia* and the *Dieci di Balìa*, to scrutinies, and to legislation concerning the *Monte* and taxation, with the express proviso that all tax bills required the assent of the statutory councils. But displeasure with the *Balìa*'s activities appears to have continued during the following year, so much so that in July 1447 the suggestion was made in a *Pratica* to dissolve the *Balìa* before its time was up, and to restore the traditional democratic liberties, *solita populi potestas*; or, failing this, at least to increase the *Balìa*'s personnel.[2] A committee consisting of leading members of the régime, and including Cosimo de' Medici himself, was set up to discuss these proposals. It advised against any change, on account of the war; once peace was concluded, the matter could be discussed once more. At the same time, the committee earnestly begs the Signoria to use the *Balìa* solely 'for those things for which the law had provided, and not for others', thus incidentally admitting the justice of the criticisms voiced against that council.[3] The final test came, however, in the following year, when, in view of the approaching end of the *Balìa*'s term of office, the Signoria of July–August, which was headed by Luca Pitti, tried to prolong its existence. Although the Signoria proposed an extension of two years only, this was defeated by the council of the People, and so was the subsequent proposal for an extension of one year.[4] Bills to this effect were presented

[1] Provv., 137, fol. 128^{r-v}. The law is significantly described, in a marginal note, as 'balie . . . limitatio'.

[2] Cons. e Prat., 52, fol. 20^r (29 July 1447): Giovannozzo Pitti '. . . dixit iterum atque iterum deliberandum si solita populi potestas reddatur. Tandem conclusit nullo modo esse augendum numerum . . .'; Filippo Carducci: 'Numerum non esse augendum; nec eo consilio amplius utendum, sed consiliis requisitorum ducentorum, et populi et communis, ut antea consuetum fuerat'; Otto Niccolini: 'esse consulendum an balia tollenda sit; et si non tollenda opus esse ut augeatur', &c. See also above, pp. 19, 23–25.

[3] 'Che considerato e temporali in che ci troviamo et ancora nella guerra, benchè ci sia speranza di pace, pure non ne siamo certi, ci pare per al presente non si faccia rinnovatione alcuna del consiglo maggiore. Et che si conforta et priega la Signoria che l'usi a quelle cose che fu ordinato et non ad altro. Et quando pace fia, allor sia da vedere et da pensare se sia da fare alcuna rinnovatione del decto consiglo . . . Et che ciascuno ne sia confortato parlarne d'una lingua per pace et quiete del reggimento.' The spokesmen are Giovannozzo Pitti, Nerone Dietisalvi, and Cosimo. Cons. e Prat. cit., fol. 20^v (31 July 1447).

[4] Libri Fabarum, 61, fol. 122^r (30 July 1448): 'Prorogatio temporis duorum annorum consilii maioris cum additionibus fiendis dicto consilio maiori'; fol. 124^r (2 Aug.):

to that council no less than thirteen times, between 30 July and 13 August, without ever reaching the council of the Commune. A final attempt to obtain a majority for an extension by proposing a limitation of the *Balìa*'s powers proved equally unsuccessful,[1] and the *Balìa* duly dissolved on 20 May 1449.[2]

We have seen how, in July 1447, it had been argued that the *Balìa* should continue in office because of the war. When it was first established, this argument was not used to justify it, for the simple reason that Florence was then at peace.[3] But war was now clearly considered a powerful argument in favour of *Balìe*. Accordingly, when hostilities broke out in 1452 between Florence on the one side and Venice and Naples on the other, the Signoria, under the Gonfalonier Giovannozzo Pitti, succeeded in persuading the councils to create a new *Balìa*, so that decisions could be taken swiftly, *diligenter et celeriter*.[4] However, the narrow majority with which the law was passed by the council of the People indicates that its members were not always convinced by this argument.[5] The *Balìa* was to last for the duration of the war plus six months, but for not more than two years altogether. It was to consist of up to 100 elected and, like the *Balìe* of 1438 and 1444, of a large number of official members. Possibly in order to avoid the difficulties its predecessor had experienced in 1446, its powers were couched in more general terms than those of either of the two preceding *Balìe*. Apart from being put in charge of the next scrutiny,[6] it could, without the assent of the other two councils, pass laws and ordinances 'in order to obtain and preserve peace', as well as 'for the defence of liberty and for the preservation of the régime'.[7] This lack of specification of its functions was evidently the reason why, as early as the following February, two attempts were made to define and limit its authority along the lines of the limiting law of August 1446.[8] These

'Prorogatio... pro uno anno...'; ibid., fols. 122ʳ–128ʳ (30–31 July, 1–3, 5–12 August). The Signoria announced fines for non-attendance of the council meetings.

[1] Ibid., fol. 129ʳ (13 Aug.): 'pro duobus annis et pro sex mensibus pro vice'.

[2] Its last decisions are of that day: Balìe, 26, fols. 227ʳ–228ʳ; cf. Libri Fabarum, 60, fol. 96ʳ.

[3] Peace with Milan had been concluded in Nov. 1441. Cf. Buoninsegni, *Storie*, p. 78.

[4] Provv., 143, fol. 197ʳ (10–14 July 1452); see also above, p. 21.

[5] It passed the law in its first reading with 186 against 84 votes. The council of the Commune passed it with 144 against 51 votes in the same reading.

[6] Provv. cit., fol. 200ʳ. For this purpose only, the Signoria in office at the time could nominate nine additional members. All the knights who had been *veduti* from 1434 onwards belonged automatically to the *Balìa*.

[7] Ibid., fols. 199ᵛ–200ʳ: 'pro... consequenda... et conservanda pace... pro defensione libertatis et conservatione status'.

[8] Libri Fabarum, 62, fols. 185ʳ, 186ʳ (22 and 27 Feb. 1453). See above, p. 76.

attempts proved, however, unsuccessful, and ten months later
the councils of the People and Commune extended the *Balìa*'s
term by no less than five years.[1] Once more, opposition to *Balìe*
was reflected in the narrow majorities, this time in the council of
the Commune, by which the law was passed: in its final reading
it received a majority of two only.[2] Possibly the councils were
only induced to pass the law at all because, as had been unsuccessfully demanded in February, the *Balìa*'s powers were once
more restricted[3] to coincide, largely, with those of its predecessor.
This restriction was, however, more theoretical than actual.
Above all, there was no reference to the assent of the ancient
councils being required to the *Balìa*'s tax legislation, as had still
been the case in 1446.[4] In fact, a large proportion of the business
transacted by the *Balìa* was of a financial nature, beginning with
its first legislation in July 1452.[5] The intention was clearly to
take advantage of the opportunities provided by the continued
state of war to restore the conciliar system which had been
abolished in 1449. It was hardly a coincidence that the Gonfalonier of Justice in office in December 1453 was the same Luca
Pitti who had headed the Signoria which, in July and August
1448, had strenuously tried to prolong its existence.[6]

However, the *Pratica* which on 16 December advised the
Signoria to seek the prolongation of the *Balìa*, 'quia sic est summe
necessarium', had evidently not reckoned with the strength of
public opinion against the conciliar policy of the régime.[7] On
23 April the peace of Lodi was ratified by Florence; on 22 and
23 May the councils of the People and Commune dissolved the
Balìa although it still had a life span of over five years.[8] This time,
the law was passed with large majorities, 'although', as a contemporary diarist writes, 'many members of the *Balìa* also
belonged to the council [of the People], because to everyone

---

[1] Provv., 144, fols. 47ᵛ–54ᵛ (18–22 Dec. 1453).

[2] The votes in the third reading were 150 to 50 in the council of the People, and 109 to
52 in that of the Commune.

[3] 'Quod auctoritas dicte vigentis balie a die qua presens provisio habebit finalem conclu-
sionem . . . sit restricta et limitata', i.e. to decisions concerning the distribution and
imposition of taxes, the preservation of the *status*, scrutinies, matters concerning the *Monte*,
and those matters that came under the competence of the councils of 200 and 131. 'Et quoad
cetera . . . sit quelibet . . . auctoritas de cetero . . . sublata' (Provv. cit., fol. 50ʳ).

[4] Above, p. 76.

[5] Balìe, 27, *passim*. The first laws passed by the *Balìa*, of 17, 21, 22, and 27 July, are
almost exclusively concerned with financial matters (fols. 9ʳ ff.).

[6] See above, p. 76.

[7] Cons. e Prat., 53, fol. 48ʳ⁻ᵛ. The *Pratica* unanimously recommended 'ut consilium
maius sive balia prorogetur'.   [8] See above, p. 22, n. 3.

who wanted the right way of life and a republican government, the present *Balìa* was, in every respect, hateful'.[1]

The aim of the conciliar policy of the régime, as it developed after 1434, was thus to delegate to *Balìe* major decisions in matters which concerned internal and external security and public revenue, as well as the scrutinies and the election of key officials such as the Eight of Ward. Since this policy was pursued within the normal framework of the constitution, that is without resorting to the plebiscitarian method of the *Parlamento*, it had to rely on the periodical votes of the statutory councils. This meant, among other things, that the councils had to be persuaded to abandon, over prolonged periods, their control of taxation. There was probably no aspect of the Medicean *Balìe* which was more unpopular with the ancient councils, and where some concessions were more imperative. Yet such concessions, as contained in the laws defining the functions of the *Balìe*, were in practice frequently, if not generally, ignored; in 1452 and 1453 they were altogether omitted.[2] The recurring state of war during the first twenty years of the Medici régime provided an important argument in favour of special powers. It was well summed up in the law of May 1454 dissolving the *Balìa*: 'Since in extraordinary cases and times it is necessary . . . to use extraordinary ways and means and to dispose of quick remedies . . . we have, in the present war, made use of the *Balìa*, to be able to provide swiftly in such cases and emergencies as might occur.'[3] But this argument was irrelevant in 1444, when Florence was at peace; moreover, before 1434 the councils had been quite capable of dealing with military situations. After initial experimenting, five-year periods were evidently considered desirable and practicable terms of office for the *Balìe*; while the attempt, in 1448, to extend the term of the *Balìa* by another two years shows that men like Luca Pitti were already looking further afield.

[1] '. . . si vinse al primo tratto, avengachè molti della Balìa fussino del consiglo, perchè da ciascuno che apetiva il ben vivere e populare governo, la detta balìa era in tutto exosa' (*Priorista* of Francesco Giovanni, Bibl. Naz., XXV. 379, fol. 162ʳ). The law was passed by 162 against 31 votes in the council of the People, and by 152 against 31 in that of the Commune. The *Balìa* appears already to have stopped meeting at the end of April: the last *provvisione* entered in its registers, which authorizes the Signoria and the Ten to ratify the peace of Lodi, is of the 23rd of that month (Balìe, 27, fols. 222ᵛ–223ʳ).

[2] See also below p. 185.

[3] Provv., 145, fol. 60ʳ: 'considerato quod in casibus et temporibus extraordinariis opportet . . . ire per vias et modos extraordinarios et habere remedia prompta . . . in guerra presenti fuimus usi consilio balie pro celeriter providendo casibus et necessitatibus occurrentibus, prout sepius consuevit . . . nunc autem, cum dei gratia facta sit pax, conveniens est redire ad vias ordinarias et modos consuetos et ordinatos per ordinamenta communis . . .'.

The advantages of the new conciliar system for the régime were obvious. Owing to their wide powers, the *Balìe* could act more swiftly and efficiently than was possible by normal legislative procedure, which required the assent of at least two, and sometimes four, councils.[1] Speedy decisions, especially where taxation was concerned, might be imperative in times of war; they were desirable under any circumstances in a city in which the difficulty of getting finance bills passed was one of the chief problems of successive governments. However, the principal advantage of the *Balìe* was no doubt of a political nature. Councils whose members were appointed for five years provided much greater opportunities of control than the councils of the People and Commune, whose members changed every four months.[2] When the *Balìe* of 1438 and 1444 were created, the election of the entire Signoria, or of part of it, was in the hands of the *Accoppiatori*; the law establishing the *Balìa* of 1452 also reintroduced election *a mano* of the Gonfalonier of Justice. *Balìe* and elections *a mano* of the Signoria represented the two principal methods by which the Mediceans had learned to exercise political control within the structure of the republican constitution.

This control depended for its effectiveness ultimately on the loyalty of the *Accoppiatori* and of the personnel of the *Balìe*. The problem of selecting these men was accordingly of the utmost importance, and clearly more difficult to solve in the case of a large council than in that of an office consisting of five or ten members. The elective members of the *Balìe* of 1433 and 1434 had been nominated by the Signoria and formally elected, *en bloc*, by the *Parlamento*. This method of election, which follows the precedent of earlier *Balìe*, was characteristic of plebiscitarian legislation and revolutionary situations.[3] When the councils came to take the place of the *Parlamento* in creating *Balìe*, they did not take over the election of their personnel, but delegated it to all, or some of the *ex officio* members of the *Balìe*.[4] The *Balìe* had always included official as well as elected members (*arroti*); in 1434 the former amounted to 46 out of a total membership of 385.[5] After 1434, however, the proportion of official members increased sharply: in 1438 they amounted to 124 out of a total

---

[1] See above, p. 69.   [2] See above, p. 69, n. 5.
[3] See above, p. 70.
[4] Among these I include the twenty-one consuls of the guilds who were chosen from among their colleagues.   [5] See Appendix, no. II.

of *c.* 348, and in 1444 to 158 out of a total of 238.[1] This increase
was due, in 1438, to the inclusion of a large number of high
magistracies, over and above those of the Signoria, the *Sedici
Gonfalonieri*, the *Dodici Buonuomini*, and the Captains of the Guelph
Party, who had been the only official members in 1434. In 1444,
it was due to the rise in the number of citizens who had served
as *Accoppiatori* or *Secretari* from 1434 onwards, and who were
made members *ex officio*. In 1438 and in 1444 all official members,
with the exception of the twenty-one consuls, were put in charge
of electing the *arroti*. To entrust the election of these men to so
large a body may, however, have proved cumbersome, and in
1452 the electoral procedure was changed: only the Signoria,
the Colleges, the *Dieci*, and the *Accoppiatori* of 1444 and of 1448[2]
—in all 67 out of a total membership of 275[3]—elected the *arroti*.[4]
This change in procedure reflects the increasingly important role
the *Accoppiatori* had come to play in the *Balìe*.

When the new *Balìa* was created in 1438, a case could have
been made for the inclusion of the *Accoppiatori* and *Secretari* on
account of the scrutiny which that council was to hold, just as the
presence in it of the *Ufficiali del Monte* and *del Banco* could be
explained on technical grounds. If so, the argument was a novel
one: according to the Statutes, the *Accoppiatori* did not serve on
the scrutiny councils.[5] In 1438 the *Accoppiatori* of the next
scrutiny were not made *ex officio* members of the new *Balìa*;
however, when it came to their election in January 1440, they
were chosen from among its personnel.[6] In this way the letter
of the law was observed: for the *Accoppiatori* of 1434, who were
official members, were not in charge of the scrutiny, and the new
Accoppiatori, who were, were not official members.

The policy of including all citizens who from 1434 onwards
had been in charge of elections *a mano* and of scrutinies was also

---

[1] See Appendix, nos. III and IV.

[2] In the case of vacancies caused by the death of *Accoppiatori*, substitutes were to be
elected by their colleagues and the Signoria.

[3] This includes the nine members nominated by the Signoria for the scrutiny (see above,
p. 77, n. 6), and five citizens chosen *quia milites*.

[4] As well as the consuls of the guilds who were to serve on the *Balìa*. When the term of
office of the *Balìa* was extended by five years in Dec. 1453, the Signoria, the Colleges, the
Captains of the Guelph Party, the Eight of Ward, the *Ufficiali del Monte*, and the *Sei di
Mercanzia* who were in office at that time were added to its personnel. This was in addition
to substitutes elected for the scrutinies in the place of deceased members under a law passed
by the *Balìa* on 5 Nov. (Provv., 144, fol. 50ʳ; Balìe, 27, fol. 158ᵛ).

[5] See *Statuta* 1415, ii, p. 481.

[6] Tratte, 60, fol. 228ᵛ.

followed in 1444 and 1452.¹ In 1444 the *Accoppiatori* who were appointed for the scrutinies of 1444 and 1448 were again not members *ex officio*, but already belonged to the *Balìa* as *arroti*.² As a result of this policy, the number of past or present *Accoppiatori* and *Secretari* in the *Balìe* increased sharply. By the end of 1434 only one scrutiny of the three highest offices, and one of the internal and external offices, had taken place since Cosimo's return; by 1444 there had been two and three respectively, as well as scrutinies for the *Mercanzia* and the Guelph Party. Moreover, new *Accoppiatori* had been appointed in 1443 to elect the Signoria *a mano*. Consequently, no less than 75 out of the 158 official members of the *Balìa* of 1444, or one-third of its total personnel, appear as *Accoppiatori* or *Secretari*.³ In the *Balìa* of 1452, only 55 out of the 161 official members belong to this category; however, their actual numbers were somewhat higher, since several of them were members by virtue of other offices.⁴ If we take these into account, the *Accoppiatori* and *Secretari* past and present provided, in July 1452, about a quarter of the total personnel of the *Balìa*.

Moreover, among the changing personnel of the *Balìe*, the *Accoppiatori*, belonging as they did to successive councils, formed something like a permanent nucleus, a unique position which doubtless enhanced their influence in the meetings of these councils. They were further distinguished from most of their *ex officio* colleagues by owing their office to election.⁵ Thus the *Accoppiatori* of 1434 had been elected by the *Balìa* of that year, those of 1440 by the *Consiglio Maggiore* of 1438, those of 1443 by the Signori and other high officials, including the previous *Accoppiatori* and Secretaries, and those of 1444 and 1448 (re-appointed in 1452) by the *Balìa* of 1444.⁶ Evidently the members of the *Balìe* who had been appointed to their offices by lot might constitute greater 'security risks' than their elected colleagues.

¹ Balìe, 26, fol. 9ʳ⁻ᵛ; Provv., 143, fols. 199ᵛ–200ʳ.

² The same does not apply to all the Secretaries of the scrutinies of the other internal and external offices of 1445 and 1448, which reflects their inferior status as compared with that of the *Accoppiatori*. For the names of the latter, see Appendix, no. I.

³ Their share is further increased after the election of *Balìa* members as *Accoppiatori* for the scrutinies of 1444 and 1448.

⁴ Thus, four previous *Accoppiatori* were members since they belonged to the *Dieci di Balìa*.

⁵ In the *Balìa* of 1438, the Signoria had been elected *a mano*, the Eight by the combined method of election and sortition, the *Dieci* by the 145; in that of 1444, part of the Signoria had been elected *a mano*, and the Eight as in 1438; in that of 1452, the new Eight had been elected by the Signoria, the Colleges, *Dieci*, and *Accoppiatori* (the *Dieci*, by the councils of the People and Commune).   ⁶ See above, pp. 8, 15, 31, and 32.

Among the *Accoppiatori* and Secretaries, the former were the *élite*, as well as a substantial and growing section: in 1452 they amounted to no less than 35.[1] There was no office which was better informed about the qualifications or disqualifications of citizens for the highest magistracies, and none which could be trusted more to give a pro-Medicean lead in the scrutinies and to elect, as members of the *Balìe*, citizens who were loyal supporters of the régime. In 1438 and 1444, the elective members were, as we have seen, chosen by the official members of whom the *Accoppiatori* constituted a substantial part; in 1452, by the Signoria, the Colleges, the *Dieci*, and the twenty *Accoppiatori* who were in charge of elections *a mano*.

. . . . . .

The continuity of service of the *Accoppiatori* and *Secretari* reflects a general pattern which also applies to the remaining personnel of the *Balìe*. Once a citizen had been a member of such a council, he stood a very good chance of being chosen as one of the elected members in the next one, unless he already belonged to it *ex officio*; and if not he himself, his sons or brothers. At the same time, it would be wrong to describe the policy in regard to admissions as narrowly oligarchical. The régime appears to have aimed at some kind of balance between the concentration of membership in the same families or citizens, and the admission of new members. Thus of about 224 elected members of the *Balìa* of 1438, 130 had belonged to that of 1434; of the remaining *arroti*, 53 had had relatives in it. The relationship between old and new members is roughly the same in the *Balìa* of 1444: 52 out of the 80 *arroti* had been in that of 1438. Most of these, i.e. 38, had already been in the *Balìa* of 1434; 4 had been members in 1434, but not in 1438, and of the remaining 28, 21 had had relatives— often father or brother—in one or other of these councils. In 1452, on the other hand, only 30 of the 100 *arroti* had also belonged to the *Balìa* of 1444, which may have been due to the criticisms that were levelled against that *Balìa*.[2] However, of the remaining 70 *arroti*, 24 had belonged to the *Balìa* of 1434 or 1438, or to both, so that the number of those who had been members of previous Medicean *Balìe* amounted to over one half of the

[1] This includes substitutes appointed to fill vacancies among the *Accoppiatori*. On the list of the *Balìa* of 1452, several *Accoppiatori* past and present are entered under other offices which they happened to occupy at the time the *Balìa* was established. See above, p. 82, n. 4.

[2] See above, pp. 75–76. Of the nine members nominated by the Signoria, one only had been previously in a Medicean *Balìa*.

total number of *arroti*. Again, most of the others had family connexions in the preceding *Balìe*; only 10 had none whatsoever.[1]

If we turn to the official members, we find a similar picture, largely owing to the many *Accoppiatori* and Secretaries among them. In 1444, 105 of the 158 official members had been in the *Balìe* of 1434 or 1438 or both; but of these, 66 had been *Accoppiatori* or Secretaries. Again, in 1452, of the 161 official members, 90 had been in previous Medicean *Balìe*, and of these, 50 appear as past *Accoppiatori* or Secretaries, or as their substitutes. Among the rest of the official members, the proportion of 'old members' was much lower: in 1444, 39 out of 83, in 1452, 40 out of 106.[2] The reason for this discrepancy was no doubt that many *Balìa* members in this category owed their membership to having been appointed to their office by lot. Thus, while election provided a strong element of continuity for the elective members, the same effect was achieved for the official ones by the presence of large numbers of *Accoppiatori* and Secretaries. As a result, in all the *Balìe* between 1438 and 1452, the 'old members' represented over one half of the total membership.[3]

To individual continuity of service we have to add that of families.[4] This was, not surprisingly, particularly pronounced among the leading families of the régime. While it reflects the social structure of the régime, it is also in keeping with the traditional pattern of Florentine government. The claim of the Florentine upper classes to be strongly represented in the principal magistracies and councils was now evidently extended to the *Balìe*, which were developing into quasi-permanent institutions. In these circumstances, it was clearly considered politic to avoid excessive representation of single families. In the magistracies, the *divieti* prevented not only the contemporaneous, but also the successive membership of relatives; in the councils of the People and Commune not more than four, in that of 200, not more than three members were allowed to be of the same

---

[1] These figures are based on the membership lists of the *Balìe*. See Appendixes, nos. II–V.

[2] To this last figure may be added the five knights who were members by virtue of their dignity: of these, four had previously been in Medicean *Balìe*. For the *Accoppiatori* and Secretaries, see above, p. 82. The incidence of *gente nuova* among the official members was, not surprisingly, highest among the twenty-one consuls of the guilds. The respective figures are 16 in 1444, and 18 in 1452.

[3] In 1438 they amounted to 193 out of *c.* 348 members; in 1444, 161 out of 238, and in 1452, 151 out of 275.

[4] See Appendixes, nos. II ff.

family or *consorteria*.[1] It would have been highly unpopular if a similar limitation had not also been applied to the *Balìe*, once these were on the way to becoming a normal institution of the régime. In fact, family representation for the elected members of the *Balìe* of 1438, 1444, and 1452 was not only limited, but kept at the lowest possible level of one per family, although exceptionally this maximum could be raised to two for a limited number of families.[2] These regulations, which were, incidentally, strictly observed, may appear democratic enough, and may indeed have facilitated the passage of the *Balìa* bills. However, they do not reveal the full extent of family representation in the single *Balìe*: if we count official as well as elective members, it could be considerably larger. Thus, in the *Balìa* of 1438 there were, from the *Quartiere* of S. Giovanni alone, ten families with two members each, five with three members, and one with five—the Medici. In the *Balìa* of 1444, there were, from the same *quartiere*, seven families with two members each, and two with three members; in the *Balìa* of 1452, eight with two members each, and three with three. Such 'over-representation' was clearly liable to render the limiting regulations somewhat illusory. Accordingly, the *Balìa* law of 1452 expressly stipulated that the total representation must on no account exceed three for any one family or *consorteria*.[3]

Despite these limitations, the leading families of the régime were not only well represented in the *Balìe*, but continuity of such representation was secured, as in the scrutinies, by the entry of younger members of these families in successive *Balìe*. Thus, a considerable number of the newcomers in the *Balìe* of 1444 and 1452 were sons or brothers of members of prominent families who had belonged to preceding *Balìe*.[4] With the passage of time, the Medicean *Balìe* underwent the same process of rejuvenation within the ruling class which had long been a characteristic feature of the oligarchical trend in Florentine government.

Yet similarly characteristic of Florentine government was the constant influx of new elements. In the *Balìe*, as in other Florentine

---

[1] *Statuta* 1415, ii, pp. 661, 769. For the 200, Provv., 99, fol. 168ʳ (4–5 Feb. 1411).

[2] Provv., 129, fol. 34ᵛ, Balìe, 26, fol. 9ᵛ; Provv., 143, fol. 200ʳ. In 1438 up to 10, to be chosen by the Signoria, the Colleges, and other offices, and in 1452 up to 5 families, to be chosen by the Signoria, could have 2 members among the *arroti* (ibid.).

[3] Provv. cit. Once more, the regulations were strictly observed.

[4] See Appendixes, nos. II–V.

institutions, social continuity was balanced against flexibility, oligarchical trends against democratic ones. After 1434 the principal consideration in the admission of new men was no doubt their loyalty to the régime, and some families, such as the Del Nero, owed their advance to Medici patronage. At the same time, the entry of *gente nuova* was probably also dictated by the desire to avoid giving the impression that the membership of the *Balìe* was too exclusive; for such an impression was liable to influence the voting in the councils on which the *Balìe* now depended for their existence.

Larger *Balìe* could provide greater scope for the entry of new men or families. According to a statement of the Milanese orator in 1458, they were more acceptable to the people;[1] and the permission given in 1438 to the new *Balìa*, to co-opt 100 additional members in 1440, has probably to be seen in this light.[2] On the other hand, large councils were more liable to give rise to factions and pressure groups. This was particularly the case when the *Balìe* were acting as scrutiny councils. Thus, Francesco Giovanni blames it on the *conventicule e congiure* and on the size of the *Balìa* that in 1448 many upstarts were made eligible, 'to the great shame of the government'.[3]

In fact, despite the trouble that was taken in selecting their personnel, the *Balìe* were occasionally capable of acting against the wishes of the leading citizens of the régime.[4] In 1449 the *Balìa* did not even shrink from defeating a proposal, which had been approved by the *più principali del reggimento*, to extend by one year the powers of the *Accoppiatori* to elect *a mano*.[5] This failure to co-operate in a matter of outstanding importance for the security of the régime was doubtless the reason why, in the next *Balìa*, an absolute majority was substituted for the normal two-thirds majority as being required for the passage of bills. Even so, the law of August 1452, which ordered the *Accoppiatori* to elect, once more, the entire Signoria *a mano*, was passed by the *Balìa* with the narrowest majority—as was also, in November 1453, the extension of these powers by five years.[6] Clearly, if even the Medicean councils could not always be trusted to secure

---

[1] See below, p. 108, n. 3.   [2] See above, p. 72, n. 3.

[3] *Priorista* cit., fol. 156ʳ: '. . . Fune cagione l'asai numero degli squittinanti ch'era circa 400, et le conventicule e congiure e il rendere le fave contro a ogni debito in pro o in contra.' See also above, p. 61, n. 2.

[4] See above, p. 73.   [5] See above, p. 19.

[6] See above, pp. 27–28.

the survival of the institutional safeguards of the régime, there were serious flaws in its conciliar policy.

However, the greatest weakness of the new type of *Balìa* was the fact that its very existence depended on the votes of the councils on whose rights and functions it was encroaching to an increasing extent. Whatever concessions were made to public opinion, these were evidently not sufficient to uproot the ancient councils' dislike of the conciliar policy of the régime; a dislike which was revealed once again in the large majorities with which they prematurely dissolved the *Balìa* of 1452.

5

THE *PARLAMENTO* OF 1458
AND THE CONSOLIDATION OF THE
RÉGIME

AFTER the abolition of the *Balìa* and the closing of the *borse* in 1454 and 1455, Florence returned to her traditional form of government. Once again, the councils of the People and Commune were fully in charge of legislation and financial policy, and the Signoria was appointed by lot. But this restoration of the pre-Medicean form of government was marred by a number of unfavourable circumstances. Moreover, it was not as complete as might be expected at first sight.

To begin with, the *borse* from which the names for the Signoria were drawn after June 1455 were those prepared by the *Accoppiatori* on the basis of the scrutiny that had been carried out by the *Balìa* in 1453.[1] If this gave the régime a considerable security margin, it also limited the extent to which electoral liberties were actually restored. It was therefore not surprising that, two years later, an attempt should have been made to abolish the scrutiny of 1453 before a new one was due; but this attempt was unsuccessful.[2]

Moreover, the difficult economic situation in which Florence found herself after the war placed a heavy strain on the restored system of government and was liable to underline any inherent weakness. The intermittent wars between 1423 and 1454 had left Florence economically exhausted; and recurring epidemics, as well as the general economic situation, added to her problems.[3]

---

[1] Above, pp. 22, 53. Also the *borse* for the other offices, internal as well as external, had been filled afresh after the scrutiny of 1453 and 1454; above, p. 55.

[2] Pietrobuoni, *Priorista*, Bibl. Naz., Conv. soppr., C. 4. 895, fol. 176ʳ: 'Al tempo de' detti Signiori tennono istretto ragionamento fra lloro d'ardere le borse dello squittino dell'anno 1453. Non andò innanzi perchè tra lloro fu chi non volle far sanza consiglio di praticha. E scopersesi e funne t[r]a principali ciptadini molti malcontenti.' The passage is used by Cambi, *Istorie*, in *Delizie*, xx, p. 351. It refers to the Signoria of Sept.–Oct. 1457.

[3] Cf., e.g., St. Antoninus, *Chronica*, tit. xxii, cap. 12, § 5 (Lyons, 1586, pars iii, p. 557): 'Anno Domini 1456 et septimo magna penuria fuit in civitate non tantum ex defectu victualium . . . sed magis ex defectu pecuniae, quia assueti vivere de laboribus manuum suarum non conducebantur ad exercitia artium, subtrahentibus se civibus a commerciis diversis ex causis. . . .' On the epidemics, ibid., cap. 13, § 3.

Tax bills met with strong resistance in the councils, which contrasted with their speedy dispatch in the *Balìe*.[1] The revision of tax assessments in January 1458 provided, for many citizens, an alleviation of the burden of taxation. The main sufferers were the wealthy citizens whose property and income had increased since the last *catasto*; hotly resisted from this quarter, the new *catasto* was correspondingly popular with the poorer classes.[2]

The passage of the *catasto* law in January 1458 was one of a series of events which gradually created an atmosphere of crisis in the city.[3] The jubilation at the end of the war seemed to recede into the distant past. The *catasto* could be considered a successful popular attack on real or alleged tax evasion by the richer classes, and was not directed against the régime as such, although many of its foremost supporters were bound to suffer. Indeed, it might serve to make the régime more popular; Cosimo, for one, unlike other rich citizens, did not oppose it, so as not to lose 'la gracia del populo minuto'.[4] In September 1457 a conspiracy against the régime was nipped in the bud.[5] At the end of the year, the *Pratica* pleaded for unity in discussing internal affairs;[6] while a number of its leading personalities took a serious enough view of the opposition to play with the idea of seizing power, of 'volersi assicurare delle cose di drento'.[7]

[1] Cf., e.g., Libri Fabarum, 64, fols. 4v–8v (14–21 Nov. 1454); fols. 23r–25r (15–24 Jan. 1455); fols. 31r–32v (3–6 March 1455).

[2] Nicodemo da Pontremoli to Francesco Sforza, 9 Jan. 1458 (Bibl. Nat., MS. ital. 1588, fol. 10v, quoted by Gutkind, *Cosimo de' Medici*, p. 135, n. 1). On the *catasto* of 1458, see G. Canestrini, *La scienza e l'arte di stato* . . . i (Florence, 1862), pp. 169 ff.

[3] Nicodemo writes, before the passage of the law: 'Et va questa città tuta sotto sopra, in modo che chi non intendesse el modo loro, extimaria fossero per venire a novità' (loc. cit.).

[4] Ibid.: all the rich are against it, 'da Cosimo in fora, che se ne porta cum summa modestia, perchè da un canto non vole dispiacere ali homini richi, da l'altro non vole perdere la gracia del populo minuto, che vole questo catasto omnino . . .'.

[5] Buoninsegni, *Storie*, p. 119: 'A dì 7 di settembre 1457 fu rivelato alla nostra Signoria un trattato, che si teneva in Firenze contro a essa per alcuni cittadini, e furonno presi due, cioè Piero di Giovacchino de' Ricci, e Carlo di Benedetto de' Bardi, i quali (facendoci alquanto la pestilenza) havevano disegniato, che s'ella multiplicasse, e i cittadini si partissono, com'è d'usanza, di far gran novità al reggimento . . .' See also Cambi, *Istorie*, pp. 349–50. Cons. e Prat., 54, fol. 155r–v (7 Sept. 1457): '. . . super negotio Caroli de Bardis et Antonii Baptista captorum pro conspiratione nuper facta contra pacificum statum et quietem in civitate . . .'.

[6] Ibid., fol. 180v (15 Dec. 1457): 'Tutti s'accordano che si metta ogni cura e diligentia alla civile unione . . . Et de' facti de' cittadini dentro si parli amorevolmente, sicchè ci sia concordia nelle parole, come si crede sia ne' facti. . . .'

[7] Guicciardini, 'Memorie di famiglia' in *Scritti autobiografici e rari*, ed. R. Palmarocchi (Bari, 1936), p. 19. On 26 April, Agnolo Acciaiuoli writes to Francesco Sforza that on his return to Florence, some citizens had discussed with him plans to 'ridurre lo stato ne' principali' (Milan, Bibl. Ambros., Z. 247 sup.). Agnolo was still in Milan on 28 Feb. 1458 (Med. av. Pr., XII, 229).

It was not the first time since the reaction against the régime
had begun in 1454 that suggestions of this kind were made.
A letter from Cosimo de' Medici, which appears to have been
written towards the end of that year, mentions a plan to use
'extreme remedies' being mooted by leading Mediceans. Cosimo
disapproved of it, both on account of such measures not being
necessary and of their being dangerous for the city and the
régime.[1] Much the same suggestion, combined with an offer of
help, was made to Cosimo by the orator of the Duke of Milan,
a few weeks after the councils had abolished, in February 1455,
elections *a mano*; to which Cosimo replied in the same vein that
the situation in Florence was 'not as dangerous as he understood
was believed' in Milan.[2] The most obvious way of recovering the
lost positions would have been to restore the *Balìa* and elections
a mano. One such attempt was, in fact, made in September 1456,
when the Signoria had tried to initiate a bill to this effect, but had
failed to do so.[3] In 1458 the creation of a *Balìa* would have been
particularly important in view of the fact that the time for the
next scrutiny was approaching. For nearly twenty-four yrears, all
the scrutinies of the *Tre Maggiori*, and all but two scrutinies of the
other offices, had been carried out by *Balìe*. There was no know-
ing what might happen if a scrutiny were to be held once more by
a statutorily elected scrutiny council.

The law of 15 April was evidently intended to thwart such
schemes by rendering the creation of *Balìe* exceedingly difficult,
and by prohibiting altogether the holding of scrutinies by them.[4]
It throws some interesting light on contemporary criticism of the
Balìa system:

[1] Carte Strozz., 1ª ser., 136, fol. 126ʳ. Sixteenth-century copy, without address, but
according to the copyist, to Jacopo Guicciardini, 'sendo de' signori l'anno 1454 di novembre'. Jacopo was Signore in Nov.–Dec. 1454. The letter is addressed to a Signore whose
late father was called Piero: so was Jacopo's.

[2] Boccaccio Alamanni to Francesco Sforza, 10 April 1455 (ASM, Pot. est., Firenze,
268): 'Ancora confortay Cosmo per parte della Vostra Illustrissima Signoria ad volersi
adsicurare et adirizare lo stato suo, offerendoli tanto quanto mi dicesti. Ringratia la Illustrissima Signoria Vostra et dice che vi diate buona vogla, chè non è tanto pericolo quanto
comprenhende [*sic*] è stato ditto costà, perchè non c'è alchuno che pensi affare delle cose
stimavano. . . .'

[3] Libri Fabarum, 64, fols. 168ʳ–172ʳ (2–6, 10–13 Sept.); *Priorista* Giovanni, Bibl. Naz.,
xxv, 379, fol. 164ʳ: 'Volsono fare balìa e ripiglare le borse a mano. Non possendo vincere
di fare balìa e riaprire le borse e dare balìa agl'otto e al capitano, essendovi molto infiamato
il gonfaloniere . . . si disse che lui era per questo uscito de' gangheri e stette a casa a buona
ghuardia più giorni. . . .' He was Donato di Niccolò Donati, son of the Gonfalonier who had
headed the Signoria that had recalled Cosimo from exile.

[4] Provv., 149, fols. 39ʳ–40ʳ (14–15 April 1458). The law was passed by 168 votes to 44
in the council of the People, and by 122 to 37 in that of the Commune.

Since every time a new Signoria is drawn and enters its office, people wonder: 'What will they do? Will they hold a scrutiny, or try to create a *Balìa*?'; and since there could not be anything more harmful to our city than revolutions [*fare novità*] and *Balìe*; and since on such occasions all the citizens and merchants and craftsmen are afraid and do not dare do any business (and in this they are truly right, for those who want to live under a good constitutional government greatly disapprove of such ventures); it is herewith decreed that the abovesaid actions may not be taken as easily as they used to be until recently. And in case they should nevertheless be necessary, their execution is to be rendered more difficult. . . . [1]

Accordingly, the law ordered that a *Balìa* could only be established by a majority vote of the councils of the People and Commune and of the council of 200, after having been passed almost unanimously by the Signoria and the Colleges; and that such a *Balìa* was not allowed to carry out a scrutiny.[2] 'No holier law against tyranny was ever passed in the Palace', commented Cambi about half a century later.[3] Some days earlier, the Milanese ambassador wrote to Francesco Sforza that Cosimo's influence with the government was no longer what it used to be.[4] The record of the Signoria of March–April,[5] which had been drawn from the purses filled on the basis of the scrutiny of 1453, was abundant evidence of the dangers for the régime of uncontrolled elections of the government, even at a time when the scrutiny had been held by a *Balìa*.

The leading citizens who were planning to recover political

[1] 'Perchè sempre nella tracta della Signoria et nella loro entrata si mormora et dice: "Che faranno questi Signori? Faranno eglino squittino overo balìa?"; et perchè alla nostra città non potrebbe essere peggior cosa che di fare novità overo balìa; et perchè ne' tempi delle novità et balìe tutti i cittadini et mercatanti et artefici stanno tutti sospesi et non s'ardiscono di fare alcuna cosa de' traffichi loro, et in verità anno ragione, perchè chi vuole ben vivere et civilmente a grandissimo dispiacere delle decte cose; però si provede di levare via ogni cagione che lle sopradecte cose non s'abbino a ffare così di leggieri et di facto come s'è usato da poco tempo in qua; et quando pure s'avessono a ffare, s'abbino a ffare con maggiore dificultà . . .' (Provv. cit.).

[2] '. . . se prima non fia deliberata per nove fave nere de' Signori et di poi obtenuta pe' Signori et collegi per fave trentasei nere . . . e di poi obtenuta pe' consigli del popolo et comune et di poi confirmata pel consiglio del dugento . . . Et quando per decta via s'ottenessi, s'intenda non potere fare alcuno squittino di nuovo nè dentro nè di fuori, anzi s'intenda per questa provisione et legge vietato. . . .' Suspension of laws regarding scrutinies was equally forbidden.

[3] 'Non si fecie mai in Palazzo la più santa leggie a volere non fare tiranni'; *Istorie*, in *Delizie*, xx, p. 354.

[4] Bibl. Nat., MS. ital. 1588, fol. 50ᵛ (4 April 1458): 'non pò Cosimo continuamente essere in palazo, e fare como solia.' Gutkind, *Cosimo de' Medici*, p. 135, mistakenly interprets this sentence to mean that 'at the moment Cosimo may not go into the Palazzo'.

[5] Under the Gonfalonier Matteo di Marco Bartoli.

power, 'ripigliare lo stato', were now waiting for a Signoria to be drawn which was favourable to their design. The next Signoria, of May–June, did not appear to them to be 'of such prudence that so great a task can be entrusted to them', as Agnolo Acciaiuoli writes on 9 May; and how much depended on the Signoria is shown by his remark that he and his friends did not feel they could act without its help.[1] But at the next drawing of the Signoria, on 28 June, chance was in their favour.

Luca Pitti, whose name was drawn for the Gonfaloniership of Justice, was at that time one of the most influential men of the régime; and during his two previous terms as Gonfalonier of Justice, he had been prominent in pressing its conciliar policy. He had headed the Signoria of July–August 1448 which had unsuccessfully tried to extend the lifetime of the *Balìa* of 1444, as well as that of November–December 1453, during whose term of office the *Balìa* of 1452 received an extension of five years.[2] On 2 July, the day after he assumed office, he addressed an unusually large *Pratica*, of no less than 220 citizens, on the wider issues which, he maintained, were raised by the financial difficulties the government had to face.[3] The city was unable to effect payments, when due, to its mercenaries, to its foreign officials, and to the guardians of its fortresses: 'nec pecunias in tempore haberi, quibus conductis militibus et urbis rectoribus et arcium custodibus satisfieri possit.' The reason for this had to be sought in the continuous economic decline. This decline, Luca Pitti said, was the more surprising as Florence had been at peace for several years, so that one might have expected just the opposite to happen, 'ut videlicet civitates bellis exhauste in priori statu atque gloria restituantur'. By now the crisis had reached a point where, if no action was taken, a débâcle was imminent.[4] The debate which follows gives a vivid picture of the

---

[1] Agnolo Acciaiuoli to Francesco Sforza (Bibl. Ambros., Z. 76 sup.): we have not changed opinion, 'nè da quello pensiero ci siamo rimossi. Et benchè noi potessimo a ogni tempo mectere a 'ssecutione questo nostro pensiero, nientedimeno questi Signori che entrorono il primo dì di questo mese non ci sono paruti di tal prudentia che tanta opera si possa rimectere in loro; et sanza il mezo loro non c'è paruto da fare, maxime non essendo le cose nostre in tale extremo che non possino aspectare qualche dì. Siamo in parere di lascare [*sic*] andare questo priorato, non accadendo altro che ci facesse mutare proposito.'

[2] See above, pp. 21, 76.   [3] Cons. e Prat., 55, fol. 23ʳ⁻ᵛ.

[4] 'Se vero nunc cernere . . . urbem . . . post pacem habitam in deterius lapsam ac continuo labi cunctaque civium exercitia, quibus augeri civitas et felix esse consueverat, imminuta esse atque eo loci adducta ut, nisi mature provideatur, penitus occasura videantur, non solum cum civitatis iactura maxima, sed etiam cum dedecore, qui liberorum animos hominum magis movere possit. . . .' (ibid.).

discontent with which leading citizens were viewing the situation. Some speakers held the lack of unity among the citizens, 'varias civium discordias', responsible, others blamed the *catasto*, which 'mercatoribus maxime onerosum esse noscitur';[1] others again criticized 'non sana consilia', possibly of earlier *Pratiche*.[2] One speaker, however, Domenico Martelli, sees the root of the trouble in the present form of government, which he condemns as contrary to the true régime of Florence, 'a vero civitatis regimine alienum esse'; 'universus regendi modus sibi vehementer displicet'. What, then, was Florence's 'true régime'? Not the traditional republican one, which had been restored by 1455; but the Medicean system of government which it had, once more, replaced.[3]

The problem raised by Domenico Martelli became the principal theme of the discussions in the *Pratica* during the following days. On 3 July the Gonfalonier of Justice opened the debate with the declaration that the *Pratica* had heard, in the previous meeting, that what was needed was a general reform of the city, rather than merely the settlement of its short-term financial difficulties.[4] The discussion which followed showed that not everyone agreed with his diagnosis of the situation and with the remedies he proposed. First of all, were things really quite as bad as all that? Great wars, says one speaker, always create this kind of problem; and another suggests that, as the city had been, at the end of the war, nearly without money, *pecuniis penitus exhausta*, there was no reason to be surprised if it was still ailing, *infirma adhuc remansit*; moreover, there was the present danger of plague.[5] Others agree that matters were going from bad to worse: the city was suffering from a dangerous disease, because the citizens were only thinking of their own, and not of the common

---

[1] Otto Niccolini: '... plures ... defectus evenisse tum propter imminentem suspitionem pestis, tum etiam ob varias civium discordias. Et si quis recensere velit iam longo tempore in civitate acta, intelliget quecunque in consiliis fere obtenta sunt per iracundiam et hodium et non in rei p. bonum fuisse constituta: si quid vero salutare ac bonum fuit propositum, nunquam obtentum fuit ...' (fol. 25ᵛ). Manno Temperani: anything *malum aut incommodum* that may happen in the city will be due to the citizens *inter se dissidentibus* (fol. 24ʳ); on the *catasto*, Guglielmo Tanaglia (fols. 23ᵛ–24ʳ). On discord also Girolamo Machiavelli, fol. 26ᵛ.

[2] Agnolo Acciaiuoli; Tommaso Salvetti (fols. 24ᵛ–25ʳ).

[3] Fol. 25ʳ⁻ᵛ: he could therefore not be accused of being an innovator who was seeking *aliam vivendi normam*.

[4] '... audivisse illos priori die opus esse reformatione civitatis in multis rebus neque enim solum stipendia militibus debita neque custodibus arcium' (fol. 28ᵛ).

[5] Tommaso Salvetti (fol. 30ᵛ); Bernardo Gherardi (fol. 33ᵛ).

interest.[1] Many abandon business altogether, 'tradentes se otio et luxui';[2] and one speaker recalls the ancient Romans who, after having subjected the other nations, 'tandem ob luxum et inhertiam se ipsos superasse'.[3] Franco Sacchetti blames disunity as the chief cause of the trouble, and so do many speakers during these debates: 'as long as our ancestors were united, the city was ruled exceedingly well; all the evils started once discord had broken out'; and 'no war is more dangerous than civil war'.[4] Another speaker attacks, more pertinently, criticism of the ruling class as the principal cause of the city's troubles: hence prominent citizens are forced to retire from public service.[5] It can hardly be by accident that he is followed by a speaker who, a few weeks later, was to be singled out as the leading personality among the opposition, Girolamo Machiavelli, whose contribution to the debate is consequently of special interest. There are many more evils in the city, he asserts, than have been accounted for; there is little patriotism about, and the lack of it usually spells the ruin of states; the decline, *labes*, of the city is the more serious as it has set in among the ruling citizens a long time ago. As for the difficulties experienced in getting constructive legislation passed, they may be due to the fact that many councillors are desperate about their economic conditions.[6]

What, then, was to be done? A few speakers still feel that financial reforms are what is needed most to deal with the immediate

[1] Giovanni Bartoli (fols. 30ᵛ–31ʳ); Mariotto Benvenuti (fol. 34ʳ): 'egritudinem civitatis maximam esse, eo precipue quo cives publica spernentes commoda sua respiciant. Unde si tandem cives ipsi postpositis privatis passionibus communem inspexerint utilitatem, fore ut omnia bene disponantur.'

[2] Otto Niccolini (fol. 32ʳ).

[3] Francesco del Benino (fol. 35ʳ).

[4] 'Si reliqua exempla deficerent, quos fructus vel concordia vel discordia parere soleant, ex presenti civitatis more exempla assumi possunt; donec enim maiores nostri concordes extiterunt, egregie ab eis civitatem administratam esse; postquam vero discordia secuta est, mala evenisse omnia. Nullum enim pericolosius bellum esse quam intestinum, ad quod removendum omni ope annitendum esse' (fol. 33ʳ).

[5] Otto Niccolini (fols. 31ᵛ–32ʳ): '. . . maledicorum voces, qui rem p. gubernantibus egregie quidem ac prudenter semper detrahere consueverunt, et sepenumero evenire illos, qui reliquis detrahunt, nequissimos omnium esse, querentes ex aliorum infamia gratiam sibi querere. Iccirco ex his evenisse, ut prestantes cives rei p. curam abicere coacti sint.'

[6] '. . . res istas eo esse graviores quo in civibus precipuum regimen habentibus labes ista iam diu fuit. . . . Dixit etiam longe plura esse mala atque incomoda que civitatem invaserunt, quam illa que relata sunt. . . . Mirari quoque se etiam dixit cives singulos hec omnia carpere, in universo vero nihil boni statuere, ob exiguum civitatis amorem; ex quo accidere solere dixit, civitates omnes facillime deperire, abiecta ipsarum cura; arbitratus quoque est multos cives, qui salutaribus propositis suffragia denegant, ea de causa ad hoc adduci, quia se nihil lucrari animadvertunt, desperatione ducti . . .' (fol. 32ʳ⁻ᵛ).

difficulties.[1] However, by now the designs of the Signoria evidently went beyond such partial measures, as is indicated by Luca Pitti's introductory speech, as well as by a remark of Dietisalvi Neroni, who as Gonfalonier in May–June 1454 had played a leading role in the dissolution of the *Balìa*,[2] and who now pleads for moderation, 'ut si qua remedia adhibentur, ea non sint extrema nec nimium aspera, sed mediocria'; for virtue, he adds in Aristotelian vein, consists in the mean.[3] What these extreme remedies were became clear in the following days.

On 4 July the first speaker informed his colleagues that he understood that a scheme for a new constitutional reform had been drafted. It should be read out and, if necessary, modified.[4] But could the councils be expected to pass any reform bills at all? This became now increasingly the central issue of the debate. If the *via ordinaria* of legislation were used, says Carlo Pandolfini, much time would be wasted; was it not perhaps preferable to try and persuade the councils to create a *Balìa* for this purpose?[5] Domenico Martelli agrees: if the principal citizens were only united, the *via ordinaria* would be adequate; but in the circumstances legislative powers should be delegated by the people to the Signoria and a number of citizens.[6] But let this be done quietly and peacefully, adds another speaker;[7] and similarly several others advise moderation.

The reform scheme was duly read to the *Pratica* on the following day, and appears to have met with general approval.[8] It contained the proposal to create a new permanent council, to

---

[1] Donato Donati (fol. 31r–v); Simone Uguccioni (fols. 32v–33r): the *catasto* should be abandoned.

[2] Francesco di Tommaso Giovanni, *Ricordanze*, Carte Strozz., 2ª ser., 16 *bis*, fol. 15v: 'A dì 22 di maggio 1454 Dietisalvi di Nerone di Nigi per gl'oportuni consigli levò e annullò la detta balìa. . . . Aquistòne . . . grande benevolenza nel popolo.' See also above, p. 22, n. 3.

[3] 'Nam in mediocritate virtutem consistere' (fol. 34r).

[4] Manno Temperani (fol. 36v): 'et quia audivit scriptum esse quandam formam novam rei p. institutionis, optimum esse duxit, ut illa forma legeretur; et si quid in ea esset reprehensione dignum, de consilio civium corrigeretur. . . .'

[5] This is clearly the meaning of his words: 'et quia intelligit, si via ordinaria in rebus mederi incipient, quum multis indigent consiliis et tempus frustra tereretur, forsitan alia via eundum esse; id est ut populus in dominorum prudentia confisus dominis potestatem tribuat una cum quibusdam civibus super huiusmodi rebus transigendi et statuendi . . .' (fol. 36v).

[6] '. . . a populo capiendam auctoritatem esse cum qua domini omnia statuere possint una cum aliis quibusdam civibus' (fol. 38r–v).

[7] Donato Donati (fol. 38v): 'civibus terror non adhibeatur, sed via quieta et pacifica, ne maius scandalum suscitetur.' His father had been Gonfalonier of Justice in the Signoria of Sept.–Oct. 1434, which had recalled Cosimo de' Medici.

[8] This emerges from the discussion in the *Pratica* of 6 July. The minutes of that of 5 July are not extant.

be chosen, for six-monthly sessions, from a group of selected citizens, and invested with wide powers over scrutinies, taxes, war, and elections. Moreover, legislation by the other councils was to require its assent.[1] The six-monthly sessions remind us of the unsuccessful proposal of August 1448 to extend the term of the *Balìa* by a 'novum modum et formam deputationis';[2] and from the debate of 6 July it transpires that the reform scheme had been under discussion among the leading citizens for some months.[3]

On that day, the Gonfalonier once more addressed the *Pratica*, and, to their surprise, seemed to be drawing back from his earlier stand. The councils, he said, were most unlikely to pass the reform bill, and its defeat would only be an embarrassment to the government. If, however, by the great efforts of the *Pratica* the bill were in the end to be passed, so much time would have to be spent to achieve this result as not to leave any for other legislation. He disclaims any intention on the part of the Signoria of trying to push the bill through by extraordinary measures and without conciliar consent, 'aliquam extraordinariam tentare viam vel violentam vel parum consuetam preter ordinariam oportunorum consiliorum'; and consequently he proposes to concentrate on short-term questions such as the payment of the soldiers, leaving the larger issues for later, if there was still time left for them.[4] Was this apparent volte-face genuine, or only intended to test the feeling of the meeting on the desirability of using such 'extraordinary means'? The general consensus of the *Pratica* was that the Signoria should try to obtain the reform by ordinary legislation. One speaker suggested that it did not imply such an innovation after all; the council of 200 had (in 1411) been established for a similar purpose[5]—a somewhat specious argument, for why not use, in that case, the existing council of 200? There was general agreement on the excellence of the plan for a new council which would serve as a

---

[1] The text of the scheme does not survive, but it is summarized by Francesco di Tommaso Giovanni in his *Priorista* (MS. cit., fol. 166r). His brother was a member of the *consiglio del Popolo* to which, as we shall see, the scheme was submitted, and he was consequently in a position to know its contents. See also below, pp. 103, n. 3, 113, n. 8.

[2] Libri Fabarum, 61, fol. 129r (13 Aug. 1448), see above, p. 77 n.

[3] Cons. e Prat., 55, fol. 46v (Francesco del Benino): 'intellexit plures iam menses provisionem illam cum prestantibus civibus et optimis fuisse examinatam.'

[4] Fols. 42v–43r.

[5] Tommaso Soderini (fol. 44v): 'sicut nunc novum consilium reperiebatur, ut hec mala emendarentur, ita iam consilium ducentorum ob eandem causam inventum fuit.'

check, *frenum esset in civitate*.[1] Legislation that in the ordinary councils could be obtained only with the greatest difficulties would be obtained more easily:[2] in fact, one speaker goes so far as to claim that experience showed that the councils were not prepared to pass any good laws.[3]

Luca Pitti's advice prevailed, and the reform bill was not presented to the councils.[4] There are no minutes of further discussions on internal policy in the *Pratica* until 21 July. On that day, the Gonfalonier asked for advice on a new project, namely to hold the scrutinies of the *Tre Maggiori* and the other offices, which were not due until the end of 1458 and the end of 1459 respectively, during the term of office of the present Signoria.[5] There was no technical reason for such a measure; nor was the argument put forward by Luca Pitti, that it would help to establish unity among the citizens, very convincing.[6] The real reasons have to be sought elsewhere. The bill proposing the creation of a new council which, like the *Balìe*, would have been in charge of scrutinies, having been defeated, the prospect had now to be faced of a scrutiny of the highest offices being carried out, for the first time since 1434, by a statutory scrutiny council. If the scrutiny could be held immediately the Signoria, which had made so valiant an effort to strengthen the régime, would at least have an important voice in the organization of that council and might, together with its Colleges, play an influential role in it. The *Pratica* approved of this proposal: nothing was more likely, it was argued, to comfort the citizens and restore unity among them;[7] but Girolamo Machiavelli observed trenchantly that had offices been distributed more fairly on previous occasions there would not now be so much disunity in the city.[8] The council of the People,

---

[1] Giovannozzo Pitti (fol. 46^r).

[2] Francesco del Benino (fol. 46^v): 'facilius civitati salutaria possent obtineri, que per consilia iam instituta difficillime obtinentur. . . .'

[3] Franco Sacchetti (fol. 44^r): 'experientia cernebatur per consilia nil boni obtineri potuisse. . . .'   [4] See Libri Fabarum, 65, fols. 128^r ff.

[5] Fol. 50^v: 'ut suo tempore scruptineum ordinarent'. He says that the initiative for this proposal came from the Colleges. The last scrutiny of the *Tre Maggiori* had been held in Nov.–Dec. 1453, that of the external offices had been completed one year later; see above, pp. 21, n. 7, 55.

[6] '. . . quod quidem futurum esset utile civitati ad concordiam retinendam in civitate' (ibid.). According to him, this was the argument of the Colleges in favour of a scrutiny being held now.

[7] Fols. 50^v–55^r (21 July). Giovannozzo Pitti (fol. 51^v): 'nil enim esse quod magis cives consoletur . . .'; Otto Niccolini (fol. 53^r): 'nec scit videre quis melior modus sit in uniendis civibus quam scruptineum facere bonum et honestum.'

[8] Fol. 53^r: 'si cives preteritis temporibus equaliter in honoribus fuissent trattati, non tot discidia in civitate evenissent.'

however, was not convinced of the desirability of anticipating the scrutiny; the bill did not obtain a majority on 24 July, nor on any of the successive days until 1 August, on which day it was presented once more.[1]

The Signoria was so anxious to get the bill passed that they encouraged the open ballot in the council of the People, evidently in the hope of being able to bring pressure to bear on recalcitrant councillors. To the Archbishop of Florence this appeared so serious a matter that, on 26 July, he issued a public protest against rendering the *fave scoperte*, which 'è contro al giuramento dato di rendere le fave coperte et segrete et contro alla ragione naturale', and prohibited it under threat of excommunication.[2] This proclamation was affixed to the doors of the Cathedral, much to the anger of the Signoria, who complained to the *Pratica* on 28 July that just when there was an excellent prospect of getting the bill passed, the archbishop, by his most unusual procedure, threatened to ruin everything.[3] Thirty-one members of the *Pratica*, including Girolamo Machiavelli, associated themselves with this protest, and promised to go the next day to the council meeting and to speak in favour of the bill, to show that there was no disagreement among them.[4]

These efforts were of no avail, but before the bill was finally abandoned, the Signoria gave yet another twist to its attempts to strengthen the régime by adding the amendment that the next Gonfalonier of Justice, whose name was due to be drawn on 28 August, was to be elected *a mano*.[5] Although only a short-term measure, it might at least help to secure continuity of government policy until the end of October, when the term of the next Signoria came to an end. The debate in the *Pratica* on 31 July provides ample evidence of how greatly elections *a mano* were valued among the ruling citizens. The election *a mano* of the Gonfalonier of Justice, says Carlo Pandolfini in initiating the discussion, is *utile et honorarium*; there is no better way of settling our difficult problems.[6] 'Those who hate the *Accoppiatori* and

---

[1] Libri Fabarum, 65, fols. 137ᵛ–141ʳ. The bill was for a scrutiny of all offices.

[2] Ser Baldovino Baldovini, *Vita* of S. Antonino, extract ed. by R. Morçay, *Saint Antonin*... (Tours–Paris, s.d. [1914]), pp. 429–30.

[3] Cons. e Prat. cit., fol. 55ᵛ (ed. by Morçay, pp. 493–4).

[4] Ibid.

[5] This emerges from the debate in the *Pratica* on 31 July (Cons. e Prat. cit., fols. 56ʳ–61ᵛ). There is no reference to this amendment in the Libri Fabarum, 65, fols. 137ᵛ–141ᵛ.

[6] Fol. 56ʳ: 'utile et honorarium, et non aptior modus ad ordinandum et componendum res nostras valde dissipatas et incompositas.'

their powers, are ill-advised', adds Agnolo Acciaiuoli;[1] seven
years later he was to take a rather different view of this matter.
If citizens were apprehensive that in this way they would stand
less chance of obtaining the highest office, they were, according
to Giovanni de' Medici, mistaken, for the *Accoppiatori* 'poterunt
nonnullos cives ad illum honorem assumere, nemini vero poterunt auferre'[2]—an observation which incidentally indicates that
it was planned to retain elections *a mano* of the Gonfalonier over
a longer period than proposed. Another speaker expresses his
surprise at the failure to pass the bill, for 'there can be hardly six
citizens in the council to whom it could do any harm, as the
number of *imborsati* for the Gonfaloniership is only small'.[3]

The debate of 31 July shows a mounting sense of frustration
among the leading citizens at the continued refusal of the council
of the People to pass the bill. It also throws some interesting
light on one of the council's motives. 'No one is justified in
opposing the bill', says Otto Niccolini, 'on the ground that it will
prepare the way for a revolution (*status mutationem*). For the
citizens who advise in favour of the bill are of such social standing
and wealth as to be unlikely to desire a revolution, which suits
rather the poor, the dishonest, and the desperadoes.'[4] And in
a similar strain Guglielmo Tanaglia exclaims: 'the bill has been
devised by those citizens who have been governing the State for
24 years in a most excellent manner. Revolutions are of no use
to men of this calibre, but rather to the poor and desperate, as
one can read in connexion with Catiline . . .'.[5]

The bill having been thrown out once more, the Signoria
summoned the *Pratica* again for the evening of the 31st, and
asked it for advice on what to do now, since 'omnia tentassent
pro provisione obtinenda, nec perfecissent'. Were they to per-
severe, or should another course of action be taken?[6] Agnolo

---

[1] Fol. 56ᵛ : 'qui aborrent copulatores et eorum auctoritatem, non bono consilio moventur.'

[2] Fol. 59ʳ.

[3] Francesco Ventura : 'Quantum ad bursam vexilliferi, dixit mirari se quod non obtineatur, cum vix in consilio sex futuri sint quibus provisio noceat; pauci enim pro vexilliferis
imborsati sunt . . .' (fol. 60ᵛ).

[4] Fol. 58ʳ: 'Nec posse aliquem dicere ideo provisionem non esse obtinendam, quia post
se alia mala paritura sit, id est status mutationem. Nam cives qui ista consulunt eius
qualitatis sunt et locupletes et magni, qui mutationem status non solent desiderare. Talia
enim cupere ad inopes, improbos et desperatos pertinet.'

[5] Fols. 59ᵛ–60ʳ: 'ab his civibus instituta est, qui per annos vigintiquatuor rem p. optime
gubernarunt. Tales quidem, quibus non conducat novitates aut mutationes fieri, sed potius
egenis et desperatis, sicut in Catilina accidisse legitur . . . .'

[6] Fol. 61ʳ: 'an vero alie vie sint tentande'.

Acciaiuoli suggests that the Signoria present the bill once more the next morning, and allow, for this occasion, the open ballot—that is, the very procedure which the archbishop had solemnly condemned only five days earlier. If the bill still fails to get a majority, the *Pratica*, which is to meet again on the following day, will advise the Signoria how to proceed further.[1] What this could involve became evident on the following day; in the meantime, nothing reflects better the feeling of impending crisis which was gathering in the *Pratica* than the words of Alessandro degli Alessandri: 'what is at stake here is whether the leading citizens of the régime should lose or retain their political influence.'[2]

When the *Pratica* met on the following day, the bill had again been thrown out. The Gonfalonier stated that the government had done everything in its power to get it passed; but nothing could be achieved because of the 'duritiem civium qui sunt discordes'. How can these civic divisions be eliminated?[3] In other words, how could the opposition be silenced? Alessandro degli Alessandri is the first to speak: the opposition to the bill is organized (and hence strictly illegal);[4] and then he interrupts his speech to ask for the following proceedings of the *Pratica* to be kept secret. The members of the *Pratica* having promised secrecy, he declared that since everything else had failed, there was no other solution but to summon a *Parlamento*,[5] that is to suspend normal conciliar procedure by an appeal to the popular assembly for emergency powers. This had not happened since September 1434. Throughout the debates in July, and despite the continued opposition of the council of the People to the bill, the Gonfalonier of Justice, as well as the members of the *Pratica*, had constantly emphasized their desire to observe the *via ordinaria* of conciliar legislation. This was in keeping with the policy of establishing a measure of control with the consent of

[1] Fol. 61r-v: 'Et quod interim cras mane consilium habeatur populi, et quod dicatur in potestate ipsorum esse dare fabam discopertam vel copertam. Et si non obtineatur, capiant illam viam domini, que per cives prestantes eis dabitur.' 'Cives prestantes' evidently refers to the members of the *Pratica*.

[2] Fol. 61v: 'attento maxime quod hic tractatur an cives precipui status vel reputationem amittant vel retineant.'

[3] Fol. 61v (1 Aug.): '. . . ab his civibus mature providendum esse, quo pacto res p. constituatur et eiusmodi civium dissensiones deleantur. . . .'

[4] On prohibition of *intelligenze*, see below, pp. 118–19, 217.

[5] Fol. 62r: he has heard 'a quibusdam civibus, quod ea forma, que ordinata est, nunquam obtineretur; talem esse inter cives datum ordinem. . . . Post datam secreti fidem prosecutus est, dicens quod quum nulla alia via reperiri potest, videtur sibi ut per viam parlamenti res ista transigatur.'

the normal legislative bodies. The advice to resort to a plebiscite as the only way left of dealing with conciliar opposition reveals, once again, the extreme gravity with which leading citizens viewed the situation, and illustrates the difficulties inherent in that policy.

In the debate which follows, Franco Sacchetti gives added weight to Alessandro degli Alessandri's analysis of the situation: what is at stake is the entire social basis of Florentine government. 'There are two alternatives: should we allow the *ottimati* to be ruled by the others, or should the others be ruled by them, as is right and just?'[1] Another speaker agrees: it must not be tolerated that popular rule replace the rule of the *ottimati*.[2] Were such fears genuine, or was Alessandro degli Alessandri intent on rallying the waverers and opponents? The debate of 1 August reveals that, while many members of the *Pratica* favoured his proposal, not everyone supported, and some opposed it.

To summon a *Parlamento*, it was argued, was *pericolosum valde*, as well as *non multum honestatis*;[3] to which Tommaso Soderini retorted that 'it was not as dangerous as some assert', nor would Florence's reputation suffer from it, but rather improve; and anyway, there was no other solution.[4] Other speakers, however, felt that, in view of the dangers inherent in a *Parlamento*, it might be preferable, at least for some time, to continue trying to achieve the desired results by normal constitutional methods. Among these 'moderates' we find Cosimo de' Medici's son Giovanni. If the councils go on refusing to pass this 'honest' law, he says, a *Parlamento* should be summoned; but before resorting to this extreme expedient, the Signori should, for two more days, attempt to get the bill passed by impressing on the council that the *Pratica* was united.[5] Was this also the advice of Giovanni's absent father?

[1] Fol. 65ᵛ: 'rem in duobus versari, videlicet ut videatur an permittendum sit prestantes cives ab aliis duci, an vero ipsi alios ducant et gubernent, sicut equum esset'.

[2] Francesco del Benino (fol. 65ᵛ). Similarly Otto Niccolini (fol. 63ʳ) and Tommaso Soderini (fol. 66ᵛ).

[3] Tommaso Deti (fol. 63ᵛ). Similarly, against the *Parlamento*, Francesco Ventura (fol. 63ᵛ), Niccolò Giugni (fol. 64ᵛ), Ugolino Martelli (fol. 65ʳ), and Bernardo Antinori (ibid.), who says that 'evenire . . . posse ut civitas, que felix est, in maximam miseriam laberetur'.

[4] Fol. 66ᵛ: 'dixit viam datam sibi placere, nec adeo pericolosam esse, sicut quidam dixerunt, nec infamiam allaturam civitati, sed reputationem, que apud omnes exteros etiam amissa est . . . unde nullam aliam viam censet esse nisi parlamentum. . . .'

[5] Fol. 67ᵛ: '. . . addidit antequam ad hec extrema veniatur, per duos adhuc dies in consiliis tentandum esse an provisio iam instituta obtineatur. Hortatus dominos, ut consilio dicerent omnes hos cives concordes esse . . . ita enim sperat fore, ut tandem pertinacia ommissa [*sic*], convertantur omnes ad provisionem obtinendam.'

It is in this meeting that his name is mentioned for the first time since the *Pratica* began its discussions on 2 July; and it is not perhaps by accident that it is mentioned by 'uncommitted' members. The first speaker to do so is Lodovico da Verrazzano: he does not know which is more dangerous, the illness or the medicine; since the matter is so dangerous, there should be more discussion on it, and Cosimo, in particular, should be consulted.[1] Another speaker suggests that a committee of eight or ten citizens be elected to discuss the matter with Cosimo *viro sapientissimo*, and that their decisions be accepted as final.[2] In the end, the *Pratica*, while accepting this suggestion, modified it in a way which was significant of the balance of power in the inner circle of the régime. There is no question of leaving the final decision altogether to another committee. The *Pratica* unanimously accepts the proposal to summon a *Parlamento*, but adds the proviso that it should be carried out on condition that Cosimo approves.[3]

There is no record of the meeting with Cosimo. But on the same day, the Milanese ambassador wrote to Francesco Sforza that in the morning Cosimo had discussed with him in utmost secrecy, and for the first time, the possibility of military support from Milan.[4] This must have been after the meeting of the *Pratica*, since Giovanni di Cosimo and Agnolo Acciaiuoli, who had spoken in it, were present at this interview. There is no reference yet to Cosimo having agreed to a *Parlamento*; on the contrary, in the same letter Nicodemo contrasts the anger of the leading citizens of the régime at the resistance of the council with Cosimo's philosophical and almost detached attitude.[5] But Cosimo was now evidently preparing to abandon this attitude of quasi-neutrality; and it was characteristic of his policy that in

---

[1] Fol. 64ʳ⁻ᵛ: '. . . duas res esse extremas, scilicet egritudinem et remedium, quod cum periculosum sit, dubitationem affert menti sue. . . . Et quia, ut dixit, res ista periculosa est, videretur sibi alios orandos cives, qui super istis rebus in idem consentiant; et precipue super hac re cum Cosma prestantissimo viro consultandum esse. . . .'

[2] Antonio da Rabatta (fol. 67ᵛ): 'deputandos esse octo vel decem cives qui cum Cosma sint viro sapientissimo, et quicquid per eos statuetur fiat. . . .'

[3] Fol. 68ʳ: 'Post predicta cives omnes singulatim de dominorum iussu interrogati an consentirent' to the proposal to summon a *Parlamento*, 'omnes unanimiter responderunt ita velle ac consulere et consentire. . . . Hoc addito quod deputentur quidam cives, qui cum Cosma sint, et cum eo super his rebus loquantur; et si ipsi Cosme idem visum fuerit, quod aliis visum est, consulta omnia executioni demandentur.'

[4] Bibl. Nat., MS. ital. 1588, fol. 109ʳ: 'Et questo non sa ancora persona del mondo, se non Messer Angelo, Zohannino de Cosimo et io, che questa matina ne facemo le prime parole fra noi in grandissimo segreto.'

[5] Ibid.: 'Reputandoselo questi de lo stato ad grande ignominia, benchè Cosimo se ne porti molto saviamente e in vista quasi neutrale.'

doing so he wished to ascertain what support he could count upon from his friend, the Duke of Milan. The ambassador did not feel empowered to make a definite promise, and Francesco Sforza's reply, in which he pledged himself to give all possible assistance, did not arrive until the 10th.[1] But already by the 5th the decision had been taken to hold the *Parlamento* on the 11th, the Signoria having secured, by that time, substantial military protection against disturbances.[2]

Two days earlier, on 3 August, Girolamo Machiavelli had been arrested, according to a well-informed contemporary source on the charge of having instigated a councillor to vote against the bill; probably Alessandro degli Alessandri had him in mind when on 1 August he complained in the *Pratica* that councillors had been 'ordered' to do so. The Milanese ambassador writes that Girolamo Machiavelli was the only prominent citizen among the opposition.[3] A lawyer of distinction, he had shown himself in the July *Pratiche* a critic of present conditions and a champion of the ordinary citizen.[4] On 4 August two other citizens were arrested, both of them relatives of exiles of 1434; and the three were tortured and subsequently exiled.[5] Shortly after these arrests the Signoria ordered about 150 citizens to go to their villas and not to return to the city without its permission; many of these belonged to the 'party of 1433'.[6] On 9 August Astorre, lord of Faenza, was expected with 300 cavalry and 50 infantry.[7] On the 10th the Signoria ordered all citizens over fourteen to come the next morning unarmed to the Piazza. When

---

[1] MS. ital. 1588, fol. 117ʳ (11 Aug.). Francesco Sforza's letter was of the 6th.

[2] Ibid., fol. 114ʳ (5 Aug.): 'Farassi questo parlamento cum Symonecto e forsi el Signore de Faenza e molti soy homini' &c. Simonetto was one of Florence's *condottieri*.

[3] *Priorista* of Francesco di Tommaso Giovanni cit., fol. 166ʳ: 'perchè avea confortato Piero d'Alesso Doni a non vincere la provisione e a contradire ancora in piaza e che arebbe compagnia' etc. Nicol di Tommaso was at that time member of the council of the People, together with Piero Doni. They belonged to the same *gonfalone*, that of Nicchio of the *Quartiere* of S. Spirito (Tratte, 165). On Alessandro degli Alessandri, see above, p. 100, n. 5. Nicodemo da Pontremoli to Francesco Sforza, MS. cit., fol. 114ʳ (5 Aug.): Girolamo 'era el da più fosse fra costoro'.

[4] See above, pp. 94, 97.

[5] *Priorista* cit., loc. cit.: 'Adì 4 fu ... preso Antonio Barbadoro e Carlo Benizi; furon tutti 3 tormentati più giorni, poi condannati e confinati.' Two of Antonio Barbadori's relatives had been exiled in 1434; so was Carlo Benizi's brother Matteo. Nicodemo da Pontremoli describes these two citizens as *de picola extima*. Cf. Buoninsegni, *Storie*, pp. 56, 57, and 121. See below, p. 109.

[6] *Priorista* cit., fol. 166ᵛ. Francesco Giovanni mentions Jacopo Baroncelli and sons, Pierozzo and Giovanni della Luna and sons, Zanobi and Guglielmo di Ser Matteo delle Riformagioni, Lipaccio and Carlo di Benedetto di Lipaccio de' Bardi, nearly all the Bardi, and Rinieri and Orso del Pace and sons.

[7] Nicodemo to Francesco Sforza, MS. cit., fol. 116ʳ (8 Aug.).

they arrived, they found the Piazza and the streets leading to it heavily guarded by mercenary troops and armed citizens. Then the Signoria appeared on the rostrum in front of their Palace, and a notary read out the text of a law creating a new *Balìa*, and asked the people three times whether two–thirds of the citizens were present and whether they were in favour of the law; and 'since only few understood what Ser Bartolomeo was saying, for he cannot speak loudly, only few citizens answered with yea. . . . Then the Signoria returned to the Palace and the citizens to their shops and the mercenaries to their billets.'[1] A new period in the history of the Medici régime had begun.

'The proposals put by the Signoria to the people were very fair, so that they were accepted gladly, and they are commended by everybody', wrote the Milanese ambassador after the *Parlamento*.[2] This was wishful thinking, but it contained a germ of truth. After the tenacious resistance of the council of the People to the Signoria's reform schemes, it would have been unwise to disregard public opinion completely, and the law of the *Parlamento* was, on the whole, more moderate than might have been expected from some of the talk in the *Pratica*. Its main purpose was twofold, to resuscitate the system of control which had been ended in 1454–5, and to put it on a permanent basis by making it part of the constitution. The former was achieved by restoring, for the time being, elections *a mano* of the Signoria and of the Eight of Ward, by granting the Eight once more special powers to proceed in political cases, and by entrusting the new scrutiny to the *Balìa*; the latter by the creation of a permanent council in the place of quinquennial *Balìe*.

The law of the *Parlamento* of 11 August[3] accordingly differed from that of September 1434, in that it did not simply delegate full powers to the *Balìa*; the *Balìa*, in its turn, differed from its

---

[1] The account in Francesco di Tommaso Giovanni's *Priorista*, fol. 166ᵛ (a slightly shorter account in his *Ricordanze*, Carte Strozz., 2ᵃ ser., 16 *bis*, fol. 29ʳ), is the most circumstantial of the descriptions of the *Parlamento* of 11 Aug. by an eyewitness. Nicodemo da Pontremoli describes it in his letter, of the same day, to Francesco Sforza (loc. cit.); however, he was not on the Piazza, but in the Medici Palace. He states that the *Parlamento* was held 'cum la maiore unione del mondo e sanza un minimo scandalo'. This is also Buoninsegni's and Agnolo Gaddi's comment (*Storie fiorentine*, p. 121; *Priorista*, British Museum, MS. Egerton 3764, fol. 189ʳ). According to the letter of the *Podestà* of Florence, Giovanni da Balbiano, to Angelo da Rieti, the people on the Piazza shouted as with one voice, 'sì, sì, fiat, fiat!' (13 Aug.; MS. ital. cit., fol. 119); but he was hardly an unbiased witness.

[2] Loc. cit.: 'Et foro le conditioni che porse la Signoria honestissime in modo che'l populo le acceptò de bona voglia, et sono commendate da ognuno.'

[3] Balìe, 29, fols. 7ʳ–11ᵛ.

predecessors in that it was appointed for less than six months.[1] The law of the *Parlamento* laid down that during the next five years the Signoria was to be elected *a mano* by the remaining *Accoppiatori* of 1452 and the *Accoppiatori* of the new scrutiny, who were to divide for this purpose into groups of five and seven respectively, each to act for six elections—a regulation which may reflect a preference for smaller committees to handle the election of the government: also, in subsequent reforms of this office, its size was kept down to five members.[2] At the same time, it was expressly stated that at the end of the five years the *Accoppiatori* were to close the purses of the Signoria in the customary manner.[3] The *Balìa* was put in charge of working out the constitution of the new council, whose creation had already been decided by the *Parlamento*; otherwise it was to have the same full powers as the *Balìa* of 1434.

This departure from the procedure followed in 1434, when the *Balìa* had been granted unlimited powers by the *Parlamento*, may be partly explained by the role of the *Pratica* of July–August. Of exceptionally large size, and including nearly all the leading citizens of the régime, it had not only, in the customary fashion, discussed and advised upon the measures proposed by the Signoria, but had made decisions on them.[4] Consequently, some of the work of the *Balìa* had already been done by the *Pratica*. Furthermore, the *Balìe* had in the past not always proved as subservient as might have been expected,[5] and it may have been considered safer to have all the fundamental issues settled by the law of the *Parlamento*.

The short term of office of the *Balìa* offers a striking contrast to the long terms granted the *Balìe* after 1434. It was closely connected with the decision to create a new permanent council. Although allegedly this council was merely intended to replace the councils of 200, 131, and 145, which were abolished by the *Parlamento*,[6] in fact it took the place of the long-term *Balìe*.

---

[1] Until 31 Jan. 1459 (ibid., fol. 8ᵛ).

[2] Ibid., fols. 8ᵛ–9ʳ. See below, pp. 168, n. 8, 180. In 1452, the office of *Accoppiatori* had consisted of no less than twenty members, of whom seventeen survived. One of the *Accoppiatori* of 1452, Lorenzo della Stufa, refused to accept his reappointment on account of old age. He nominated as his substitute his son Agnolo, who was duly elected by the Signoria (Tratte, 17, *ad* 11 Aug. 1458).

[3] 'Et finitis dictis quinque annis dicti coppulatores . . . et eorum substituti et dicti novi coppulatores . . . debeant claudere dictas bursas . . . secundum consuetum' (Balìe, 29, fol. 9ʳ).

[4] See above, p. 102.   [5] See above, pp. 86–87.

[6] Balìe cit., fol. 10ʳ⁻ᵛ.

The leading citizens of the régime had evidently learnt their lesson from the opposition to these *Balìe* in 1446, 1448, 1454, and 1458.[1] The most impressive result of this opposition, the law prohibiting *Balìe* of April 1458, was still in force, and had to be suspended by the *Parlamento* for the occasion.[2] It was clearly going to be difficult, if not impossible, to continue persuading the councils of the People and Commune to create new *Balìe* of this type. These difficulties were avoided by using plebiscitarian methods to decide on the creation of a permanent new council. How much this council was, at the time, considered a continuation, in a different form, of the *Balìa* of 1458, is shown by the remark of a contemporary diarist that it was called 'el consiglio maggiore in chanbio della balìa', 'the greater council to replace the *Balìa*'.[3]

The composition of the *Balìa* was in keeping with earlier developments, by which the *Accoppiatori* and Secretaries past and present had provided a large proportion of the official personnel, while the Signoria and the *Accoppiatori* had increasingly taken over the selection of the elective members of the *Balìe*. The 200 *arroti* of the *Balìa* of 1458 were to be chosen by the Signoria, the *Accoppiatori* of 1452,[4] and the *Accoppiatori* and Secretaries of the new scrutiny, who were also to be members of the *Balìa* together with all the other past *Accoppiatori* and Secretaries of the Medici régime and a large number of magistrates.[5] By including the twenty new *Accoppiatori* and Secretaries, the proportion of all past and present holders of those offices was raised to nearly one-half of the *ex officio* personnel. One incidental effect of this was to raise the ratio of official members who had previously belonged to *Balìe*, a further contributory factor being the absence of consuls

---

[1] See above, pp. 22, 75–77, 90–91.

[2] Balìe cit., fols. 7ᵛ–8ʳ: '. . . quod omnes . . . leges et quecumque ordinamenta tam generalia quam specialia que infrascripta in dicto parlamento . . . proponenda et firmanda modo aliquo impedirent, aut illis obstarent . . . sint pro hac vice et pro infrascriptis rebus dumtaxat sublata et seu suspensa. . . .' See above, pp. 90–91.

[3] *Priorista* of Agnolo Gaddi, MS. cit., fol. 189ᵛ. Agnolo Gaddi had been a member of the *Balìa* of 1452, as one of the *Sei di Mercanzia* (see Appendix, no. V). Nicodemo da Pontremoli's remark, in his letter to Francesco Sforza of 8 August (Bibl. Nat., MS. ital. 1588, fol. 116ʳ), to the effect that 'a poco a poco quel numero de la balìa se minuerà e redurassi a pochi' probably refers to the projected new council, which in fact turned out to be much smaller than the *Balìa*; see below, p. 113.

[4] One of them, Luca Pitti, was already an elector in his capacity of Gonfalonier of Justice.

[5] The *Sedici Gonfalonieri*, the *Dodici Buonuomini*, the Captains of the Guelph Party, the Eight of Ward, the *Ufficiali del Monte*, the *Massai della Camera*, the *Sei di Mercanzia*, the *Ufficiali del Catasto*, and the past and present *proconsul* of the guild of Judges and Notaries. The official personnel totalled 152.

of the Lesser Guilds, who had always provided a substantial number of newcomers.[1] Accordingly, while the proportion of such men among the elected members was roughly the same as in the preceding *Balìe*, i.e. about one-half, it was considerably lower—about one-third[2]—among the official members. A similar bias against newcomers appears also in the regulations of the *Parlamento* law concerning the size of family 'representation': up to eight families were allowed to have as many as three of their members among the elective members, or *arroti*, as against a maximum of two for five families in 1452, while the other families or *consorterie* were not allowed more than one *arroto*, with the exception of those of them which were not represented among the *ex officio* members; these could have two *arroti*. No limit was set to the total representation in the *Balìa*, as in 1452.[3] The Signoria and the *Accoppiatori* and Secretaries selected as the privileged families the Canigiani, Pitti, Salviati, Rucellai, Tornabuoni and Popoleschi, Bartoli, Acciaiuoli, and Albizzi.[4] However, when it came to the election of the *arroti*, only two of these privileged families received the maximum of three *arroti*, which shows the caution with which the Signoria and *Accoppiatori* used their powers. If the raising of the maximum was due to pressure from the great families, there were strong arguments against allowing too high a family representation. The absence of an upper limit for the entire *Balìa* made it possible for some families to be represented by more than one or two members: thus the Medici and the Pitti had five of their members in the *Balìa*.[5]

One of the principal tasks of the *Balìa* was the scrutiny; a case could have been made on these grounds for the unusually large number of *Accoppiatori* and Secretaries among its personnel.[6] The scrutiny was to be completed by the end of the *Balìa*'s

---

[1] See Appendix, no. VI. Only the *proconsul* of the guild of Judges and Notaries and his predecessor were admitted.   [2] 52 out of 152. See above, p. 84, n. 2.

[3] Balìe, 29, fol. 8ʳ (11 Aug. 1458). The privileged families were selected by the Signoria, the *Accoppiatori* of 1452 and the *Accoppiatori* and Secretaries of the new scrutiny on 14 Aug. (Tratte, 17). See above, p. 85.   [4] Tratte, 17.

[5] Both families were represented by four members among the *ex officio* personnel of the *Balìa*, and by one among the *arroti*. Pierfrancesco di Lorenzo de' Medici does not appear to have been elected immediately, for he does not figure on the list of forty-three *arroti* for the *Quartiere* of San Giovanni (Tratte, 61, fols. 164ʳ–169ʳ), which was compiled on 17 Aug., the election having taken place on the 14th (Tratte, 17). He was presumably elected between 17 and 22 Aug., on which day the *Balìa* met for the first time.

[6] The *Balìa* decided on 26 Aug. that the scrutiny, which was to comprise all offices, was to begin in the first week of Nov. and was to be completed by 31 Jan. 1459 (Balìe, 29, fol. 26ʳ). The scrutiny of the *Tre Maggiori* was, in fact, completed by 28 Dec., when it was described as 'noviter celebratum' (Tratte, 17).

session. In fact, there was now no longer any need to anticipate it, as had been unsuccessfully tried in July, the régime having obtained from the *Parlamento* permission to have it carried out by a *Balìa*.[1] The decisions on the organization of the scrutiny and the subsequent filling of the bags were delegated by the *Balìa* to the Signoria in office, the Signoria of August–September 1458, the *Accoppiatori* of 1452, and the *Accoppiatori* and Secretaries of 1458.[2] They decided, on 28 December, that the candidates who had been successful in the scrutiny of the *Tre Maggiori* were to be given one *polizza* for each of these offices, to be added to those they already possessed. The unsuccessful candidates, on the other hand, were to lose their earlier qualifications, unless the *Accoppiatori* specially decided to restore (*reducere*) them to individual candidates.[3] As in 1434, 1440, 1444, and 1453, the scrutiny acted as a check on previous qualifications, while being, in its turn, as that of 1434 had been, subject to a further check by the *Accoppiatori*.[4] Such checks were particularly important at the present moment; the events of the preceding years and months had shown that the scrutiny of 1453 was no guarantee against an uncommitted or even hostile Signoria being appointed, and the new scrutiny would thus serve to eliminate from the ballot bags undesirable elements. As emerges from the complaints made in 1465–6, many citizens did lose their electoral qualifications in this way.[5] According to Benedetto Dei, their number amounted to over 1500.[6] He adds that, as a result, the Medici and Pitti and their

[1] By virtue of its full powers. See above, pp. 97, 105.

[2] Balìe cit., fol. 26ᵛ (26 Aug.).

[3] Tratte, 17. On *reducere*, see above, pp. 42 ff.; on the loss of previous qualifications, above, pp. 40 ff. See also below, pp. 123–4.

[4] See above, pp. 7–8, 40–41, 59–60. The *Accoppiatori* had been expressly granted the same powers as had been granted to the *Accoppiatori* of 1434 (Balìe cit., fol. 9ʳ (11 Aug.): 'habeant omnem aliam auctoritatem et baliam, que . . . data fuit coppulatoribus' of 1434).

[5] Cons. e Prat., 58, fol. 92ʳ (9 Jan. 1466): 'quibus ablati sunt honores' in the scrutiny of 1458; fol. 95ᵛ (18 Jan.): 'restituerentur honores, quibus in anno 1458 ablati fuerunt'. Since the *Accoppiatori* had been granted the same powers as their predecessors of 1434, they also claimed the right to *extrahere* twenty names from the bags before closing them, as the latter had done (see above, p. 43). However, in the end they do not seem to have availed themselves of it; see their register, Tratte, 17.

[6] *Cronaca*, Manoscritti, 119, fol. 22ʳ: 'feciono lo schuittino e fferono che chi non vinciessi el detto isquittino dell'anno 1458 s'intendessi avere persso ogn'altra poliza, sicchè si tolse per questa tal chosa lo stato e riggimento a più di 1500 cittadini, li quali per detta leggie perderono ogni loro poliza. . . .' Owing to the lack of scrutiny lists for 1458, it is impossible to check this statement. However, in view of the fact that in the scrutiny of 1453, which was not considered to be particularly harsh, 210 citizens of the *Quartiere* of S. Maria Novella who had previously been *imborsati* were not again qualified (some of these, however, had died in the meantime) Benedetto Dei's figure is probably not far off the mark. (For

followers were now in full enjoyment of political power, while many of their enemies left Florence in despair and disgust.[1]

Hand in hand with this electoral revision went legal action against political enemies. For this purpose the Eight made use of the extraordinary powers the *Parlamento* had restored to them. The arrest of Girolamo Machiavelli and his two companions was followed, after the *Parlamento*, by their exile; and a number of their relatives, and a few other citizens, shared their fate.[2] Compared with the persecutions of 1434, these measures were mild enough, and show that the fears of an organized opposition had been much exaggerated. On the other hand, in extending the sentences of the exiles of 1434,[3] and banishing their sons and descendants,[4] the Mediceans revealed a sense of mistrust which had already become apparent in the security measures before the *Parlamento*,[5] and which was doubtless due to the belief that any organized opposition against the régime would find natural allies among these men and their families.

After the persecutions of 1434–5,[6] there had been remarkably few criminal proceedings against political enemies. This was consonant with the Medicean policy to secure and strengthen the régime by peaceful means within the framework of the constitution; in June 1444 some citizens, among them the *Accoppiatori* of 1433, had been newly deprived of political rights, and a few others had their earlier prison sentences commuted into exile;[7] but the chief action of the *Balìe* in this matter concerned the

comparison between the *imborsazione* of 1449 and the scrutiny of 1453, cf. Tratte, 49 and 1151, fols. 406ʳ–419ᵛ.)

[1] Ibid.: '. . . e la parte de' Medici e de' Pitti e de' Ridolfi e Ghuicciardini e Medici e Martegli e Chorbinegli e Ssoderini e Tornabuoni e Chapponi e Pazzi e Gianfigliazzi e Bartolini e Biliotti e Bartoli e Vespucci e Salviati e altri infiniti chasati e partigiani de' Medici e de' Pitti si ghoderono lo stato e gli ufizi e lo regimento e drento alla città e ffuori della città di Firenze; e passato e posato tutto, s'attendea nella città a llavorare, ma tutto era invano pegli animi pregni de' cittadini, li quali si vedeano essere istati mondi e netti e ttosati d'ogni honore et d'ogni utile, di modo che assai de' principali se n'andorono fuori della città . . . per disperazione e per dispetto che gli avieno ogni giorno di vedere inimici loro avere il chanpo libero e ogni giorno ufizi e onoranze e ttenere il chapo senpre nella mangiatoia. Cierto questa fu gran chosa . . . che lla non fu meno che quella dell'anno 1433 e 1434 e 1444. . . .'

[2] See above, p. 103. Sentences of exile were pronounced by the Captain of the People on 18 Aug. against Girolamo d'Agnolo Machiavelli, Piero d'Agnolo Machiavelli, Niccolò di Bartolomeo Bartolini, Antonio di Giovanni Barbadori and sons, Carlo di Piero Benizi, Antonio and Filippo di Piero Benizi, Giovanni di Matteo di Piero Benizi, Francesco and Matteo di Domenico Caccini, Domenico di Giuliano Ginori, Bono di Jacopo Ristori, Lorenzo di Giovanni della Stufa, Jacopone di Bartolomeo Gherardini, and Giovanni and Piero di Tommaso Borghini (Otto di Guardia e Balìa, 224, fols. 80ʳ–84ʳ). See also Buoninsegni, *Storie*, p. 122.

[3] See below, p. 110.
[4] Ibid.
[5] See above, p. 103.
[6] See above, pp. 2–3.
[7] See above p. 18.

exiles of 1434. At the beginning of its session, the *Balìa* of 1444 extended their term by ten years;[1] and when these were nearly over, the next *Balìa* decreed, in March 1454, a further extension until March 1465.[2]

These measures were now carried further, first by the law of the *Parlamento*, and then by a decree of the *Otto* of 6 November 1458. By the law of 11 August, the sentences of exile, although they had over six years to run, were once more extended by ten years. This term was raised by the Eight to no less than twenty-five years.[3] Over and above this, the Eight banished, equally for twenty-five years, the sons and descendants of exiles who had been declared rebels or had not observed the terms of their sentences, and of citizens who had been executed for political reasons;[4] and the same fate befell the sons and descendants of a number of specifically named families which had been prominent under the past régime and had been hit by banishments in 1434 or later, among them the Strozzi.[5] As if this were not enough, they were all deprived for life of the right to hold office; and so were, for twenty-five years after the expiry of their sentences, the citizens who had been condemned for political reasons from 1434 onwards.[6] Evidently, after its successful recovery, the régime was determined to eliminate, once and for all, any danger that might accrue from a return of the exiles to political life: in many cases, the new sentences amounted to banishment, or at least disqualification, for life.[7]

[1] Ibid.

[2] Balìe, 27, fols. 217ᵛ–218ʳ (13 March 1454): the sentences were now to run until 24 March 1465.

[3] Balìe, 29, fol. 10ʳ (11 Aug.); Cons. e Prat., 55, fol. 87ʳ: report of the decision of the *Otto* to the *Pratica*, 6 Nov.

[4] Ibid. The sentences of the Captain of 13 Nov., under the ordinance of the Eight, are in Otto di Guardia e Balìa, 224, fols. 85ᵛ–86ʳ. At the same time the duration of the sentences of Aug. was raised by ten years.

[5] Ibid. They are the Castellani, Bardi, Ardinghelli, Belfredelli, Strozzi, Peruzzi, Guasconi, Rondinelli, Brancacci, Guadagni, Baldovinetti. In the case of men who were already banished, the sentence was increased by 25 years. Among the citizens to whom this decree applied was Filippo di Matteo Strozzi: on Filippo Strozzi, see Alessandra Macinghi-Strozzi, *Lettere di una gentildonna fiorentina del secolo XV ai figliuoli esuli*, ed. C. Guasti (Florence, 1877), esp. pp. 143 ff.

[6] Otto, 224, fol. 85ᵛ. Moreover, the Eight declared thirty-nine citizens rebels, and condemned five citizens to be beheaded 'per facto di stato dell'anno 1434', ibid., fol. 86ʳ⁻ᵛ. Cf. Cambi, *Istorie*, pp. 364–5.

[7] The *Balìa* made, in Jan., some small concession to the newly-exiled sons and descendants of the families named by the *Otto*, by reducing the distance from Florence at which they were to live outside Florentine territory from 100 to 50 miles (Balìe cit., fols. 101ᵛ–102ʳ; 19 Jan. 1459; ed. in Alessandra Macinghi-Strozzi, *Lettere*, pp. 148–50).

Nor were the security measures limited to proceedings against single citizens and families. The law of the *Parlamento* had granted the Eight of Ward, for two years, the same extraordinary powers or *balìa* as those granted to the Eight in October 1434.[1] This remained the legal basis for the powers the *Otto* exercised after August 1458; as we shall see, these extraordinary powers were renewed for five years in 1460, when it was alleged that 'experience showed clearly that the authority of the Eight is more effective in preserving the peace and liberty of Florence when they possess *balìa*'.[2] Before 1458 the Eight of Ward had, in fact, only occasionally been granted full powers or *balìa* to proceed in political offences. Although no ordinance granting these powers in autumn 1434 is extant, the Eight who were elected for six months at the end of September certainly possessed *balìa*, as their sentences of exile show.[3] But this was by no means the normal situation after 1434 as is shown by the fact that the Eight continued to be called simply *Otto di Guardia*, without the addition *e Balìa*.[4] In order to prevent disturbances in connexion with the scrutiny, the *Balìa* decided, in November 1453, to let the next Eight be elected 'cum ea auctoritate et balia . . . de qua dictis eligentibus videtur'; and the subsequent grants to the Eight by the Signoria, Colleges, and *Accoppiatori* of 'balia libera et plenissima' in matters of exile and civic disqualification, though limited to a maximum of six months altogether, were considered sufficiently important to serve as precedents for the future powers of the Eight.[5] In or soon after 1458 a register was compiled to

---

[1] Balìe cit., fol. 9^{r-v}. At the same time it had also followed the precedent of 1434 by granting *balia* to the Captain of the People, whose term it extended by one year.

[2] Provv., 151, fol. 77^r; see below, p. 121.

[3] The law of the *Parlamento* speaks of the 'octo custodie facti auctoritate balie' of 1434; but the *provvisione* of that *Balìa* of 29 Sept.(Balìe, 25, fols. 19^v–20^r) which regulates the method of electing the next Eight, does not grant them *balia*, but specially lays down that they were to have the same authority as their predecessors who were appointed by lot ('cum officio auctoritate et aliis concessis . . . Octo custodie qui per viam extractionis deputantur'). The grant of *balia* was probably made by the Signoria, between 1 and 10 Oct., for on that day they call the Eight in the register of their deliberations, 'officiales octo custodie et balie' (Signori e Collegi, Deliberazioni, ordinaria autorità, 46, fol. 35^r). The register of the *Deliberazioni* by special authority, 25, fol. 83^r, does not mention the Eight in October.

[4] There does not appear to be sufficient evidence for the statement in G. Antonelli's valuable study of this office, 'La magistratura degli Otto di Guardia a Firenze', *Arch. Stor. Ital.*, cxii (1954), p. 17, that 'dal 1434 in poi ebbero quasi sempre la balìa'.

[5] Balìe, 27, fol. 170^r (19 Nov. 1453); Signori e Collegi, speciale autorità, 30, fols. 190^v–191^v (21 Nov. 1453), partly ed. by Antonelli, p. 18, n. 44. The Eight were elected for two months. On 11 Dec. 1453, the Signoria and their colleagues extended the term of office by another four months, with the same *auctoritate et balia* (Tratte, 225 bis, fol. 95^r). The importance subsequently ascribed to this grant of *balia* is borne out by the note added to the entry in the *Tratte* register 225 bis by Bartolomeo de' Dei, who was notary of the Signoria in

contain their sentences for political offences from 1434 onwards.[1] It is preceded by a collection of laws by which, from that year onwards, special powers had been granted to their office; and the only entry referring to their *balìa* is precisely the ordinance of the Signoria of 21 November 1453 containing the law of 19 November.[2] These powers to proceed arbitrarily against political enemies were revived in 1458, but not, as in 1453, for six months only. The grant of *balìa* to the Eight for two years was an innovation which proved to be a fresh point of departure for the régime; so much so that seven years later a critic of the excessive powers of the Eight demanded a return to the authority they had possessed before 1458, which seemed to him extensive enough.[3]

In view of their greatly increased powers, it was clearly more important than ever to control the appointment of the *Otto di Guardia e Balìa*, as they are now regularly called. To substitute election for statutory sortition of the Eight had been an aim of Medicean policy ever since 1434, which, as we have seen, had met with varying fortunes. While, between 1434 and 1440, the Eight had nearly always been appointed by election or combined election and sortition, the latter had been restored in 1440 and 1447, and continued almost uninterruptedly until the establishment of the next *Balìa*. The Eight who began their office in September 1452 and in March 1453 were again elected, and so were those in office from November 1453 to May 1454.[4] In that month election by lot was restored, and remained in force until August 1458, when the *Parlamento* revived election by the Signoria, *Accoppiatori*, and Secretaries, following the practice introduced first in 1434. This remained the electoral procedure until 1459, when the new council of One Hundred took over election of the Eight.[5]

The law of the *Parlamento* had decreed that the new council should be completed by the end of November.[6] But the *Balìa*, which had been put in charge of legislation to this effect, had not yet done anything substantial by the beginning of that month,

---

1489 (Marzi, *La cancelleria*, p. 506), to the effect that the text of this *balìa* was contained in the register of the deliberations of the Signoria ('ut ego Bartholomeus de Deis vidi et legi': fol. 95ʳ).

[1] Otto di Guardia e Balìa, periodo repubblicano, 224.
[2] Fol. 8ʳ⁻ᵛ.
[3] Cons. e Prat., 58, fols. 27ʳ–28ʳ (5 Sept. 1465; Manno Temperani); see below, p. 141.
[4] See above, pp. 50–52.
[5] Tratte, 80, fol. 21ʳ⁻ᵛ, 30ʳ; 81, fols. 3ʳ–4ʳ; see also above, p. 50, and below, p. 114.
[6] Balìe cit., fol. 10ʳ.

as emerges from a *Pratica* of 3 November, consisting of the *Accoppiatori* and Secretaries, which warned the Signoria not to hurry too much with this matter, but to discuss it first with a small committee.[1] Nothing more is heard of it until 26 November, that is four days before the deadline, when the Gonfalonier again asked the *Accoppiatori* and Secretaries what to do about it. They advised appointing a committee for this purpose.[2] The latter, which consisted exclusively of *Accoppiatori*, appears to have suggested that the drafting of the law be delegated to the *Accoppiatori*, the Secretaries, and the Signoria in office; for we find these men completing the draft three days later, on 29 November.[3] On the same day, the law was passed by the *Balìa*.[4]

The new council of *Cento* was to be the first in matters concerning 'statum seu bursas aut scructinea aut . . . onera vel conductas gentium armigerarum', and the last in all other matters.[5] Bills concerning the present form of government, elections, taxes, and mercenary troops had therefore to be passed by it before being sent to the councils of the People and the Commune, while the remaining bills required its consent in the last instance in order to become law.[6] It was to be composed of 100 members appointed for six months, and the Signoria and Colleges in office.[7]

This follows closely the reform bill defeated in July 1458; the functions are the same, with the exception of the election of members of the councils of the People and Commune: this part of the reform scheme was not adopted, probably because it was considered too extreme a proposal.[8] It had been argued that the

---

[1] Cons. e Prat., 55, fol. 86^v: they had been asked 'utrum tertium consilium nunc fiendum esset,' and answer that 'tempus dominis satis super est . . . ipsi non festinent in ordinando eo, sed loco et tempore oportunis de aliquorum consilio civium illud ordinent et statuant. . . .'

[2] Ibid., fol. 89^{r-v}. The eight citizens who were elected were Luca Pitti, Tommaso Soderini, Otto Niccolini, Francesco Orlandi, Giovanni Bartoli, Francesco Ventura, Alessandro Alessandri, and Dietisalvi Neroni (fol. 89^v).

[3] The corrected draft of the law is in the register of the *Accoppiatori*, Tratte, 17.

[4] Cento, 1, fols. 5^r–13^r.   [5] Ibid., fol. 11^v.

[6] A special committee, to be elected every two months by the Signoria, three days after it had assumed office, was to decide into which of these two categories a bill fell. This committee was to consist of two members of the XVI *Gonfalonieri*, two of the XII *Buonuomini*, and four of the *Conservatori delle leggi* (ibid.).

[7] For the first two sessions of the new council also the previous VIII *di Guardia e Balìa* and their successors elected on 21 Aug. 1458 respectively were to be *ex officio* members.

[8] See above, pp. 95–96. From Francesco di Tommaso Giovanni's account, it is not clear whether the decisions of the new council, as proposed in July, had equally required the assent of the ancient councils; if not, this would imply a further amendment of the original scheme in the final law. *Priorista* cit., fol. 166^r: 'Questo consiglo facessi gl'altri, e avessi a riformar tutti gli squittini e l'ordinare graveza . . . e di piglare impresa e tutte

new council would greatly facilitate the passage of legislation, as well as acting as a check on the ancient councils[1]; and this was precisely what the council of *Cento* was designed to achieve. In contrast to the temporary *Balìe* which it was meant to replace, it was built into the fabric of the Florentine constitution—not unlike the former council of 200, but with much wider powers. The matters for which the *Cento* was to be the 'first council' were largely identical with those with which the *Balìe* had dealt, either by their own authority or in conjunction with the statutory councils; and in matters concerning war and finance it also superseded the councils of 200, of 131, and of 145, which, as we have seen, had been abolished by the *Parlamento*.[2] If specially authorized, it could, like the *Balìe*, carry out by its sole authority certain elections to offices which were normally filled by lot. The new council was, in fact, increasingly used for this purpose. In 1458 it was put in charge of electing the *Ufficiali del Monte*; in 1459 of the election of the officials of the *Catasto*, of the Eight, and of the *Conservatori delle leggi*, as well as a few particularly exposed officials of the territorial administration, such as the Captain of Leghorn; finally, in 1460, of that of the Sea Consuls.[3] The *Cento* thus came to occupy an important place in the system of electoral controls, and to fulfil also in this respect functions which the *Balìe* had fulfilled before over much shorter periods. But in one respect it was closer to the council of the 200 than to the *Balìe*: however great its powers, they were not absolute.[4] It could not legislate without the assent of the ancient councils, as the *Balìe* could do in some matters, and had successfully attempted in others, much to the dissatisfaction of the statutory councils.[5] If the *Balìe* had shown, after 1434, two distinct trends, one towards collaboration, in a position of

l'electioni d'ufici a mano o ambasciadori, e le provisioni de' consigli s'approvassino per questo consiglo. Non ottenendosi in più volte questo che andò a partito nel popolo, si fè poi parlamento.'

[1] See above, pp. 96–97.   [2] See above, p. 105.

[3] For the *Ufficiali del Monte*: *provvisione* of the *Balìa* of 25 Sept. 1458, i.e. before the constitution of the new council was ready, to be valid from 1460 onwards (Tratte, 81, fol. 65ʳ; the next *Ufficiali*, for 1459–60, were to be elected by the *Balìa*); for the *Ufficiali del Catasto*: Cento, 1, fols. 18ᵛ–19ᵛ (28 March 1459); for the Eight, the *Conservatori delle leggi*, and the *Ufficiali del Monte*: Cento, 1 fol. 25ʳ⁻ᵛ (6 Nov. 1459); for the *Capitano* and two *castellani* of Leghorn, the *Capitano* of the fortress of Pisa and the *castellani* of the *Palazzotto* of the fortress of Pisa, those of Stampace, of S. Marco, of the new fortress of Pisa, of Vicopisano, and of Motrone: ibid., fol. 32ʳ⁻ᵛ (6 Dec.; for three years); for the Sea Consuls, and the *provveditori* of the customs office at Pisa: ibid., fol. 34ʳ⁻ᵛ (4 Jan. 1460).

[4] The 200, on the occasions on which they were summoned, always acted as the council of first instance; cf. Provv., 99, fol. 168ᵛ (4–5 Feb. 1411). See also above, p. 96.

[5] See above, pp. 75–76, 79.

superiority, with the existing councils, and the other towards exclusive power, it was the former which triumphed with the creation of the *Cento*. This abandonment, at least for the time being, of the more radical policy was probably due, to no small extent, to the opposition to which the *Balìe* had been subjected in the past; but it was counterbalanced by the creation of a new permanent council, which limited the legislative powers of the ancient councils of the People and Commune. As happened so often in Florentine politics during this period, the constitution of the *Cento* was the result of a compromise. Despite the great advance it meant for the Medici régime, it also showed the limits of its power.

As in the case of the *Balìe*, the value of the new council for the régime depended on the loyalty of its members. The method by which the *Balìe* had been appointed had been gradually perfected, with the *Accoppiatori* playing an increasingly important role in the appointment of the elective members.[1] It is therefore not surprising to find them in charge, together with the scrutiny secretaries of 1458 and the Signoria of November–December, of the election of the first 100 councillors for January–June 1459. The councillors for the second half of 1459 were to be appointed by lot from candidates selected by the same officials,[2] after which the normal regulations, which will be discussed presently, came into force. That special ones should have been considered advantageous for the appointment of the first two councils doubtless reflects preoccupations with the critical period after the *Balìa* had ended its session on 31 January 1459, as does the fact that during 1459 the *Otto di Balìa* who had been in office in August 1458 were to be members of the council. At the end of 1459, the normal regulations came into force.

Every December, the Signoria was to summon the citizens of at least thirty-five years of age who since October 1434 had been *seduti* or *veduti* for the Gonfaloniership of Justice, that is who had either held the highest office in the State, or had had their names drawn for it but had been temporarily disqualified.[3] These

---

[1] See above, pp. 81–83.

[2] The council of *Cento* for the second half of 1459 was to be elected in the following way: the Signoria, *Accoppiatori*, and Secretaries nominated 360 candidates who were at least thirty-five years old and were *veduti ai Tre Maggiori* since 1434. These were then put to the vote. The candidates who had obtained a two-thirds majority, but not more than three per family, were *imborsati* in special bags, from which the members of the council were drawn in June 1459.   [3] *Cento*, 1, fols. 8ᵛ–9ᵛ.

citizens, together with the Signoria, were then to vote, provided a quorum of two-thirds was present, first on the *seduti* and *veduti* for the Gonfaloniership, and then on those for the three highest offices, the *Tre Maggiori*, of thirty-five or over. The names of the candidates who had obtained a two-thirds majority were placed in three bags per *quartiere*, the third being for the *seduti* and *veduti* for the *Tre Maggiori* of the Lesser Guilds, to be valid for one year. In December and June, thirty-two names would be drawn from the first bags, forty-eight from the second, and twenty from the third; their owners would form the personnel of the *Cento* for six months. After the June sortition, the bags would be destroyed, to be replaced by new ones in the following December; and supplementary bags would provide for possible deficiencies in the principal ones.[1] Furthermore, the Gonfalonier of Justice of July–August 1458 and all the citizens of at least thirty-five years who were subsequently *seduti* or *veduti* for the Gonfaloniership of Justice were to be admitted, with full voting rights, to those meetings in which the *Cento* acted by its sole authority.[2]

While the composition of the *Cento* follows closely the proposals made in July 1458, the proportion of the *seduti* and *veduti* Gonfaloniers of Justice is raised by the law from one-fifth to one-third of the elected members, and all these citizens gain the right to vote in the elections that were carried out by the *Cento*.[3] By thus giving this group of citizens a prominent position in the *Cento*, the reform institutionalized their *de facto* prestige. This was to have important repercussions on the structure of Florentine politics during the following decades. The men whose names had been drawn for the highest office in the State after 1434 could well be expected to constitute lesser security risks than any other clearly definable section of the population—including the much more numerous *seduti* and *veduti* for the *Tre Maggiori*. At the same time, their status also involved potential dangers.

---

[1] They were to be used in case the ordinary bags did not contain more than 75 names.

[2] This meant that they could take part in the elections to offices which were made by the *Cento* by virtue of some special authority. Cento 1, fol. 11ʳ: 'quod in cunctis rebus que deliberari et fieri debebunt per dictum Consilium Centum per se solum absque aliis consiliis ... possint intervenire et fabas reddere ... per omne tempus futurum ... Ita ut si voluerint, possint se ... ad dictum consilium congregare ... ultra alios. ...'

[3] Francesco Giovanni, loc. cit., on the July proposals: 'Che tutti e seduti e veduti gonfalonieri di justitia s'imborsasse [*sic*] e traessisi 5 per quartiere; e questi 20 insieme con Signori e Collegi mandino a partito tutti veduti dal 34 in qua d'anni 35 e imborsasine 200, cioè 50 per quartiere, delle più fave; poi si cavassi 20 per quartiere e 20 de' gonfalonieri di justitia e tutti cavalieri e artefici stati x di balìa e Signori e colegi che pe' tempi saranno. ...'

Even before 1434, the *veduti ai Tre Maggiori*[1] had enjoyed certain political privileges. When the new council of 200 was created in 1411, its personnel had to be recruited by lot from those citizens who, since 1382, had either been appointed to one of the *Tre Maggiori*, or who had been 'visi fore imbursati per extractiones factas ad aliquod ex dictis officiis'.[2] 1382 was the year in which the 'oligarchical' régime had definitively asserted itself after the Ciompi rising, and in which its first scrutiny had been held; citizens of this status might therefore be expected to be loyal to it. Buoninsegni accordingly calls the council of 200 'un nuovo consiglio di 200 huomini scelti, e conformi al reggimento'.[3] As the passage just quoted shows, the citizens 'qui vulgariter nuncupantur e veduti'[4] were, apart from those who had actually held the office, the only ones of whom it was expected to be publicly known that they had been qualified for the *Tre Maggiori*, since results of scrutinies were meant to be kept strictly secret.[5] It was natural for Florentine citizens to expect that the special status of the *veduti* should also reflect on their families, so that even to belong to a family which included, or had included, such men could be a qualification for office.[6]

In 1433, the Albizzi faction had hoped to prevail in the councils of the People and Commune by giving the *veduti* the same privileges in these councils as they possessed in that of 200.[7] The *Balìa* of 1434 restored the statutory method of election, by which the Signoria and the Colleges qualified candidates, final

---

[1] Following contemporary administrative terminology, this term may be used instead of *seduti e veduti*. Strictly speaking, all *seduti* were also *veduti*.

[2] Provv., 99, fols. 168ʳ–169ʳ (4–5 Feb. 1411). See above, p. 69.

[3] *Storie*, p. 2. In 1415 it was laid down that in all scrutinies the names of the *veduti ai Tre Maggiori* should be voted on separately and before the names of the *non veduti* (Provv., 105, fols. 152ᵛ–153ᵛ; 6–10 Oct. 1415). See also the regulations for the scrutiny of 1440 in Tratte, fols. 229ʳ, and above, p. 56.

[4] Provv., 120, fol. 271ᵛ (3–4 August 1429).

[5] See, e.g., Balìe, 29, fol. 27ʳ (26 Aug. 1458): 'Tenghasi il segreto dello squittino . . . de' tre maggiori . . . solamente per gli accopiatori che di nuovo sono stati facti . . . insieme cogli ufficiali del palagio usati', and the friars who assisted them.

[6] In 1429, a law was passed by which all those who were either themselves *veduti ai Tre Maggiori*, or whose father, paternal grandfather, brother *ex eodem patre*, or paternal uncle, were *veduti*, had to inform the *Conservatori delle leggi* of their age, in order to facilitate the administration of the minimum-age regulations for offices (Provv., 120, fol. 271ᵛ–272ᵛ). Laws to the same effect were passed in 1435 (Provv., 126, fols. 3ᵛ–4ʳ; 6–7 April), 1444 (Provv., 134, fols. 255ʳ–256ʳ; 3–7 April), and 1452 (Provv., 143, fols. 195ᵛ–196ʳ; 6–12 July). The register of the *Conservatori*, Tratte, 39, was compiled following the law of 1429, and was continued until the middle of the century. Cf. also Tratte, 41, for 1457–72.

[7] Balìe, 24, fol. 17ᵛ (23 Sept. 1433). All the *veduti ai Tre Maggiori* who were *imborsati* for the 200 were also to be so for the councils of the People and Commune. To these the Signoria and Colleges could add up to 10 *non veduti* per *gonfalone*, i.e. up to 160 in all.

appointments being made by lot.[1] But in 1448, shortly before the unsuccessful attempt to extend the lifetime of the *Balìa*, a bill was presented to the councils which aimed at resuscitating, in a modified form, the electoral reform of 1433.[2] The bill was not passed at the time, but was revived after the creation of the new *Balìa* in 1452, when it was laid down that those citizens who had been *veduti ai Tre Maggiori* since October 1434 were to have their names automatically placed in the ballot bags for the two councils.[3] October 1434 had been the month during which the first Medicean scrutiny had been held. Just as, in 1411, only those citizens whose names had been drawn during the period of the 'oligarchy' had been given the privilege of *veduti*, so now did the year 1434 become the *terminus post quem* for the *veduti* of the new régime.[4] However, the behaviour of the councils between 1454 and 1458, with their recurrent opposition to Medicean policy, must have given rise to second thoughts; for the law of the *Parlamento* of 11 August 1458 once more gave the Signoria with its Colleges full powers to select the candidates for the councils of the People and Commune.[5]

That the potential or real influence of the *veduti* could, in fact, be viewed with some apprehension is shown by two laws, of February 1444 and June 1455, by which all citizens over twenty-four who had been *veduti* or who belonged to a family of *veduti* were barred for five years from membership of confraternities.[6] The law of 1455 did so expressly 'per obviare agli scandali che potrebbono nascere nella nostra città'. In fact, the first law was

---

[1] Balìe, 25, fol. 24[r] (4 Oct. 1434): 'imbursentur ... eo modo et prout fiebant ... ante diem primum mensis septembris' 1433. See *Statuta* 1415, ii, p. 660.

[2] Libri Fabarum, 61, fol. 110[v] (12 April 1448): 'quod pro consilio populi et communis fiant burse de vedutis et non veduti scrutinentur'. See above, p. 19, n. 4.

[3] Balìe, 27, fol. 14[r] (27 July 1452). All the *veduti ai Tre Maggiori* who were 'abili ad dicta consilia' to be *imborsati*; the XVI *Gonfalonieri* to nominate sixteen *non veduti* each, to be voted on by the Signoria and the Colleges, and qualified by two-thirds majority.

[4] Henceforth, it will be understood that the term *veduti*, as used for the Medicean period, normally implies this time limit.

[5] Balìe, 29, fol. 10[r]: 'Item quod Consilia populi et communis Florentie possint et debeant deinceps per omne tempus deputari et fieri ... per viam scrutinei et in omnibus ... quemadmodum fiebat et observabatur hactenus. . . .'

[6] Provv., 134, fols. 208[v]–209[r] (19–20 Feb. 1444): 'Quod quilibet maior etatis annorum vigintiquatuor completorum, qui aut cuius pater, frater carnalis ex eodem patre, aut patruus aliquo tempore esset extractus ad aliquod trium maiorum officiorum, videlicet *fusse veduto*, qui in posterum conveniret aut se congregaret in aliqua societate laudantium vel disciplinantium sub quocumque nomine censeretur in civitate Florentie, vel infra quinque miliaria, ipso facto incidat in penam florenorum mille auri pro qualibet vice, et ultra hoc habeat devetum a quocumque officio ... annis quinque proxime futuris. . . .' This prohibition does not apply to the *Societas nigrorum*. Provv., 146, fols. 147[r]–148[r] (19–20 June 1455), is practically identical, but the age limit is reduced to twenty and sons are included.

passed after the controversial scrutiny of 1443, and the second just before the closing of the bags in June 1455. They were evidently designed to prevent the formation of pressure groups, and were confirmed, together with earlier legislation against confraternities, by the law of the *Parlamento* of 1458.[1] The extent to which such confraternities could serve as pressure groups is illustrated by a revealing entry in a contemporary diary. Domenico di Niccolò Pollini, who was a member of the *compagnia* of Gesù Pellegrino, records how on 26 December 1454, while the scrutiny for the internal and external offices was in progress,[2] the captains of his confraternity decided that those of its members who were *deboli a lo squittino*, that is who stood little chance of being successful in the scrutiny, should be assisted by their brethren. For this purpose, special proposers (*sollecitatori*) were appointed for all electoral districts.[3]

Among the *veduti* for the three highest offices, those who were *veduti* for the Gonfaloniership of Justice formed an *élite*. They also could be regarded as safer, from the point of view of the régime, than the ordinary *veduti*. For even when elections were not *a mano*, the names of the Gonfaloniers of Justice would be drawn from bags that had been specially filled by the *Accoppiatori*.[4] Not surprisingly, the *veduti* for the Gonfaloniership were a relatively small group: in 1458, about 200 as against 1600-odd *veduti ai Tre Maggiori* of twenty-five years or more.[5] This was due, in the first place, to the fact that only 6 Gonfaloniers of Justice were elected every year, as against 48 Priors and 96 members of the Colleges, that is of the *Sedici Gonfalonieri* and *Dodici Buonuomini*. Furthermore, when elections of the Signoria were *a mano*, the *Accoppiatori*, before 1458, nearly always showed a marked

---

[1] Balìe, 29, fols. 10v–11r. In Oct. 1419, in order to suppress 'scandals' and eliminate their roots, all confraternities except those specially licensed by the government were prohibited (Provv., 109, fols. 160r–162v; 19–20 Oct.).

[2] See above, p. 55.

[3] *Ricordanze* of Domenico di Niccolò Pollini, Bibl. Naz., Magl. VIII. 1282, fol. 45r: '. . . determinarono che in ogni ghonfalone fossino ai[u]tati e deboli a lo squittino e anche gl'altri e sono quegli del ghonfalone de lion biancho gl'infrascripti . . .' (the writer is among the twenty-three named). 'Sollecitatori a detto squittino furono nominati gl'infrascripti per ogni gonfalone' (fol. 45v).

[4] See above, p. 46.

[5] These figures are based, for the Gonfaloniership of Justice, on the sortition registers between 1434 and 1458 (Tratte, 198 to 201), and, for the Tre Maggiori, on Tratte, 1074, which is entitled 'Registrum visorum ad aliquod trium maiorum de scrutineo celebrato in anno 1434 aut de aliis postea factis, etatis legitime, qui omnes sunt imborsati pro consiliis populi et communis'. Internal evidence indicates that this register was compiled in 1458. I have deducted from its lists, apart from the names of the dead, those of the *veduti* that are cancelled on account of their owners being *religiosi*, *banniti*, &c.

reluctance to select, for the final sortition of the Gonfalonier of
Justice, citizens who were temporarily disqualified, and who
would therefore be liable to be *veduti* instead of *seduti*. Between
October 1434 and December 1440, three citizens only were
veduti for the Gonfaloniership;[1] but as soon as sortition was
restored, the number of *veduti* shot up: in the year 1441 alone it
amounted to no less than twenty-eight.[2] Between June 1444 and
February 1446, and again in 1448, not a single citizen was *veduto*
for that office; but after the closing of the bags in May 1449,
eighteen citizens were *veduti* for it in the four remaining elections
of 1449.[3]

After August 1458 there was a striking change in the procedure
of the *Accoppiatori* in this matter. The *seduti e veduti* for the Gonfaloniership of Justice having been given a position of considerable responsibility in connexion with the *Cento*, it was evidently
considered necessary to increase their numbers. Consequently, on
29 November 1458, that is on the day of the creation of the new
council, the *Accoppiatori* decided that up to six citizens could be
newly *veduti* for the Gonfaloniership at every election of the
Signoria.[4] Over and above these, they could *far vedere* citizens
who were already *veduti*: a procedure which was probably intended
as a check on those citizens who had been *veduti* while elections
were by lot. As a result, the number of newly *veduti* between
December 1458 and December 1459 came close to the total
for the twelve years of *a mano* elections between 1434 and
1449.[5]

There were evident dangers in this policy. With growing
numbers, the group of *veduti* for the Gonfaloniership was bound
to lose some of its exclusiveness, but was also liable to create
fresh problems for the régime. The drastic reduction of the
maximum figures for the newly *veduti* from six to two, which the
Accoppiatori decided on 20 December 1459,[6] may have been due
to apprehensions of this kind. A maximum of twelve a year
would fill the gaps caused by death, and provide for a moderate
increase in numbers, while giving the *Accoppiatori* the opportunity of raising the social status of families. Although far in

---

[1] See above, p. 37.   [2] Tratte, 198, 199.
[3] Tratte, 200. See above, p. 38.   [4] Tratte, 17.
[5] 26 as against 27. In the Dec. election of 1458 there were three newly *veduti* (among them,
Piero di Cosimo de' Medici).
[6] Tratte, 17: 'possint imbursare tantum usque in duos . . . pro faciendo videri de novo
pro Vexilliferis Iustitie . . .'.

excess of the average number of *veduti* during the periods of elections *a mano* before 1458, it would keep the group of *Gonfalonieri seduti e veduti* small and exclusive. With this group acting as electors of the *Cento* and providing one-third of its personnel, the remaining two-thirds being chosen from among the *seduti e veduti ai Tre Maggiori*, the new council might well be considered as safe an institution as the régime could have devised, without pushing exclusiveness too far for the liking of the ordinary Florentine citizen.

.   .   .   .   .

As we have seen, the reforms of August–November 1458 were permanent only so far as the council of *Cento* was concerned. Following the precedent of 1453, the *Accoppiatori* were given authority to elect the Signoria *a mano* for five years.[1] In July 1460 the councils extended elections *a mano* by another five years. Probably in order to make the extension law more palatable, it contained the promise of a new scrutiny in autumn 1463, that is, after the statutory quinquennium had elapsed.[2] But this was not the only way in which the initiators of the law showed their anxiety about the councils' response to their proposal.

In the summer of 1460 Girolamo Machiavelli was captured in the Lunigiana, where he had been conspiring against the régime. He was imprisoned in Florence, and died in July, 'o per disagi, o per tormenti'; 'and as a result of his confession, about twenty-five citizens were banished'.[3] Already on 7–11 June, the councils had extended the special powers of the Eight of Ward, which were due to expire in August, by no less than five years.[4] Now, a *Pratica* summoned on 9 July, after Girolamo's examination, advised that elections *a mano* should be extended by five years.[5] This move was doubtless due less to a genuine sense of apprehension than to the desire to take the utmost advantage of the discovery of the conspiracy: electoral controls had still three years to run, and it would have seemed reasonable to leave the problem of extending them to a date nearer to their

---

[1] See above, p. 105.

[2] Provv., 151, fol. 138ʳ (10–12 July 1460): '. . . finiti e cinque anni pe' quali furono facti gli accoppiatori . . . si debbi fare uno nuovo squittino.'

[3] Buoninsegni, *Storie*, p. 127. Cons. e Prat., 56, fol. 84ʳ (9 July 1460): the *Otto di Guardia*, having examined Girolamo 'per multos dies', had discovered 'ipsum multa molitum esse adversus libertatem et salutem civitatis et imprimis exules omnes aut relegatos excitasse adversus civitatem qui prius quiescebant, et eos una secum conspirasse, ut rem publicam invaderent'. A number of exiles were declared rebels: Otto di Guardia e Balìa, 224, fol. 104ʳ.

[4] Provv., 151, fols. 76ᵛ–79ʳ.   [5] Cons. e Prat. cit., fols. 85ʳ–90ᵛ.

expiry. The circumstances that arose in summer 1460 must have appeared particularly favourable for persuading the councils to prolong elections *a mano* for another five years, as well as to extend the special powers of the Eight. That the leaders of the régime should eagerly seize upon this opportunity not only reveals, once again, their concern with public opinion, but also reminds us that, in spite of the great success the régime had achieved in 1458, its principal means of control still depended for its continued survival upon the votes of the councils of the People and the Commune. Accordingly, the preamble of the law of 12 July makes the most of the threat to the benefits of peace which the government was helping the citizens enjoy. It had been known for some months, and had now become evident, that a number of persons had been preparing disorders. They had got so far with their sinister plans that, had they not been closely watched, they would have been able to carry them out. Everyone realized that the best way to consolidate the present peaceful condition of the city, so that all citizens could feel safe and free to attend to their various businesses, was to elect *a mano*, for to do so gives a great sense of security to the supporters of the régime, and makes its enemies tremble and despair.[1] In 1463, ten new *Accoppiatori* were to be elected, to act jointly with the present ones for the new scrutiny, and to carry out with them elections *a mano* during the following quinquennium.[2] But in January 1462 the scrutiny was in its turn postponed for five years.[3]

Scrutinies had, for some time, been considered a potential source of trouble. The scrutiny of the external offices of 1443

---

[1] Provv. cit.: 'E s'è inteso già più mesi sono et hora nuovamente si toccò con mano, che mentre che questa Magnifica Signoria attende quì a ordinare i facti del Comune, et a cercare che si possa godere questa pace che Dio ci a data, per alcuni altri molto cautamente s'è atteso et attende a volervi mettere in disordine et a farvi schandolo grande dentro et di fuori; et avevono già tanto tirato inanzi e loro captivi pensieri, che se non fussino stati ben veghiati, arebbono potuto in brieve tempo quelli mettere ad effecto. Ma essendo stati veghiati et attesi bene i loro processi, sono infine venute a luce le loro perverse intentioni et operationi, le quali sono tante et tali che ogni buono cittadino ne debba tremare et desiderare et rechare che si provegha per modo che non possino avere effecto. . . . Et intenden-dosi per ciaschuno unitamente, che per conseguitare tale effecto non si può fare più utile provedimento che di tenere le borse a mano, come per experientia più volte s'è veduto et vede, però che questo tale provedimento, sicome dà grande animo et sicurtà et speranza di pace et di riposo a quelli che amano il presente stato, così *e converso* invilisce et fa tremare et priva d'ogni speranza gli adversari di quello . . .'. Cf. Buoninsegni, loc. cit.: 'e per più sicurtà di stato si raffermarono le borse a mano per cinque anni'. The law was passed by the *Cento* by 98 votes to 18, and by the councils of the People and Commune by 153 votes to 59 and 126 respectively.

[2] Provv. cit., fol. 138ʳ.   [3] Provv., 152, fols. 261ᵛ–262ᵛ (22–25 Jan. 1462).

had been annulled in the following year; that of 1453 had been suspended until after the end of the war.[1] It finally took place, in 1454, after an unsuccessful attempt had been made to postpone it once more, on the grounds that the citizens were not united among themselves, or as one citizen put it, almost in Machiavellian terms, 'quia materia corrotta est'.[2] In November 1453, the Eight had received full powers to enable them to deal with disturbances that might result from the scrutiny which was then being held.[3] In January 1462, on the other hand, the postponement was justified by the Signoria on economic grounds: scrutinies and *imborsazioni* take up a great deal of the citizens' time and interfere with their business for at least one year; moreover, a scrutiny was not at present necessary.[4] This last argument had also been used in 1454, when it was pointed out that the bags were still full.[5] In fact, from a technical point of view, it does not normally appear to have been necessary for scrutinies to be held every five years, and a case could be made for longer intervals in the interest of business and internal order. But such arguments touched at the roots of the republican system. It remained to be seen whether the Florentines would accept, without opposition, this further reduction of their electoral rights; the more so as the last scrutiny, of 1458, had resulted in many citizens losing their earlier qualifications for the three highest offices.[6]

Perhaps in order to meet criticisms on this score, the *Accoppiatori* decided, in December 1463, to use powers granted to them in December 1458, which authorized them to requalify for the three highest offices citizens who in 1458 had had *polizze* in the old

[1] Above, pp. 55, 58.

[2] Cons. e Prat., 53, fol. 112ᵛ (1 Aug. 1454; Giovannozzo Pitti); 110ʳ (31 July; Tommaso Salvetti).

[3] See above, p. 111.

[4] Provv., 152, fol. 261ᵛ: 'la quale opera, come per experientia s'è veduto, tra nell'ordinare prima lo squictino et poi squictinare et ultimamente imborsare, toglie molto tempo a tucti i cittadini di qualunche qualità sieno, e sviagli assai da' loro exercitii, sichè si può dire che tucta la terra ne stia inferma per lo meno uno anno; et pertanto acciò che questa opera dello squictino non abbia ad interrompere i vostri exercitii nè la buona condictione in che al presente per la gratia di dio si truova la città vostra, ma piutosto quegli e quella si possino migliorare e accrescere; et finalmente inteso sopra ciò i pareri e conforti di più vostri savi cittadini . . .' On 9 Jan., Carlo Pandolfini had advised, in the *Pratica*, that 'scruptineum per aliquot annos differatur' (Cons. e Prat., 56, fol. 182ᵛ).

[5] Cons. e Prat., 53, fol. 109ʳ (31 July 1454); Agnolo Acciaiuoli: 'marsupia plena sunt.'

[6] See above, p. 108. The law of 25 Jan. postponing the scrutiny was passed with narrow majorities by the councils of the People and of the Commune. The votes were, in the *Cento*, 93 to 17, in the council of the People, 141 to 66, and in that of the Commune, 136 to 45.

bags, but who had not been successful in the scrutiny of that year.[1] They had already occasionally made use of these powers: in December 1459 in favour of twelve citizens, and in April 1463 in favour of one.[2] But these were small matters in comparison with the *reductiones* carried out by them in December 1463 and January 1464. On this occasion, they added the names of no less than 385 citizens to those contained in the *borse* for the *Tre Maggiori* of 1458, which was nearly twice the number of *reductiones* carried out before the closing of the bags in 1455.[3] This action may have reconciled some citizens to the postponement of the scrutiny. Indeed, *reductiones* on such a scale might almost be regarded as a minor substitute for a scrutiny. For the Mediceans, on the other hand, they had the great advantage of being carried out by the *Accoppiatori*, in contrast to a scrutiny that would have to be held by a large council. At the same time, they could represent only a temporary expedient, for the *Accoppiatori* had no authority to qualify newly for the *Tre Maggiori*; and this applied to young members of ruling families just as much as to *gente nuova*. However, while not creating new qualifications for the *Tre Maggiori*, they substantially modified past ones by placing 140 out of the 385 names they had selected in the *borse* of the Gonfaloniership of Justice, the remaining 245 being placed in those of the Priorate, of the XVI *Gonfalonieri*, and of the XII *Buonuomini*. They had already qualified three citizens for the Gonfaloniership in December 1459,[4] and now adopted this procedure on a large scale. Such a procedure constitutes an important innovation.

To qualify for the Gonfaloniership of Justice was an altogether

---

[1] See above, p. 108. Tratte, 17 (28 Dec. 1458): since the *Accoppiatori* who last closed the *borse* and the new *Accoppiatori* 'sint illi qui habent penes se secretum dicti novi scrutinei trium maiorum officiorum et bene noverunt errores predictos [i.e. which happened at the scrutiny of 1458, when a number of citizens who had been qualified in or after 1434 did not obtain a majority] et nomina et pronomina civium in quibus fuit erratum et qui digni essent ut reducentur', the *Accoppiatori* may, on one or more occasions, add (*reducere*) all or some of the old *polizze* of such citizens to the new *borse* of the *Tre Maggiori*. See also Balìe, 29, fol. 26ᵛ (26 Aug. 1458).

[2] Tratte, 17 (29 Dec. 1459). The *reducti* are Lorenzo di Larione Larioni, Lionardo di Niccolò Manelli, Bernardo di M. Giannozzo Manetti, Alamanno di Filippo Rinuccini, Benedetto di Giampaolo da Panzano, Francesco di Altobianco degli Alberti, Antonio del Maestro Lorenzo Sassoli, Giovanni di Ser Paolo, Gino di Giuliano Ginori, Francesco di Niccolò Martelli, Papi di Tedaldo Tedaldi, and Agnolo di M. Palla Strozzi. To these they added, on 19 April 1463, Giovanni di Paolo Rucellai.

[3] See above, p. 44.

[4] They were Mariotto di Dinozzo Lippi, Giuliano di Lapo Vespucci, and Piero di M. Andrea de' Pazzi (Tratte, 17; 29 Dec. 1459).

different process from the *reductio* by which previously existing qualifications were simply restored to the *borse*. It was normally carried out by the *Accoppiatori* immediately after the scrutiny;[1] in 1449 and 1455 it preceded the closing of the *borse* and the restoration of the election by lot.[2] By 1463 practically no such qualifications had taken place since June 1455. Elections *a mano* having been restored in August 1458, the *Accoppiatori* were consequently at liberty to place the name of any citizen who had been qualified for the *Tre Maggiori* in 1458 in the two-monthly bags for the Gonfaloniership. In fact, they virtually always chose citizens who had been qualified for it in 1455.[3] Had elections *a mano* not been extended in 1460 by a further period of five years, the *Accoppiatori* would have made the statutory qualifications for the Gonfaloniership in 1463, before closing the bags. The *reductiones* for the Gonfaloniership took, to some extent, the place of this procedure. At the same time, the *Accoppiatori* confirmed the eligibility of all those citizens who had been qualified for the Gonfaloniership in 1455 and for the *Tre Maggiori* in 1458, and whose names had been drawn (*veduti*) between August 1458 and December 1463.[4]

The addition of these new names provided Florentine citizens with fresh opportunities, if not of being actually elected to, at least of being *veduto* for, the highest office in the state. The electoral records after December 1463 show that the *Accoppiatori* lost no time in having newly-added names drawn for the Gonfaloniership, and in doing so usually exceeded the maximum of two they had set themselves, in December 1459, in the matter of *far vedere* for that office.[5] At the same time the *Accoppiatori*, while following the traditional policy of their office in respecting social continuity, showed a relatively liberal attitude towards new 'admissions' to the coveted status of *veduto Gonfaloniere di Giustizia*: about one-third of the newly *veduti* between August 1458 and August 1465 belonged to families which had not yet

---

[1] See above, pp. 6, 45–46.   [2] Above, pp. 20, 22, 40.

[3] Tratte, 16, fols. 16ᵛ–20ʳ, 17, and 202, *passim*.

[4] Tratte, 17 (17 Dec. 1463). Moreover, the *Accoppiatori* reserved their right 'declarandi, nominandi et reducendi alios . . . ad dictas bursas Vexilliferi Iustitie semel vel pluries, quos et quotiens eisdem videbitur et placuerit . . . '.

[5] See above, p. 120. No formal suspension of this regulation appears in their register, which, however, breaks off in Jan. 1464 (Tratte, 17). As a result, between Dec. 1463 and Sept. 1465, when the *borse* were once more closed, twenty-five newly *reducti* were *veduti*, and one appointed to the office. In that period, the total of newly *veduti* was twenty-eight. At the same time the *Accoppiatori* saw to it that citizens who had already been *veduti* before 1458 were so once more (Tratte, 202).

been singled out for this honour.[1] How much the social status of a family was considered to be raised by one of its members being *veduto* for the Gonfaloniership may be illustrated by an entry in the diary of Carlo di Salvestro Gondi, who was among the *reducti* of January 1464. Shortly after that date he heard that one of the *Accoppiatori* had decided to have his name drawn at one of the next elections, *per far vedere*. Carlo was overjoyed because of the great prestige this would bring to his family— 'perchè desideravo questo onore, che mi pareva dare principio grandissimo alla casa.'[2]

In 1463 the political scene may have appeared calm enough. There was a slight flurry in July, when it was realized that, according to the text of the law of July 1460 extending elections *a mano* until 1468,[3] new *Accoppiatori* had to be elected in 1463 for the scrutiny which was then to take place. The scrutiny had now been postponed; but special legislation was required to dispense with the election of the ten additional *Accoppiatori*.[4] The incident is chiefly interesting for the almost pedantic concern with legality, which was characteristic of the régime after, as before, 1458. The *Accoppiatori* of 1458 were to remain, for another five years, in sole control of electing the Signoria *a mano*. In 1458, they consisted, as we have seen, of the surviving *Accoppiatori* of 1452, nearly all of whom had already served between 1444 and 1448, and of 10 new *Accoppiatori* appointed in 1458, amounting to 27 in all.[5] By April 1463 their number had been reduced to 20, of whom 6 were momentarily absent.[6] Of the 20, 6 had been

---

[1] Tratte, 201, 202.

[2] *Ricordanze* of Carlo di Salvestro Gondi, Florence, Archivio Gondi, busta XI, fols. 18ᵛ–19ʳ. The passage is included in the extracts from the *Ricordanze* ed. by J. Corbinelli, *Histoire généalogique de la maison de Gondi* (Paris, 1705), i, Preuves, p. cxcviii. Carlo's ambition was fulfilled at the election of the Signoria which took place at the end of June 1465 (Tratte, 202). See also below, p. 138. The following are the families which, between 1458 and 1465, obtained this honour for the first time since 1434 : in the *Quartiere* of S. Spirito, the Alamanni, Antinori, Bini, Cicciaporci, Deti, Ilarioni, and Nerli; in the *Quartiere* of S. Croce, the Bagnesi, Dini, Mancini, Mellini, and Pepi; in the *Quartiere* of S. Maria Novella, the Gianfigliazzi, Gondi, Nobili, Rustichi, Da Sommaia, Tebalducci, Tornabuoni, Del Vigna, and Vespucci; in the *Quartiere* of S. Giovanni, the Cresci, Inghirami, Lapi, Pazzi, Sostegni, and Taddei (based on Tratte, 199 to 202).   [3] See above, p. 121.

[4] Provv., 154, fols. 105ʳ–106ᵛ (9–13 July 1463) : since in the law of Jan. 1462 postponing the scrutiny, 'niente fu per expresso dichiarato' concerning the *Accoppiatori*, 'sichè non si provedendo altrimenti, s'arebbono a ffare hora di proximo i decti dieci nuovi Accopiatori oltre a quelli che sono al presente, benchè non s'abbia affare hora nuovo squittino, come è decto, che sarebbe contro alla intentione principale della provisione' &c.

[5] See above, pp. 32, 105.

[6] Tratte, 17, 19 April 1463 : 'quatuordecim ex viginti copulatoribus . . . hodie superviventibus et restantibus' — Luca di Bonaccorso Pitti, Luigi di Piero Guicciardini, M. Otto di Lapo Niccolini, Lodovico di Cece da Verrazzano, Giovanni del Zaccaria di Jacopo,

Accoppiatori from 1445 and 4 from 1448 onwards, with the exception of the years 1449–52, when there were no elections *a mano*.[1] Among them, we find leading personalities of the régime like Luca Pitti (who had already been in office from 1434 to 1439), Tommaso Soderini, Luigi Guicciardini, Agnolo Acciaiuoli, Otto Niccolini, and Piero di Cosimo de' Medici.

After 1460, the constitutional foundations of the régime were more solidly established than ever, with the *Accoppiatori* in charge of electing the Signoria until 1468, with the *Cento* acting permanently as first legislative council and electing such key officials as the *Otto di Guardia*, and with the *Otto* having full powers to proceed in political offences until 1465. The anniversary of the *Parlamento* of 1458 was fittingly celebrated by a ceremony in the palace of the Signoria, during which official orators might extol the benefits which, in terms of peace, liberty, and unity, the *Parlamento* had brought the town.[2] That it had restored peace, unity, and prosperity to Florence was also the theme of Piero di Cosimo de' Medici's address to the *Pratica*, a few days after he had assumed, for the first time, the office of Gonfalonier of Justice in January 1461:[3] 'The State finds itself in such peace and happiness as not only the present citizens, but also their ancestors, had never witnessed or recalled. Business and public revenue are constantly growing, and bestowing greater glory and dignity upon the city'; but this happy state of affairs will last only as long as the citizens remain united in concord. Internal unity was a traditional theme of Florentine political rhetoric, which had now assumed fresh significance. After a

M. Manno di Giovanni Temperani, M. Agnolo di Jacopo Acciaiuoli, Giovanni di Domenico Bartoli, Piero di Cosimo de' Medici, Dietisalvi di Nerone di Nigi Dietisalvi, Agnolo di Lorenzo della Stufa, Matteo di Marco Palmieri, Niccolò di Zanobi Bonvanni, Bartolomeo di Francesco di Ser Andrea. 'Absentibus ex ipsis viginti' Tommaso di Lorenzo Soderini, Matteo di Morello Morelli, Martino di Francesco dello Scarfa, Lionardo di Bartolomeo Bartolini, Antonio di Lenzone di Simone, and Ugolino di Niccolò di Ugolino Martelli.

[1] See Appendix, no. I.

[2] One such oration given on 11 Aug. 1462, by Alamanno Rinuccini in the name of the *Dodici Buonuomini*, is in his *Lettere ed orazioni*, ed. V. R. Giustiniani (Florence, 1953), pp. 191–3.

[3] Cons. e Prat., 56, fols. 123ʳ–124ʳ (5 Jan. 1461): '. . . rem publicam in ea pace ac beatitudine reperiri qualem nedum qui vivunt cives, sed maiores eorum nunquam viderunt aut meminerunt. Augerique continuo civium exercitia et redditus publicos, ex quibus maior accidat gloria et dignitas civitati.' This felicity is to be preserved, 'ac niti ne amictatur'. The Signoria has to see to it first of all, 'ut cives quesito bono in perpetuum frui possint, iustitiam scilicet observare ac ministrare, cum ea neglecta nulle res publice, nulla imperia . . . diuturna esse possunt . . . deinde ut cives ipsi concordiam et unanimes animos habeant . . . Sic enim agendo non solum que nunc adest felicitas conservabitur, sed etiam rei publice opes ac gloria continuo magis ac magis augebuntur. . . .'

period of dissensions, the Mediceans had closed their ranks, and recovered and consolidated their power; would they succeed in maintaining unity? This question concerned not only the survival of the régime, but also the position in it of Cosimo de' Medici.

. . . . .

If, after August 1458, the régime could be considered more firmly established than ever before, the same also applied to Cosimo's position. When, in 1459 and 1463, the *Accoppiatori* met to decide on additions to the new *borse*, they did so in Cosimo's palace in the Via Larga, 'quem locum ante omnia sibi ad infrascripta gerenda elegerunt', instead of their official meeting place, the Palace of the Signoria.[1] These were hardly the only official meetings of magistracies that were, in those years, held at the Medici palace. Pius II, who visited Florence in the spring of 1459, states in his *Commentaries* that after August 1458, state affairs were debated at Cosimo's house and records this as evidence of his ascendancy in Florence.[2]

A visitor to Florence after 1458 might well make a judgement of this kind, although the Pope was too shrewd an observer not to notice 'that there were some who asserted that Cosimo's power was intolerable'.[3] There was always a temptation for non-Florentines to analyse Cosimo's position in terms of contemporary Italian despotism, and this temptation was doubtless greater between 1458 and 1464 than before. 'Although Cosimo is practically Signore of the town, he behaves in such a way as to appear a private citizen, and prefers facts to appearances', writes Pius elsewhere.[4] Cosimo liked to emphasize his private status at Florence when this was convenient to him: thus in reply to Pius's request, in 1463, that he should see to it that Florence contributed to the crusade, he pointed out that the Pope knew very well 'quid in libera et populari republica possit privatus civis'.[5] A ruler like Pius II might consider this to be not more

---

[1] Tratte, 17 (20 and 29 Dec. 1459, 19 April and 17 Dec. 1463). On 31 Jan. 1464, on the other hand, when they carried out their final *reductiones*, they met again in the Palace of the Signoria. See also above, p. 124.

[2] *Commentarii* (Rome, 1584), p. 89; 'consilium de republica domi suae agitari'.

[3] Ibid.: 'qui potentiam Cosmae ferendam negarent'.

[4] 'De viris aetate sua claris', in Pius II, *Orationes politicae et ecclesiasticae*, ed. J. D. Mansi, iii, Appendix (Lucca, 1759), p. 169: 'Sed Cosmus quamquam Dominus civitatis exstat, ita tamen se gerit, ut privatus videatur, et esse potius quam videri vult.' This work was composed between 1444 and 1450: C. M. Ady, *Pius II* (London, 1913), p. 293. Cf. Jacopo Ammanati, 'Commentarii', in Pius II, *Commentarii* (Frankfurt, 1614), p. 379: 'obtinuerat in civitate Florentina principatum annos prope triginta Cosmus . . .'.

[5] Fabroni, *Cosmi vita*, ii, pp. 242–3 (3 Nov. 1463), 245.

than an empty excuse. It was nevertheless quite true that Cosimo's authority in Florence was of an entirely different kind from that of a despot. Cosimo's outburst, on another occasion, when hearing of Francesco Sforza's dissatisfaction over a refusal of financial help, shows genuine exasperation at such sweeping simplifications: 'a republic cannot be run in the same way as a despotic régime.'[1] There was probably some wishful thinking in the attitude of Italian rulers to Cosimo. Francesco Sforza, for one, would doubtless have preferred dealing with a Florentine despot whose interests were closely linked to his own, to negotiating with a republic whose policy might change overnight with a change of government, and whose proceedings were necessarily far less secret.[2] His envoys were perhaps not always above exaggerating Cosimo's influence in order to please their master and vindicate his policy. Even so, some of their observations on Cosimo's position in Florence reflect, by their vagueness and ambiguity, the difficulties in assessing it correctly. Thus when Nicodemo da Pontremoli writes, in July 1458, that Cosimo *guida tuto*,[3] he clearly refers to the decisions of the leading citizens of the régime. In 1464, he states that 'sine ipso factum est nihil'.[4] Here too, the precise nature of Cosimo's influence remains undefined.

Vespasiano da Bisticci did not have, like the Milanese orator, access to secrets of state; but he had the Florentine's sense of the possibilities and limitations of Florentine politics, besides possessing many friends among the ruling class. Cosimo, he says in his *Lives*, 'knew how difficult it was to exercise political power (*tenere uno stato*) as he had done, owing to the opposition of so many great citizens who in former times had been his equals. He acted with the greatest skill to preserve his power; and whenever he wished to achieve something, he saw to it, in order to escape envy as much as possible, that the initiative appeared to come from others and not from him'.[5] This indirect approach seems

[1] Nicodemo to Francesco Sforza, 13 June 1462, Bibl. Nat., MS. ital. 1589, fol. 61ʳ: 'El non se pò governare un populo como se governa un particulare signore.'

[2] Nicodemo to Francesco Sforza, ibid., 1588, fol. 10ᵛ (9 Jan. 1458): 'li stati populari non se sano nè possono governare cum quella discretione et secreto che se converia. . . .'

[3] Ibid., fol. 94ʳ (15 July 1458).

[4] Ibid., 1590, fol. 262ʳ (2 July 1464).

[5] *Vite di uomini illustri del secolo XV*, ed. P. d'Ancona and E. Aeschlimann (Milan, 1951), p. 417: 'conosceva la difficultà ch'era a tenere uno stato, come aveva tenuto lui, avendo tante opposizioni di cittadini potenti nella città, trovatisi grandi come lui in altri tempi. Usocci drento una grandissima arte, a potersi conservare; e in tutte le cose che voleva, sempre procurava, paressi ch'elle procedessino da altri e non da lui proprio per fuggire la invidia quanto poteva.'

to have increased during the last ten years of his life. Between 1434 and 1455 he had often held high office, but not more often than some other leading citizens of the régime. He had been three times Gonfalonier of Justice, in 1435, 1439, and 1445,[1] and seven times of the *Dieci di Balìa*.[2] But he had only once been *Accoppiatore*, from October 1440 to February 1441, in place of his brother who had died in office, and only twice one of the Eight, from March to July 1445, and from May to July 1449—probably he did not wish to be personally too closely connected with these two key instruments of Medici power.[3] While his membership of the Ten reflects his role in Florentine diplomacy, his long terms of office as one of the *Ufficiali del Monte*, from 1445 to 1448, and from 1453 to 1455, bear out his influence on financial policy.[4] He belonged to the *Balìe* of 1438, 1444, and 1452,[5] and frequently spoke in *Pratiche*, often as spokesman of special committees.[6] But from 1455 onwards, Cosimo not only ceased to hold high office; his name also disappears from the minutes of the meetings of the *Pratiche*, although he still belonged to the *Balìa* of 1458.[7] His illness was doubtless to a large extent responsible for this withdrawal from official public service; already in 1450, he had declined a fourth election to the Gonfaloniership on grounds of illness;[8] and in 1453, he was relieved of an office in the financial administration because 'adeo est impeditus et infirmitate detentus, quod non posset attendere ad ea que sunt opportuna pro dicto officio'.[9] His advancing age—he was sixty-five in 1454—was doubtless an additional reason. However, his gout and age

---

[1] During the same period, Domenico di Lionardo Buoninsegni was three times, Bernardo di Bartolomeo Gherardi and Manno di Giovanni di Temperano Manni were four times Gonfalonier of Justice. Luca Pitti was three times Gonfalonier between 1448 and 1458, and Ugolino di Niccolò Martelli between 1449 and 1458. Bernardo Gherardi was again Gonfalonier in 1459.

[2] Tratte, 80, fols. 441ʳ⁻ᵛ, 454ʳ⁻ᵛ. See also *Delizie*, xiv, pp. 302–7.

[3] See above, p. 32, and Appendix, no. I. For the Eight, Tratte, 80, fols. 17ᵛ, 18ᵛ. In 1445 he had been elected by the *Balìa* for six months, but had to resign on 25 July on account of being appointed to the *Ufficiali del Monte*.

[4] Tratte, 80, fols. 393ᵛ–394ʳ.   [5] See Appendix, nos. III–V.

[6] Cons. e Prat., 50–53. The year 1447 may serve as an example. In this year, Cosimo appears fourteen times in the minutes of the *Pratiche* (ibid., 52), including eight times as spokesman. After 1454, the Medici were 'represented' mainly by his son Giovanni, and his distant cousin Bernardo di Alamanno. Piero di Cosimo appears occasionally, Orlando di Guccio de' Medici frequently (ibid., 53).

[7] See Appendix, no. VI.

[8] Signori e Collegi, Deliberazioni, speciale autorità, 29, fol. 81ᵛ (29 April 1450). On Cosimo's medical history, see G. Pieraccini, *La stirpe de' Medici di Cafaggiolo* (Florence, 1924), i, pp. 28 ff.

[9] Balìe, 27, fol. 109ʳ⁻ᵛ (5 March 1453). The office is that of 'exgravium distributionis oneris'.

might also have served as pretexts. Was it mere coincidence that his withdrawal from official service in government and administration coincides with the setbacks the régime suffered after the conclusion of the peace of Lodi?[1] In November 1456 he told the Milanese ambassador that he would like to retire from public affairs;[2] and in April 1458 Nicodemo reported that Cosimo could no longer be constantly in the Palace of the Signoria, 'e fare como solia', although if he so wanted he could still determine matters, and 'faràlo meglio che may'.[3] But in a moment of supreme crisis the *Pratica* of July–August of that year sought his final decision *in absentia*, not however without indicating which way they wished it to go.[4] After August 1458 his political action seems to have mainly centred in his palace in the Via Larga.[5] No minutes exist of the discussions that took place there, and none may ever have existed; and in the virtual absence of direct evidence on this subject, it is difficult properly to assess the amount of political control Cosimo exercised after the successful consolidation of the régime. But up to 1454 the numerous meetings of *Pratiche* in which he took an active part allow us an insight into his position among the leading citizens of the régime.

The minutes of the *Pratiche* are our fullest documentation on the political views of the Florentine ruling set. Although Cosimo certainly did not need to be present in the meetings to make his influence felt, the differences of opinion we often find in the debates should serve as a warning not to exaggerate the extent of such indirect influence. The debate, in December 1446, on the question of whether the *borse* should be closed, may illustrate this point.[6] Cosimo follows on a number of speakers most of whom are in favour of restoring election by lot of the Signoria, and he agrees, with some reservations, provided that 'principes civitatis in hoc concordes essent'. However, the majority of the subsequent speakers do not accept Cosimo's advice; only at the

---

[1] See above, p. 22.

[2] Nicodemo da Pontremoli to Francesco Sforza, 15 Nov. 1456, ASM, Pot. est., Firenze, 268: 'Confortolo a credere a li amici e servitori soy, e non se abandonare etc. Loy desideria el posare; ma se vorà in tuto posare, gli s'erano furate le mosse; e se non fosse l'ombra vostra, gli seria cercato fare la bucca cum altra presteza e efficacia che non si fa. . . .'

[3] Nicodemo to Francesco Sforza, 4 April 1458, Bibl. Nat., MS. ital. 1588, fol. 50ᵛ: 'Et non pò Cosimo continuamente essere in palazo, e fare como solia. Ma quando direte, egli è da far cossì, so che'l potrà e saperà fare, e faràlo meglio che may.' See also above, p. 91, n. 4.

[4] See above, p. 102.   [5] See above, p. 128.

[6] Cons. e Prat., 52, fols. 1ʳ–4ᵛ; see above, pp. 23–25.

next meeting do most, though not all, of these come round to it. Four days later, Cosimo and Otto Niccolini report the conclusion of the committee of ten to the effect that elections should remain *a mano*, and now the vast majority approves, although there are again dissenting voices. Some speakers do so because the committee had recommended it, and one, 'cum videret primores civitatis' to be of this opinion. In matters of policy, Cosimo's influence was perhaps most effective in the field of foreign policy, where his diplomatic successes and outstanding reputation had given him a position of great authority. The most serious challenge to his influence in this field occurred after 1446 over the question of the alliance with Francesco Sforza, and the consequent realignment against Venice.[1] His success in making his policy prevail in Florence against strong opposition may have helped more than any other event after 1434 to strengthen his prestige at home and abroad. Also in matters of internal policy Cosimo did not always see eye to eye with the other leading citizens of the régime. In January 1458 he alone among the *ottimati* was not up in arms against the new *catasto*, with the result that he gained much popularity among the lower classes.[2] Later in the year, during the critical weeks before the *Parlamento*, he seems to have been more moderate in his views than some of his friends: as late as 1 August the Milanese orator writes that Cosimo behaves as 'in vista quasi neutrale'.[3] Francesco Sforza's support stood the régime in good stead during those dramatic days: 'se aiutano principalmente cum la spada vostra', writes Nicodemo to the Duke on 5 August;[4] and Cosimo could command the Duke's friendship and loyalty more than anyone else in Florence.[5] This doubtless helped in rallying the leading citizens around Cosimo, and in discouraging waverers. Two events during those early August days spotlight the situation: the citizens flocking to Cosimo's palace to protest their allegiance to the régime, 'in modo che pare habia la sagra a

---

[1] See B. Buser, *Die Beziehungen der Mediceer zu Frankreich während der Jahre 1434—1494...* (Leipzig, 1879), pp. 21 ff.; Gutkind, *Cosimo de' Medici*, pp. 154–60. Diplomacy is considered here only in so far as it affected domestic policy.

[2] Nicodemo da Pontremoli to Francesco Sforza, 9 Jan. 1458, Bibl. Nat., MS. ital. 1588, fol. 10ᵛ: the *Dieci* were trying to push it through 'contro la voglia di tuti li richi, da Cosimo in fora, che se ne porta cum summa modestia...'. The same to the same, 9 Feb. 1458, ASM, Pot. est., Firenze, 269: 'Cosimo... de questo catasto ha facto grandissimo acquisto presso al populo minuto.' See also above, p. 89.

[3] To Francesco Sforza, Bibl. Nat., MS. ital. cit., fol. 109ʳ. See above, p. 102.

[4] Ibid., fol. 114ʳ.

[5] Ibid., fol. 109ʳ (1 Aug. 1458): '... infinite fiate me habiate comandato che sempre e in omne caso obedisca Cosimo non altramente che vostro padre....'

casa',[1] and his lonely watch at home on the day of the *Parlamento*, alone with his soldiers—and with the Milanese ambassador.[2]

The events of July and August 1458 throw into relief the problems of the position not only of Cosimo, but also of the other leading citizens of the régime. The Medici 'party' was, like the Albizzi faction before 1434, a loosely-knit group, by no means always completely united, subject to personal tensions and rivalries, and not necessarily committed to following consistently the leadership of Cosimo, or indeed of any single citizen. The debates in December 1446, as well as those of July 1458, show that they could be divided on such fundamental issues as that of electoral controls. At the same time, the *cittadini principali* appear to have been fully aware how damaging internal disunity could be to their status, and to the régime in general. There is no single theme which occurs more often in the discussions of July 1458 than the need of unity, or at least of a show of unity, in order to present the image of a united régime to the people of Florence.[3] Cosimo may have derived as much influence from his ability to bridge differences among the *uomini principali* as from any effective leadership of them.

The *uomini principali* of the régime formed the inner circle of the *uomini del reggimento* or *uomini dello stato*. We find them in the *Balìe*, among the *veduti* and *seduti*, and as regular members of the *Pratiche*. The composition of the unusually large *Pratica* summoned by Luca Pitti on 2 July 1458 to discuss the critical situation of the régime is particularly enlightening on the subject of their personalities, since it was clearly intended to provide conditions for a full-scale debate. It does not come as a surprise to find that three-quarters of them had belonged to Medicean *Balìe*.[4] The inner core of the *uomini principali* was formed by the *più principali*;[5] it was this group which Cosimo must have had in mind when, in December 1446, he talked about *principes civitatis*, and which, in July 1458, Girolamo Machiavelli described as *cives praecipue regimen habentes*.[6] But contemporaries were not

---

[1] Ibid., fol. 114ʳ (5 Aug.).

[2] Ibid., fol. 117ʳ (11 Aug.). See above, p. 104, n. 1.

[3] See above, pp. 92 ff.

[4] Cons. e Prat., 55, fols. 27ʳ–28ᵛ.

[5] Thus, when the question of the closing of the *borse* was debated in 1449, it was proposed to summon forty citizens 'de' più principali del reggimento' (ibid., 52, fol. 75ʳ; 27 March 1449).

[6] See above, pp. 24 and 94, n. 6.

always consistent in their social terminology. In April 1462 Nicodemo da Pontremoli reports that Cosimo had called to his house the *cittadini principali*, and names Agnolo Acciaiuoli, Luca Pitti, Giovanni Bartoli, Luigi Ridolfi, Francesco Ventura, Otto Niccolini, Bernardo d'Alamanno de' Medici, and Tommaso Soderini.[1] These, then, were the citizens who at the time could be considered as forming an innermost circle around Cosimo. All but one of them were *Accoppiatori*.[2] It was through such friendships and loyalties that the key controls of the régime could become instruments of Cosimo's personal power. Whether Cosimo regularly determined, when its election was carried out *a mano*, the composition of the Signoria, is another matter. It might be more to the point to regard, in general terms, the *Accoppiatori* as 'representative' of the inner circle of the régime, and the *Balìe* of the larger group of *uomini del reggimento*.

It would have been surprising, in a society like that of Florence, if the loosely-knit group of leading citizens had not been subject to tensions and rivalries. We have pointed to the differences over general issues such as the alliance with Milan and the problem of electoral controls. Personal tensions among the most prominent figures of the régime could also tie up with the question of its 'leadership'. If such antagonism existed, in the early years of the régime, between Cosimo and Neri di Gino Capponi,[3] in later years Cosimo did not always see eye to eye with Luca Pitti,[4] although this never seems to have impaired their friendship. However, in the last years of his life, two of his closest collaborators drifted away from him. In August 1463, Agnolo Acciaiuoli was trying to replace Cosimo in Francesco Sforza's diplomatic relationship with Florence; in the same month, Nicodemo da Pontremoli described Dietisalvi as Cosimo's greatest and most ambitious enemy.[5] Cosimo was an old and sick man, and his death might be imminent.[6] It was perhaps understandable that leading *cittadini principali* should, in the event of his death, consider the friendship of the Duke of Milan essential for their

---

[1] Bibl. Nat., MS. ital. 1589, fol. 55ʳ (4 April 1462).

[2] The exception was Bernardo de' Medici. See Appendix, no. I.

[3] Although Cavalcanti doubtless exaggerates it: *Istorie fiorentine*, ii, pp. 159 ff.

[4] See e.g. Gutkind, *Cosimo de' Medici*, p. 164.

[5] Nicodemo da Pontremoli to Francesco Sforza, 25 Aug. 1463, Bibl. Nat. MS. ital. cit., fol. 196ʳ; 17 Aug. 1463, ibid., fol. 190ʳ: 'Cosimo e li soy non hanno quì maiore nè più ambitioso inimico che Dietisalvi.' Agnolo Acciaiuoli had been for many years in Francesco Sforza's service; in Bibl. Ambros., Z. 247 sup., there is a list of payments made to him by the ducal treasury between 1453 and 1460 (fols. 355ʳ–366ᵛ).

[6] See Pieraccini, *La stirpe de' Medici*, i, p. 30.

own position in Florence. In this they were, after all, only following in Cosimo's footsteps.

According to a contemporary diarist, Carlo Gondi, the tensions during the last years of Cosimo's life went beyond the level of a few personal rivalries. On his return from Arezzo at the beginning of 1462, Carlo found the situation in Florence so disturbed that citizens had begun to form *intelligenze*, one of these political groups having been created by Luca Pitti at the behest of Piero de' Medici.[1] Yet there was no reason why Cosimo's death, which occurred on 1 August 1464, should seriously affect the continuity of the régime itself. For six years it had now been firmly based on the reforms of 1458. The *Cento* was a permanent institution, and the *Accoppiatori* were in charge of electing the Signoria *a mano* until 1468. The chief problem which Cosimo's death created for the régime was that of his 'succession'. Would his son Piero inherit, together with his wealth, his position in the state? And if so, would he be able to command the united support of the *uomini principali*?

[1] Extracts from his *Ricordanze* in Corbinelli, *Histoire généalogique*, i, Preuves, p. cxcvii. Carlo Gondi had been appointed Captain of Arezzo on 30 May 1461; his successor's name was drawn on 5 Dec. 1461 (Tratte, 305).

PART II

Piero di Cosimo: Republican Reaction and Medicean Restoration

PALLA STROZZI, when asked by Girolamo Machiavelli to join, together with other exiles, in a conspiracy against Cosimo, had declined on the ground that as long as Cosimo was alive, it was impossible to get rid of him; once he was dead, within a few days conditions would develop according to their wishes.[1] The veteran exile had been away from Florence too long to assess the situation correctly. The crisis which he had prophesied developed only gradually over the next two years. After Cosimo's death, Piero's position seemed secure enough. 'Since he died', wrote a Florentine citizen, on 15 September 1464, to his exiled brother-in-law, 'things continue smoothly, and I believe that those in power will remain so. May God keep them united.'[2] The unity of the régime was to prove at least as important a problem as that of Piero's 'succession'.

The situation was complicated by the fact that criticism of Cosimo during the last years of his life had also been extended to Piero. The month before Cosimo's death, Agnolo Acciaiuoli had called both of them *huomini freddi* 'whom illness and old age have reduced to such cowardice that they avoid anything that might cause them trouble or worry'.[3] It was unlikely that a man like Agnolo Acciaiuoli, who had lately been so critical of Cosimo[4] and Piero, should now accept Piero's ascendancy unquestioningly. The more so as, after Cosimo's death, he was considered

---

[1] Nicodemo da Pontremoli to Francesco Sforza, 6 July 1460 (ASM, Pot. est., Firenze, 270): 'diceva erano rasonamenti e pensieri vani, perhochè vivendo Cosimo gli pareva impossibile de smeterlo, ma morto lui la cosa per se medesima se adapteria in pochi dì al bixogno e desiderio loro. . .'.

[2] Giovanni Bonsi to Filippo Strozzi, 15 Sept. 1464, in Alessandra Macinghi-Strozzi, *Lettere*, p. 327.

[3] To Francesco Sforza, 12 July 1464 (ASM, Pot. est., Firenze, 271): 'huomini freddi come è Cosimo e Piero, e quali e dalle infirmità e dall'età sono tanto inviliti che fugono ogni cosa che habbi arrecare loro fatica o cura d'animo'. In another letter of the same date he makes this point even more strongly (Bibl. Ambros., Z. 247 sup.): 'sono più vili de' conigli, e per l'essere infermi, e per non dispiacere a qualchuno'.

[4] See also above, p. 134.

one of the three most powerful citizens beside Piero, the other two being Luca Pitti and Dietisalvi Neroni.[1] The way these men visualized their relations with Piero is strikingly revealed in a letter Dietisalvi wrote to Francesco Sforza a week after Cosimo's death. 'While Cosimo was alive, decisions were left to him; now those who remain at the head of the régime [are] Piero and a number of citizens supporting him, who were brothers to Cosimo and who will now be fathers to Piero.'[2] It remained to be seen whether Piero would be satisfied with this role.

The pattern of power within the régime was further complicated by the relations of Florentine citizens with the Duke of Milan. Already during the last years of Cosimo's life, Milanese reliance on him as the principal instrument in Florence of Sforza diplomacy had been liable to be affected by the Duke's friendship with other leading citizens. Agnolo Acciaiuoli, who had been in his service during several years, enjoyed his favour in particular.[3] On 1 August, before learning of Cosimo's death, Francesco Sforza especially instructed his ambassador in Florence to consult with Agnolo on everything.[4] At that moment the Duke seemed almost to have been more concerned with the unity of the régime than with the personal ascendancy of Piero. While ordering Nicodemo to treat Agnolo with all due respect, he called upon the latter to collaborate with Piero and his friends.[5] As late as November 1465, he advised Piero to act with the restraint and humanity of his father, and, while trying to acquire new friends, to temporize towards his enemies.[6]

[1] Alessandra Macinghi-Strozzi to Filippo Strozzi, 13 Dec. 1464 (*Lettere*, p. 334): 'e principali sono e quattro di sopra'.

[2] 8 Aug. 1464 (Bibl. Ambros., Z. 247 sup.): 'dove in vita di Chosimo si lasciava il pensiero a llui, hora questi che rimanghono nel ghoverno dello stato, che è Piero chol favore di parechi cittadini i quali erano fratelli ad Cosimo, ora hanno ad essere padri ad Piero'.

[3] Cf. Vespasiano da Bisticci, *Vite*, p. 493: 'Avendo avuto il duca Francesco Milano. . ., volle ch'egli andassi a stare a Milano, dove istette col duca Francesco, con grandissima provisione e molto onorato'. See above, p. 134. The Duke protected him at Florence against his critics and enemies, including the Milanese ambassador: see next note.

[4] Nicodemo da Pontremoli to Francesco Sforza, 6 Aug. 1464 (Bibl. Nat., MS. ital. 1590, fol. 328r), reply to letter of 1 Aug. ordering Nicodemo 'ch'io participi tucto cum M. Angelo e ch'io l'honori e reguardi &c'. Nicodemo adds that Angelo 'essi messo a gran pericolo; solo el vostro mantello l'ha aiutato, e so ne certo, e hoglelo aiutato a ssectare adosso. . .'.

[5] Agnolo Acciaiuoli to Cicco Simonetta, 14 Aug. 1464 (Bibl. Ambros., loc. cit.): 'Io ho inteso lo scrivere vostro, e quello mi dite del parere vostro, e del volere del Signore del intendermi con Piero e con sua amici. Farò e comandamenti della Signoria Sua come m'è debito. . . .'

[6] 27 Nov. 1465; ed. A. Municchi, *La fazione antimedicea detta del Poggio* (Florence, 1911), App., doc. 1. The letter deals with developments after Cosimo's death, and shows the line

Piero's position was, at first, strengthened by the support he received from Luca Pitti. There was, after Cosimo's death, no citizen to whom the régime owed more than to Luca, and none who had, next to Piero, a stronger claim to leadership. A contemporary diarist says that in accordance with Piero's wishes, Luca Pitti had created a political group (*intelligenza*), to which belonged 'the flower of Florence'.[1] The principal obstacle to lasting unity in the régime was Agnolo Acciaiuoli, despite his protestations to the contrary. 'They believe that my attitude has changed', he writes to Francesco Sforza on 23 April 1465, 'but this is not true. What is true is that I am no longer as keen to agree with them.' He had followed the Duke's advice and had kept peace with Piero, 'who is honoured as his father had been and is in no danger whatsoever'; but Piero is a sick man and may become unable to cope with all his work and worries.[2] To what extent such personal tensions could affect the political situation depended upon the loyalty and co-operation of the leading citizens. Agnolo Acciaiuoli was one of the five *Accoppiatori* in charge of elections *a mano* in 1464–5,[3] and could consequently influence the composition of the Signoria during that period. Nor was this the only trouble a hostile *Accoppiatore* could cause Piero, as Carlo Gondi's diary vividly illustrates.[4] Agnolo, to whom Carlo Gondi had in the past rendered certain services, was determined to use this opportunity to make him a *veduto* Gonfalonier of Justice.[5] Carlo was greatly pleased when he heard about this, the more so as he had just been made Signore for January and February 1465, again without asking for it. Although Piero, who was one of the *Accoppiatori*, was not in charge during that year, he went to him to thank him for his election. 'We have elected you to suit us rather than you,' replied Piero, but Carlo too would get

of action which Francesco Sforza wished Piero to adopt to preserve the régime. There is no question of his advising Piero to aim at despotic rule. In this respect his policy contrasts with that of his son Galeazzo Maria towards Lorenzo, after Piero's death. See below, p. 180, n. 3.

[1] Carlo Gondi, *Ricordanze*, in Corbinelli, op. cit., p. cxcvii.

[2] 23 April 1465 (ASM, Pot. est., Firenze, 272): 'non pare loro che la mente mia sia qual la soleva; e questo è falso. È bene vero ch'io non mecto il tempo come solevo a seguire e pensieri loro. . . Piero è honorato in questa città quale era il padre, nè è in alcuno periculo e sono certo che non c'è huomo che habbi intellecto che pensi diminuirgli uno iota di reputatione. Dubito bene parlando con la S. V. come posso, che per la infirmità lui medesimo non invilisca in tale fatica e in tanta cura. . . .'

[3] i.e. of the group of five (*quinquina*) in office for 6 elections, from Aug. to the following June; see above, p. 105. Giovanni Bonsi to Filippo Strozzi, 15 Sept. 1464 (in Macinghi-Strozzi, *Lettere*, pp. 327–8), gives the names.

[4] Op. cit., pp. cxcvii ff.   [5] See above, p. 126.

something out of it by being *veduto* Gonfalonier in the near future. The last election during Agnolo's term of office took place on 28 June; but by June, the situation in Florence had changed for the worse; and thus, 'considering that the great division between Piero di Cosimo and those other *cittadini principali* had already begun, I decided to go and tell him what Messer Agnolo Acciaiuoli had said to me'. This he did on the 11th; but when Piero heard him mention Agnolo's name, he became agitated, sent away his company, and had the doors locked; and when he learned what Agnolo had told Carlo Gondi, he complained bitterly about the former. 'When I saw that he had blown off steam, I said how sorry I was to have caused him trouble; but that now I would tell Messer Agnolo not to meddle any longer in my affairs, &c. To which he replied that he did not want me to do this.' In the end, Carlo was *veduto* on the 28th, though not without difficulty, 'la quale cosa m'arecò grande onore, ma fu con grande invidia'.[1]

It would be a mistake to accept at its face value the official version of the events of the following year, according to which the rift in the régime was confined to a few citizens who opposed Piero's power.[2] On 15 September 1464, Alessandra Macinghi-Strozzi writes that as a result of Cosimo's death a number of citizens were having 'tra loro nuovi pensieri del governo della terra'.[3] The economic situation may have contributed to this. Piero's decision, after his father's death, to carry out a general revision of the bank's accounts and to avoid new business transactions for some time, may have been one of the causes of the series of bankruptcies which began in November 1464.[4] At any rate, it

---

[1] Op. cit., pp. cxcviii–cxcix: '. . . e andando io a Piero di Cosimo a ringraziarlo mi disse: Noi t'abiam fatto più per nostro commodo, che per tuo, ma e' sarà anche commodo a te, perchè, innanzi che tu esca del divieto, tu sarai veduto Gonfaloniere. . . E venendo presso alla tratta, e considerato io che di già era cominciato gran dissensione tra Piero di Cosimo e questi altri cittadini principali, diliberai andare da Piero di Cosimo, e digli quello m'aveva detto Messer Agnolo Acciaiuoli, e così fu. . . il quale, come lui sentì nominarmi Messer Agnolo, si turbò, e dette licenza a ogni persona. . . e partito fu ognuno, fè serrare la camera. . . e restammovi lui ed io. E avendo inteso quello avevo detto di Messer Agnolo lui vi cominciò a entrare, dicendomi molte doglienze di lui, e anche d'altri cittadini de' principali. . . e finalmente quando io vidi, che lui s'era sfogato, ripigliai le parole, e dissigli, che mi sapeva male avergli dato scandolo, ma che da ora io direi a Messer Agnolo, che di ciò non sene impacciasse per me, &c. A che lui mi rispuose, che non voleva facessi così, ma che seguitassi. . . Il perchè, quando venne il tempo della tratta, furono alla disputa, e fuvi gara e non piccola, e pure in fine s'accordorono fossi veduto Giovanni di Pagolo Rucellai ed io, la quale cosa m'arecò grande onore, ma fu con grande invidia, come si dirà. . . .'

[2] See below, p. 158.   [3] *Lettere*, p. 323.

[4] Piero de' Medici to Francesco Sforza, 21 Aug. 1464 (Bibl. Ambros., Z. 247 sup.): 'mi sono tutto rivoltato a rassettare le cose nostre et intendere quanto si può di conservarle; et

can hardly have helped to improve his position in Florence. It was characteristic of Agnolo Acciaiuoli's attitude to assert that no greater crisis had occurred in Florence for over 100 years;[1] but his view may have been shared by others.

Events in June 1465 reveal the extent of the rift in the régime which had developed by that time. The special powers that had been granted to the *Otto di Guardia* in August 1458 for two years had been extended by five years in June 1460.[2] These five years were now up, and a further extension for the same period was proposed by the Signoria, but rejected by the council of *Cento*, which is the more surprising as that council had been in charge of electing the Eight from 1459 onwards.[3] After 1458, the *Cento* was one of the institutional cornerstones of the régime; it now emerged that it could not always be trusted to back Medicean policy. The *Cento*'s opposition to the bill also shows that the division within the régime had begun to affect its security. The new ideas on government, the 'nuovi pensieri del governo della terra', of which Alessandra Macinghi-Strozzi had written in September 1464, were evidently beginning to bear fruit. At the same time, Agnolo Acciaiuoli, whose opposition to Piero seems to have hitherto been mainly on personal grounds, appears as an exponent of a liberalization of government. While Piero informed the *Pratica* of 1 June of his desire to renew the special powers of the Eight for another five years, Agnolo opposed this: 'baliam esse mortem civitatum.'[4] Agnolo Acciaiuoli had, in 1458, supported the restoration of controls, as well as the use of the *Parlamento* to bring this about:[5] but as he had pointed out in his letter of 23 April, he was no longer prepared to follow Medicean policy all

per fare questo ho fatto quello che sempre in simil casi anno fatto i miei progenitori, scritto a tutti i luoghi dove abbiamo affare, che per certo tempo non interprendino cose alcune. . . .' Nicodemo had written already before Cosimo's death (to Francesco Sforza, 29 July 1464; ASM, Pot. est., Firenze, 271) that 'Piero sospenderà el murare tucto per uno anno, e forse li trafichi'. Cf. R. de Roover, *The Rise and Decline of the Medici Bank, 1397–1494* (Cambridge, Mass., 1963), p. 360.

[1] To Filippo Strozzi, 22 Dec. 1464 (in *Lettere*, p. 350); on the bankruptcies, cf. also Alessandra Macinghi-Strozzi to the same, 3 Jan. 1465, ibid., p. 342, and Rinuccini, pp. xciv–xcv. I have found no evidence for Machiavelli's story (*Storie fiorentine*, vii, 10) that Dietisalvi persuaded Piero, in order to undermine his popularity, to call in loans. It seems, incidentally, to be the source of H. Sieveking's statement ('Die Handlungsbücher der Medici', *Sitzungsber. Akad. Vienna, Phil.-hist. Kl.*, cli (1905), p. 65) that Piero 'forderte in nichtpolitischer Genauigkeit die Rechnungen des Hauses ein'.

[2] See above, pp. 111, 121.

[3] Libri Fabarum, 67, fols. 233ʳ–235ʳ (8, 9, 10, 14, and 15 June). See above, p. 114.

[4] Cons. e Prat., 57, fols. 12ᵛ (1 June), 15ʳ (12 June).

[5] Cons. e Prat., 55, fol. 62ᵛ (1 Aug. 1458); fol. 73ʳ (17 Aug. 1458): 'postquam et balia remota est et burse clause sunt, sicut poscebat populus, omnia in deterius lapsa sunt.'

the way; whether he was quite sincere in asserting that he had really never changed his views was a different matter. But it is true that both in 1446 and 1455 he had been in favour of closing the *borse*.[1] One must not expect too much consistency from Florentine politicians. On the other hand, changes of opinion need not necessarily be due to personal interest, but could also be determined by changed assessments of the political situation.

The debate on the *Otto* was resumed in the *Pratica* at the beginning of September.[2] It was pointed out by one of the Eight that their present powers were hardly sufficient to ensure the safety of the city; Agnolo Acciaiuoli retorted that they did not require special powers for this purpose.[3] But a few days later, the *Pratica* began to discuss much wider issues. On 5 September, Dietisalvi Neroni had written to Francesco Sforza that 'la cittadinanza vorrebbe più libertà et più universale governo, come si conviene nelle città popolari come è la nostra'.[4] On 10 September, Manno Temperani, a veteran supporter of the régime and, like Dietisalvi, one of the *Accoppiatori*, opened the debate of the *Pratica* with the statement that the immediate reason for the failure of the *Otto* bill was the unpopularity of the term *balìa*. But the roots of the difficulties went deeper: the people had lost its freedom: 'in paucorum animis positam esse omnem potestatem, et in eorum arbitrio omnia gubernari'.[5] The cause has to be sought in the powers of the *Accoppiatori* who, by electing *a mano*, 'omnia habere in sua potestate'; the present officials should be allowed to resign from their office. Other *Accoppiatori* in the *Pratica* of 10 September were in favour of closing the *borse* altogether. On the 11th, Manno Temperani agreed, although somewhat reluctantly, to this proposal, and so did two other *Accoppiatori*, Otto Niccolini and Tommaso Soderini, who on the 10th had opposed it.[6] Agnolo Acciaiuoli was not present in the *Pratica*,

---

[1] Cons. e Prat., 52, fol. 1ʳ (6 Dec. 1446); 53, fols. 155ᵛ–157ʳ (22 Feb. 1455).

[2] Ibid., 58, fols. 22ᵛ–24ᵛ (4 Sept.).

[3] 4 Sept.: ibid., fols. 22ᵛ, 23ʳ (Luigi Guicciardini, Agnolo Acciaiuoli).

[4] Bibl. Ambros., Z. 247 sup.

[5] Op. cit., fol. 28ᵛ. Manno Temperani had been *Accoppiatore* in 1444–9, 1452–5, and from 1458 onwards. He had belonged to the *Balìe* of 1434, 1444, 1452, and 1458.

[6] Ibid., fols. 29ʳ–33ᵛ (10 and 11 Sept.). The other *Accoppiatori* who spoke were Dietisalvi Neroni, Luigi Guicciardini, Giovanni Bartoli, Luca Pitti, Agnolo della Stufa, and Matteo Palmieri. Otto Niccolini, like Tommaso Soderini a staunch Medicean, had pointed out, on the 10th, that he remembered 'antequam marsupia haberentur manibus, multam fuisse civium discordiam. Hec mala non habere originem a marsupiis . . .' (fol. 29ᵛ). In the second meeting of the *Pratica* on 11 Sept., Manno Temperani could state that all its members had now agreed 'sortes emittendas esse manibus' (fol. 32ᵛ).

but was certainly of the same opinion. We seem to be back in February 1455, when the *Accoppiatori* had advised the closing of the *borse*. As in 1455, they were doubtless influenced by considerations of expediency rather than of principle. It emerges from the debate that both electoral controls and *Accoppiatori* had become so unpopular that nothing short of their removal might be sufficient: 'palam in foro et curia, in coronis et circulis cives omnes libertatem sortium desiderent', said one of them.[1] Another 'not only advised, but prayed that the purses be closed, since this matter had begun to be hateful to the people'.[2] He hoped in this way to facilitate the passage of a new tax bill which was being discussed in those days,[3] and other speakers shared this view. For precisely the same reasons, the restoration of sortition had been advised in 1455.[4] This combination of political concessions with financial legislation provides further evidence for the unpopularity of electoral controls, which was abundantly confirmed by the large majorities by which, on 16–18 September, the councils passed the bill restoring elections by lot of the Signoria.[5] Even the *Cento* passed it by 90 against 20 votes; in the council of the People it obtained 175 against 19, in that of the Commune 146 against 6 votes.[6] These large majorities are strikingly similar to those by which, ten years earlier, elections *a mano* had been abolished for the last time.[7] They are the more impressive as the bill also contained the imposition of a tax of three *catasti*.[8] The *Accoppiatori*[9] were to close the purses within one month. Agnolo Acciaiuoli wrote on 21 October that they had put back into the purses the names of nearly all those citizens who had been made eligible from 1434 onwards, in other words, of those who had

---

[1] Giovanni Bartoli, 10 Sept. (fol. 30^r).

[2] Agnolo della Stufa, 10 Sept. (fol. 30^v): 'claudi marsupia non solum censuit sed oravit . . . cum ea res populo odio esse cepit.'

[3] '. . . quod si fiat, cetera omnia et de provisione expensarum et ceteris de rebus que utilitatem rei p. [spectent], facillima reddi . . .' (ibid.).

[4] Above, p. 28.

[5] Provv., 156, fols. 148^v–149^v.

[6] Libri Fabarum, 68, fol. 11^{r-v}. In the case of the *Cento*, it will be remembered that it had refused, in June, to extend the full powers of the Eight (see above, p. 140); the present voting returns are particularly interesting in view of the fact that in the meantime its personnel had been changed for the second half-yearly session of 1465.

[7] On that occasion the voting had been 218 to 22 in the council of the People, and 169 to 7 in that of the Commune; above, p. 29.

[8] Loc. cit., fol. 151^r.

[9] That is, all the *Accoppiatori*, and not only the five in office for the two-monthly elections: the regulation of the law of 11 Aug. to this effect was now operative (Balìe, 29, fol. 9^r: 'finitis dictis quinque annis, dicti copulatores, qui ultimo clauserunt bursas, et eorum substituti, et dicti novi copulatores . . . debeant claudere bursas . . .').

not been successful in the scrutiny of 1458, nor in the additions made to it in 1463–4.[1]

The closing of the bags, as well as the requalification of these citizens, had, according to Agnolo, been *gravissimo* to Piero de' Medici, although the whole city was pleased with it, 'a tutta la ciptà è piaciuto'. This was no doubt closer to the truth than Piero's explanation to the Milanese orator that he himself had ordered the bags to be closed, in order to forestall his enemies who, instigated by Dietisalvi, had planned to have Luca Pitti elected the next Gonfalonier; by restoring free elections, Luca would have greatly enhanced his own popularity, and undermined that of Piero.[2] But in this case, it would hardly have been reasonable to propose this reform nearly seven weeks before the election of the Gonfalonier was due to take place. Piero's version of the events is clearly influenced by his desire to prove to his Milanese protector that he was still in control of the situation. Luca Pitti, on the other hand, told Nicodemo that he had already for some time 'publicato per la città che vivano più honestamente che per lo passato'.[3] As to Dietisalvi, he wrote, a few days later, to Francesco Sforza that the restoration of free elections would reunite the leading citizens, and particularly Piero and Luca Pitti, who would need each other more than in the past and thus secure their power and prestige more firmly than ever.[4] Jacopo Ammanati, writing a few years later in his *Commentarii*,[5] bears out Luca's and Dietisalvi's version: together with Agnolo Acciaiuoli, they had been frequently

[1] 'Noi seràmo le borse, e ritiràmo quasi tutti quelli che aveano vinto il partito dal 1434 in qua. . .' (to his son Jacopo, in *Lettere* cit., p. 484). See above, pp. 108, 123–4.

[2] Nicodemo to Francesco Sforza, 14 Sept. 1465 (Bibl. Nat., MS. ital. 1591, fol. 191ʳ): Piero had told him that night that 'più dì fa se audè e intese che M. Luca Pitti e alcun'altri de questi soy gli andavano a mal gioco . . . et che da poco in qua, instigati da M. Detesalvi, se son coniurati contra de lui, sopratucto de meterlo in vostra disgracia, e de questo populo. . . In quella del populo se refidavano metterlo cum fare M. Luca Gonfaloniero quest'altri doy mesi, et col serare le borse remanese in gracia del populo, e Piero in disgracia. . . Il perchè gli è necessario pigliare lui [i.e. Piero] questo cappo. . . de serare le borse; cossì ha ordinato che omnino se serino; et essene facto cappo cum sequella de molt'altri de' migliori citadini de questa città; per la qual cosa a M. Luca e quest'altri è stato necessario consentire. . . .'

[3] Ibid. This agrees with what his son had said, on 11 Sept., in the Pratica: 'Patrem suum D. Lucam diu iam in ea sententia fuisse; voluisse etiam se abdicare magistratui.' (Cons. e Prat. cit., fol. 33ʳ). See above, p. 141, n. 6.

[4] 23 Sept. 1465 (ASM, Pot. est., Firenze, 272): the closing of the *borse* 'è stata cosa molto grata al populo, che pare loro havere riavuta la libertà. Ma ella sarà anche cagione di grande unione et benivolentia tra i principali. . . Piero et Messer Lucha insieme con li altri principali cittadini si ristringhono insieme con molti altri cittadini, et saranno con più amore et fede l'uno con lo altro fussino mai; perchè hanno magiore bisognio l'uno dell'altro che per il passato. Et manterrannosi insieme quella grandigia et reputatione havessono mai, perchè fa per caschuno di loro.' [5] Op. cit., p. 379.

complaining that 'satis iam diu uni civi servisse rempublicam. . .
non id agi his eorum studiis ut civitate pellatur Petrus, quem sal-
vum velint; sed ut posito dominatu civilem aequalitatem accipiat'.
Whatever the personal enmities and ambitions of these men,
there is no evidence that at that time they wanted more than to
preserve the régime on a basis of equality among the leading
citizens. If they were hoping to achieve this by liberalizing its
political structure, they may perhaps have been mistaken: according to Nicodemo da Pontremoli, they were rashly jeopardizing
their 'bello e bono stato'.[1] But *ottimati* like Agnolo Acciaiuoli
might point to the oligarchical régime before 1434, which appeared to some as a golden age of good government and civic
patriotism. 'In those days the whole city enjoyed the utmost
happiness', says Manno Temperani in a long speech in the
Pratica of 2 January 1466 about the years around 1418.[2]

Sentiments of this kind found a programmatic expression in
the speech with which the new Gonfalonier of Justice, whose
name had been drawn on 29 October, addressed his first *Pratica*:
'Not without cause did our ancestors ordain that high offices be
filled by lot, and not be handed over.'[3] The speech of Niccolò
Soderini is one long and enthusiastic plea for Florence's traditional form of government. Niccolò was brother of Tommaso
Soderini, who was related to Piero by marriage and a good
Cosmiano;[4] but Nicodemo da Pontremoli was mistaken when he
thought that this would make him choose what he called the *bona
via*.[5] In the ensuing debate it emerged that a number of influential citizens considered the abolition of elections *a mano* to be
only the beginning of a reform of Florence's government, and
were prepared to go beyond a restoration of the system in force

[1] To Francesco Sforza, 14 Sept. (Bibl. Nat., MS. ital. 1591, fol. 191ᵛ); he had told Luca
and his friends that they would be 'li primi a pentirsi del serare le borse, e non havere
cognossuto el bello e bono stato loro. . .'.

[2] Cons. e Prat., 58, fol. 73ᵛ: 'Tum etiam omnis civitas maxima felicitate utebatur.' The
minutes of the *Pratiche* dealing with domestic affairs between 3 Nov. 1465 and 5 Sept. 1466
are now ed. by G. Pampaloni, 'Fermenti di riforme democratiche nelle consulte della
Repubblica fiorentina', *Arch. Stor. Ital.*, cxix (1961), pp. 242–81, and 'Nuovi tentativi
di riforme alla Costituzione Fiorentina visti attraverso le consulte', ibid., cxx (1962),
pp. 521–81 (henceforth referred to as Pampaloni, I and II). Manno Temperani's speech:
Pampaloni, II, p. 522.

[3] Cons. e Prat., 57, fols. 49ᵛ–51ᵛ (3 Nov. 1465; Pampaloni, I, pp. 242–4): 'Non sine causa
patres nostri sortiri, non tradi, honores instituerunt.' The entry of Soderini's election is
in Tratte, 202. His name was the fifth to be drawn; the first four were temporarily disqualified from accepting the office.

[4] Nicodemo to Francesco Sforza, 23 Nov. 1465 (ASM, Pot. est., Firenze, 272). He was
married to Dianora, sister of Lucrezia Tornabuoni.

[5] To the same, 5 Nov. 1465 (ibid.).

before 1434. Agnolo Acciaiuoli, supported by Dietisalvi Neroni, Dietisalvi's brother Francesco, and Roberto Altoviti, demanded (thirty years before Savonarola) that the Signoria and the *Otto* be deprived of their power to pronounce sentence without recourse to the ordinary tribunals.[1] To preserve these powers, says Roberto Altoviti, means to destroy the liberty, 'quam esse restitutam gaudemus'.[2] This was one of the most sensitive points of the Medicean system of government. The judicial powers and competence of the executive had been gradually increased after 1434, especially for political offences.[3] Judgement by 'six beans' or votes of the Signoria or the *Otto* could accordingly come to stand for arbitrary jurisdiction, as a result of the transfer of powers from the judiciary to the executive. That such powers could be abused for personal ends was evident; Agnolo Acciaiuoli wants them abolished, 'ne possit quis per iniuriam cives expellere, ut factum est alias'. This would go far beyond the refusal, in June, to renew the *balìa* of the *Otto*,[4] and the majority of the *Pratica* was not prepared to follow him.[5] Other speakers suggest that no offices should henceforth be filled by election instead of sortition.[6] A general measure to this effect had to wait until the following May,[7] but on 8–12 November the councils decreed that the *Conservatori delle leggi*, the *Otto di Guardia*, and the *Ufficiali del Monte* were, 'pro omni tempore futuro', to be appointed by lot, thus reducing the authority of the *Cento* who since 1459 had been in charge of electing to these, as well as to other, magistracies.[8] Finally, on 13 November, the Gonfalonier proposed that a new scrutiny should now be held—'a matter that had been neglected for many

[1] That is, by two-thirds majority; hence these powers were called those of the six beans, or votes. 'Auctoritas sex suffragorium auferatur' (ibid., fol. 35ᵛ). See also Pampaloni, 'Fermenti di riforme democratiche nella Firenze medicea del Quattrocento', *Arch. Stor. Ital.*, cxix (1961), pp. 28–31, 57.

[2] Cons. e Prat., 58, fols. 35ᵛ (Agnolo Acciaiuoli); 36ʳ⁻ᵛ (Dietisalvi Neroni); 37ᵛ (Francesco Neroni); 38ᵛ (Roberto Altoviti); Pampaloni, I, pp. 246, 249, 251.

[3] See above, pp. 111–12, and Antonelli, 'Gli Otto di Guardia', pp. 18 ff.

[4] See above, pp. 140–1.

[5] Cons. e Prat. cit., fols. 36ʳ–41ᵛ (3 and 4 Nov.). Matteo Palmieri, the historian, pointed out (fol. 41ʳ; Pampaloni, I, p. 254) that the powers of the six beans went as far back as 1283 when they were introduced to protect the people against the magnates—a somewhat anachronistic argument. Nicodemo reports 'M. Angelo, M. Detesalvi, Francesco suo fratello, e uno o doy altri . . . consigliarono che se togliesse la balya a la Signoria de potere confinare per le sey fave' (5 Nov., ASM, loc. cit.).

[6] Andrea Minerbetti: 'sortiri magistratus ceteros censuit', Giovanni Canigiani: 'sortibus creentur omnes magistratus' (fol. 38ᵛ, 38ʳ; Pampaloni, I, pp. 251, 250). These were probably the 'altre strane proposte' to which Nicodemo refers in his letter of 5 Nov.

[7] See below, p. 156.

[8] Provv., 156, fols. 210ʳ–212ʳ, 218ʳ⁻ᵛ. See above, p. 114.

years to the great detriment of the city'.[1] If accepted, this proposal
would complete the destruction of the system of electoral controls built up by the Mediceans: for the first time since 1434,
a scrutiny of the highest magistracies would not be carried out
by a *Balìa*.

No scrutiny had, in fact, been held since 1458, and after the
postponement in 1462 the next one was not due until 1468.[2]
That of 1458 had deprived many citizens of their previous qualifications. The *reductiones* of 1463–4 had already reversed this trend,
and the *Accoppiatori* had continued this process when they closed
the *borse*.[3] But this still left the citizens who before 1458 had not
yet been qualified for the *Tre Maggiori*, and who would now have
to wait for such an opportunity until 1468. The same applied to
the *borse* of all the other offices, and in particular to those of the
territorial administration, some of which were much sought after
because of their emoluments.[4] To these no additions had been
made since 1458. Moreover, a number of important offices were,
for scrutiny purposes, linked with the *Tre Maggiori*, so that qualification for the latter automatically brought with it that for the
former.[5] Citizens who in 1458 had lost their previous qualifications
for the *Tre Maggiori* by not obtaining a majority in the scrutiny
had also been disqualified for those offices. As for the younger
generation, Giovannozzo Pitti doubtless voiced the feeling of
many of the *ottimati* when he pointed out that it was necessary
'for the sake of our sons' that, as no scrutiny had taken place for
a long time, one should be held by the end of the year, or by the
end of February at the latest.[6] Most speakers agreed, but there
were dissenting voices: as in the past, it was argued that scrutinies
had often been the cause of troubles.[7]

Niccolò Soderini, however, not content with proposing a new
scrutiny, suggested that all citizens who were twenty-five years

---

[1] Cons. e Prat. cit., fol. 43ʳ (Pampaloni, I, p. 256): 'rem grandem se esse propositurum
et insolitam multos annos, quod maximam utilitatem adlatura sit civitati. . . .'

[2] See above, p. 122.

[3] See above, pp. 142–3. The closing of the *borse* had to be completed by 25 Oct.: *provvisione*
of 16 Sept. cit., fol. 149ᵛ.

[4] See above, pp. 57–58.

[5] These were the so-called *uffici appiccati al priorato*.

[6] Cons. e Prat. cit., fol. 50ʳ; Pampaloni, I, p. 261 (14 Nov.): 'Quum autem diu est ex quo
squitinium non est factum, propter filios nostros necesse est ut fiat, si non per vos, per eos qui
succedent vobis', i.e. the Signoria of Jan.–Feb. 1466.

[7] Franco Sacchetti, fol. 53ʳ; Pampaloni, I, p. 265 (15 Nov.): 'squitinia sepe causam
fuisse malorum multorum. Itaque hoc quidem tempore damnandam censuit squitiniorum
mentionem.' See above, pp. 122–3 and below, p. 150.

old and who had been qualified in any of the preceding scrutinies from 1444 onwards should automatically become eligible for the same offices—i.e. without having been requalified in a subsequent scrutiny.[1] This proposal struck at the element of electoral revision which had become one of the most important aspects of the Medicean scrutinies.[2] If put into effect it would have made eligibility for government a permanent privilege of all those citizens who had been qualified for the *Tre Maggiori* in any of the scrutinies held during the last twenty years.[3] Niccolò Soderini's revolutionary proposal, which was supported by Dietisalvi and by Giovannozzo Pitti, is of considerable interest for the political aims of some of Piero's opponents; Niccolò was doubtless right in the belief that it might displease the leading citizens of the régime.[4] According to Manno Temperani, it was nothing less than an attempt to introduce the aristocratic régime of Venice into Florence.[5] The refusal of the majority of the *Pratica* to accept it reflects the traditionalist opposition both to the Medicean policy after 1458 and to oligarchical innovations. As one speaker puts it: 'laudare se consuetudinem patrum nostrorum, qui singulis quinquenniis voluerunt iudicium fieri de civibus, ut esset ille stimulus ad virtutes.'[6]

[1] Those of minor age, on reaching that of twenty-five: 'dal 1444 qui obtinuerint imbursentur pro tribus maioribus, si xxv annum aget [*sic*]; si non aget, cum ad eam pervenerit' (fol. 45ᵛ; Pampaloni, I, p. 257). It will be remembered that for qualification in scrutinies, it was not necessary to have reached the minimum age required for appointment to the office in question.   [2] See above, p. 108.

[3] That this was the meaning of the proposal emerges also from an observation made by Otto Niccolini on 15 Nov.: 'quod de perpetuitate honorum additur novum, se non satis intellexisse' (fol. 53ʳ; Pampaloni, I, p. 264).

[4] 'Etsi nolint principes, vos tamen velle debetis bene agere et quieti consulere (13 Nov., loc. cit.).

[5] Ibid., fol. 49ᵛ (14 Nov.; Pampaloni, I, p. 261): 'affere videatur statum optimatum et imitationem quandam rei p. Venetorum'. Others denied this: the Venetian electoral system was different from that of Florence; the Venetians 'nihil habent a sortibus, sed in dies eligunt ad honores et magistratus' (Mariotto Lippi, fol. 51ʳ; Pampaloni, I, p. 263).

[6] Carlo Pandolfini, 15 Nov. (fol. 52ʳ; Pampaloni, I, p. 263). Dietisalvi says that the idea that quinquennial scrutinies are a stimulus to virtue 'movere quamplurimos', but not him (fol. 52ᵛ; Pampaloni, I, p. 264). Alessandra Macinghi-Strozzi refers to these discussions on 15 Nov. (to Filippo Strozzi, in *Lettere*, p. 512): 'tutti gli uomini sono in pensiero di quello che s'ha a fare in Palagio nel dirizzare lo Stato, e'n che modo s'ha vivere: e tutto dì si pratica. . . .' Pampaloni, op. cit. (see above, p. 145, n. 1), pp. 34 ff., believes that what Soderini was proposing was the creation of a great council on a democratic basis. The minutes of his speech of 13 Nov. are admittedly somewhat obscure; but neither this speech, nor the subsequent debate, appears to bear out this interesting suggestion. The references, in the *Pratiche* of 14 and 15 Nov., to reforms of the councils seem to concern only the method of appointing the council members (for a reform of this kind in 1458, see above, p. 118); and they do not seem to have been made in Soderini's speech of 13 Nov., for Carlo Pandolfini, who had replied to it, says two days later 'quod de immutatione consiliorum *dicitur* audire' (loc. cit.).

The bill ordering the scrutiny was passed, with considerable difficulties and narrow majorities, between 18 and 27 November.[1] According to the Milanese ambassador, opposition to the scrutiny came from members of the régime who had been persuaded by Piero that they might not do so well in it.[2] The fact that the bill was passed by the *Cento* immediately does not seem to tally with this interpretation. At least some of the opposition may have been due to the pronouncedly oligarchical character of the council which was to be put in charge of the scrutiny. Instead of restoring the statutory regulations which had been in force until the scrutinies were entrusted to *Balìe*,[3] and of recruiting the council from official and elected members, the citizens whose names had been drawn for the Gonfaloniership of Justice since 1434 were to form its nucleus.[4] Once more, we find this group singled out for a prominent political role; and the regulation that sons or near relatives could be elected by the Signoria and Colleges as substitutes for deceased *veduti* shows how this honour was beginning to be recognized as a privilege. For the substitutes, the minimum age was twenty-five (for the *veduti* themselves, it was twenty-eight), but the Signoria and Colleges were authorized to elect, in exceptional cases, younger men. Among the five citizens whom they chose was Piero's son Lorenzo.[5] Since members of the Lesser Guilds could not become Gonfaloniers of Justice, it was decided, in order to keep the customary one-to-three

---

[1] While it was passed immediately by the *Cento*, by 80 to 40 votes, on the 18th, it was rejected by the council of the People on each successive day until 24 Nov., when it was passed by 193 to 88 votes; the council of the Commune passed it on the 27th by 124 to 62 votes, after rejecting it on the 25th and 26th (Libri Fabarum, 68, fols. 21ᵛ–24ʳ). The law is in Provv., 156, fols. 222ʳ–225ʳ.

[2] Nicodemo da Pontremoli to Francesco Sforza, 23 Nov. 1465 (ASM, Pot. est., Firenze, 272): 'Piero. . . ha cum bon modo mostrato a quest'altri del stato che'l non fa per loro, perchè ne verano a cadere molti di loro. . . per la qual cosa è sequito che may questo confaloniero l'ha possuto vencere nel Consiglio del popolo. . . .'

[3] See above, p. 67.

[4] The law says, all *veduti e seduti* Gonfaloniers of Justice from 1 Oct. 1434 onwards, of at least twenty-eight years of age; but the list of members shows that the *terminus post quem* which was actually used was Aug. 1458. The reason for this may have been that many of the citizens who had already been *veduti* before that date had been *veduti* once more after it (see above, p. 120). It may have been considered wise not to ignore this additional check. Sons, brothers, cousins, or nephews of deceased *veduti* could be elected as substitutes, provided the family was not already represented by more than three, or, in the case of sons of *seduti* and of *Accoppiatori*, four members.

[5] 'Item che in luogo di tutti quegli che fussino stati tracti Gonfalonieri di Justitia dal 1434 in qua che fussino morti, i decti Signori et Collegi possino torre. . . che sia figliuolo o fratello carnale o cugino o nipote carnale o nipote cugino. . . tra' quali possino essere insino in quatro minori d'anni xxv. . . .' For the names, see the list referred to below, p. 149, n. 3.

proportion between Lesser and Greater Guilds, to admit all those artisans who from 1434 onwards had been in offices of great responsibility, such as that of the *Accoppiatori* and the *Otto*.[1] On the other hand, there were to be only 83 *arroti*, to be elected by the Signoria and the Colleges, as against 200 in the *Balìa* of 1458.[2] The point of gravity lay decidedly with the *veduti* Gonfaloniers, and their sons, brothers, or cousins, who contributed 270 members, that is over one half of the total of 507.[3] The vast majority of the former (119 out of 151) had been members of the *Balìa* of 1458, and thus provided the continuity which was so important a feature of the régime; but they did so on social rather than political grounds.[4] The constitution of this electoral council, whose decisions might be vital for the future of the régime, thus reflects the same conservative trend as Niccolò Soderini's proposal. Free elections had been restored but the men who had a decisive voice in determining eligibility had risen to a prominent position under the Medici régime or were near relatives of men who had done so. Piero de' Medici, like Luca Pitti and other leading citizens, belonged to the council on the same terms as other aristocrats; and if Piero's sixteen-year-old son Lorenzo was by way of exception admitted to it, so were a few other young men, including Piero de' Pazzi's son Renato.[5]

The council began its work on 6 December with the scrutiny of the *Tre Maggiori*, the *Accoppiatori* for it having been elected previously.[6] Successful candidates were to gain two *polizze*

---

[1] All members of the Lesser Guilds who, since 1434, had been *Accoppiatori* or Secretaries, or had been of the Ten, of the Eight, or of the Officials of the *Monte*. If these numbers were not sufficient to provide the customary ratio (*ragguaglio*), the Signoria and the Colleges were to elect additional artisans.

[2] See above, p. 106. The *ex officio* members were the present Signoria and Colleges, as well as those in office at the time, the Captains of the Guelph Party, the *Otto*, the *Sei*, twenty-one consuls of the guilds, &c.

[3] A contemporary copy of the list of members is in Bibl. Naz., MS. Capponi 105, fols. 119ʳ–123ʳ. A number of members are counted twice, as *veduti* and as *ex officio* members: this must be the reason for the figure of 537 given by Leonardo Morelli, *Cronaca*, in *Delizie*, xix, p. 181, which represents the total if these double entries are not taken into account. Rinuccini, *Ricordi storici*, p. xcvii, has 'c. 530'.

[4] The proportion was, for obvious reasons, much lower for the substitutes: 14 out of 119.

[5] See the list quoted above.

[6] Their—fragmentary—register is in Bibl. Naz., II. IV. 345, fols. 67ʳ–72ᵛ (for their names see Appendix, no. I). Entry for 5 Dec. (fol. 71ᵛ): 'che per più contento di ciaschuno si faccia ...lo squittinio del priorato'. 485 (out of 507) members of the scrutiny council attended on the 4th (ibid.). Marco Parenti to Filippo Strozzi, 7 Dec. 1465 (Carte Strozz., 3ᵃ ser., 180, no. 73): the scrutiny 'ieri si cominciò'.

instead of the usual one,[1] and these were to be added to the existing *borse* (*rimbottate*). This may have been intended to compensate for the long interval since the last scrutiny; by adding them to the existing *borse* the scrutiny was deprived, like that of 1440, of its function of revision: any qualifications gained from 1458 onwards remained valid. This was clearly a reaction to the way in which, in the scrutiny of 1458, that revision had been carried out: we remember the complaints about qualifications lost on that occasion.[2] Yet the scrutiny soon ran into difficulties. There were pressure groups and *sottoscrizioni*, and although it was pointed out that this was customary during scrutinies, this time they were doubtless of a more serious and far-reaching nature than usual.[3] According to Luigi Guicciardini, a staunch Medicean, these troubles showed where the new régime was leading them: it encouraged licence rather than liberty.[4] However, Piero and his followers appear to have had their full share in catching votes.[5] Only three days after the scrutiny bill was passed, it was suggested in the *Pratica* that only the scrutiny of the *Tre Maggiori* should be carried out now, while that of the external offices should be deferred; for these, the *Accoppiatori* might restore qualifications to those citizens who had lost them in 1458 and who were now clamouring to get them back.[6] Dietisalvi wanted to put the deadline at 1445.[7] Such proposals were of considerable

---

[1] Provv. of 27 Nov. cit. The acquisition of two *polizze* instead of the customary one *polizza* had been introduced in 1453, but had again been abandoned in 1458 (see above, pp. 60–61, 108).   [2] See above, pp. 108–9.

[3] *Sottoscrizioni*, that is signed agreements by which groups of citizens pledged themselves to take specified actions, had begun to be made before the bill was passed. Agnolo Acciaiuoli says in the *Pratica* of 24 Nov. (Cons. e Prat., 58, fol. 64ᵛ; Pampaloni, I, p. 274. For the date, see 57, fol. 85ᵛ): 'Subscriptiones etiam fiunt, ut renuntiatum est heri, et maiorem annis quam ego sim . . . subscriptum audio.' Dietisalvi Neroni, 29 Nov. (fol. 67ᵛ; Pampaloni, I, p. 277): 'commotum fuisse propter mentionem subscriptionum, quae cum audiat fieri propter squitinium . . .'; Tommaso Soderini, 29 Nov. (fol. 68ʳ; Pampaloni, loc. cit.): 'discordiam non oriri a subscriptionibus, sed a squitinio. Et multa esse genera subscriptionum; neque aliter fieri posse in squitiniis, nam id vetus est.' Agnolo Acciaiuoli to Francesco Sforza, 13 Dec. 1465 (ASM, Pot. est., Florence, 272): 'queste congregationi che hanno facto e M. Luca e Piero, so che le sono dimonstrate alla S. V. che le siano nate da una benivolentia di partigiani; questo è falso, e conosceretelo posati che siano questi squittini in brieve'.

[4] 29 Nov. (fol. 68ᵛ; Pampaloni, I, p. 277): 'Novum regiminis modum videri licentiam afferre volentibus aberrare.'

[5] See Agnolo Acciaiuoli's letter quoted above, n. 3.

[6] Giovannozzo Pitti, 30 Nov. (Cons. e Prat. cit., fol. 70ʳ; Pampaloni, I, p. 279): 'quum iam cepta res est, perseverandum in eo quantum ad summum magistratum . . . quantum ad preturas provinciarum, supersedendum usque ad tempus trium annorum; et quod presentes coppulatores auctoritatem haberent restituendi honores his, qui in 1458 ablati indigne fuerunt'.

[7] Ibid., fol. 70ᵛ (30 Nov.; Pampaloni, I, p. 279): 'ut quibus ab anno 1444 ablati fuerint

importance for acquiring, or losing popularity, since the distribution of the external offices affected many more citizens than
that of the three highest magistracies. The opposition to the
scrutiny, which seems to have abated during December,[1] again
gathered momentum after Niccolò Soderini had ended his term
of office at the end of that month. This time, it was for the
Mediceans to lament the 'sickness of the body politic', which
was bound to end in its death, if no remedy could be found.[2] He
had hoped, said Tommaso Soderini, that the restoration of free
elections might bring some help: but now 'scrutinium omnia
perturbavit'.[3] The council for the scrutiny was too large,[4] and
there were also other flaws in its execution.[5]

As a result of this criticism, the Signori who entered office on
1 January sent to the councils a bill containing fresh regulations
for the scrutiny, which had previously been discussed by the
Pratica in utmost secrecy.[6] It met with strong opposition in the
councils. Having been rejected by the *Cento* on 22 and 23 January,
and by the council of the People five times between 25 and 29
January, it was finally passed by the councils of the People and

honores restituerentur'. This doubtless refers to the scrutiny of the external offices which
started in Jan. 1445 (= 1444 according to Florentine style).

  [1] There are no further references to it in the *Pratiche* of 15, 22, and 23 Dec.; there are no
minutes of other meetings of the *Pratica* for that month in Cons. e Prat., 57 and 58.
Alessandra Macinghi-Strozzi writes on 19 Dec. to Filippo Strozzi (*Lettere*, p. 524):
'ogn'uomo attende a squittinare'.

  [2] Tommaso Soderini, 2 Jan. 1466 (Cons. e Prat. cit., fol. 77ʳ): 'cum multi morbi afficiant
corpus civitatis, ut nisi remedia adhibeantur, ducant ad interitum'; Luigi Guicciardini
(fol. 74ᵛ; Pampaloni, II, pp. 523, 526): the city 'menses xiiii postquam decoctiones incepe-
runt adeo infirma est, ut iam de interitu omnes addubitare cogantur'.

  [3] 3 Jan. (fol. 79ᵛ; Pampaloni, II, p. 528): 'Existimavi ex liberatione sortium aliquid
remedii adlatum fuisse: scrutinium omnia perturbavit.'

  [4] This was also admitted by citizens who had been in favour of the scrutiny, e.g. by
Manno Temperani: 'Numerus scrutinatorum amplissimus est . . . omnis fere civitas
occupatur in scrutineis' (fol. 78ʳ; Pampaloni, II, p. 527; 3 Jan.).

  [5] This view, which in the debate of 8 Jan. (fols. 88ʳ–90ᵛ; Pampaloni, II. pp. 534–7) is
expressed by Tommaso Soderini, Antonio Ridolfi, Luigi Guicciardini, Otto Niccolini, and
Domenico Martelli, is also shared by Dietisalvi Neroni, who at that time seems to have
come closer to Piero (Nicodemo to Francesco Sforza, 3 Jan., ASM cit.). Agnolo Acciaiuoli,
on the other hand, insists that 'eas rationes que afferuntur de vitio legis scrutinii ego non
novi' (fol. 89ᵛ). For further criticisms of the scrutiny, cf. the debate of 18 Jan. (fols.
95ʳ–98ᵛ; Pampaloni, II, pp. 541–6): in it, Franco Sacchetti makes the scrutiny responsible
for all the troubles of the city. Similar views are expressed by Luigi Guicciardini and
Giovanni Lorini, while Mariotto Benvenuti complains that things were different in past
times, when their ancestors 'scrutineis concordiam querebant'.

  [6] Alessandra Macinghi-Strozzi to Filippo Strozzi, 11 Jan. 1466 (*Lettere*, p. 550): 'Ha
questa Signoria fatto parecchi dì pratica, e nulla si può intendere: chè hanno fatto pena di
rubello a chi rivela nulla, a chi si truova di questa pratica. . . .' The *Pratica* discussed the
scrutiny on 3, 4, 8, 9, and 11 Jan., on which day it unanimously approved the new scrutiny
bill (Cons. e Prat., 58, fols. 77ᵛ–94ʳ; Pampaloni, II, pp. 526–41; for the date of the last
meeting, see Cons. e Prat., 57, fol. 116ʳ).

Commune on the 30th and 31st.[1] Apart from the abolition of substitutes for *veduti* Gonfaloniers and the appointment of new elective members, the composition of the scrutiny council remained practically unchanged.[2] The results of the scrutiny of the *Tre Maggiori*, which had already been completed, were to remain intact, but successful candidates were to receive one instead of two *polizze* each.[3] The scrutiny of the other offices, on the other hand, was to be started all over again, following the precedent of 1444.[4] This was clearly a compromise: it was rumoured that the Mediceans would have liked to annul the entire scrutiny.[5] According to information received by Alamanno Rinuccini from one of the Signori in office at the time, the situation was so critical that 's'era dato ordine di fare parlamento, se non si fusse vinto quella petizione di fare nuovo squittino'.[6] There is no reference to such a scheme in the minutes of the debates in the *Pratica*; however, the idea of repeating the policy that had proved so successful in August 1458 may well have been mooted among the Mediceans. They could certainly congratulate themselves on the final passage of the scrutiny bill. Alessandra Macinghi-Strozzi says that it was passed, in the teeth of popular opposition, because 'questi principali si sono rappacificati en pochi dì ensieme';[7] yet there was trouble again over the election of the new members of

---

[1] Libri Fabarum, 68, fols. 30ᵛ–32ʳ; Provv., 156, fols. 266ᵛ–269ʳ. The votes by which the law was passed were 81 to 39 (*Cento*), 143 to 47 (council of the People), and 134 to 59 (council of the Commune). One of the reasons for the opposition in the council of the People was the fear of members of the Lesser Guilds that their representation in the new council might be reduced: 'in lege scrutinii . . . esse aliquid quod vehementer turbat opifices: quod non quartum habeant in recompensatione cum vexilliferis Justitie sed quintum' (Cons. e Prat., 58, fol. 100ʳ; Pampaloni, II, p. 547; 31 Jan.). In fact, the law granted them the former ratio of one to three.

[2] There were to be 83 *arroti*, to be nominated by the Signoria and Colleges from among the *veduti ai Tre Maggiori* from 1440 onwards, and to be elected by the *Cento*; the *veduti* to the Gonfaloniership from 1440 onwards of at least 30; and as many artisans as to constitute one-quarter of the number of the latter, who had to be *veduti ai Tre Maggiori* from the same date. *Ex officio* members were the Signori, the Colleges, the Captains of the Guelph Party, the Eight, the Officials of the *Monte*, the *Sei di Mercanzia*, twenty-one consuls of the guilds, and the *Accoppiatori*, Secretaries, and *Dieci di Balìa* from 1434 onwards, &c. *Accoppiatori* for the scrutiny were to be elected by the *Cento*, which however re-elected the existing *Accoppiatori*, who had been appointed under the law of 27 Nov.: see above, p. 149, and Rinuccini, p. xcviii.

[3] Cf. also Rinuccini, p. xcviii.

[4] See above, p. 55. Cf. Alessandra Macinghi-Strozzi to Filippo Strozzi, 30 Jan. (*Lettere*, p. 564): 'Èssi vinto nel Consiglio del Popolo, questa mattina, . . . di gittare a terra parte dello squittino fatto, e gli squittinanti.'

[5] Ibid., p. 565: '. . . fra l'altre frottole, dicono: "Piero di Cosimo e Tommaso Soderino. . . vogliono gettare a terra lo squittino".'

[6] p. ciii.

[7] *Lettere*, pp. 567–8 (to Filippo Strozzi, 1 Feb.).

the scrutiny council, which took place on 8 February after long and confused debates in the *Pratica*.[1]

The results of the distribution of qualifications for the Gon-faloniership, which the *Accoppiatori* carried out in February on the basis of the scrutiny, seem to bear this out.[2] Perhaps its most striking feature is the relatively large number of newly *imborsati*, considering that only about two years earlier many citizens had been newly qualified.[3] Thus, in the *Quartiere* of S. Spirito, the number of newly qualified rose from 11 in 1455 to 13 in 1463–4 and 22 in 1466; in S. Maria Novella from 16 to 26 and 28; and in S. Giovanni from 16 to 20 and 23.[4] In other words, between December 1463 and February 1466, no less than 35, 54, and 43 citizens respectively were newly admitted to the highest office-holding qualifications in Florence, that is about three times as many citizens as at the closing of the *borse* in 1455. Moreover, since, as in 1463–4, there does not appear to have been any limita-tion of the family ratio, the representation of single families increased considerably. An impression of the size it had attained by 1466 may be gained from the totals of the citizens, whether newly qualified or not, who in February were given a *polizza* for the Gonfaloniership (*rimbottati*). The Pitti are represented by no less than 10 members, the Medici by 9, that is half as many again as in 1455 (6); the Ridolfi by 7, as against 5, the Acciaiuoli and Bartoli by 7 each, as against 4 and 3, the Giugni, Pandolfini, and Della Stufa by 6 each; and there are 7 families (among them the Dietisalvi) with 5 members, and 12 with 4 members each. The prominence of the Pitti and the Medici reflects their position in the city. A fragmentary list of voting returns for the Medici's *Gonfalone* of Lion d'oro shows how much the *Accoppiatori* favoured the Medici. Of the 29 candidates entered, six are qualified unani-mously for the Gonfaloniership. Of these, three are Medici—

---

[1] Marco Parenti to Filippo and Lorenzo Strozzi, 8 Feb. 1466, Carte Strozz., 3ª ser., 180, no. 78: 'istamani si fanno pure gli uomini di 83 [*scil.* arroti], ch'è durata la pratica 8 dì', &c.

[2] Bibl. Naz., II. IV. 346, fols. 135ʳ–141ᵛ (a later copy is in Carte Strozz., 3ª ser., 3, no. 5): '. . . In hoc quaterno continentur illi, qui de mense februarii anni 1465 per quinque copula-tores tunc existentes vigore auctoritatis eis concesse de mense ianuarii dicti anni, videlicet XXXIª die . . . fuerunt declarati debere rimbottari et imbursari pro vexilliferis iustitie pro una apodissa . . . super bursis tunc vigentibus pro officio vexilliferorum iustitie . . .', i.e. those closed in Oct. 1465.

[3] See above, pp. 123 ff.

[4] These figures are based on a comparison between the *imborsazioni* of 1449 and 1455 and the *reductiones* of 1463–4 with the *rimbotto* of 1466. For S. Croce, no such lists exist for the *imborsazione* of 1449. See above, p. 61, n. 4.

Lorenzo and Giuliano di Piero and Averardo di Bernardo. Dietisalvi's son Lorenzo is qualified with four votes against one.[1] It is not surprising, then, to find once more the emphasis on continuity: of the 97 successful candidates for the Gonfaloniership who do not appear on the lists of 1455 and 1463–4, nearly half are sons or brothers of citizens who do.[2] Only about one in seven belongs to new families;[3] but of these citizens, eight had belonged to the scrutiny council of November 1465. If the passage of the scrutiny law on 31 January found the *cittadini principali* temporarily reunited, the policy of the *Accoppiatori* reflected the interests and ambitions of the aristocracy.[4]

Even so, in the long run, tensions over the scrutiny probably contributed more than anything else to the hardening of the division in the régime. Agnolo Acciaiuoli was doubtless right in prophesying that the political groups created for it by Piero and Luca Pitti would not so easily be disbanded, once the scrutiny was over.[5] Diplomacy continued to play a significant role in this pattern of personal and political relationships. The spectre of a Florentine *rapprochement* with Venice had been haunting Milanese diplomacy ever since Cosimo's death, and had done so increasingly after the September events.[6] Such apprehensions were, naturally enough, encouraged by Piero.[7] In fact, however much his opponents protested their loyalty to Francesco Sforza, there was an

---

[1] Tratte, 61, fols. 176^r–177^v. The list has no title, but a comparison with that of the *rimbotto* of Feb. 1466 shows that it belongs to it. Lorenzo had been *imborsato* as Gonfalonier of Justice in Jan. 1464 (see above, p. 124); Giuliano is qualified for the first time now.

[2] Thirty-four sons and thirteen brothers. These figures are based on a comparison of the lists of 1455 (Tratte, 16) and 1463–4 (Tratte, 17) with that of Feb. 1466.

[3] Nerozzo di Piero di Filippo del Nero, Ruberto di Piero da Mezzola, Pegolotto di Bernardo Balducci, Alamanno di Filippo Rinuccini, Bernardo di Giovanni Jacopi, Girolamo d'Andrea and Zanobi di Riccardo Borgognoni, Tommaso di Lorenzo Ceffi, Giuliano di Franco Viviani, Bindo d'Agnolo Vernaccia, Tommaso di Bartolomeo di Ser Tino, Bono di Giovanni Boni, Zanobi di Domenico di Cecco Frasca, Stagio di Lorenzo Barducci. Altogether, 339 citizens were qualified.

[4] There were, doubtless, some who would have been personally disappointed by the results. The outstanding example of these is Niccolò Soderini, whose term of office had in the end made him unpopular with friend and foe alike: cf. Agnolo Acciaiuoli to Francesco Sforza, 17 Dec. 1465 (ASM, Pot. est., Firenze, 272): 'questo gonfalonieri è una bestia'; 22 Dec. (Bibl. Ambros., Z. 247 sup.): 'questo gonfalonieri è una imprudente persona'. Cf. Alessandra Macinghi-Strozzi, letters of 4 and 11 Jan. 1466 (*Lettere*, pp. 540, 550).

[5] See above, p. 150, n. 3.

[6] Cf. e.g. Nicodemo's dispatch of 14 Sept. (Bibl. Nat., MS. ital. 1591, fol. 191): Piero's enemies even envisage the possibility of 'recolligarsi cum Venetiani, como sempre hano desiderato e cercato alcuni de loro'.

[7] Nicodemo to Francesco Sforza, 24 Nov. 1465 (ASM, cit., 272): 'Essendo io hogi col Magnifico Piero, me disse. . . che ha da bon loco che questi soy adversarii voltariano questa loro rabia e passione contra la V. Celsitudine cum mettervi in disgracia quì, et poy proponere l'amicicia de' Venetiani. . . .'

increasing tendency among them to make Florentine policy independent of Milan, which, despite Francesco Sforza's continuous attempts to reunite the régime,[1] remained the traditional foreign supporter of the Medici. While Piero, with the help of the Milanese ambassador, would use the alliance with Milan to defend his position in Florence,[2] Luca Pitti declared, in December, that rather than be ruled by the Duke of Milan, he would give himself to the devil.[3] Although he denied any intention to 'redurre questo populo alla via de' Venetiani', the leading citizens opposed to Piero seem to have made, towards the end of 1465, tentative approaches to Venice, as well as to the Marquess of Ferrara, who was hostile to the Sforza.[4] Thus the death, on 8 March 1466, of Francesco Sforza proved a turning point. The disappearance of his powerful protector weakened Piero's position, while his opponents and rivals felt less bound to heed Milanese interests and susceptibilities. Nothing shows better the change in the situation than the determined opposition voiced in the *Pratica*, between the end of March and the beginning of May, to the subsidy requested by the Duchess of Milan. Luca Pitti's complaints about the constant demands for money from Milan were bearing fruit.[5] While the majority was in favour of the subsidy, Agnolo Acciaiuoli, for so long a loyal servant of Francesco Sforza, as well as Dietisalvi Neroni and Niccolò Soderini, opposed it from the start, on the ground that the Sforza were not threatened, and consequently not in need of it, and their view finally prevailed; although a reduced sum had at first been

---

[1] Cf. Nicodemo's dispatches of 11 Nov. 1465 (ASM, cit.): 'l'unione mi havete facta predicare'; and of 23, 25, and 29 Nov. (ibid.).

[2] Agnolo Acciaiuoli to Francesco Sforza, 22 Oct. 1465 (ASM, cit.): 'Piero dice che. . . sarà grande quanto il Duca vorrà; Nicodemo minaccia e cittadini: dice per parte del Duca che la Signoria Sua harà a male che le borse si serrino'; 17 Nov. (ibid.): 'Piero usa dire che la Signoria Vostra gli manda ad offerire cose assai, e crede con queste parole farsi temere e più reputato nella città'.

[3] Nicodemo to Francesco Sforza, 16 Dec. (Bibl. Nat., cit., fol. 223): '. . . M. Luca diceva non volere a verun modo essere governato dal duca de Milano. . . Et che sempre stava nel chiedere denari de quì, e omne dì diceva de beneficare questo populo, et non attendeva se non a le soe specialità. Et che non che'l cercasse de redurre questo populo a la via de' Venetiani; ma se daria al patron de l'inferno per ussire el compromesso del duca.'

[4] Agnolo Acciaiuoli to Francesco Sforza, 17 Dec. (ASM, cit.): Nicodemo had asked him 's'io havevo sentito niente di pratiche che si fussino tenute quì co' Venitiani per alcuno privato cittadino'; according to what Agnolo had heard, Niccolò Soderini had written to Venice. Dietisalvi told Nicodemo on 21 Dec. (ibid.) that Niccolò and others had 'principiata gran spianata a l'amicizia o reintegrarsi cum Venetiani'. As to Borso d'Este, Nicodemo writes on 18 Nov. (ibid.) that 'molto fa travagliare questo suo M. Jacopo qual tien quì. . . et fa omne dì visitare M. Luca, M. Angelo e M. Detesalvi. . . pur a le fiate fa visitare Piero ancora'.

[5] See above, n. 3.

promised, the Signoria declared on 14 May that the loan would not now be made.[1]

By that time, the internal situation had become so critical that the new Signoria, after summoning on 4 May a *Pratica super unione*, ordered a few days later that all *veduti ai Tre Maggiori* over fourteen years of age should swear an oath to keep the peace and renounce all private political pacts. Any such agreements were declared null and void; political debates and decisions were to remain confined to the Palace of the Signoria, where the citizens should content themselves with the right to speak in the councils.[2] 'Tutte le cose del comune s'abbino a praticare nel Palazzo de' Priori'—this repeats almost literally a statement made in December by Luca Pitti, to the effect that 'ad omne modo bixognerà che le cose del comune si agit[ino] in palagio', and that more attention should be paid than had been done in the past to the constitutional organs of government and to the people.[3] There was clearly more in the oath than an attempt to end faction. That 'il governo delle cose publiche era necessario che si governassi in palazzo, e questo perchè era ragionevole e l'universale lo voleva'[4] had been all along the view of the opposition to Piero. Two further events which took place during the days following show the determination to preserve and strengthen the new régime. On 24–31 May the councils passed a law extending elections by lot, by laying down that henceforth, with the exception of a number of specified offices, all offices were 'for ever' to be filled by lot.[5] Four

---

[1] Cons. e Prat., 58, fols. 115^r–154^r (31 March, 1, 7, 9, 14, 17, and 20 April, and 2 May). Cf. also Municchi, pp. 43–47. The sum was first reduced from 60,000 to 40,000 florins: ibid., fols. 119^v–125^r (1 April). On 2 May Niccolò Soderini pleaded for the withdrawal of the promise which 'reprehensum est a multis' (fol. 152^r; Pampaloni, II, p. 553).

[2] Cons. e Prat., 58, fol. 154^{r-v}; Pampaloni, II, p. 555. Manno Temperani and the other members, among them Dietisalvi and Agnolo Acciaiuoli, want the matter referred to a smaller committee: 'fuisse delectos decem, Lucam Pictum et Petrum Medicem intelligens in eorum numero'. The proposal takes us back to the days of the struggles beween the factions of the Albizzi and Medici before 1434. On 21 Feb. 1431, a *Pratica circa unionem* was held (cf. Pellegrini, *Sulla repubblica fiorentina*, pp. 65–66, and Appendix, nos. 14–16, 19). The ordinance of the Signoria (not the oath itself) has been published by Municchi, Appendix, no. 4, from Carte Strozz., 2^a ser., 96, no. 1. Cf. Rinuccini, p. xcix: the oath was sworn in the Palazzo della Signoria on 9 and 10 May.

[3] Nicodemo to Francesco Sforza, 22 Dec. 1465 (ASM, cit.): '. . . et che facessino più segno del palasio et de l'universa[le] de' citadini che non havevate facto per lo passato'. Luca Pitti was one of the committee 'super unione': above, n. 2.

[4] Agnolo Acciaiuoli to Francesco Sforza, 17 Nov. 1465 (ASM, cit.). See also above, p. 128.

[5] Provv., 157, fols. 41^r–43^r: 'per ogni tempo advenire di qualunche officio del quale al presente non si fa tracta per qualunche cagione si sia, si possa e debba fare o far fare tracta. . . non obstante etiamdio qualunche consuetudine in contrario observata'. The exceptions include the officials of the chancery. See above, p. 145. Election to offices which should

days before its final passage, a large number of citizens, headed by Luca Pitti, swore yet another oath, but this time not to the Signoria, to help to protect the republican régime.

While endorsing the action of the Signoria, this new oath goes beyond it. The government's initiative had been ineffective: 'nientedimeno si vede che più che mai raghunate, intelligentie e compagnie publiche e segrete' take place.[1] Consequently the citizens who swear the new oath promise to observe the previous one *realmente et con effetto*.[2] But over and above this they swear to uphold the republican system of government ('che la città si governi come consueto di giusto e populare governo'), with the Signoria being elected by lot; to prevent illegal pressure being brought to bear on private citizens ('che nessuna violenza o novità sarà fatta a nessuno cittadino straordinariamente'); and to protect the citizens' freedom to counsel and decide in public affairs ('che ta' cittadini intendino essere liberi et a consigliare et a giudicare le cose publiche'). In no other document of the Medici period is the constitutionalist programme formulated so incisively and so comprehensively.

The oath is signed by over 400 citizens, headed by Manno Temperani, Luca Pitti, Agnolo Acciaiuoli, Giovannozzo Pitti, and Dietisalvi Neroni. Of the first 50 citizens, 37 had been on the scrutiny council of November 1465, 32 as *veduti* Gonfaloniers of Justice.[3] As we go down the list, we find more men of lesser status, but we also find many members of the great Florentine families. This doubtless reflects the structure of the 'republican party' in May 1466; led by Luca Pitti, its nucleus is formed by men who had acquired a prominent position under the Medici régime. Many of the signatories had belonged to the *Balìe* after 1434. Some families are represented by several members; the Pitti by 7, the Acciaiuoli by 4, the Dietisalvi by 5. Of the Soderini, on the other hand, there is only one, Niccolò, who appears as the seventh

have been filled by *tratta* were at that time often carried out by the councils by way of special authority. The usual formula in such cases was 'neque etiam obstante quod pro dicto officio non sunt facte extractiones requisite secundum ordinamenta, et maxime secundum provisionem' of 25 Aug. 1459. On that day, a law had been passed to the effect that 'nullus impetret officia imbursata, nisi ad ea fuisset decies facta extractio' (Provv., 150, fols. 86ᵛ–87ᵛ). Further legislation against such petitions was passed on 19 Aug. 1466 (Provv. 157, fols. 119–20). See also above, pp. 57–58.

[1] Bibl. Naz., II. I. 106, fols. 60ʳ–75ᵛ (text fols. 60ʳ–61ᵛ), sixteenth-century copy.

[2] The promoters must nevertheless have had some qualms about the legality of their procedure, for Manno Temperani stated expressly that the oath was identical with that sworn in the Palazzo of the Signoria: '. . . perchè si vede ch'è il giuramento fatto in Palagio de' Signori in sulla pietra sagrata'.

[3] Cf. the list quoted above, p. 149, n. 3.

on the list: his brother Tommaso was a prominent follower of
Piero's. The Soderini are not the only family with divided alle-
giances. The most notable instance of this are the Medici themselves, who are represented by Pierfrancesco di Lorenzo, Piero's
wealthy cousin. His sons were to play an important part in the
downfall of Piero's grandson;[1] it thus appears that he too had
republican sympathies.[2] At the other end of the scale, there is a
sprinkling of men whose families had, under the Medici régime,
lost their political status; thus we find two Strozzi, one Brancacci.
They may have hoped that a republican régime might be more
liberal towards them.[3] But the large number of signatures belonging to men who had held high office under the Medici régime
shows that there was, as late as May 1466, a powerful group of
cittadini dello stato who were determined to defend the recent
restoration of the traditional system of government, and who
clearly did not share the Milanese ambassador's view that election
by lot would be detrimental to their interests.[4] They were led by
Luca Pitti, who had now definitely broken with Piero.[5] Yet whatever the personal ambitions of men like Luca Pitti and Agnolo
Acciaiuoli, the oath does not contain the slightest hint at an
organized attempt to oust Piero from his position as a *cittadino
principale*, let alone from Florence.[6] At the same time, the large
number of citizens who were backing Luca Pitti in his constitutionalist policy contradicts the 'official' Medicean version that the
opposition consisted of 'five or six' men who were motivated by
private ambitions.[7]

[1] See below, p. 231.

[2] A. v. Reumont's statement (*Lorenzo de' Medici, il Magnifico*, 2nd ed., (Leipzig, 1883), i,
p. 130) that he was 'von allen politischen Angelegenheiten ferne', is evidently not correct.

[3] Alessandra Macinghi-Strozzi did not share such hopes: cf. her letter to Filippo Strozzi,
26 Oct. 1465 (*Lettere*, p. 498): 'Della mutazione fatta del serrare le borse, certo che dà
impaccio al fatto vostro; che ora sono gli uomini più liberi di loro, e tireranno ciascuno
alla sua volontà. E i' sono di contradio openione che tu.'

[4] See above, p. 144.

[5] Cf. Rinuccini, p. xcix (May 1466): 'essendo già nella città manifestamente dissensione,
e videsi esserci due parti, che dell'una era capo M. Luca Pitti e dell'altra Piero di Cosimo'.
He adds that this had not been known during the debate on the loan to Milan, i.e. in
April.

[6] See also below, p. 161.

[7] Nicodemo to Francesco Sforza, 14 Sept. 1465 (Bibl. Nat., MS. ital. 1591, fol. 151):
according to Piero 'sono in tucto cinque o sey'. Agnolo della Stufa writes on 8 Nov. 1465
that those who were not 'dedicati' to Piero were 'pochissimi e non passano il numero di dua',
induced by 'non so qual si sia o invidia o ambitione o paura per non esser così vixuti come
lui', &c. (to Francesco Sforza, ASM, Pot. est., Firenze, 272). Piero de' Medici to Francesco
Sforza, 7 Dec. 1465 (ibid.): 'questi pochi che hanno voluto indebitamente caricare et mio
padre et me'. This is also the official version after the *Parlamento* of 2 Sept. 1466 (see below,

The attempt, at the beginning of July, by Luca Pitti and his friends, to abolish the last remnants of the Medicean system of government was probably responsible for bringing about the final crisis. The powers of the *Cento* had been curtailed in November 1465,[1] but had been temporarily increased in January, when that council was put in charge of electing the new *arroti* for the scrutiny.[2] It had not always given Piero all the support he might have expected from it;[3] nevertheless, its abolition would have been the last blow to the system of government that had been patiently built up over thirty-two years. It was not surprising that Piero and his followers should resist such a plan to the utmost.[4]

From the debate in the *Pratica* it emerges that criticism of the *Cento* came both from the aristocrats and the people. Many *ex nobilissimis familiis* were excluded from it, said Manno Temperani, who, in September 1465, had initiated the debate on electoral reform, because their names had not been drawn for the Gonfaloniership. The members of the Lesser Guilds, on the other hand, did not have their customary ratio in that council.[5] Niccolò Soderini similarly criticized it 'propter inequalitatem opificum et invidiam vexilliferatus',[6] and Agnolo Acciaiuoli did so on the ground that it owed its existence to the *Parlamento* of 1458, to which, he said somewhat surprisingly, he had always been opposed.[7] It was first suggested that the *Cento* should be reorganized to meet these criticisms; in Agnolo's view, the reform should not,

p. 164, n. 6: the Signoria to the King of France, 23 Sept.): 'Nonnulli enim cives nostri, inflati superbia atque avaritia et pessimis occecati libidinibus, dum sibi ad facinora et explendas cupiditates miseras adaperire tentant viam, etiam libertatem nostram in summum periculum adduxere. . . .'

[1] See above, p. 145.

[2] See above, p. 152, n. 2.

[3] See above, p. 140. However, when the *Cento* passed the bill restoring the *tratta* of the Signoria, in Sept. 1465, it did so by considerably less votes than either the council of the People or the council of the Commune (see above, p. 142).

[4] Rinuccini, p. c: 'Al tempo di questi Signori, e nel principio dell'ufficio loro, si tenne pratica di levare via il consiglio del Cento, e l'autorità di quelli che erano veduti gonfalonieri di giustizia; ma . . . la città era divisa, e parte de' cittadini teneva con Messer Luca Pitti, i quali erano quelli che volevano levare via tale consiglio e ridurre il popolo a libertà, parte teneva con Piero di Cosimo de' Medici, e resisteva a tale impresa. . .' It may be added that Rinuccini, who had been *imborsato* for the Gonfaloniership, for the first time, in Feb. of that year, had not yet been *veduto* for it. See above, p. 154, n. 3.

[5] Cons. e Prat., 58, fol. 168ʳ; Pampaloni, II, p. 560 (6 July 1466): '. . . a quo multi de nobilissimis familiis excluduntur propter vexilliferatum iustitie quem non obtinuerunt; opifices etiam pro consueta rata non interesse possunt.' See above, p. 116.

[6] Ibid., fol. 169ʳ; Pampaloni, p. 562.

[7] Ibid., fol. 169ᵛ: 'cui ego semper obstiti quantum potui'. In the *Pratica* of 1 Aug. 1458 (see above, p. 140), he had spoken in favour of the *Parlamento* (Cons. e Prat., 55, fol. 62ʳ).

as usual, be discussed by a select committee, but by the councils of the People and Commune, 'ut populus de suis rebus, non pauci decernant'.[1] Dietisalvi subsequently considered abolishing the *Cento* altogether, although he admitted that this might be against the interests of his class: 'I like the council of *Cento* but if it causes trouble, it should be abolished.'[2] Agnolo Acciaiuoli put the case even more strongly: 'the *Cento* is all right for me, but not for the lower classes, and it can serve as an instrument for despotic government.'[3]

Neither proposal was presented to the councils—according to Rinuccini, because the Signoria was divided.[4] It was rumoured at the time that Piero had succeeded in having the *polizze* of his enemies eliminated from the ballot bags of the Gonfaloniership of Justice.[5] Similarly, it was subsequently believed that before the *tratta* of the next Signoria on 28 August, the names of the citizens who were suspect to Piero were taken out of the *borse* for that office, with the result that Piero was provided with the opportunity to squash his enemies.[6] But it is more likely that the upholders of the *tratta* system were now simply suffering in their turn from the element of chance which was its principal characteristic. The discomfiture of the opposition after the election by lot of a Signoria favourable to Piero on 28 August demonstrated once more, if such a demonstration was still required, the wisdom of the Medicean policy of controlling the elections of the government.

Of the dramatic events of August–September there are two versions, that of the victors and that of the vanquished. Of these two versions the latter seems, on the whole, to be the more reliable, being less influenced by propagandistic motives. The main question is whether Luca Pitti and his friends had, over a long

[1] Agnolo Acciaiuoli, ibid. The debate on the *Cento* continued on 8 July (fols. 171ʳ–175ʳ).

[2] Ibid., fol. 177ʳ (July s.d.): 'El consiglio del cento a me piace, ma havendo a fare scandolo, sarei di parere che si levasse. . . .' Pampaloni, II, p. 571.

[3] Ibid., fol. 176ᵛ; p. 570 (July): 'Noi stiamo nel consiglio del cento che per me fa, ma non pe' populari, et fa il bisogno di chi vuol tirannizare la città.' He adds the warning that 'el vivere populare richiede altro vivere; et se non si rimedia, sarà necessario che altri ci governi'.

[4] Rinuccini, loc. cit.: '. . . ed i signori anche erano divisi, sicchè cinque erano da una parte e quattro dall'altra; non si potè mettere a esecuzione tale impresa. . . '.

[5] Ibid.: '. . . e dissesi anche palesemente che Piero di Cosimo avea avuto mezzo nella presente tratta de' priori, benchè le borse non fossino a mano, di fare trarre della borsa del gonfaloniere della giustizia le polizze di quelli che lui non si riputava amici; la quale cosa gli dette grande incarico e infamia appresso il popolo. . .'.

[6] Ibid., p. ci.: '. . . e tennesi che innanzi si traessino detti signori, furono trassinate le borse delle tratte, e cavatone tutti quelli di chi Piero avea sospetto, e così si disse pubblicamente'.

period, been planning to seize power and expel Piero with the help of Borso d'Este, or whether they appealed to Borso only when, in August, they felt themselves threatened by Piero's designs and the military preparations of the Duke of Milan. That Piero's opponents had been conspiring against him for a long time became, after Piero's victory, the official Florentine version and has been generally accepted by later historians; but no evidence has hitherto come to light of any definite military or diplomatic arrangements directed against Piero between his opponents and the Marquess of Ferrara, or Venice, before the crisis of July–August 1466.[1]

According to Rinuccini, after the new Signoria had entered office there were rumours that Piero 'avea fatto venire a Imola, e quivi attorno circa 1500 cavalli delle genti del duca di Milano'.[2] This is confirmed by a detailed account of some of the events leading up to the final crisis, which was written by Francesco Neroni after his arrest on 8 September.[3] On 12 August he was called to Luca Pitti, who told him that he had been informed of Milanese troop concentrations around Imola. Shortly afterwards the Ferrarese envoy showed Francesco a letter from his master offering help and protection and suggesting that 'Piero fussi levato della città' and exiled. Borso d'Este would have welcomed a change of régime in Florence which would lead to the abandonment of the Milanese alliance, and was doubtless plotting in this direction. But there is no evidence that the initiative came from Luca Pitti and his friends, nor that they accepted offers of military protection before they believed their position in Florence to be seriously threatened. It was rumoured that the Milanese troops were concentrated in order to allow Piero to stage a *coup d'état*, 'cioè fare parlamento e cacciare cittadini';[4] Luca Pitti is said to have feared that the *borse* might be tampered with.[5] According to a letter by a supporter of Luca Pitti, of 6 September,[6] five or six citizens had asked Borso d'Este that 'tenesse le sue genti in ordine bisognando loro', since they feared that if the new

---

[1] I intend to devote a special study to this question.   [2] Loc. cit.

[3] Med. av. Pr., XCVII, no. 249. The long (3 pp.) letter was written after his arrest and torture, and addressed to 'Lionardo and Giovanni'. See below, p. 165, n. 5.

[4] Loc. cit.

[5] In the same conversation of 12 Aug.; letter cit.: 'dubitò che a Santa Croce alle chasse non si fan direttamente'. The bags of the *Tre Maggiori* were kept in boxes at S. Croce.

[6] Partly ed. by Fabroni, *Laurentii Medicis Magnifici Vita* (Pisa, 1784), ii, pp. 30–32, from Med. av. Pr., LXVIII, 74, as written by a 'Ser Luca'. But the signature is 'Lo.'. Municchi suggests (p. 62) that the writer may have been Lorenzo di Tommaso Soderini, who was subsequently exiled.

Signoria, whose names were to be drawn on 28 August, were favourable to Piero, he might attempt 'qualche novità'.[1]

Fear was probably the decisive element in the final crisis. On 27 August Piero received news from Bologna that the Marquess of Ferrara was moving troops towards Florence, and thereupon requested the Sforza troops in the Romagna to be held in readiness, and to be sent to Florence in the event of a further advance of the Este troops.[2]

Three days later, on 30 August, he asked the Sforza *condottieri*, in the strongest terms, to withdraw, and on no account to enter Florentine territory.[3] For in the meantime a pro-Medicean Signoria had been drawn on the 28th; and on the 29th Luca Pitti had once more reconciled himself with Piero.[4] Shortly afterwards, however, Piero received news that the Este troops were still advancing, and consequently countermanded, on 31 August, his orders to the Milanese *condottieri*:[5] an order which was in its turn countermanded by the Signoria on the following day, when it was learned that the troops of the Marquess of Ferrara, which had been sent towards Pistoia, were being withdrawn.[6]

---

[1] That these fears were not unfounded is shown by Nicodemo's postscript, of 28 Aug., to his letter of the 27th (below): 'aspectassi la trata de' signori, in la quale porta periculo nasca qualche inconveniente, posto che Petro et li soy deliberano honestarsi per dare mala conditione a li adversarii loro presso al populo.'

[2] Nicodemo to Bianca Maria and Galeazzo Maria Sforza, 27 Aug. 1466 (ASM, Pot. est., Firenze, 272): Piero 'hebbe lettere dal regimento di Bologna, da D. Johane Bentivogli', and others, informing him that troops of the Duke of Modena 'già erano mossi in buona parte per venire quì ad instantia de li adversarii d'esso Piero, et cussì certi cavalli et fanti de Bartholomeo Colione...'. Piero asked that the Sforza troops should stay put for the moment, but to 'inviarle in qua quando [their commander] intendessi dicte gente del duca de Modena venire verso qua'. (The Marquess of Ferrara was also Duke of Modena.)

[3] Piero and Nicodemo to Orfeo da Ricavo and Antonio da Pesaro, 30 Aug. (ASM. cit.): 've preghiamo vogliati essere contenti per omne modo tornare indereto cum dicte gente tucte...'; postscript by Piero: 'Io Piero iterum vi prego e stringo, che *visis presentibus* pro nulla resti che le gente d'arme torneno indreto, et a nisuno modo entrino in su' terreni nostri....'

[4] Nicodemo to Orfeo da Ricavo, 29 Aug. (ASM, cit.): 'questa matina è stato D. Lucha a visitare Piero e reconciliatossi adsieme'. See below, p. 163, n. 5.

[5] Piero and Nicodemo to Orfeo da Ricavo and Antonio da Pesaro (ASM, cit.): 'havendo noy de certo le gente del Illustrissimo duca de Modena sonno calati presso a Pistoia', &c. Postscript to a letter of 30 or 31 Aug. (ibid.): 'Fatto la lettera, è arrivato uno messo ad Orpheo de uno suo amicho che è cum quelle gente del duca de Modena, el quale advixa che ali xxviiii de questo erano sotto Fiumalbo in campo cum circa viiim. persone per passare l'alpe. Luy ha presto advixato el Magnifico Piero....'

[6] Orfeo da Ricavo and Sacramoro to Bianca Maria and Galeazzo Maria Sforza, Firenzuola, 1 Sept. (ASM. cit.). A few hours earlier, a Florentine emissary had arrived at the camp who had confirmed Piero's orders but had asked the commander of the Sforza troops to swear obedience to the Signoria: 'el quale giuramento le V. Cel. possono intendere a che fine lo fanno; et è da piacere che più tosto el sia chiamato per la Comunità che per particulare ciptadino'—in other words, to save Piero's face; indeed, he will thereby gain 'più riputatione' (ibid.).

If fear seems to have been the main motive for the appeals for foreign military help by either party, much the same applies to their preparations in Florence itself. 'Noi habbiamo divisa la terra' exclaimed Agnolo Acciaiuoli in yet another *Pratica super unitatem reducendam*, on 1 August, 'et le divisione fanno i capi. I capi temono. . . .'[1] On the 28th, the Signoria had appealed to Luca and Piero to disarm; shortly before, the citizens had sworn yet another oath, in terms of utmost solemnity, 'di non offender l'uno l'altro'.[2] According to the Milanese ambassador, both Luca and Piero obeyed;[3] according to others, only Luca, who also refused to follow Niccolò Soderini's plea for revolutionary action.[4]

Was Luca Pitti's apparent neglect in arming himself during the days that followed due to a secret understanding with Piero? This was rumoured in Florence,[5] and is confirmed by a letter written a fortnight later by Piero himself. On 1 September Luca had been to see him and had told him that he was prepared 'to live or die' with him.[6] His decision was no doubt influenced both by the result of the drawing of the new Signoria's names on 28 August and by the military situation.[7] To the dismay of his former companions it was none other than Luca Pitti who, in the *Pratica* of 2 September, proposed that the Signoria should be advised to call a *Parlamento* on the same day, 'to remedy the upheaval in the city'.[8] All the members of the *Pratica* accepted this proposal, although, as Carlo Gondi writes, 'una grandissima parte dicessino

---

[1] Cons. e Prat., 58, fol. 180ᵛ; Pampaloni, II, p. 575.

[2] Letter of 'Lo.' of 6 Sept., cit.; 'si fece quello terribile obligo fra tutti di non offendere l'uno l'altro'; Agnolo Acciaiuoli refers to it on 26 Aug., to Bianca Maria and Galeazzo Maria Sforza (ASM, cit.), and adds: 'Non m'è honesto dire il modo per il sacramento ho facto.' Cf. also Vespasiano da Bisticci, *Vite*, p. 496.

[3] To Orfeo da Ricavo (ibid.), 29 Aug. 1466.

[4] Letter of 6 Sept., cit.: 'e così Messer Luca ubidì, et Piero finse', &c. Rinuccini, p. cii. The extent of Piero's military preparations may be gathered from Nicodemo's letter of 1 Sept. (to the Sforza, ASM, cit.), in which he states that Piero could send, to strengthen the advancing Sforza army, 4,000–6,000 of the 'perhaps 8,000' troops which he had by that day in Florence and its surroundings. See also, below, p. 164, n. 4, and below, n. 8.

[5] Rinuccini, p. cii, on Luca's visit on 29 Aug.: 'dubitossi, anzi fu certo, che segretamente non fussino rimasi d'accordo loro due, perchè si vide che sempre poi Messer Luca andò a rilento in fare provedimento alcuno per sua difesa'.

[6] Piero de' Medici to Pigello Portinari, his manager at Milan, 13 Sept. 1466 (ASM, cit.): '. . . Et adciò che tu intenda bene il tucto, t'aviso che M. Luca Pitti il dì inanzi al parlamento [i.e. on 1 Sept.], veduto come le cose andavano, fu quì a me dicendomi essere disposto vivere et morire con meco. . . .'

[7] See preceding note: 'veduto come le cose andavano'.

[8] Cons. e Prat., cit., fol. 182ᵛ; Pampaloni, II, p. 578: 'che voglia porre remedio alla perturbatione della città per via di parlamento con presteza et farlo oggi. . .'. Benedetto Dei, *Cronaca*, Manoscritti, 119, fols. 23ᵛ–24ʳ: Niccolò Soderini, 'homo diavoloso e grande', wanted to 'levare a romore Firenze'; having 'raunato il popolo al ponte alla charaia con suoi masnadieri e satelliti', he tried in vain to persuade Luca to join him.

contro all'animo loro e contro al bene della città'.[1] The Signoria
may still have hesitated to take so momentous a step; according to
another contemporary source, they saw themselves compelled
to do so by Piero's military power.[2] Of this the *Pratica* could get
a first-hand impression, for its meeting took place in his palace—
a fact which shows perhaps better than anything else which way
the wind was blowing in Florence.[3]

The extent of Piero's military preparations was revealed on
the afternoon of the same day. The Piazza della Signoria, on
which the *Parlamento* assembled, was lined with about 3,000 of
his soldiers; Lorenzo di Piero came on horseback.[4] The success
of the *Parlamento* was thus, as in 1458, a foregone conclusion.
The Signoria asked for a *Balìa* to be created for four months, and
the people shouted 'yea'. After all was over, Lorenzo remounted
and returned with the soldiers to the Medici palace, 'cum grande
trionffo'.[5] That Piero's victory was due largely to his military
resources he himself admits in a letter written a few days later
to his Milanese agent: 'ma certamente. . . non si può negare che
le forze di cotesti Illustrissimi Signori e l'altre nostre ce habbiano
giovato assai'. But, he adds, 'messere domenedio è quello ch'a
operato tucto'.[6]

The fate of Piero's opponents still hung in the balance for

---

[1] *Ricordanze*, extract ed. by R. Ridolfi, *Gli archivi delle famiglie fiorentine* (Florence, 1934),
p. 87: 'E come era ordinato, M. Lucha Pitti, quale se ne fusse la chagione nollo so, benchè
molte chagione si dicesse che llui avea preso etc., e fattogli gran profferte, finalmente
lui consigliò si facesse parlamento. . . e così fu seghuitato da ogni altro', &c. Cf. also
Piero's letter of 13 Sept., cit. above: 'non potresti credere nella disgratia et contumacie in
che si truovono alji adversarii [i.e. after Luca's defection] . . . ciaschuno grida vendetta. . .'.
The members of the *Pratica* had to sign the minutes of the meeting to confirm their acceptance
of the proposal, as happened sometimes after specially important meetings; their signatures
are in Cons. e Prat., cit., fols. 182ᵛ–183ᵛ; Pampaloni, II, pp. 578–80.

[2] Letter of 'Lo.' of 6 Sept. (Fabroni, *Laurentii vita*, II, p. 31): 'Vedendo costoro e signori
a modo di Piero e appresso le genti che lui ce avea, furono costretti fare parlamento. . .'.

[3] Cons. e Prat., cit., fol. 182ᵛ; Pampaloni, II, p. 578: 'a casa Piero di Cosimo che per
essere impedito, non può venire'. He had also excused himself on 28 Aug. when summoned
by the Signoria, and had sent Lorenzo instead; however, on the 27th he had been well
enough to make a return journey to Careggi (Nicodemo to Bianca Maria and Galeazzo
Maria Sforza, 27 Aug., ASM, cit.).

[4] Antonio da Pesaro to Orfeo da Ricavo (ASM, cit.; partly printed in *Storia di Milano*,
vii, pp. 234–5): '. . . oggi ad hore xviii Piero mandò circha tremilia fanti armati in suso la
piazza, e lo fiolo a cavallo armato de tute arme luy.' Rinuccini, p. cii, has about 4,000. The
figures given by the professional soldier are probably more accurate.

[5] Antonio da Pesaro, letter cit.

[6] Letter to Pigello Portinari of 13 Sept., loc. cit. The official version of the events was
somewhat different: the people had taken up arms, wrote the Signoria to the King of France
on 23 Sept., had quashed the conspiracy, and restored freedom (Missive, Reg., 45, fols.
106ᵛ–107ᵛ, ed. Municchi, App. no. 18, p. 134). The law passed by the *Parlamento* is in Balìe,
30, fols. 5ʳ–7ʳ.

a few days. It was not finally decided until 6 September when the *Balìa* elected the new *Otto di Guardia*, 'homini amicissimi di Piero',[1] who were granted once more the special powers they had been deprived of in 1465.[2] On the following day they summoned to their presence leaders of the opposition, among them Niccolò Soderini, Agnolo Acciaiuoli, and Dietisalvi Neroni.[3] On the 8th a number of other citizens were arrested, among them Carlo Gondi, whose diary contains a vivid account of the persecutions of the anti-Mediceans,[4] and Francesco Neroni, whose confessions throw much light on the events preceding them.[5] All he had done, exclaims Carlo Gondi, was to have signed the declaration 'in difensione degli stati', but so had several hundred citizens, some of them of higher and others of lower social status: and now he and his family had with one stroke lost honour, wealth, friends, and relatives.[6] Proceedings against the anti-Mediceans evidently took account of the *sottoscrizione* of 27 May[7] where men of lesser standing were concerned; as for the leaders, they were, with the exception of Luca Pitti, exiled by the *Balìa* on 11 September on the grounds of having taken up arms against the fatherland and having called in *maximos exercitus*, thus threatening *dulcissimam ac*

[1] Nicodemo to Bianca Maria and Galeazzo Maria Sforza, 6 Sept. 1466 (ASM, cit.): '. . . il perchè questi adversarii de Piero hano preso spavento'.

[2] See above, pp. 111, 140. On 5 Sept. the *Balìa* decreed that 'per ann idieci . . . l'uficio degl'otto che pe' tempi saranno . . . habbino quella medesima o simile auctorità, potestà et balìa, la quale . . . hebbono gl'otto fatti per l'auctorità della balìa dell'anno 1434' (fol. 12ᵛ).

[3] Atti del Capitano del Popolo, 3984, fol. 23ʳ.

[4] See above, pp. 163–4. Only part of this account has been published by Ridolfi, *Gli archivi*, pp. 87–88; I quote from the MS. in the Gondi archives, which has been copied for me, with the kind permission of the late Marchese Giuliano Gondi, by Dr. E. Corti.

[5] There are extant three versions of Francesco Neroni's confession. One of these, of 10 Sept., has been edited by Fabroni, *Laurentii vita*, ii, pp. 32–34, from Med. av. Pr., LXVIII, no. 76. A much shorter version, of 9 Sept., is in Med. av. Pr., LXVIII, no. 75, and a considerably longer one is contained in the letter to Lionardo and Giovanni which has been mentioned above, p. 161, n. 3 (Med. av. Pr., XCVII, no. 249).

[6] Once arrested, 'io chonoscieva a uno tratto avere perduto l'onore e lla roba e gl'amici e parenti, e non tanto di me, ma di Mariotto e de' suoi e miei figluoli, e sanza manchamento alchuno fatto per me: solo m'ero soscritto, e così Mariotto mio fratello, a una scritta, come ò detto di sopra, in difensione degli stati, alla quale v'erano soscritto nel medesimo modo chome savamo noi, parechi cientinaia di cittadini de' magiori di noi e anche de' minori'. But, as many people told Carlo, the real reason for his downfall was his success in being *veduto* Gonfalonier of Justice in 1465, by favour of Agnolo Acciaiuoli and against Piero de' Medici's will (see above, pp. 138–9): 'La quale cosa. . . molti mi dissono che questa fu chagione della mia rovina, perchè Piero di Cosimo dimostrava volere altri. E benchè e' fusse veduto anchora Giovanni Rucellai che llo voleva lui, di meno si disse non ll'ebbe per bene. E chi metteva tale dubio, non sapeva come io era stato prima da Piero di Cosimo e ffattogli nota della voglia di mess. Agnolo verso di me di farmi vedere, offerendogli ne farei quello volesse. Lui mi rispuose che andasse dirieto al fatto mio. . . .' (*Ricordanze*, fols. 7ʳ–8ᵛ, in Archivio Gondi, discendenza di Bartolommeo di Bernardo).

[7] See above, pp. 156–8.

suavissimam libertatem.[1] Among these was Francesco Neroni, whose confession played an important role in these proceedings, although it was considerably less incriminating than the official version of the 'conspiracy'.[2] It probably also contributed to a number of other citizens, among them Carlo Gondi, being banished outside Florence or deprived of political rights for up to twenty years, on 12 September.[3] But on the whole the repression was relatively mild, and this was due largely to Piero, who showed himself to be less vindictive than some of his friends, among them the Milanese ambassador.[4] Evidently in order to counterbalance the impression created by the banishments and arrests, and to strengthen the popularity of the régime, an amnesty was granted on 20 September to a number of citizens who had been condemned to exile and deprived of political rights from 1434 onwards.[5]

However, Piero's clemency in dealing with the vanquished[6] was not matched by concessions in the matter of the political régime. Should there still have been any doubts about this at the time of the *Parlamento*, they were soon dispelled. In contrast to the previous *Parlamento*, of 11 August 1458, which had itself decreed the restoration of electoral controls,[7] all such decisions were now left to the *Balìa*,[8] with the sole proviso that it must on no account reduce the powers of the *Cento*.[9] This was clearly an

---

[1] Balìe, 30, fols. 15ᵛ–17ʳ. The condemned were Agnolo Acciaiuoli and his son Neri; Dietisalvi, Francesco and Agnolo di Nerone Dietisalvi, and Niccolò Soderini and his son Geri (cf. also Otto di Guardia e Balìa, periodo repubblicano, 224, fols. 126ʳ–127ᵛ). Except Francesco Neroni, they had, when the sentence was passed, already fled Florence. On Agnolo Acciaiuoli, see also Vespasiano da Bisticci, *Vite*, p. 497, who believes that Agnolo would have been spared exile if he had not fled.

[2] Letters of Piero de' Medici to Pigello Portinari, 13 Sept., and of Nicodemo to Bianca Maria and Galeazzo Maria Sforza, of the same date (ASM, cit.). Piero writes that Francesco Neroni had confessed that the conspirators 'mi dovevano tagliare a pezi et sachegiarmi la casa', &c.: this does not emerge from his confession.

[3] Otto di Guardia e Balìa, cit., fols. 128ᵛ–135ᵛ, 136ᵛ–138ʳ.

[4] Nicodemo to Bianca Maria and Galeazzo Maria Sforza, 4 Sept. (ASM, cit.): he, Nicodemo, does not have 'l'animo bene securo che'l faza el bisogno vostro e suo'. Cf. Guicciardini, *Memorie di famiglia*, op. cit., p. 42.

[5] Balìe, 30, fols. 20ᵛ–22ᵛ, ed. in Alessandra Macinghi-Strozzi, *Lettere*, pp. 581–2. Some of these had been exiled in 1458 (see above, pp. 109–10). Alessandra's son Filippo, who benefited from this measure, comes under this category. Nicodemo writes on the same day (to Bianca Maria and Galeazzo Maria Sforza, ASM, cit.): I would have advised Piero to do this but not so soon, 'nè fin che questa nova piagha fosse stata meglio curata. . .'.

[6] Cf. Guicciardini, *Storie fiorentine*, pp. 17, 20.

[7] See above, p. 105.

[8] Balìe, 30, fol. 5ᵛ (2 Sept. 1466).

[9] '. . . intelligatur confirmata et roborata omnis auctoritas circa consilium quod vocatur consilium del Cento . . . et contra tamen in ipsius diminutionem nihil disponi, provideri vel ordinari possit quoquomodo; sed in augmentum et favorem sic' (ibid.).

attempt to safeguard the *Cento*, whose authority was at the same time *confirmata et roborata*, against any attempt at reform or abolition like those made in July.[1] Such a safeguard was, incidentally, also implied in the short term of office of this *Balìa* (it was to last until 31 December), in contrast to the long-term *Balìe* between 1438 and 1455; this type of *Balìa* was evidently considered to have, once and for all, been replaced by the *Cento*. That it was felt necessary to protect the latter from interference by the *Balìa* is not without interest. If it was due to uncertainty about the *Balìa*'s future behaviour, a similar uncertainty may well have been responsible for the absence, in the law of the *Parlamento* itself, of any reference to the restoration of controls.

For while, in view of the suspension of conciliar assent to the decisions of the *Balìa*, there was no immediate need to pay much attention to public opinion as expressed in the councils of the People and the Commune, the same does not apply to the *ottimati*. Indeed the very composition of the *Balìa* shows that it was considered desirable to humour them: for instead of conforming to the pattern of the *Balìa* of 1458, with its large element of elected members, the new *Balìa* follows that of the scrutiny council of February 1466, which in its turn had constituted an amended version of the scrutiny council of the previous November.[2] The *Balìa* was similarly composed of two main sections, the *veduti* Gonfaloniers of Justice and the elected members, the *ex officio* members being reduced to a minimum, in contrast to earlier *Balìe*.[3] The *veduti* Gonfaloniers of Justice were thus automatically admitted, as they had been to the two scrutiny councils of 1465–6: in September 1466 they provided *c.* 46 per cent. of the total membership, only little less than the elected members, who provided *c.* 48 per cent.[4] Since nearly all the *veduti* Gonfaloniers and many elected members had belonged to the scrutiny councils, the social structure of the *Balìa* did not differ significantly from that of the

---

[1] See above, pp. 159–60.   [2] See above, pp. 148, 152.

[3] The elected membership was to consist of seventy-five members of the Greater and twenty-five of the Lesser Guilds, to whom were to be added so many additional members of the latter as to amount to one quarter of the total number of *veduti* Gonfaloniers: in this way, the normal one-to-three ratio for the artisans was preserved. The elected members were to be chosen by the Signoria and the Colleges from among the citizens who had been *veduti ai Tre Maggiori* since 1434. In the *Balìa* of 1458 there had been 152 official members, as against 200 *arroti*, i.e. elected ones (see above, p. 106); in that of 1466 there were, in fact, only 17, since most of the Colleges already belonged to the *Balìa* in the capacity of *veduti* Gonfaloniers or *arroti*. After the new Colleges entered their office on 8 and 14 Sept. respectively, the number of official members rose to 32; cf. list in Appendix, no. VII.

[4] 149 and 156 respectively out of a total of 322 at the beginning of the session.

latter: it shows the same oligarchical trend, over and above the social continuity that had been characteristic of the *Balìe* since 1434.[1] Like the preservation of the *Cento*, this may well have been designed to conciliate the *ottimati*. When the *Balìa* began its session it included many citizens who had signed the republican declaration of May 1466, among them all the leading opponents of Piero.[2] Yet there could be little doubt that the vast majority of the *Balìa*, whatever their political sympathies in the past months had been, would now back the victorious party in restoring the Medicean controls that had recently been abolished; the more so as the past leaders of the opposition set the example: it was Luca Pitti himself who, on 5 September, proposed the opening of the *borse*, Agnolo Acciaiuoli having, in his turn, offered to do so.[3] The law passed on 5 September by the *Balìa*[4] restored, in fact, all the former controls, judicial as well as political. The *Otto di Guardia* recovered the special powers they had lost in 1465,[5] and were granted *balìa* for ten years; and *balìa*, or special powers, was also given, for up to five years, to the *Podestà* or the Captain of the People.[6] At the same time, the *borse* of the Signoria were once more put in the hands of *Accoppiatori*.

The restoration of elections *a mano* was explained in terms of what had become official Medicean theory: the *borse aperte* bring peace and unity, the *borse chiuse* discord and civil strife.[7] During the next ten years the Signoria was to be elected *a mano* by annually appointed *Accoppiatori*.[8] This period is twice as long as

---

[1] 167 out of its 322 members had belonged to the *Balìa* of 1458.

[2] See above, p. 157. Eleven of these appear in the *Balìa* list with the marginal note *privatus* added after its compilation; see Appendix, no. VII. They had all been exiled or deprived of offices.

[3] Cons. e Prat., 58, fol. 184ʳ (5 Sept.). Nicodemo to Bianca Maria and Galeazzo Maria Sforza, 5 Sept. (Bibl. Nat., MS. ital. 1591, fol. 369): Agnolo 'usò parole submissive' towards Piero and told him 'che voleva essere el primo in palasio a consigliare che le borse se repigliassero a mano. . .'.

[4] Balìe, 30, fols. 12ᵛ–15ᵛ.   [5] See above, pp. 140, 165.

[6] The decision was left to the Signoria in office. This *provvisione* made it possible for the *Podestà* or the Captain to deal with political cases without recourse to the normal judicial channels, and was accordingly designed as an additional safeguard. For precedents, see above, pp. 3, n. 7, 111, n. 1. On the strength of this decree, the Captain of the People, Giovanni di M. Paolo da Gubbio, was granted *balìa* on 6 Sept. (Signori e Collegi, Deliberazioni, speciale autorità, 32, fol. 131ᵛ). His term of office having been extended by six months by the *Balìa* (Balìe, 30, fol. 48ᵛ; 21 Oct. 1466), the Signoria extended his *balìa* for the same period (Deliberazioni, cit., fol. 137ᵛ; 10 Jan. 1467). On 9 July 1467 they granted it, instead, to the *Podestà* (ibid., fols. 155ʳ–156ʳ).

[7] 'Et considerato in quanta pace et unione sia stata la cittadinanza ne' tempi passati, quando le borse de' Signori erano aperte, et in quanta discordia et civili dissensioni tutti i cittadini siano venuti poi se serrono' (Balìe, 30, fol. 14ʳ). See also above, pp. 25, 26–27, 122.

[8] Their number was to be ten in the first year, and five in each of the following years.

that for which elections *a mano* had been reintroduced in 1458; but as the first quinquennial term had been extended for another quinquennium in 1460,[1] it could be argued that in fact a ten-year term was not an innovation. To secure an even longer one does not seem, at the time, to have been considered feasible or advisable; but by the end of December the Mediceans clearly felt strong enough to be able to obtain from the *Balìa* an extension for another ten years.[2] If, in July 1460, the discovery of Girolamo Machiavelli's conspiracy had been used to persuade the councils to pass the quinquennial extension,[3] to have such an extension decreed by the *Balìa*, before it dissolved on 31 December, was doubtless a much safer procedure. By opening the *borse* for twenty years, elections *a mano* of the Signoria became practically a permanent institution, and the development that had begun in October 1434 was all but completed. In fact, the *borse* of the Signoria remained open until the fall of the régime in 1494.

In August 1458 the *Accoppiatori* of 1452–5 and those of the scrutiny had been put in charge of the elections *a mano*, and had for this purpose been divided into annual groups of five.[4] They had closed the bags in October 1465, and new *Accoppiatori* had been appointed for the scrutiny of 1465–6.[5] There was no reason why the *Accoppiatori* of 1452–5 should not now be reappointed as they had been in similar circumstances in 1458. Instead, the law of 5 September laid down that, while the first *Accoppiatori* were to be elected by the Signoria of September–October 1466, in each subsequent year the Signoria in office in October had to see to it that the election took place (*debbino far fare*).[6] The Signoria was implicitly authorized to delegate its powers to elect and did so to the *Cento*, who even held the election of the first *Accoppiatori* on 26 October 1466, the candidates having probably been nominated by the Signoria.[7] This reform, which constituted a sharp departure from earlier practice, may have been inspired by the experiences of the past year, when four of the *Accoppiatori* had played a leading role in the opposition to Piero.[8] To elect new officials every year might, in the end, be less risky than to let the

---

[1] See above, pp. 121–2.
[2] Balìe cit., fols. 85ᵛ–86ʳ (24 Dec. 1466).
[3] See above, pp. 121–2.
[4] See above, p. 105.
[5] See above, pp. 142, 149, and 152, n. 2.
[6] Balìe, 30, fol. 14ʳ–ᵛ.
[7] The fact that the Signoria could delegate its authority is emphasized by the opening sentence of the following paragraph: 'Le sopradecte electioni degli accopiatori tempo per tempo si faccino per chi n'a auctorità....' For the election on 26 Oct., Tratte, 19, fol. 1ʳ–ᵛ.
[8] They were Luca Pitti, Agnolo Acciaiuoli, Dietisalvi Neroni, and Manno Temperani.

office rotate among the same group of men; to entrust the
election to the *Cento* could be considered a further safeguard. In
this way the election of the *Accoppiatori* was given an oligarchical
twist which was in keeping with previous tendencies. Even so,
the law of 5 September met with considerable opposition in the
Balìa—an opposition that was the more significant as the city was
still under the shadow of the past events, and the enemies of
Piero were cowed into submission. According to Alamanno
Rinuccini, the rate of absenteeism at the meeting of 5 September
was fairly high; only 276 out of the 322 members of the *Balìa*
were present (this contrasts with the almost complete attendance
at the scrutiny council in December 1465); and of these 276, no
less than 77 voted against the granting of special powers to the
Captain or the *Podestà*.[1]

Supplementary regulations concerning the method of *far vedere*
for the Gonfaloniership of Justice and the Priorate were passed
on 14 October, and may have been designed to conciliate the
opponents to the restoration of electoral and other controls. 'Per
consolare quanto si può nelle cose honeste et usate i nostri cittadini che desiderano che i loro figliuoli o altri congiunti che non
sono anchora veduti ad alcuno de' tre maggiori sieno veduti', the
Accoppiatori were henceforth authorized to have as many names
as they wished drawn from the *borse* of the Priorate at the two-
monthly elections, for the purpose of *far vedere*; for the Gonfaloniership of Justice, on the other hand, the maximum of two
veduti per election, laid down in 1459, was maintained.[2] This concession affected a much wider section of the citizenry than the far
more exclusive matter of *far vedere* for the Gonfaloniership, and
was thus doubtless aimed at increasing Piero's popularity. The
Accoppiatori loyally followed suit by having an uncommonly large
number of names drawn from the *borse* of the Priorate at the next
two-monthly elections, for the purpose of making their owners
veduti. While during the twelve months preceding the closing of
the *borse* in September 1465, the number of *polizze* drawn for the
Priorate averaged about 27 and during the twelve months following, under free elections, 42, it shoots up to 166 at the election

[1] Rinuccini, p. ciii. The *Balìa* registers, unlike those of the statutory councils, do not
contain voting returns. See also above, p. 149, n. 6.

[2] Balìe, 30, fol. 38ᵛ: '. . . che i detti accoppiatori . . . possino . . . di quegli che fussino
imborsati nelle borse del priorato o del notariato de' priori che pe' tempi vegghiaranno,
che fussino minori o avessino divieto, deliberare che sieno imborsati per fargli vedere . . .
quanti e quali a loro parrà che si convenga. . . .' For the Gonfaloniership of Justice, see
above, p. 120.

of December 1466, and rises to 173 and 227 respectively at those of February and April 1467.[1]

To complete its electoral legislation the *Balìa* decreed, on 11 December, that the next scrutiny be started in November or December 1468, and issued additional regulations for it on 22 December.[2] 1468 was the year in which, according to the *provvisione* of January 1462 postponing the scrutiny,[3] one had to be held in any case: this meant that the scrutiny of 1465–6 assumed, implicitly, an irregular appearance. Owing to the abandonment of the system of long-term *Balìe* after 1458, the holding of a scrutiny presented, however, fresh problems to the régime: for if there was no *Balìa* to carry it out, decisions on its technical organization reverted automatically to the statutory councils. The laws of 11 and 22 December were designed to provide a short-term as well as a long-term answer to this problem. On 11 December it was decided that the *Balìa* would be reconvened in 1468 for the scrutiny, when its size was to be increased by the addition of eighty members, to be elected by the *Cento*, and of the citizens who had been *veduti* Gonfaloniers of Justice after 1 September 1466.[4] Ten days later, the *Balìa*, 'essendosi veduto più volte che il mezo degli squittini induce facilmente a obtenere qualunche deliberatione etiamdio non honesta, di che risurge grande alteratione alla città', permanently regulated the procedure to be adopted in future scrutinies. After 1468 scrutinies were to be carried out, at intervals of not less than five years, by the Signoria and Colleges in office, the citizens who had been *veduti* Gonfaloniers from 1434 onwards, plus members of the Lesser Guilds numbering a quarter of these *veduti*, and 100 elected members (*arroti*).[5] This closely resembles the composition of the scrutiny council of February 1466.[6] The decision to hold scrutinies *se non passato* five years was bound to be popular, as it might

[1] Tratte, 202. After the April election, the number of *polizze* decreases again: during the twelve months following they average 66 per two-monthly election, and during the next two years 22 and 12 respectively.

[2] Balìe, 30, fols. 74r–75r (11 Dec.); 83v–84v (22 Dec.).

[3] See above, p. 122.

[4] Balìe, 30, fols. 74r–75r. The official members were the Signoria and the Colleges in office in Dec. 1466, the preceding Colleges who had been members of the *Balìa*, as well as the Signoria and the Colleges in office at the time. The minimum age for the *veduti* was to be thirty.

[5] Of these *arroti*, one quarter was to belong to the Lesser Guilds, and all of them were to be chosen from among the *veduti ai Tre Maggiori*. The minimum age for the *veduti*, the artisans, and the *arroti*, was to be thirty-five. The artisans and the 100 *arroti* were to be elected by the *Cento*. Balìe, 30, fols. 83v–84v. See also Rinuccini, p. cv.

[6] See above, p. 152, n. 2.

appear to revive the traditional quinquennial scrutinies. In this way it was also understood by well-informed citizens;[1] but the wording of the law was perhaps intentionally ambiguous. On the other hand, the oligarchical features of the new scrutiny councils may have been a concession to the patriciate. The principal novelty of the law was the settlement of the scrutiny procedure on a permanent basis, instead of the *ad hoc* legislation passed from time to time after 1434. 'Fu cosa violenta e vinta per forza', comments a member of the *Balìa*,[2] a remark which probably refers both to the form and the contents of the law.

The *Balìa* duly dissolved on 31 December;[3] but it was not reconvened for the scrutiny in 1468. The Signoria of November–December 1468, which was due to initiate the scrutiny, asked a *Pratica* for advice on whether it should be held then; and while opinions in the *Pratica* were at first divided, there was finally general agreement in favour of postponing it.[4] The usual argument that scrutinies were liable to create disturbances, 'si fieret scrutinium, multa mala et incommoda civitati sequerentur',[5] prevailed over the view that the scrutiny should be held 'honoris causa',[6] a query as to whether the text of the law contained some loophole which could make postponement possible having been answered in the affirmative by the lawyer Domenico Martelli.[7] There was, as we have seen,[8] an ingrained dislike among the Mediceans of an institution which preserved, even under the controls introduced after 1434, some of its original democratic characteristics by affecting large sections of the population, and which was thus liable to upset the delicate balance created by the régime.

[1] Rinuccini, p. cv: 'che da ora innanzi per ogni tempo si avessi a fare squittino di cinque in cinque anni, intendendosi detto termine cominciare immediate finito lo squittino che si avea a fare nel 1468. . . .' Rinuccini was a member of the *Balìa*, as *arroto* for S. Croce.

[2] Ibid.

[3] Its last deliberations are of that date: Balìe cit., fols. 95^r–99^v.

[4] Cons. e Prat., 60, fols. 41^v–42^r (23 Nov. 1468): 'super scrutineo petitum consilium lecta lege', 42^{r-v} (26 Nov.), 43^{r-v} (1 Dec.), and 44^{r-v} (6 Dec). On 6 Dec. Otto Niccolini states for the *Otto* that while opinions had at first been divided, 'nunc videntur omnes consentire ut supersedeatur in scrutinio' (fol. 44^v).

[5] Giovannozzo Pitti (fol. 44^r), who on 23 Nov. had been in favour of observing the law.

[6] Giovanni Lorini (fol. 42^r; 26 Nov.): the Colleges 'honoris causa desiderare, ut scruptineum fieret; sed nullo modo velle ea que sint noxia civitati'. On 6 Dec. they backed Otto Niccolini's advice (see above, n. 4).

[7] On 1 Dec. Luigi Guicciardini having asked 'si quid est subterfugium in lege, ut vitari pene posset et non celebrari scrutinium', Domenico Martelli 'iureconsultus aperuit cartam legis et disputando eo rem adduxit ut concluderet illo exemplo prorogationis [*sic*] utiliorem esse' (fol. 43^r).

[8] See above, pp. 122–3.

The legislation of the *Balìa* thus not only restored the system of government that had been revived and consolidated in 1458, but also strengthened it in its turn by extending the period of electoral controls to an unprecedented degree. The ultimate success of this system, however, depended, after 1466 just as before, on the collaboration of the leading citizens of the régime. The militant opposition to Piero had collapsed, and the security measures taken by the *Balìa* were more than sufficient to ward off any dangers at home. But in 1467 and 1468 Niccolò Soderini and other leading exiles were striving to bring about Piero's downfall by war, with the help of the *condottiere* Bartolomeo Colleoni, and with the tacit backing of Venice;[1] and there were doubtless people in Florence who would have welcomed their victory. It is highly unlikely that all the 400-odd citizens who in May 1466 had signed the republican declaration should have changed their minds so soon; Alamanno Rinuccini is probably a not untypical example of citizens who, while taking part in administration and government under the Medicean régime, were harking back to the good old times before 1434. Considerable concessions had been made to the *ottimati*, but the problem remained of how to reconcile their traditional political ambitions with the ascendancy of one family. Success depended, to a large extent, on the tact and diplomacy of the Medici; and Piero proved, despite his comparative mildness towards his opponents, to be less capable in this respect than his father.[2] When he died, on 2 December 1469, Medici ascendancy could therefore appear less secure than it had been after Cosimo's death. The youth and inexperience of his sons Lorenzo and Giuliano created a further problem, and there were many people in Florence who believed that constitutional government would be fully restored within a few days.[3]

---

[1] On the Colleoni war, see *Storia di Milano*, vii, pp. 237 ff.

[2] It was later believed, probably correctly, that shortly before his death Piero had been planning an amnesty for the exiles. See Vespasiano da Bisticci, *Vite*, p. 497, and Francesco Altoviti's letter to Lorenzo di Piero de' Medici of 16 Sept. 1475 (Carte Strozz., 1ª ser., 3, fol. 91): 'come sapete, se fossi vissuto più alquanti dì, haveva ordinato che noi tornassimo.' Cf. also Machiavelli, *Istorie fiorentine*, vii, 23.

[3] Letter of the Ferrarese orator, Niccolò Roberti, to Borso d'Este, 4 Dec. 1469 (ed. A. Cappelli, 'Lettere di Lorenzo de' Medici . . . con notizie tratte dai carteggi diplomatici degli oratori Estensi a Firenze', *Atti e Memorie delle Deputazioni di storia patria per le provincie modenesi e parmensi*, i (1863), p. 250): 'che fra pochi dì si abbia a ridurre ogni cosa al palazzo.' See also above, p. 156.

PART III

Lorenzo di Piero: The Medici at the Height of their Power

ON the evening of 2 December[1] about 700 citizens met at the church of S. Antonio to discuss the situation created for the régime by Piero's death on the same day. The meeting had already been decided upon in the morning, when Piero's condition appeared grave, by Tommaso Soderini and other leading citizens.[2] Originally, only about 150 citizens were to be invited to it, but after Piero's death, their number was doubled, and in the end over 700 came to S. Antonio.[3] The meeting was not a *Pratica* summoned by the Signoria—a *Pratica* did take place three days later—but an unofficial meeting of supporters of the régime. Its large numbers reflect the desire to make it as representative as possible; as the Milanese orator put it, it included men of all kinds, *de omne sorte*. The gravity of the situation was evidently felt to warrant exceptional measures. However, it could be argued that, since the meeting had no constitutional standing, whatever it decided would be of little practical consequence. This was Marco Parenti's view: he writes, on the following day, that it was not more than a ceremony—'fu una cirimonia, e stimasi atto di poco pondo'.[4] But the Medicean leaders knew what they were about: after receiving the support of the rank and file, a small number of *veri amici* of the Medici were intended to take matters into their hands.[5] Tommaso Soderini, who had so loyally supported Piero and who was now the prime mover in these proceedings, initiated the discussion; and the meeting unanimously demanded the preservation of the Medici, that is of Lorenzo and Giuliano, 'in

[1] Not, as the Ferrarese orator writes, after his funeral on the 3rd (Niccolò Roberti to Borso d'Este, 4 Dec. 1469, loc. cit.).

[2] Sacramoro to Galeazzo Maria Sforza, 2 Dec. 1469 (ASM, Pot. est., Firenze, 277).

[3] The same to the same, writing later on the same day (ibid.): 'faranno questa sera quello raxonamento fra loro et saranno circa .CCC., benchè prima havessino ditto de' .CL.' In his third letter of that day (ibid.), he writes: 'dove credevano essere .CCC., sonno stati circa VII^c e più. . . .'

[4] To Filippo Strozzi, in Alessandra Macinghi-Strozzi, *Lettere*, p. 609.

[5] Sacramoro, 2 Dec., first letter, loc. cit.

reputatione e grandeza'.[1] In its studied vagueness this decision reflects the nature of Medici ascendancy; but its political intention was clear enough. 'Intendesi', writes the Ferrarese ambassador, 'così passeranno per le mani di Lorenzo le cose secrete di questa Signoria, come passavano per le mani del padre';[2] and the Milanese envoy reports after the meeting that all the *principali cittadini* had decided to avoid a change of government.[3] The memory of the events of 1465–6 must have been still fresh in their minds, and there was little doubt that the Duke of Milan would once more be prepared to back the Medici by force of arms.[4] Giovannozzo Pitti and Domenico Martelli probably voiced the general feeling of the meeting when they pointed out that the regime stood or fell by the leadership of one man.[5] Three days later the Signoria summoned a *Pratica* of about sixty to seventy leading citizens to discuss measures to protect the régime.[6] As Tommaso Soderini had predicted, political decisions had once more passed to a small group of loyal Mediceans.

Lorenzo, on the other hand, could hardly have failed to accept when, on 3 December, the 'principali della città e dello stato', the leading men of the city and the régime, asked him to assume the care of both, which in the past had been entrusted to Cosimo and Piero.[7] Lorenzo states that he did so reluctantly, and there was indeed much that drew him away from public affairs. Yet the day before his father's death, he had written to the Duke of Milan asking him to extend the protection which he had hitherto accorded to the *stato e grandezza* of the Medici, also to him.[8]

---

[1] Sacramoro, 2 Dec., third letter, loc. cit.

[2] Niccolò Roberti, 4 Dec., loc. cit. According to Niccolò Roberti's account of the meeting, Tommaso Soderini described Cosimo's and Piero's ascendancy as *principato*, but Sacramoro does not say anything of this sort, and it is highly unlikely that Tommaso would have used this term, which, on the other hand, would be familiar to an Italian ruler.

[3] To Galeazzo Maria, 3 Dec. 1469 (ASM, cit.): 'la volontà de tutti quisti principali è de non volere alteratione in la ciptà. . . .'

[4] The Duke wrote on 6 Dec. to the Signoria that he was keeping troops in the territory of Parma, in readiness to intervene if necessary (ASM, cit.). There were fears that the anti-Mediceans and the exiles might stage a coup: Sacramoro to Galeazzo Maria, 6 Dec. (ibid.). See also G. Soranzo, 'Lorenzo il Magnifico alla morte del padre e il suo primo balzo verso la Signoria', *Arch. Stor. Ital.*, cxi (1953), pp. 47–48.

[5] Again, the formulation is doubtless Niccolò Roberti's: 'che si aveva a riconoscere uno signore e superiore che . . . avesse unanime a trattare tutte le cose concernenti lo stato di questa Ecc. Signoria' (loc. cit.).

[6] Sacramoro to Galeazzo Maria Sforza, 6 Dec. 1469 (ASM, cit.).

[7] *Ricordi* of Lorenzo di Piero de' Medici, ed. Fabroni, *Laurentii vita*, ii, p. 42. Fabroni published the *Ricordi* without indication of provenance, but no doubt from the sixteenth-century copy in the Bibl. Naz., II. IV. 309, fols. 1ʳ–2ᵛ. The meaning of the term *stato* in this context is 'régime', and not, as modern historians commonly translate, 'state'.

[8] ASM, cit. (1 Dec. 1469); ed. Buser, *Die Beziehungen*, p. 442.

The Duke had, in December 1469, special reasons for backing Lorenzo, whose youth might be expected to make him even more amenable to Milanese influence than his father had been. The Papacy was at war with Roberto Malatesta over the succession in Rimini, and Galeazzo Maria Sforza was bent on non-intervention by the triple alliance of Milan, Florence, and Naples; an attitude that was not shared by the King of Naples, who had his own reasons for desiring energetic action against Paul II. The discussions between representatives of the league, which began in Florence about a month after Piero's death, were not only overshadowed by these contrasting aims, but also revealed similar differences of opinion among the leading citizens of the régime.[1] However much these differences might be due to genuine assessments of the diplomatic situation, opposition to Sforza diplomacy was always liable to be taken, rightly or wrongly, as prompted by the desire to weaken Medici ascendancy. The brave show of unanimity which the régime had put up at the time of Piero's death was thus put to a severe test almost immediately after it. Tommaso Soderini, in particular, now toed the Aragonese line; nor was he alone in doing so.[2]

Moreover, Tommaso Soderini, and some other elder statesmen of the régime such as Luigi Guicciardini, may well have felt that it was their right and duty to guide the young Lorenzo, and thus to assume a leading role in the régime, at least during the first years of his ascendancy. The events of 1466 made it highly unlikely that they would, if thwarted, follow the example of Luca Pitti; but there were more subtle ways of bringing pressure to bear on Lorenzo. Foreign policy was foremost among these.[3] It was consequently just as imperative for Lorenzo as it had been for his father to be able to rely upon the loyalty of the Signoria. However, the electoral controls, which had been developed so carefully over the years, were not considered, in 1470, to be wholly satisfactory.

Neither the *Accoppiatori*, nor the *Cento* who elected them, had proved, in 1465, as reliable as could have been expected after the reforms of 1458; and the *Balìa* of September 1466, while restoring Medicean controls, had done nothing to strengthen them. According to Francesco Guicciardini, whose grandfather and great-uncle

---

[1] See Soranzo, op. cit., pp. 500 ff.
[2] Ibid., pp. 56–57.
[3] Ibid., p. 62.

had been many times on the council of *Cento*,[1] Lorenzo and his friends could not always muster enough votes on the occasions when elections were held by that council, and feared that this might also happen one day when the *Cento* elected the *Accoppiatori*.[2] The bill which the Signoria proposed on 5 July 1470 was designed to make such an occurrence impossible by depriving the *Cento* of the right to elect these key officials of the régime. For the rest of the time in which elections of the Signoria were to be *a mano*, that is until 1486, the *Accoppiatori* were to be appointed by lot from among the citizens who had served in this capacity from October 1434 onwards.[3] As Giovannozzo Pitti explained in the *Pratica* of 3 July, the ruling citizens could not have *certitudinem status*, unless the *Accoppiatori*, who were in charge of electing the Signoria, had their approval. The method to achieve this was to recruit them in the proposed fashion. Tommaso Soderini added that this proposal did not constitute an innovation. In fact, it closely resembles the method by which the *Accoppiatori* were selected between 1458 and 1465; but while in 1458 this method of appointing the *Accoppiatori* had been adopted, in the first place, for five years, and had only subsequently been extended by another five years, the present reform was to remain in force for sixteen years.[4] This went considerably beyond any precedent of this kind, and may help to explain why Rinuccini condemns the reform bill as setting up forty-five tyrants.[5] 'They maintained', he continues, 'that the proposal required the assent of the *Cento* only' to become law. The argument was doubtless that the reform concerned elections which had previously been delegated to the *Cento*;[6] in fact, since

---

[1] Up to 1470 Jacopo Guicciardini had been three times, Luigi Guicciardini five times, a member of the *Cento* (Tratte, 336).

[2] *Storie fiorentine*, p. 24. The voting returns for the elections that were held in the *Cento* are not extant.

[3] Libri Fabarum, 69, fol. 45^r: 'Quod pro residuo temporis, quo burse debent stare ad manus, intelligantur electi in copulatores illi qui fuerunt'. Cf. Rinuccini, *Ricordi storici*, p. cxiii, who says that five newly-elected citizens were to be added to their number, which at that time amounted to about forty. See above, pp. 126, 149.

[4] Cons. e Prat., 60, fol. 110^{r-v} (3 July): Giovannozzo Pitti 'censuit gubernatores habeant certitudinem status; et id fiat hoc modo quod copulatores, quibus potestas est creandi summum magistratum, hi sint qui gubernatoribus et primis grati sint. Occurrere autem dixit id quod audisset a nonnullis, ut ille magistratus copulatorum a paucis fiat, id est a copulatoribus qui ab anno 1434 ad hanc diem fuerint . . .'; Tommaso Soderini: 'neque novum esse quod nunc inducitur, sed usitatum a maioribus quandocumque opus fuit; et exemplo anni 1458 usus est. . . .' See also above, pp. 105, 121.

[5] Loc. cit.

[6] There were precedents for this: thus on 6 Nov. 1459, the *Cento* had passed, by its sole authority, regulations concerning elections to offices with which it had been previously entrusted (Cento, 1, fol. 25^{r-v}). But the present bill went much further by depriving the *Cento* altogether of their powers to elect the *Accoppiatori*. See also below, p. 178, n. 2.

it concerned the *status*, it should also have been presented to the councils of the People and Commune. But if its promoters were hoping that the *Cento* would be more amenable than the ancient councils, they were mistaken, for the *Cento* rejected the bill twice,[1] and the Signoria did not insist further. All it could obtain was that the next *Accoppiatori* were to be elected before its term of office came to an end, and even this the *Cento* granted only with difficulty.[2] This temporary expedient in its turn bears witness to the crisis of the system of electoral controls: if all Signori could not be equally trusted to participate in the annual election of the *Accoppiatori*, not all *Accoppiatori* could be trusted to elect the right Signori. The Signoria of July–August having proved themselves loyal supporters of Lorenzo's reform scheme, it could be hoped that at least the next *Accoppiatori* would be, as Sacramoro puts it,[3] 'tali che sian de Lorenzo': for on this is founded his political power, 'in questo consiste el suo stato'.

The dispatches of the Milanese ambassador throw some interesting light on Lorenzo's aims and motives in this first attempt after his 'succession' to carry out constitutional reforms.[4] 'If I understand matters correctly,' Sacramoro writes on 3 July,[5] 'whether or not Lorenzo will preserve his ascendancy depends on the reform of the *Accoppiatori*; for Lorenzo is determined to follow his grandfather's example and use, as much as possible, constitutional methods.' According to his design, the *Accoppiatori* were to be appointed from a group of about forty citizens, who in their turn would be selected from those families which had been represented in that office since 1434. Each of these families was to provide one of this group, with the exception of

---

[1] Libri Fabarum, loc. cit.

[2] Cento, 1, fols. 72ᵛ–73ʳ (30 July 1470). The *provvisione* was passed with the narrow majority of 106 votes to 48, after having been rejected on the 27th (Libri Fabarum, loc. cit.). That it became law without the assent of the councils of the People and Commune appears to bear out Rinuccini's observation on the bill of 5 July (above, p. 177). The new *Accoppiatori* were elected on the 31st: see next footnote.

[3] To Galeazzo Maria Sforza, 31 July 1470 (ASM, Pot. est., Firenze, 279).

[4] Soranzo, following Guicciardini, ignores this episode altogether, and accordingly does not quote from the Milanese dispatches concerning it.

[5] ASM, Pot. est., Firenze, 279 (to Galeazzo Maria Sforza), 'el modo che andava per la mente a Laurenzo è questo per seguire li modi del avolo suo, che era di far tal cose cum più civilità si potesse. Designava Sua Magnificentia che se ne facesseno XL dove ce mettesse tutti quisti cavalleri principali . . . cioè uno per caxa, tollendo solum le caxate de quilli sonno stati accopiatori dal 34 in qua . . .', with the exception of the above-mentioned families, which were to provide two members each, i.e. Ugolino and Domenico Martelli, Luca and Giovannozzo Pitti, Bernardo and Antonio Ridolfi, and, evidently, Luigi and Jacopo Guicciardini, who had all been *Accoppiatori* since 1434. 'El resto autem fino al ditto numero de 40 o 44 metterci de quilli che siano amici soy e pur reputati in la terra. . . .'

the Guicciardini, the Martelli, the Pitti, and the Ridolfi, which were to provide two. Although slightly more flexible than the bill proposed two days later to the *Cento*, Lorenzo's scheme was criticized by Bartolomeo Scala for being too oligarchical. The Florentine chancellor and client of the Medici who, as Sacramoro puts it, knew as much about Florentine politics as any man in the city, told him confidentially that he did not like the reform scheme: for as long as the leading citizens remained disunited, as they were at present, all was well, but once they were united the situation would be very dangerous, for in that case they could acquire so much power that one might find oneself at their discretion. Consequently he would have preferred the *Accoppiatori* to be chosen from a larger number of citizens, including among these many middle-class Miceceans; or alternatively, he would exclude anybody who was suspect.[1] Lorenzo, when warned about these dangers, replied that discussions on the reform bill were already too far advanced for him to be able to draw back. As for the suspects, many of them were old men and would soon die, and would then be replaced by 'good men'; and to increase the number of potential *Accoppiatori* by adding twenty to thirty middle-class citizens would create new jealousies: for there were so many of this class that the more of them one qualified, the more one would incense those who were left out.[2]

Bartolomeo Scala's apprehensions touch upon one of the permanent problems of the régime, which Lorenzo in his turn had now to face. Despite Piero's success in 1466, there still remained the danger of oligarchical tendencies among the ruling group becoming too strong. As long as the Medicean system of government remained within the framework of the constitution—and Lorenzo was, as we have seen, determined to follow Cosimo's

---

[1] Ibid.: Bartolomeo Scala, 'che è vero partixano de Laurenzo . . . el quale credo habbia li termini de questo fatto civile così bene come homo de Fiorenza per sapere li loro secreti et per essere sapientissimo homo, hammi ditto in secreto non li piacere molto questo partito, perchè non ci conosse tutto el sicuro. Perchè stando quisti principali desuniti como hora sonno, non c'è pericholo; ma reunendosi como potriano fare col tempo, essendosi pure veduto qualche loro mala volontà . . . li pareria cosa molto pericholosa, perchè se vene a mettere quì troppo a loro discretione. . . . Haveria voluto . . . o maior numero, et metterci assay de quisti amici veri de caxa sua de meggia mano . . . overo . . . arecharsi in picholo, et lassare fore li sospetti . . .'.

[2] Ibid.: 'essere tanto inanti in quisti raxonamenti cum quisti principali, che mo non si pò retrare, et allega sue raxioni che quisto suo pensero è bono, cum dire che volendoci mettere xx o xxx più di li homini de quista conditione, che l'è tanto el numero de quilli, che quanto più ce ne mettesse, tanto più sdegnaria chi non ci fusse, et che quisti bastano. Allega etiam che de quisti principali sospetti ce ne sonno de' vecchi assay che finiranno presto, et renovarà de li bony. . . .'

policy in this matter—an effective and permanent tightening of controls required the further concentration of power in an inner circle of the régime, whose members were liable to claim power by right. Scala's case was, to some extent, borne out by the fact that Lorenzo evidently considered it inevitable to qualify as *Accoppiatori* citizens who might not be wholehearted supporters of his, in the hope that they would soon disappear; and his rejection of Scala's more cautious approach was probably due less to youthful rashness than to the conviction that, at least for the time being, his freedom of action in this matter was limited. His 'amici veri et boni' were thus greatly pleased, according to the Milanese ambassador, when, three days later, the *Cento* rejected the reform bill;[1] and Sacramoro adds, confidently: 'one will find some other way.'[2]

The opportunity for this arose six months later, after a Signoria headed by Agnolo della Stufa, a staunch supporter of the Medici and partisan of the Sforza, had been elected.[3] On 9 January 1471 it proposed that for the next five years the new *Accoppiatori* were to be elected annually in July or August by the *Accoppiatori* and the Signoria in office.[4] On 1 January the membership of the *Cento* had been changed for the first six-monthly session of 1471, which may explain the timing of the proposal; even so, it was unlikely, after the experiences of the previous July, that the *Cento* would pass the new bill without being granted some concessions. The limitation of its validity to five years, and, in particular, the provision that the candidates elected by the *Accoppiatori* and the Signoria had to be approved by the *Cento*, were doubtless designed to serve this purpose; although by requiring only an absolute, instead of the customary two-thirds majority, the law deprived this concession of much of its effective value. In fact, the bill met with considerable opposition in that council, which passed it with a majority of two votes only.[5] It was not presented to the councils of the People and Commune, and this

---

[1] Libri Fabarum, loc. cit. (5 and 6 July 1470).

[2] To Galeazzo Maria Sforza, 6 July 1470 (ASM, cit.): 'l'è suta gettata a terra, cum modo che li amici soy veri et boni restano molto consolati; et è fatto senza torre de reputatione al stato. Trovarasseli altra forma.'

[3] Galeazzo Maria Sforza expressed to his ambassador his pleasure at the election of Agnolo as Gonfalonier of Justice: 'Tu non potresti credere el piacere et contentamento havemo havuto ad intendere che'l nostro M. Angelo sii stato electo confallonero; et parhe hora che Lorenzo comenzi ad intendere la medicina che gli bisogna. . . .' (4 Jan. 1471; ibid.).

[4] Libri Fabarum, 69, fol. 73ᵛ.

[5] Cento, 1, fols. 73ʳ–74ʳ (9 Jan. 1471); Libri Fabarum, loc. cit.: 126 votes to 60.

was probably justified with the same arguments that had been used in July.[1]

It would have been difficult to devise, in the circumstances and within the framework of the republican constitution, a more efficient centralization of electoral controls. The new law places the main responsibility for the election of their successors squarely on the shoulders of the *Accoppiatori*; for though they shared this responsibility with the Signoria, the latter had in turn been elected by them. In the view of Lorenzo de' Medici, to achieve an absolute majority in the *Cento* did not constitute a problem for him and his friends.[2] 'In questo modo venirà sempre ad essere quella Signoria che luy vorrà', wrote the Milanese ambassador on 9 January; thus his ascendancy would be safer than that of his father and grandfather.[3]

The 'mala dispositione de molti che sonno del dicto consiglio', which, according to Sacramoro, was 'imbastardito assai',[4] had evidently been the principal motive for the reform of the election of the *Accoppiatori*. The next step was the reform of the *Cento* itself. Lorenzo's observations on the majorities obtainable in the *Cento* spotlight the problems with which the Mediceans were faced as late as 1471 when it came to voting in the councils, including their own creation, the *Cento*. As the average attendance in that council during 1470 was 115,[5] Lorenzo was accordingly confident of mustering about 60 votes, but not the 75 or so required for the normal two-thirds majority. The legislation of July 1471 was designed to remedy this flaw.

Since the *Cento* could, especially after the recent experiences, hardly be expected to be amenable to reforming itself, the Signoria of July–August[6] proposed, on 3–5 July, to the councils the creation of a *Balìa*, on the somewhat vague grounds that 'al presente gli animi di tutti e cittadini si truovano sospesi dubitando di varie cose', and that it was necessary to 'ordinare et correggere molte cose nella città, donde nascere può e nasce continovamente sementa di molti scandali'.[7] There is no specific reference to a

---

[1] See above, p. 177.

[2] Sacramoro to Galeazzo Maria Sforza, 9 Jan. 1471 (ASM, 281; Soranzo, p. 71): 'chè reducendosi a questo numero largo, introvenendoce la maiore parte de li soi de la croceta, se confida havere sempre chi luy designarà ... questa largeza de le fave remedia a la mala dispositione de molti che sonno del dicto consiglio.' [3] Ibid.

[4] Ibid. [5] Libri Fabarum, 69, *passim*.

[6] Galeazzo Maria Sforza praised it for being composed of 'seguaci de la voluntà de Lorenzo' (to Sacramoro, 4 July; ASM, cit.).

[7] Provv., 162, fol. 93ᵛ.

reform of the *Cento*, or indeed to any other constitutional reform; the only function of the *Balìa* which is explicitly mentioned is to hold the general scrutiny, which had been postponed in 1468, and which 'desiderasi universalmente'.[1] As usual, the *Balìa* was to have *pienissima et libera autorità*, as much as the three councils together; but at the same time these were to retain while it was in session, that is until 31 October, their normal powers in those matters that did not belong to the competence of the *Balìa*: a concession which, in view of its vagueness, had little practical value. More explicit were the prohibition against the *Balìa* increasing the gabelles or changing the present distribution of taxes, and the promise of a scrutiny. It was probably felt that in this way the councils could once more be persuaded to create a *Balìa*, and that it would be unnecessary to consider resorting to a *Parlamento*, as had been done in 1458 and 1466. The gamble just came off, but the large number of votes cast against the bill indicates the strength of the opposition, which may have been sharpened by the January reform.[2]

The *Balìa* was to include 240 elected members, of whom the first 40 were to be chosen by the Signoria and the newly-appointed *Accoppiatori* for 1471–2;[3] these 40 were, together with the Signoria and the *Accoppiatori*, to co-opt the remaining 200; official membership was confined to the Signoria, the Colleges, and the five *Accoppiatori*.[4] In this way, the Signoria, which, as Sacramoro writes on 5 July,[5] 'è tucta de uno pezo et nostra da vero', and the

---

[1] Provv. 162, fols. 93ʳ–95ᵛ, and Balìe, 31, fols. 12ᵛ–14ᵛ (3–5 July). This meant, incidentally, that the regulation on the composition of scrutiny councils adopted in Dec. 1466 would not be observed: see above, p. 171.

[2] Cf. Sacramoro to Galeazzo Maria Sforza, 11 Jan. 1471 (ASM, cit.; Soranzo, p. 72): 'sonno stati de quelli che hanno demostro quanto pesi questo partito preso de li accopia-tori. . . .' While the *Cento* passed the bill of 3 July with the not too comfortable majority of 8, the councils of the People and the Commune did so with a bare majority and a majority of two respectively (Libri Fabarum, 69, fol. 101ʳ). The *Balìa*'s term was subsequently ex-tended: below, p. 186.

[3] These were, accordingly, the first *Accoppiatori* to be elected as a result of the January reform, by the Signoria of July–Aug. and the *Accoppiatori* in office. The election took place on 5 July: Sacramoro to Galeazzo Maria Sforza, 5 July 1471 (ASM, cit.). Unlike earlier *Balìe*, not more than two members of a family or *consorteria* could belong to the *arroti*, un-less the Signoria granted special exemptions from this rule. The minimum age for the 200 was fixed at thirty, for the 40 at thirty-three years, with the proviso that one of them could be younger ('potendo nondimeno in detto numero de' quaranta diputarsi uno di qualunche età'): accordingly Lorenzo was elected. He had already, despite his age, been a member of the 1466 *Balìa*, having been chosen as a substitute by his father (Balìe, 30, fols. 6ʳ and 73ʳ; 2 Sept. and 4 Dec. 1466; in V. Ricchioni, *La costituzione politica di Firenze ai tempi di Lorenzo il Magnifico* (Siena, 1913), p. 2, n. 1, and p. 145; cf. pp. 42–43).

[4] i.e. the Signoria and the Colleges in office, while the Signori of July–Aug. were to remain members after 31 Aug.   [5] To Nicodemo da Pontremoli (ASM, cit.).

new *Accoppiatori*, 'che possite pensare che sonno nostri', occupy a key position in choosing the personnel of the *Balìa*. 'You will understand', adds Sacramoro, 'that from the first to the last, it will consist of picked men';[1] in fact, 163 of the 240 *arroti* had belonged to earlier *Balìe*.[2] However, in the event the election proved to be a more complex matter than had been anticipated, and showed that Lorenzo and his friends were anxious not to exploit their success too much. On 5 July Sacramoro reports to the Duke of Milan that, while Luca Pitti had been chosen, his cousin Giovannozzo, being pro-Aragon, was to be left out; and that the same would probably happen to Jacopo de' Pazzi and his followers, who in this way would remain practically 'mezo amoniti', half excluded from offices. In fact, if Lorenzo followed those who were advising him well, he would put his brother-in-law Guglielmo de' Pazzi in Jacopo's place, thus adding to the latter's discomfiture.[3] But four days later he had to report, to his great annoyance, that Jacopo de' Pazzi and Giovannozzo Pitti, as well as Domenico Martelli, had in the end been made members of the *Balìa*, after first having been discarded. Lorenzo had justified himself to Sacramoro by explaining that he wished to avoid the accusation that the *Balìa* was causing unrest, and that he was certain that these few men could not do him any harm, 'especially as power will be centred in those first forty and the five *Accoppiatori*'; but the Milanese ambassador was not so sure.[4]

What Lorenzo meant by his last remark became clear three days later when the *Balìa* passed a law reforming the council of *Cento*.[5] For the law of 8 July, which was valid until the end of 1476, extended the prominent position of the forty far beyond the lifetime of the *Balìa*. Together with two co-opted members and the five *Accoppiatori* of 1471–2, they became permanent members of the *Cento*, as well as of its electoral college. The *veduti* Gonfaloniers of Justice lost their right to attend the electoral meetings of the *Cento*, and their place in its electorate; however,

---

[1] '... sichè de primo ad ultimum intendete che li ellecti seranno homini scelti.'

[2] See Appendix, no. VIII, and below, pp. 193–4.

[3] '... metterà suo cognato Guglielmo in locho del dicto d. Jacomo per più sua confusione' (ASM, cit.). Guglielmo was married to Lorenzo's sister Bianca.

[4] To Galeazzo Maria Sforza, 9 July 1471 (ASM, cit.): '... demostra dicto Lorenzo haverlo facto perchè non si possa dire che questa balìa sia cum schandolo et cum alteratione de la città ... et dice che per questo non è da dubitare che possano condurre una minima cosa ... contraria agli bisogni nostri ... et tanto mancho quanto l'auctorità si redurrà in quelli primi quaranta et li cinque accoppiatori.'   [5] Balìe, 31, fols. 15ʳ–17ʳ.

eighty of them were to be chosen every year by the forty-seven, and the Signoria and *Accoppiatori* in office, to join the forty-seven as additional members of the *Cento*,[1] and of its electoral college which in its turn appointed the 200 members for the Cento's two six-monthly sessions.[2]

The reform is a masterpiece of political compromise, and a striking example of Florentine constitutional technique. While the oligarchical features of the *Cento* are preserved, the *veduti* Gonfaloniers of Justice no longer attend by right but by election; while a permanent nucleus is maintained, it is made more manageable and, above all, more reliable. The right of all *veduti* Gonfaloniers to attend the electoral meetings of the *Cento* was evidently felt to be a serious flaw in its constitution, and may well have substantially contributed to the difficulties Lorenzo and his friends had experienced in that council.[3] Moreover, the greatly increased authority to act alone, which was granted the *Cento* shortly afterwards, made it advisable to admit to such meetings only citizens who had been specially selected.

The law of 9 January had drastically curtailed the *Cento*'s powers in electing the *Accoppiatori*. The *Balìa* now compensated it by granting it, on 23 July,[4] exclusive competence in all those matters in which it had previously been acting as council of first instance, that is in those concerning 'statum seu bursas aut scructinea aut . . . onera vel conductas gentium'[5]—in other words, in all the more important political, military, and financial decisions. There was no doubt that, as the bill claimed, this would speed up legislation;[6] but at the same time the reform drastically reduced the powers of the old statutory councils which had time and again opposed Medicean policy. Their original function as sole source of legislation had been gradually whittled down, first

---

[1] This applied only to the meetings in which the *Cento* acted by virtue of its sole authority, and hence to those in which it held elections ('in tutti quegli casi e deliberationi che solo per decto consiglio senza gli altri fare si possono . . . et nel fare delle electioni'). This clause acquired new significance in the light of the increased powers vested in the *Cento* a fortnight later; see below, and above, p. 116.

[2] 'Per rispetto di quegli che manchassino et per dare parte et speranza a' più', the annual *Accoppiatori* were to remain electors after their office had come to an end. The 80 were chosen by placing the names of the 100 *veduti* who had received most votes in a bag, and drawing from it 80. The election of the *Cento* was made for two sessions at a time, the personnel of each of the two six-monthly councils being then appointed by lot.

[3] See above, pp. 176–7.

[4] Balìe, 31, fol. 25ᵛ; ed. Ricchioni, pp. 147–8, with the wrong date of 13 July.

[5] See above, p. 113.

[6] '. . . considerantesque in deliberationibus ad statum ac libertatem pertinentibus plurimum prodesse celeritatem in illis expediendis'.

by long-term *Balìe*, and then by the *Cento*; the law of 23 July was a further, and as it turned out decisive, step in this direction; for although, like that of 8 July, it was to be valid for five years only, its validity was, as we shall see, extended repeatedly until the end of the Medici régime.[1]

No aspect of the increased authority of the *Cento* is more far-reaching than the powers of financial legislation it acquired at the expense of the councils of the People and Commune, by being made the sole council competent to pass tax laws. The reform of the *Cento* thus constitutes a landmark in the history of the Medici régime, and the culmination of earlier, and not always successful, attempts in this direction.[2]

It will be remembered that already during the early years of the Medici period, the *Balìa* of 1444 had tried to take over tax legislation at the expense of the statutory councils.[3] This policy, which was contrary to the *Balìa* law, met with determined resistance on the part of the councils, which in 1446 passed supplementary legislation to keep the *Balìa* within the limits of its competence, without, however, achieving complete success. The *Balìa* of 1452 was given full powers to impose taxes and was thus enabled to continue, without being hampered by any restrictions, the financial policy of its predecessor, and practically monopolized tax legislation, a procedure which was justified in terms of military requirements.[4] The *Balìa* of 1458, on the other hand, while making a number of decisions regarding expenditure and financial administration, did not impose any new taxes;[5] it must, however, be remembered that it lasted for a few months only. The *Balìa* of 1466, equally of short duration, confirmed the distribution of the *catasto* then in force, and imposed one *aggravo*, as well as allowing tax reliefs (*sgravo*).[6] But at the same time it granted the *Cento* new fiscal powers. Having, on 7 November, authorized the Signoria, together with the Colleges and the *Otto*, as well as the *Cento*, to hire soldiers during the following

---

[1] See below, pp. 194, 206, 207, 209. The regulations on the election of the *Cento* of 8 July did not come fully into force until 1 Jan. 1472 (see above, p. 183), and consequently did not expire until 31 Dec. 1476.

[2] See above, pp. 75 ff.

[3] Above, p. 76.

[4] Provv., 143, fol. 199ᵛ (see above, p. 79). Tax laws followed each other in rapid succession: cf. e.g. Balìe, 27, fols. 9ʳ–11ᵛ (17 July 1452); 46ᵛ–48ᵛ (27 Sept.); 55ᵛ–56ᵛ (26 Oct.); 57ʳ–59ʳ (16 Nov.); 85ᵛ–88ʳ (14 Jan. 1453), &c.

[5] The only specific tax law concerned reduction of previous taxation (Balìe, 29, fols. 46ᵛ–47ʳ; 7 Sept. 1458). On 23 Sept. it reformed the *Monte* for five years (fols. 51ʳ–55ʳ).

[6] Balìe, 30, fols. 63ʳ–64ʳ (14 Nov. 1466).

twelve months in view of the military situation, it also authorized
them to levy enough taxes to pay for these troops, but no more.[1]
However, the financial powers of the *Cento* were greatly increased
on 18 December, when the *Balìa*, in view of the 'grandi aparecchi
che si fanno delle genti dell'arme', vested full authority over
taxation in the *Cento*, the Signoria, and its Colleges, until the end
of 1468.[2] By virtue of these decrees the *Cento* passed tax legislation
during 1467 and 1468, or confirmed taxes that had been decided
upon by the Signoria, the Colleges, and the *Otto*, in execution of
their special military powers.[3] The last finance bill passed by the
Cento only, that is without the other councils, is of 16 November
1468;[4] all tax bills were once more passed by the councils of the
People and Commune in 1469 and 1470, after having received
the assent of the *Cento*.[5] The reform of 23 July 1471 thus restored
to the *Cento* the fiscal powers it had already possessed in 1467–8,
and for the period of five, instead of two, years.[6] Repeated
renewals rendered them all but permanent, and thus deprived
the councils of the People and Commune of their most effective
instrument of opposition. The *Monte*, the gabelles, and certain
other matters of financial administration still remained, however,
within the competence of all three councils, but, as we shall see
presently, not for long.[7]

The work of the *Balìa* of 1471, whose term of office was
extended by the *Cento* until the end of February 1472,[8] was completed by the promised scrutiny. Planned to begin on 8 November,
it was postponed until the 20th: even now there were doubts as
to its advisability; but the view that the law should be observed

---

[1] Balìe, 30, fols. 59ʳ–61ʳ, and 61ʳ–62ʳ (7 and 8 Nov. 1466). The taxes were to be imposed
on the distribution of the *catasto* in force.

[2] '. . . etiamdio se fusse tale che ne bisognasse fare quì spezial menzione et expressa . . .
havendo intorno acciò tutta quella auctorità che a la presente balìa' (Balìe, 30, fol. 81ʳ⁻ᵛ).
At the same time, the decree of 8 Nov. remained in force.

[3] 3 Jan. 1467: confirmation of the *condotta* and the imposition of taxes made by the
Signoria &c. (Cento, 1, fols. 58ʳ–59ᵛ); 11 May: imposition of nine *catasti* (fols. 62ᵛ–63ᵛ);
1 Aug.: imposition of one million fiorini 'pro negociis belli', to be spread over three years,
and to be abolished if peace is concluded in the meantime (fols. 64ᵛ–65ʳ); 16 Nov. 1468:
new distribution of taxes = *ventina* (fols. 68ᵛ–70ᵛ).

[4] Libri Fabarum, 68, fol. 146ʳ.

[5] 10–15 April 1469 (Libri Fabarum, 68, fols. 164ʳ–165ʳ); 16–21 June (fols. 173ᵛ–174ʳ,
175ᵛ–176ᵛ); 13–17 July 1469 (fols. 178ʳ–179ʳ); 9–13 Dec. (69, fols. 9ʳ–10ᵛ).

[6] The *Cento* did not use these powers until after the dissolution of the *Balìa*; in the meantime, the *Balìa* used its own powers to impose taxes, on 8 July 1471 and 27 Jan. 1472 (Balìe,
31, fols. 17ᵛ–20ʳ, 77ᵛ–79ᵛ). The first tax bill passed by the *Cento* in exercise of its new authority
is of 11 Jan. 1473 (Cento, 1, fols. 78ʳ–79ʳ).

[7] See below, pp. 195, 199, 204–6.

[8] Cento, 1, fol. 74ʳ⁻ᵛ; 27 Sept. 1471. The last deliberation of the *Balìa* is of 29 Feb. 1472.

prevailed.[1] On 14 November the *Balìa* co-opted a number of official members for the scrutiny;[2] the customary ten *Accoppiatori* (as distinct from those in charge of elections *a mano*) were to be elected by the *Cento*.[3] As in 1458, they were, together with the Signoria, to determine the technicalities of the scrutiny as well as the number of new *polizze* which were to be given to successful candidates; moreover, they were empowered to qualify for all other public offices citizens selected by them for the Gonfalonier-ship of Justice, and to determine the procedure *per far vedere* for the Gonfaloniership at the two-monthly elections *a mano* of the Signoria.[4] Rinuccini was right in emphasizing their *grandissima autorità*,[5] which was further increased when, on 8 August 1472, the Signoria delegated its own powers over the scrutiny to them.[6] Their increased responsibilities are thrown into relief by the fact that they acted without their colleagues who were in charge of electing the Signoria *a mano*. In 1458 the two offices had still collaborated in the scrutiny;[7] by now their separation had become final.[8] In view of their extensive powers, it does not come as a surprise to find that six of the ten *Accoppiatori* of the scrutiny belonged to the forty.[9] One of these was Lorenzo de' Medici.

The ten *Accoppiatori*, having been given full powers by the Signoria on 8 August, got down to work on 9 August; and

[1] Balìe, cit., fol. 68^r. Cons. e Prat., 60, fol. 136^{r-v} (8 Nov.): 'Super scrutineo an faciendum sit'. Luca Pitti: 'Scrutinium faciendum ut leges iubent . . . sed prorogandum principium scrutinei usque ad diem xx mensis huius.' Giovanni Canigiani: 'maxime celerandum . . . quia longum negotium sit, et pro quo suspensa civitas esse soleat plures menses' (fol. 136^v; 9 Nov.).

[2] The Signoria and the Colleges in office—the Signoria of July–Aug. and the five *Accoppiatori* of 1471–2 already belonged to it—, those later in office during the scrutiny, and the Colleges who had been in office in July. The Signoria was also to elect one additional member, 'etiamdio sia di minore età', a provision which can hardly refer to Lorenzo de' Medici, since he was already a member of the *Balìa*.

[3] Balìe cit., fols. 71^r–73^r. The office of the *Accoppiatori* was to last two months after the completion of the scrutiny.

[4] Ibid. See above, p. 108.   [5] Op. cit., p. cxix.

[6] The decision of the Signoria is contained among the minutes of the proceedings of the *Accoppiatori*, Med. av. Pr., LXXXVI, fols. 317^r–334^r (fol. 317^r). The scrutiny having been completed on 13 March (ibid.), the powers of the *Accoppiatori* would have expired on 13 May; but on 30 April, the *Cento* extended them by two months, with authority to the Signoria to grant further extensions, which, however, must not exceed two months altogether (Cento, 1, fol. 75^v). The Signoria accordingly extended their term of office until 13 Sept. (Med. av. Pr., loc. cit.). The new bags of the *Tre Maggiori* were used for the first time in October 1472 (Tratte, 202); but the entire scrutiny had not yet been *imborsato* by that time; in Feb. 1474, the *Accoppiatori* were recalled for one day only to tidy up loose ends (Cento, 1, fol. 83^{r-v}).   [7] See above, p. 108.

[8] However, five of the *Accoppiatori* of the scrutiny had had previous experience in electing the Signoria *a mano*.   [9] See Appendix, no. I.

during the following days they determined not only the qualifications for the Gonfaloniership of Justice, but also many other
questions relating to the *imborsazioni*, as well as how to *far vedere*
at the two-monthly elections of the Signoria. The exceptionally
detailed records of their deliberations are extant and allow us
a unique insight into the working of the electoral system. They
are preceded and concluded by technical observations and his-
torical notes on scrutinies and *imborsazioni* after 1434, which in
their turn throw interesting light on the kind of problems the
officials in charge of scrutinies had to tackle.[1]

The first impression one gains from this document is one of
almost pedantic concern with legality and technical efficiency.
Regulations on preceding scrutinies are carefully examined in the
light of their administrative efficiency. Whatever the ultimate
political motives and purposes of these officials, the minutes of
their proceedings show the officials as civil servants who are
reluctant to depart too much from precedent, and do not reveal
any arbitrary abuse of authority. The only occasion on which
the *Accoppiatori* appear to depart from the scrupulous observation
of the rules is when they grant some minor concessions to a few
leading chancery officials. At the same time it must be remembered that by virtue of their authority they had, like the *Accoppiatori* of preceding scrutinies, vast powers in selecting citizens
for qualification for the highest office; and their treatment of the
Pazzi shows how they could use their powers to penalize a great
family.

The decisions on the methods of *imborsare* and of *far vedere*, to
be adopted in the two-monthly election of the Signoria,[2] provide
ample evidence for the mechanism of elections *a mano* at that time.
The term, it appears, had by then become a figure of speech,
since the five *Accoppiatori* in charge of these elections were not
supposed to know the results of the preceding scrutiny, nor, for
that matter, the contents of the bags that had been filled after it.
Before the two-monthly sortition each *Accoppiatore* was to nominate, with exceptions, at least sixteen candidates for the Priorate
from among those 'che chredessino avere ottenuto' in the scrutiny,
and at least one for the Gonfaloniership of Justice.[3] After a

---

[1] Med. av. Pr. cit., fols. 316^{r-v}, 335^r. The scribe and author of the above-mentioned
notes was doubtless a member of the chancery.

[2] Ibid., fols. 318^v–319^r (8 Aug. 1472).

[3] The *Accoppiatore* of the *quartiere* which happened to provide the two members of the
Lesser Guilds was likewise to nominate at least sixteen citizens. Since there were five

secret ballot by the *Accoppiatori*, the names of those candidates who had received more than half of the votes were placed in the special *borse* for the final sortition by the *Podestà*—provided they could be found in the scrutiny bags by the Palace officials, who were in charge of the secret registers of the scrutiny. As for the names that were to be *imborsati per far vedere*, each *Accoppiatore* was allowed to select, every two months, five names to *far vedere* for the *Tre Maggiori*, again from among those he assumed to have been qualified; and if his candidates fulfilled this condition, the Palace officials had to add their names to the special sortition bags. If the *Accoppiatori* decided to *far vedere* for the Gonfalonier-ship of Justice, each of them had to nominate two citizens who had not yet been *veduti* for that magistracy. From the four nomi-nees who had received most votes, two were selected by lot, again provided that they were already *imborsati* for the Gonfalonier-ship; and their names were likewise added to the final bags for the sortition of the Signoria. In this way, an element of chance survived in the elections *a mano*: assuming that the *Accoppiatori* nominated only the minimum number of candidates, and that all of these were passed by them with the requisite majority, and cleared by the Palace officials, the final bags would contain sixty-eight names for the eight Priors and seven for the Gonfalonier, plus up to twenty-five and two respectively *per far vedere*. The registers of the *tratte* of the Signoria[1] show that the average number of *polizze* drawn every two months for the Signoria, including the Gonfalonier of Justice, was 36 in 1473, 35 in 1474, 36 in 1475, and 32 in 1476. The downward trend continued during the following years: in 1477 the two-monthly average was 28, in 1478 20, in 1479 14, in 1480 18, in 1481 16, in 1482 13, and in 1483 14. It may be argued that at this point the *Accoppiatori*, for all practical pur-poses, appointed the Signoria, the drawing by lot having become a farce. However, to some extent the low number of names drawn may have been due to the fact that the bags that had been filled after the scrutiny of 1471 would be progressively emptied. The effective field of choice of the *Accoppiatori* would therefore be reduced progressively, as fewer names would be found in the bags for subsequent clearance by the Palace officials. In fact, after the

---

Accoppiatori, two of them would belong to the same *quartiere*; of these, each was to nominate at least ten instead of sixteen. As for the Gonfaloniership, the *Accoppiatore* for the *quartiere* whose turn it was to provide the Gonfalonier of Justice was to nominate at least three candidates instead of one.

[1] *Tratte*, 202, 203.

scrutiny of 1484[1] the average number of names drawn at the two-monthly elections rose sharply: during the twelve months after the new scrutiny was used for the first time, it amounted to fifty, as against sixteen in the preceding twelve months.

The ten *Accoppiatori* had been authorized to determine how many *polizze* the citizens who had been qualified in the scrutiny of the *Tre Maggiori* of 1471 were to receive. They decided that those who had already been qualified in the scrutiny of 1458, or whose fathers had been, were to acquire two *polizze*, the rest one.[2] This procedure followed that adopted in 1453 and in 1465,[3] and was also applied to many other offices, so that citizens who had already previously been qualified for them received two *polizze* instead of one.[4] Since citizens who had recovered their civic rights in September 1466 were accordingly at a disadvantage, some of them were, by way of special concession, granted more than the normal number of *polizze*.[5] On the other hand, as in 1458, the citizens who had not been successful in the scrutiny lost their previous *polizze* for the offices in question, unless the *Accoppiatori* decided specially to add them to the new bags.[6] The *Accoppiatori* were further entitled to accord citizens they had qualified for the Gonfaloniership of Justice qualification for other offices as well,[7] and they used these powers in favour of forty-two citizens.[8] Among these were several members of the chancery or relatives of chancery officials.[9] We find some favouritism in the interest of the chancery in other respects as well; thus the First Chancellor, Bartolomeo Scala, and two sons of the notary of the *Tratte*, Ser Antonio di Adamo, were allowed more

---

[1] See below, pp. 210 ff.

[2] '. . . che qualunche a ottenuto in questo nuovo isquittino il partito del priorato, c[h]'egli o suo padre ottenne allo isquittino 1458 il partito del priorato, s'intende dovere essere e sia imborsato chon dua polize, e gli altri chon una . . .' (fol. 317ᵛ).

[3] See above, pp. 60–61, 149–50.

[4] 'E quegli ch'anno ottenuto gli altri partiti, cioè Pisa, e sedici ufici, gli otto ufici e gli undici e i providoratichi e il marzochio, siano imborsati in questo modo: quegli ch'anno ottenuto alchuno di detti partiti in questo nuovo isquittino e avessino quello medesimo partito ottenuto altra volta nello isquittino 1448 o del 54, siano imborsati in nelle borse degli ufici [per due polizze]; e similmente siano imborsati per due polize quegli che in questo nuovo isquittino avissino ottenuto alchuno tal partito in quello medessimo partito avesino otenuto nel 65, e questo in chaso che nello isquittino del 58 non avessino auto l'età che ssi richiedeva a tal partito . . .' (ibid.).

[5] Fols. 319ʳ, 320ᵛ. Some of these were allowed three *polizze*, provided they had been qualified in the scrutiny of 1448 or later; others were automatically given two *polizze* for any office they had been successful for (fol. 319ʳ; 9 Aug.).

[6] Fol. 318ʳ.   [7] Balìe, 31, fol. 72ʳ.

[8] Fols. 319ᵛ–320ᵛ (11 Aug.).

[9] Bartolomeo Scala, Ser Giovanni di Ser Bartolomeo Guidi, Giuliano di Ser Niccolò di Feo Dini, and Matteo di Michele di Feo Dini.

polizze for the *Tre Maggiori* and the offices linked with them than they were entitled to by the regulations that had been laid down by the *Accoppiatori* themselves.[1] These were not very important concessions, but the greater opportunities to obtain political and administrative posts outside the chancery, which they provided for practically permanent officials like Bartolomeo Scala, who owed his career largely to Medici patronage, were enough to incense the *ottimati*.[2]

However, in selecting the names for the Gonfaloniership of Justice the *Accoppiatori* showed that, like their predecessors after previous scrutinies, they had no intention of departing from the traditional policy of respecting the status of the *ottimati*.[3] The only substantial difference, in this respect, between their list of qualifications and that of February 1466,[4] concerns families that had been involved in the 'conspiracy' of 1466. The Dietisalvi are entirely absent, the Acciaiuoli are reduced to three, from seven in February 1466, the Pitti from ten to three. In the supplementary *borse*, which were to be used in case of deficiencies in the principal ones, the Acciaiuoli are represented by two further members, the Pitti by six; however, as it turned out, this was not worth much since these supplementary bags do not appear to have been used. The Soderini remained stationary at three, plus one in the supplementary bags; the Gondi disappeared altogether. As in 1434, these changes are of a political nature; as a social group the *ottimati* continue to occupy the prominent position they considered their due. At the same time several of the Medicean families increased their representation considerably: in the principal *borse*, the Ridolfi are represented by ten members as against five in 1455[5] and seven in 1466, the Canigiani by eight as against two and four respectively, the Guicciardini by six as against two and four, the Capponi by ten as against six and six,

---

[1] Bartolomeo Scala, Ser Giovanni di Ser Antonio d'Adamo, and Adamo di Ser Antonio, who had been qualified for the first time for the *Tre Maggiori*, were to receive two *polizze* instead of one for these offices, 'come s'eglino o lor padre avessino 1448 [*corr.* 1458] ottenuto il priorato saviamente e rettamente' (fol. 320ᵛ).

[2] Bartolomeo Scala had been reappointed for ten years in 1466 (Marzi, *La cancelleria fiorentina*, p. 243). On 12 Oct. 1471 the Signoria had decided that, while he was to remain, as chancellor, barred from all external offices, he could hold any internal one to which he was appointed, together with his office in the chancery (Deliberazioni dei Signori, speciale autorità, 34, fols. 88ᵛ–89ʳ). Cf. Guicciardini, *Storie fiorentine*, p. 79.

[3] Fols. 321ʳ–328ʳ (12 Aug.). On this day they made the final arrangements for the *borse* of the Gonfaloniership; the selection of the names was probably made by them on the previous day.   [4] See above, pp. 153–4.

[5] See above, pp. 47–48; for the Ridolfi, p. 48, n. 1.

the Pucci by seven as against two and three. The Medici, on the other hand, increased their representation only to ten, from nine in 1466 and six in 1455. Other families were less fortunate. The Donati and Albizzi remain stationary at three as compared with 1455 (two and four respectively in 1466), while the Pazzi are represented by three, as in 1466. In some cases the size of the representation was affected by that of the families, in others it was doubtless the result of favouritism. Such favouritism was even more marked when it came to *gente nuova*: thus the Del Nero, who had been qualified for the Gonfaloniership of Justice for the first time in 1466, trebled their representation. There are also a number of new names, due to individual citizens having risen to political influence, such as the lawyer Bernardo Buongirolami, who was beginning to play an important role in Lorenzo's counsels.[1] However, most of these are to be found in the supplementary bags only, where we also find the names of a few members of the chancery, including that of the First Chancellor. While the number of citizens qualified for the first time is considerably greater than in the *rimbotto* of 1466, the percentage of newly-qualified families in the principal *borse* is only about one-half of what it had been in 1466.[2] This difference is due to the fact that most of the citizens in these *borse* who were newly qualified in 1472 belonged to 'established' families, ninety, that is over one-half, being sons or brothers of men who were already qualified for the Gonfaloniership in 1455.[3]

At the same time, while there is no departure from the policy of social continuity, the rise in the total number of those qualified for the highest magistracy from 227 in 1455 and 339 in 1466 to 383 in 1472 (or, including the supplementary *borse*, to 493), reflects the increased importance and prestige attached to the *veduti* Gonfaloniers of Justice.[4] Thus, although the general picture is the traditional one of continuity tempered by a measure of mobility, individual *ottimati* families might well feel that they were receiving less than their due, or indeed were being penalized for political reasons. The representation of the Pazzi, one of the richest families in Florence, in the principal *borse* of the Gonfaloniership, remained stationary at three. However secret

---

[1] On his membership of the *Balìa* of 1471, see below, p. 193.
[2] *c.* 7·5 per cent. as against *c.* 15 per cent.   [3] They totalled 162. See above, pp. 47–48.
[4] The creation of supplementary bags may, however, indicate that the *Accoppiatori* were preparing for the possibility of the next scrutiny being postponed, with a resulting shortage in the principal bags.

the results of these selections were kept, the results of the two-monthly *tratte* were bound to make known such discriminations sooner or later.

No new scrutiny took place until 1484, so that the *borse* filled in 1472 remained in force until then. As had been the case after 1458, this blocked new admissions to the most select of them, and consequently the *Cento* reappointed, on 23 August 1482 and for that day only, the *Accoppiatori* of 1472, to make additional qualifications for the Gonfaloniership of Justice, given the fact that 'molti a' quali tale qualità era suta conceduta sono morti, et molti . . . sono di qualità che hora meritano essere aggregati agli altri'.[1]

The policy of the *Accoppiatori* in distributing qualifications for the Gonfaloniership of Justice had its counterpart in the composition of the *Balìa* of 1471.[2] Of its 240 elected members, 163 had belonged to earlier *Balìe*, and of these, 145 to that of 1466.[3] This presents the by now familiar picture of social continuity in the councils. At the same time the proportion of new men is relatively high—nearly one-third of the total;[4] yet nearly all of these had relatives in earlier *Balìe*.[5] But the picture changes when we turn to the forty original members of the *Balìa* who were to belong permanently to the *Cento* and its electorate: of these no less than thirty-eight had been in the *Balìa* of 1466, and twenty-eight in that of 1458.[6] All of them had been members of the scrutiny council of 1465, and were consequently particularly qualified to take part in the new scrutiny, as well as, for that matter, in the annual selection of the members of the *Cento*. Twenty-three out of the forty had not been in pre-1458 *Balìe*, but most of them had had near relatives in them. Only one had never been a member of a *Balìa*, Bernardo Buongirolami; Guicciardini mentions him as one of those citizens 'spogliati di parenti e credito' whom Lorenzo favoured at the expense of the aristocrats.[7] At the same time,

---

[1] Cento, 2, fol. 76ʳ. I have been unable to find the list of these additional qualifications.

[2] The list of its members is in Balìe, 31, fols. 9ʳ–12ᵛ. See Appendix, no. VIII.

[3] Cf. Appendix, nos. II–VII. 113 had been members of the scrutiny council of 1465 (Bibl. Naz., MS. Capponi 105, fols. 119ʳ–122ᵛ). The family maximum for the 240 was, similarly to earlier *Balìe*, two, the Signoria being allowed to grant exemptions in special cases. It did so for only four families, the Medici, Ridolfi 'di Ferza', Carducci, and Tornabuoni, who were represented by three members each, with the exception of the Medici, who were represented by five.

[4] 77 out of 240.   [5] Of the 77, 45 had their fathers and 9 had brothers in earlier *Balìe*.

[6] Cf. Appendix, nos. VI and VII.

[7] *Storie fiorentine*, pp. 24–25. See above, p. 192. Another of them was Bernardo del Nero, who was, like the former, one of the forty.

there was clearly no desire to increase the influence of the Lesser Guilds, whose share in either section of the *Balìa* was reduced to one-fifth.[1] A number of prominent families, though represented among the two hundred, are missing from the forty, who are clearly selected on strictly political grounds. In view of their special responsibilities, they may be considered the inner circle of the régime; and it is not surprising to find many of them again in the council of Seventy in 1480.[2]

The validity of the reform laws of 1471 expired in 1475 and 1476: the law of 9 January 1471 in August 1475; those of 8 and 23 July, on the *Cento*, in December and July 1476 respectively; moreover, the law of 5 September 1466, granting *balìa* to the *Otto* for ten years, was not valid after September 1476.[3] 'We are preparing ourselves', writes Lorenzo de' Medici on 29 June 1476 to Jacopo Guicciardini, 'to renew these powers, that were granted five years ago, for another five years. I had thought that some other method might be devised, but since there is some danger of plague, this seemed to be the best.'[4] Three days later a *Pratica* unanimously advised in favour of continuing the existing system of government; and on 2 and 4 July the laws on the *Cento* and the *Otto* were extended by another five years, and that on the *Accoppiatori* for the entire period during which the elections of the Signoria were still to be *a mano*, i.e. until 1486.[5] The councils of the People and the Commune passed the extension law with fairly comfortable majorities, although there was a good deal of opposition to it in the former. On the other hand, the large majorities in the *Cento* offer a striking contrast to the few votes by which that council had passed the *Accoppiatori* law in 1471: the reform of the *Cento* was evidently having its effect.[6] But if the councils of the

---

[1] As against the customary one-quarter.

[2] See Appendix, nos. VIII–X.

[3] See above, pp. 180, 183, 184–5, and 165, n. 2.

[4] Med. av. Pr., LXXII, 371 : 'Noi ci addirizziamo, mancando quelle autorità che si preseno cinque anni fa, a prolungarle per altri cinque anni. Credetti che si piglassi qualche altro modo, ma è paruto meglo questo per qualche suspitione di peste . . . Cessando questo sospetto, forse si farà qualche pensiero, e io ho caro che s'indugi per haverne anche il parere vostro. . . .'

[5] Cons. e Prat., 60, fol. 153ᵛ: 'Super prorogandis legibus quae de auctoritate consilii centumvirorum et potestate octovirorum et potestate coppulatorum loquuntur.' The five speakers are for it; Domenico Martelli: 'ut ita vivatur et administretur res publica ut hactenus'. Provv., 167, fol. 74ʳ⁻ᵛ (2–4 July); Cento, 1, fols. 90ᵛ–91ᵛ (2 July). The law of 23 July 1471, on the *Cento*, had to be extended by all three councils, the others by the *Cento* only.

[6] Extension of the law concerning the powers of the *Cento*: 147 to 58, and 124 to 30. The *Cento* passed it with 102 votes to 13. Extension by the *Cento* of the law on the *Accoppiatori*, and of that on the election of the *Cento*: 142 to 11, as against 126 to 60 in Jan. 1471 (Libri Fabarum, 70, fol. 60ʳ; see above, p. 180).

People and Commune could be persuaded without much difficulty to accept the continuation of the pre-eminent position of the
Cento for another five years, they put up considerable resistance
to the further extension of its financial powers, as contained in
a bill presented on 11 July, by which the *Cento* was granted
exclusive authority for one year, from 1 August, to legislate on
the affairs of the *Monte*.[1]

The legislation of 1471, as renewed in 1476, had still a considerable time to run, with the strong likelihood of its being
extended again, when the Pazzi conspiracy and the war which
followed it created a new situation. The significance of these
events for the constitutional development of the Medici régime is
twofold. While they impressed on the Mediceans the desirability
of a further concentration of political power, Lorenzo's success
in concluding peace with the King of Naples strengthened his
hand at home and encouraged him and his friends to carry out
reforms which otherwise they might not, or not yet, have
attempted.

The contemporary Florentine evidence on the conspiracy is
almost exclusively pro-Medicean; and the minutes of the *Pratiche*,
in contrast to those of 1465–6, yield nothing on the origins, and
little on the effects, of the upheaval.[2] The only contemporary
Florentine source which decidedly takes the side of the Pazzi is
Rinuccini's *De libertate*, composed early in 1479;[3] but this work
is, in its way, just as rhetorical and biased as is, in the opposite
camp, Poliziano's *Coniurationis commentarium*.[4]

According to the Medicean version published after its failure,
the conspiracy was motivated, at Florence, exclusively by the
selfish interests of the Pazzi and some of the Salviati.[5] However

[1] Libri Fabarum, 70, fols. 60ᵛ–62ʳ (11–19 July): 161 to 77, 120 to 54 respectively. The
Cento passed it, naturally, with a large majority, 86 to 21 (19 July). The council of the People
had rejected it on 11, 12, 13, and 15 July, that of the Commune on 17 July. Provv., 167,
fol. 80ʳ⁻ᵛ (16–19 July). The *provvisione* specifies: 'intendendosi potere usare tale auctorità
solo pe' casi appartenenti al comune di Firenze et non a private persone principalmente.'
The *Cento* did not, however, enact its reform of the *Monte* until 7 June 1477, that is just
before its special authority expired (Cento, 2, fols. 9ʳ–12ʳ).

[2] Cons. e Prat., 60. The dispatches of the Milanese ambassador, Filippo Sacramoro, also
yield little on the background of the conspiracy; while the papal letters and encyclicals are
too biased and propagandistic to be of much use for an appreciation of the internal situation
of Florence. Even so, the Pazzi conspiracy would well deserve a detailed study, which,
however, falls outside the scope of the present work.

[3] Ed. F. Adorno, in *Atti e Memorie dell'Accademia Toscana di Scienze e Lettere La Colombaria*,
xxii (1957), pp. 270–303.

[4] Ed. A. Perosa (Padua, 1958).

[5] Poliziano, op. cit., pp. 4–5: 'invidebant enim Medicae familiae eiusque summam nostra
in re publica auctoritatem et privatum decus . . . obterebant.'

much a sense of injury and rivalry induced members of the Pazzi and Salviati families to conspire with Girolamo Riario, who had good reason for disliking Lorenzo's foreign policy, Rinuccini's treatise (as well as his diary) shows that there was at least one citizen who described their attempt as being directed against a tyranny and designed to restore the traditional republican régime.[1] He praises not only Jacopo and Francesco Pazzi for emulating the ancient tyrannicides, but also the Milanese conspirators who, in December 1476, had assassinated Galeazzo Maria Sforza.[2] Rinuccini bore a personal grudge against Lorenzo;[3] but so did other citizens. Although few might follow his praise of the 'tyrannicides', his strictures on the present political régime, though doubtless intentionally exaggerated, resemble too much those voiced by the opposition in 1465–6 to be dismissed as purely rhetorical.[4] Conversely, his praise of the good old times is inspired by much the same republican conservatism as the speeches of Manno Temperani and Niccolò Soderini in 1465.[5]

It was clearly to this latent opposition that Jacopo de' Pazzi tried to appeal when he rode to the Piazza della Signoria shouting the ancient republican slogan of *popolo e libertà*.[6] But there was no organized opposition, as there had been in 1466,[7] and the Signoria, elected *a mano* by the *Accoppiatori*, was unquestioningly on Lorenzo's side. If in August 1466 it had been touch and go which of the two parties was to prevail, in April 1478 the victory of the Medici party was, after Lorenzo had escaped death, a foregone conclusion.

[1] Op. cit., p. 273. Accordingly, the war waged by Sixtus IV and Ferrante of Naples against Florence was 'non contra Florentinum populum, sed contra Laurentium Medicem Florentinum tyrannum pro libertate populi susceptum' (p. 302). This was the papal claim: cf. Sixtus IV's bull of 1 June 1478 (ed. Fabroni, *Laurentii vita*, ii, p. 125), and the reply of the Signoria to Sixtus's accusations against Lorenzo, of 21 July 1478 (ed. L. Pignotti, *Storia della Toscana* (Livorno, 1820), iv, pp. 117–18). See also Niccolò Modrussiense, *Defensio ecclesiasticae libertatis*, extracts ed. by G. Mercati, *Opere minori* (Città del Vaticano, 1937), iv, pp. 255–6. See also below, pp. 218–19.
[2] Op. cit., p. 273. The Milanese conspirators had, in their turn, been compared at Florence with Roman heroes. See Luca Landucci, *Diario fiorentino . . .*, ed. I. del Badia (Florence, 1883), pp. 14–15: 'Feciono come Scevola romano, ch'anno messo la vita per la vita. Molto tardi si truova simili uomini.'
[3] According to Rinuccini, it dated from his embassy to Rome in 1475–6: *De libertate*, pp. 300–1. Cf. Rinuccini, *Lettere ed orazioni*, pp. 215–17; *Ricordi storici*, pp. 249–50.
[4] *De libertate*, pp. 282–6.   [5] See above, p. 144.
[6] Landucci, *Diario*, p. 18.
[7] That this was realized at the time is borne out by Sacramoro's dispatch of 27 April (ASM, Pot. est., Firenze, 294): 'In questo tractato scelerato non se sono retrovati de casata alchuna inbratata fin adesso altri cha [*sic*] Pazzi, Salviati, et uno di Baroncelli che era cassero d'epsi Pazzi, et un altro Andrea Pandino, che haveva per moglie una de la casata di Pazzi bastarda, et quisti de Poggio [i.e. of Poggio Bracciolini].'

However, the military set-backs during the war which followed created fresh and increasing difficulties; and Sixtus IV's argument that the war was not directed against Florence, but against Lorenzo, does not appear to have been entirely lost on Florentine public opinion.[1] Lorenzo went out of his way to prove it wrong; thus he pointed out, in a letter of October 1478, that public affairs must be dealt with by the government and not by him personally, his own interests being identical with those of the state.[2] Lorenzo's decision to go to Naples was doubtless appreciated at Florence both for its courage and the promise of success it held out,[3] yet according to Guicciardini, whose grandfather and great-uncle held prominent positions during the war, Lorenzo's absence placed a serious stress on the cohesion of the régime.[4] This was probably one of the reasons why the peace with the King of Naples, which was proclaimed shortly after Lorenzo's return to Florence on 15 March 1480,[5] was almost immediately followed by constitutional reforms.

On 8–10 April, a bill creating a *Balìa* was presented to the three councils, allegedly to heal some of the wounds inflicted by the war, particularly as far as taxation and the *Monte* were concerned. The bill promised a fairer distribution of taxes, and described the situation as being so serious that, unless something radical was done quickly, the *Monte* would have to stop payments. Furthermore, there had been no scrutiny for nine years, and one was now to be held by the *Balìa*.[6] As in 1471, Lorenzo and his friends no doubt hoped that the councils could be persuaded to pass the bill

[1] Cf. e.g. Sixtus's letter of 25 July 1478 (in Fabroni, *Laurentii vita*, ii, p. 130): 'Non enim agimus quicquam contra alios nisi contra illum ingratum, excommunicatum et haereticum filium iniquitatis Laurentium de Medicis.' On 7 Aug. 1478 Lorenzo writes to Girolamo Morelli in Milan: 'perchè la brigata dice che spendo troppo [on the war, &c.], . . . la boce è ita che questa guerra è facta a me proprio, e per questo rispecto è bisognato giuchare del rattenuto' (Med. av. Pr., L, 4). See above, p. 196, n. 1.

[2] To Girolamo Morelli, 30 Oct. 1478 (ibid., XCVI, 223), on peace overtures by the Duke of Calabria through the Count of Pitigliano: 'Hogli risposto che quello che apartiene alli stati nostri mi pare si debba trattare con quelli a chi apartiene, et non mecho; quanto alle specialità mia, non ne fo difficultà alcuna, perchè acconce le cose publiche, le mie sono ancora acconce. . . .'

[3] Cf. the letters of Bartolomeo Scala, Agnolo della Stufa, and Antonio Pucci to Lorenzo, of Jan. 1480, in Fabroni, ii, pp. 201–13.

[4] *Storie fiorentine*, p. 52; *Memorie di famiglia*, p. 37.

[5] The peace was proclaimed in Florence on 25 March (Landucci, *Diario*, p. 34), and ratified by the Signoria on 14 April (Signori e Collegi, Deliberazioni, speciale autorità, 34, fols. 70^v–73^r). Lorenzo arrived in Florence on 15 March: Landucci, loc. cit.

[6] Provv., 171, fols. 1^r–4^r, and Balìe, 31, fols. 91^r–92^r (ed. G. Capponi, in *Arch. Stor. Ital.*, i (1842), pp. 321–6). The regulations for future scrutinies, which had been laid down in 1466, could be taken to imply that scrutinies should be held at intervals of five years; however, no scrutiny had been held in 1476. None was held in 1480 either; see below, p. 199.

by the promise of financial and electoral gains; and as in 1471, the bill contains no mention of a specific political reform to be undertaken by the *Balìa*, except a vague reference to 'many shortcomings', for which it was to find remedies.[1] Even so, the proposal to create a *Balìa* met again with considerable opposition, which this time was strongest in the *Cento*.[2] In view of the increase in its powers in financial matters since 1471, and the special authority it had been granted in 1476, for one year, to reform the *Monte*,[3] that council may well have considered itself competent to deal with such matters, and may also have been apprehensive of the ulterior political purpose of the *Balìa*. If this was the case, its fears proved certainly justified, for the creation of the Seventy dislodged the *Cento* from the position of first council it had hitherto occupied.

In the election of the members of the *Balìa* the precedent of 1471 was closely followed. The Signoria elected the first 30 members, who jointly with it co-opted 210; for the scrutiny, 48 additional citizens could be elected.[4] Thus apart from the *ex officio* members (i.e. the Signoria and the Colleges), the *Balìa* was composed, as in 1471, of 240 citizens, with the only difference that its first members were thirty instead of forty. But the continuity between the two *Balìe* becomes even more evident when one examines the names of the thirty; for twenty-one of them had been among the forty of 1471 (including Lorenzo de' Medici), and all of them had been in the *Balìa* of 1471.[5] Similarly, the conservative selection of the first members contrasts, as in 1471, with the more liberal attitude to newcomers in the case of the co-opted

---

[1] '. . . tanti mancamenti . . . che in nessuno modo siano da differire più oltre i salutiferi rimedi; e quali ricercando si truovano difficili et lunghi, se non si piglia di quei partiti quali per voi et pe' vostri padri et progenitori . . . si sono usati fare', i.e. to create a *Balìa* with powers to enable it 'a tutto possino et presto et bene porre conveniente rimedio, et poi la vostra città pacificamente et rectamente riformare. . . .'

[2] Libri Fabarum, 70, fol. 168^r. It was passed by the *Cento* by 81 votes to 39, that is by a majority of 1, by the council of the People by 180 to 87, and by that of the Commune by 145 to 40. The scribe adds to the entry regarding the voting in the *Cento*: 'in primo partito obtentum, cum tamen animi civium prius fluctuare viderentur'.

[3] See above, p. 195.

[4] By the Signoria in office and the 30. The *Balìa* was to be reconvened for the scrutiny in November 1480. No one who had relatives among the members of the *Balìa* could be elected, and only one per family or *consorteria*. The family maximum for the 210 was fixed at two per family, and one for those families that were already represented among the 30 by more than one member. However, the Signoria and the 30 could exempt up to two families from these regulations—and, if they wished, also from those concerning the minimum age, which was 30. The one family which was allowed to have more than three members in the *Balìa* was the Medici (Balìe cit., fols. 92^v-95^v; Appendix, no. IX). There was no minimum age for the 30.

[5] See Appendix, nos. VIII and IX.

members: of these, only about 40 per cent. had belonged to the *arroti* of the preceding *Balìa*.[1]

By the law of 10 April the *Balìa* received full powers, until the end of June, to decide on financial reforms, as well as on any matters 'necessarie et oportune al buon governo della città'.[2] But it passed its first finance bill only on 7 May, when it decided to grant a tax relief (*sgravo*), and also to impose fresh taxation.[3] The 'reform' of the *Monte* was not passed until 3 June, and was so inadequate that as soon as the following year full powers to re-order the *Monte* had to be granted to the *Cento*.[4] As for the scrutiny, the *Balìa* altogether omitted to carry it out.[5] But if the promises that had been held out were thus hardly fulfilled, the significance of the somewhat obscure phrase relating to matters 'necessarie et oportune al buon governo' soon became clear. For the principal achievement of the *Balìa* was the creation, less than a week after it had begun its session, of the Council of Seventy.[6]

The new council was composed of the first thirty members of the *Balìa*, and of forty citizens of at least forty years of age co-opted by them, and was to last for five years. There was to be no change of personnel during this period, except that the Seventy could fill vacancies caused by death or other causes, and co-opt Gonfaloniers of Justice after they had completed their term. Legislation remained confined to the three councils of the *Cento*, the People, and the Commune, but the Signoria was no longer allowed to initiate any bills of importance (i.e. on 'cose appartenenti allo stato o alle borse o alli squittini o alle gravezze . . . o alle condocte . . . o al Monte') without first obtaining the consent of the Seventy.[7] The Seventy, moreover, replaced the five *Accoppiatori* in electing the Signoria *a mano*. For this purpose they were to divide each year into committees of thirty-five, and each of these was to be in charge of six elections. Finally, every six months the thirty were to elect from among their members two new magistracies, the *Otto di Pratica* and the *Dodici Procuratori*, the first of which was to be responsible for foreign policy and

---

[1] 89 out of 210. See above, p. 193.

[2] Its last deliberation is of 30 June. For the purpose of the scrutiny it was to reassemble in Nov.

[3] Balìe, 31, fols. 101^r–102^v.   [4] Ibid., fols. 110^r–113^r. See below, p. 204.

[5] It was not held until 1484: see below, pp. 211 ff.

[6] Balìe cit., fols. 97^v–100^v (19 April); ed. Capponi, op. cit., pp. 329–40, and Ricchioni, *La costituzione fiorentina*, pp. 166–79.

[7] The same applied to private bills, which now required the consent of the Seventy before being presented to the *uditori delle provvisioni*.

matters concerning the régime, the second for internal, and especially financial, affairs.[1] In view of their control of foreign and internal policy, it is not surprising to find that it was left to the Seventy to decide how the ambassadors and commissioners, the *Dieci di Balìa*, and the *Otto di Guardia* were to be elected.[2] The powers of the Eight of Ward, who tended to encroach more and more on the ordinary course of jurisdiction, had been defined by a law of 18 November 1478.[3] They remained wide enough to make control over the appointment of the Eight particularly important, the more so as the obstinate resistance the Eight had put up in October 1478 to the reform of their office had shown that the present method of election by the *Cento* was not wholly satisfactory.[4] Accordingly, after 1480 we find the Seventy and the Signoria electing the Eight, the *Cento* being reduced to giving the final approval.[5] As for the *Dieci di Balìa*, the *Otto di Pratica* replaced them, for all practical purposes, in times of war, just as they also replaced the Signoria in the conduct of foreign affairs in times of peace. When, at the beginning of the Ferrarese war in 1482, new *Dieci* were appointed, they consisted of the *Otto di Pratica* in office, plus two members elected by the Seventy.[6]

The council of Seventy thus became the supreme agency of control and, through its committees, the principal organ for all important decisions. The Signoria, though it still preserved its executive authority, lost its right to initiate, with the assent of the Colleges, legislation in the councils, which it had possessed

[1] 'E sopradecti octo habbino a vegghiare tutti e casi occorrenti e quali appartenessino allo stato, et ogni caso ancora el quale havessi dependentia fuori della giurisditione del comune di Firenze . . . i decti dodici habbino la cura di tutti e casi appartenti al Monte, o ad alcuno suo membro, et all'uficio de' consoli del Mare, et agli altri casi della città et sua giurisditione.' In a letter to the Florentine ambassadors in Rome, of 2 May 1480, the Signoria informed them that the *Otto di Pratica* were henceforth to be in charge of the *cose di fuori et dello stato*, and the 12 of the *cose dentro* (Signori, Legazioni e Commissarie, 21, fol. 8ʳ, to Antonio Ridolfi and Pier Lutozo Nasi; Ricchioni, pp. 103–4). Similarly, on the same day, to Pier-filippo Pandolfini (fol. 8ᵛ): 'Habiamo creato uno nuovo magistrato di LXX, et di questo facto deputatione di octo sopra le cose externe et dello stato, e quali haranno nelle mani le cose più secrete. Quando ti accaderà qualche cosa più secreta, potrai scrivere a questo deputati . . . nelle altre cose tucte scriverrai a noi, essendo mancato l'uficio de' x per beneficio della pace.'

[2] Fol. 100ʳ; Ricchioni, pp. 176–7.

[3] Cento, 2, fols. 44ʳ–46ʳ; ed. Ricchioni, pp. 151–65. See Antonelli, 'La magistratura degli Otto di Guardia', pp. 24–27.

[4] Ibid., p. 24. See above, p. 114, on the election of the *Otto*.

[5] Deliberazioni dei Signori &c., Tratte, 283 (old shelfmark), fol. 12ʳ⁻ᵛ, *et passim*.

[6] Cento, 2, fols. 76ᵛ–77ʳ (4 Sept. 1482). Their term of office was to end on 30 April 1483, unless peace had been declared in the meantime, in which case it was to end one month after peace had been published in Florence. It was repeatedly extended until 1486, when the Seventy elected new officials (Cento, 2, fols. 84ʳ⁻ᵛ, 88ʳ⁻ᵛ, 92ʳ–93ʳ, 94ᵛ–95ʳ, 97ᵛ–98ʳ, 98ᵛ, 101ʳ⁻ᵛ, 102ʳ, 102ʳ⁻ᵛ, 102ᵛ–103ʳ, 104ᵛ–105ʳ), whose term came to an end in Dec. 1486. They were once more replaced by the *Otto di Pratica* (ibid., fol. 109ʳ⁻ᵛ).

since the thirteenth century; the *Cento*, while it remained the first legislative council, ceded its place in the conciliar hierarchy to the Seventy; both the Signoria and the *Cento* were deprived of their previous role in the most important elections. Yet even this did not seem enough to the leading citizens of the régime; for shortly before the *Balìa* concluded its session on 30 June 1480, they made a determined attempt to have it transfer its extensive powers to the Seventy.[1] This would have meant a return to the five-year *Balìe* of Cosimo's time, but with greatly reduced size and increased authority. The failure to persuade a majority in the *Balìa* to accept this proposal shows that there were limits beyond which, even in 1480, many of the prominent members of the Medici party were not prepared to go. Nor is it difficult to believe the Este ambassador that there was much popular discontent with recent developments. In his dispatch of 3 July, he quotes a citizen who had asked Tommaso Soderini, a member of the *Balìa* and of the Seventy, why he no longer said, as he used to do, 'you will run into danger', *periculareti*; to which Tommaso replied: 'because we are in danger', *perchè siamo periculati*.[2] If the story is true, this was a gloomy view to take, which may have pleased Ercole d'Este, whose brother and predecessor had supported the opposition to Piero.[3] This had been fourteen years earlier; fourteen years later the Medici régime was to be swept away by a revolution. Despite the great success achieved in saving and consolidating that régime, an elder statesman like Tommaso Soderini might wonder even now how solidly it was founded, and what the future was holding in store.

[1] The only source for this attempt is the dispatch of the Este ambassador, Antonio Montecassino, of 3 July 1480 (to Ercole d'Este, ASMo, Est., Firenze, 2) which has hitherto been ignored by historians (it has not been published by Cappelli, op. cit.). There is no reference in the *Libri Fabarum* to a bill to this effect being presented to the statutory councils, and there can be no doubt that Antonio Montecassino was referring to a proposal in the *Balìa*, which in fact had been given authority to delegate its powers: 'potendo et ad altri tale loro autorità, in parte et in tucto et come volessino, committere' (see above, p. 197, n. 6). The councils, which passed the *Balìa* law on 8–10 April, could hardly have visualized the possible implications of this passage; it will be remembered that that law did not contain any mention of the creation of a new council. 'Trovo questo populo', writes Antonio Montecassino, 'pezo contento che mai. Et uno segno dimostra asai et non pocho: a questi dì se è facto conselgio ogni zorno, … et se volea obtenire per questi che regono che la autorità la quale havea quelli 210 con Signori et collegii, che era quello può al populo, fusse data ali setanta. Et mai mai [*sic*] non si potè obtenire; poteno fare praticha aposta, mai non se obtene cosa alcuna. … Solo obteneno se potese per certi homini farsi servire de danari sopra a le graveccie imposte, per potere fare per la utilità comune quanto li bisogni. …' In fact, the last decree of the *Balìa*, of 30 June, delegated to the Signoria, the Colleges, and the Seventy, authority 'faciendi vivam impositionem factam'.

[2] Ibid.   [3] See above, p. 161.

The two outstanding aspects of the reform of 19 April are the concentration of power in the new council, and the permanent character of its membership. On both counts historians from Guicciardini onwards have rightly considered it a landmark in the development of the Medicean régime under Lorenzo; but they have invariably overlooked the fact that it constituted the final stage in a development that went back to the time of Cosimo, thus reflecting the continuity which was so characteristic of the Medicean régime. The extensive powers of the council, as well as the permanence of its membership, recall the *Balìe* of Cosimo's days; but the closest links are with the reforms of 1471. Apart from the similarities in the appointment of its members, the very concept of a small permanent council was, in a sense, a logical development of the political programme underlying the creation of the 47 in 1471. Although the reform was, in 1480 as in 1471, valid for five years only, it was probably a foregone conclusion that it would be renewed, just as that of 1471 had been in 1476.[1] Yet this limitation to a quinquennium, which followed earlier precedents, indicates that even in 1480 Lorenzo and his friends did not consider themselves strong enough, or were not willing, to establish a senate for life. As we shall see, the subsequent extension of the reform did in fact, though not in law, give the Seventy a lifespan that lasted until the fall of the régime in 1494.

If the quinquennial validity of the law creating the Seventy was a concession to republican sentiments, the abolition by the *Balìa* of the regulations of 8 July 1471 concerning the annual election of the *Cento*[2] may well have been due to the desire to conciliate the *ottimati*. The 47 ceased to function, and once more all *veduti* Gonfaloniers of Justice were to act as electors, as well as being admitted to the meetings the *Cento* held independently of the councils of the People and the Commune;[3] and since the powers of the *Cento* to act alone had been extended in July 1471 to cover legislation, this constituted in fact an increase in the influence they could exercise. Their position was rendered slightly less exclusive by the admission, on the same terms, of the members of

---

[1] See above, p. 194.   [2] See above pp. 183–4.

[3] 'Il consiglio del Cento per l'advenire si squittini . . . come innanzi a dì primo di luglio MCCCCLXXI . . . s'observar doveva, cioè pe' veduti gonfalonier di giustitia d'anni XXXIIII forniti . . . et . . . vi possino intervenire . . . come potevano innanzi a decto dì primo di luglio' &c. (fol. 100^{r-v}; ed. Ricchioni, p. 179). The justification of this measure is significant: 'per allargare i beneficii quanto più si può et negl'uomini degni . . .' (fol. 100^r; not ed. by Ricchioni).

the Seventy belonging to the Lesser Guilds, which was clearly designed to appeal to the latter, but in fact did not amount to a great deal.[1] As to the Seventy itself, the thirty had been expressly forbidden to co-opt anyone for the forty who had not been *veduto* Gonfalonier of Justice,[2] with the exception, of course, of the artisan members, who as such were ineligible for the Gonfaloniership. Contrary to custom, no ratio was laid down for the artisans, and in the event their share turned out to be considerably lower than the traditional one to three.

This breach with tradition may in its turn have been a concession to the *ottimati*; but it probably also reflects the desire not to let artificial social restrictions interfere with the selection of what were considered the most suitable councillors.[3] Loyalty to the régime and administrative ability shown by past service were, as in the *Balìe*, doubtless overriding considerations; so were family connexions with Lorenzo.[4] At the same time, there appears to have been some difference in the selection of the two sections of the Seventy. While the appointment of the thirty appears to have been determined entirely by considerations of individual qualification, as a result of which a number of leading Medicean families were not represented, an attempt was clearly made to redress the balance in the case of that of the forty.[5] Only five of the Seventy had never been in a *Balìa*.[6] This exceptionally low proportion[7] is perhaps the most remarkable testimony to the desire to reduce to a minimum the security risks in the membership of the council which was henceforth to constitute the pivot of the Medici régime—even at the expense of the time-honoured principle of social mobility.

After the creation of the Seventy there still remained one gap

[1] 'Et perchè due soli del membro delle XIIII arti intervenivano, cioè solo quelli due e quali di dicembre si trovavano de' Signori, intervenganvi . . . oltre a' predecti tutti quelli e quali pel membro di predecte XIIII . . . arti saranno in tal tempo del numero de' Septanta et saranno habili.' In 1480 there were ten members of the Lesser Guilds among the Seventy, seven of whom were among the forty.

[2] Fol. 98r; Ricchioni, pp. 167–8.

[3] It is significant that two of the three members of the Lesser Guilds among the thirty, Antonio di Bernardo Dini and Ser Niccolò di Michele Dini, occupied important administrative positions. Both were clients of Lorenzo's.

[4] See Ricchioni, p. 65.

[5] This procedure resembles that adopted in the selection of the 40 of 1471; see above, pp. 182–3, 193.

[6] All of these were among the forty. They had all been *imborsati* for the Gonfaloniership of Justice in 1472, and four of them had been members of the scrutiny council of 1465 as substitutes of *veduti* Gonfaloniers (see above, p. 148).

[7] Cf. the respective percentages in the *Balìe*, including that of 1480 (above, pp. 83 ff., 183, 198–9).

in the conciliar system of the régime. The *Cento* had since 1471 had full authority to impose taxes, but not to deal with the *Monte*, which was the cornerstone of the financial administration of fifteenth-century Florence. In 1476, however, the *Cento* was granted special powers to this effect for one year,[1] and this was repeated in July 1481, with the proviso that the *Cento* could delegate these powers, which were now extended to include also matters affecting the gabelles and the Sea Consuls.[2] The explanation given for this measure was the disastrous condition of the *Monte*,[3] which was due to the war, to the rise of the value of gold in terms of silver, to the large payments of interest, to tax evasion and fraud,[4] and which the legislation of the *Balìa* of 1480 had evidently not done much to alleviate. On 4 August the *Cento* made use of its new authority by delegating its special powers, until July 1482, to a commission consisting of the five *Ufficiali del Monte* and twelve additional members elected by the *Cento*.[5] The Seventeen *Riformatori*, as they came to be called, duly ended their term of office in that month;[6] but 'especially in view of the danger of war' which might necessitate rapid decisions, the councils renewed the *Cento*'s special powers for another year,[7] and much the same argument was used in the following year, when

[1] See above, p. 195.

[2] Provv., 172, fols. 81ᵛ–84ᵛ (24–26 July 1481). The powers concerned the Monte, the office of the *Consoli del Mare*, and all gabelles, 'sì per agiugnere et crescere entrata . . . sì per limitare l'uscite et spese . . . sì anchora per riformare ciaschuna tal cosa . . . in meglio. . . .'

[3] 'Essendo suto ricordato da' principali et più savii cittadini in quanto disordine si truovi el Monte et tutti e suoi membri, et quanto quanto [*sic*] sia il suo grande debito per le paghe insino a oggi, et per le dote per insino al primo di marzo MCCCCLXXnono . . . et per le dote da detto dì primo di marzo . . . in qua . . . Et examinato che a volere satisfare a' creditori del Monte . . . di quello che in tale anno corressi . . . non ragionando il sopradetto debito vecchio di paghe et dote, l'uscita sopravanzerebbe l'entrata ogn'anno migliaia et migliaia di fiorini, et continuamente multiplicharebbe il debito, et crescerebbono gl'inconvenienti . . . Il che anchora torna grandissimo danno et dispiacere . . .' &c. See also above, p. 199.

[4] 'Le cagioni de' disordini sono manifeste: le insopportabili spese della guerre per le quali s'è adoperato tutte l'entrate del Monte, lasciando indrieto le paghe et dote; l'altra la mutatione et varietà che a fatto la moneta, perchè l'entrate del Monte per la maggior parte sono lire et l'uscita fiorini; gli assai interessi pagati, et finalmente la licentia di ciascheduno in non pagare le graveze più che si voglia, et fraude commesse et che si commettono tutto dì sotto varii modi per disobligarsi dallo specchio et da gravamenti personali, et licentia di chi piglia e danari del commune . . .' &c.

[5] Cento, 2, fols. 63ᵛ–64ᵛ. See L. F. Marks, 'The financial oligarchy in Florence under Lorenzo', in *Italian Renaissance Studies*, ed. E. F. Jacob (London, 1960), p. 138.

[6] See their register, Monte Comune, 884 (provisional number). The first deliberation entered in their register is of 11 Aug. 1481, their last of 24 July 1482. Their official name was 'Riformatori del Monte et delle gabelle del comune di Firenze' (ibid., fol. 8ʳ). The twelve additional members were nominated by the Signoria.

[7] Provv., 173, fols. 73ᵛ–75ʳ (13–19 July 1482): '. . . presertim propter belli suspitionem . . . et tamen multa possent in dies occurrere presertim ad salutem libertatis spectantia, que et celeriter et cum facilitate expediri convenerit. . . .'

a further extension for one year was granted.[1] In July 1484 the special powers were renewed for a further year.[2] Two months later they were extended until 1490, and were now also to include the *casi della camera del Comune*; and in this form they were renewed in 1489, to be valid until 1495.[3] The ancient councils of the People and the Commune were thus deprived of the last shred of their original power. They continued to deal with matters of minor importance, especially with private bills,[4] and retained the authority to pass constitutional reforms, as long as this had not been vested in the *Cento*.[5] Their decline is reflected in the decrease in the number of their meetings. The meetings of the two councils which actually completed legislation declined from an annual average of 22·2 during the decade 1470 to 1479, to an annual average of 14·3 during the decade 1480 to 1489.[6] On the other hand, the annual average of the meetings in which the *Cento* passed legislation by its sole authority rose from 5·8 in 1470–9, to 8·4 in 1480–9.[7] But also the *Cento*, in spite of its increased powers, suffered from the fact that the Seventy would now deal with decisions not involving legislation which previously would have come within the competence of the older councils. As we have seen, in 1481, when a systematic settlement of financial problems was attempted, the *Cento* delegated its extraordinary financial powers to a small commission; and this procedure was repeated in July 1490, when the *Cento* once more appointed a commission of Seventeen to reform the affairs of the *Monte* and

---

[1] Provv., 174, fols. 57ᵛ–58ᵛ (26–28 June 1483): '. . . et propter bellum minime potuit intendi illis rebus, que fieri debuissent per dictam auctoritatem . . . et insuper multa possent in dies occurrere presertim ad salutem libertatis spectantia, que et celeriter et cum facilitate expediri utile est. . . .'

[2] Provv., 175, fols. 90ᵛ–92ʳ (8–13 July 1484).

[3] Provv., 175, fols. 114ᵛ–118ʳ (15–17 Sept. 1484); Cento, 2, fols. 146ʳ–147ʳ (12 Feb. 1489). See also below, p. 207.

[4] Cf. Libri Fabarum, 71, *passim*.   [5] See below, p. 208.

[6] These figures are based on Provv., 160 to 180. Since the registers of *provvisioni* contain completed legislation only, the *Libri Fabarum*, which also contain entries for the meetings which rejected bills, would have given a more complete picture of the frequency of council meetings, were it not for the fact that there is a lacuna in the extant *Libri Fabarum* between April 1481 and April 1491. Nevertheless, the following figures, derived from Libri Fabarum, 69 to 71, may provide some additional evidence.

	Cento	Council of the People	Council of the Commune
1470	44	54	38
1475	27	24	21
1480	19	18	15
1493	13	14	14

[7] Cf. Cento, 1 to 3.

to deal with other pressing financial problems.[1] The Seventeen *Riformatori* of 1490 have been wrongly described as a permanent institution with unlimited powers which replaced, for all practical purposes, the Seventy as the apex of Florentine government, and hence as a decisive step in the direction of despotic rule. But if their appointment, for a specific purpose and a limited term, repeats the procedure adopted in 1481, it also reflects the tendency to delegate important decisions to committees which could deal with them more effectively and, in the case of the Seventeen, could be more easily controlled than the *Cento*.[2]

In fact, even after the reform of 1470, bills did not always have a smooth passage in the councils.[3] Thus the law of July 1481, granting the *Cento* special financial powers, met with stiff opposition, the council of the Commune only passing it with a majority of one;[4] and this opposition had by no means abated when these powers were to be renewed; if anything, it had increased.[5] Somewhat surprisingly, although not as strong as in the councils of the People and the Commune, it was also substantial in the *Cento*. But the *Cento* had also passed, on 9 February 1481, with the narrowest majority, the bill extending for the second time the law of 23 July 1471 to which it owed its exclusive powers of legislation.[6] The *Cento* represented, more than the ancient councils, the views and

[1] Cento, 3, fol. 1^{r-v} (15 July 1490). The term of office of the Seventeen expired at the end of Feb. 1491; but having been extended twice, they remained in office until 31 July 1491. On 10-13 June 1491 the three councils also put them in charge of economic and administrative reforms in Pisa and its *contado* (Provv., 182, fols. 29^{r}-30^{v}). See Rubinstein, 'The *Storie fiorentine* and the *Memorie di famiglia* by Francesco Guicciardini', *Rinascimento*, iv (1953), pp. 222-5.

[2] See above, pp. 199-200, on the *Otto di Pratica* and the *Dodici Procuratori*. Lorenzo belonged to the Seventeen of 1481 and 1490. Somewhat ironically, the argument of efficiency and speed, which was used to obtain the additional financial powers for the *Cento* (above, p. 204), was also put forward in 1481 to obtain the delegation of these powers to the Seventeen ('examinato . . . quanta utilità habbia a seguire di tale auctorità se sarà chi . . . sollecitamente procuri quelle cose le quali sono necessarie al presente bisogno'; loc. cit.).

[3] We do not possess registers of the proceedings of the Seventy. All that remain are a few decrees entered at the end of Balìe, 31 (fols. 124^{v}-127^{r}; 24 Nov. 1480-21 March 1481), which were passed by the Seventy by virtue of special authority granted to it by the *Balìa* before its dissolution in order to 'far vivo quello che resta della impositione facta del mese di maggio' (ibid., fols. 123^{v}-124^{r}; 30 June 1480). See above, p. 201, n. 1.

[4] Council of the People: 176 to 80; council of the Commune: 105 to 51; *Cento*: 92 to 33 (24-26 July 1481).

[5] 13-19 July 1482: 155 to 74, 104 to 49, and 76 to 37; 26-28 June 1483: 134 to 67, 103 to 50, and 88 to 23; 8-13 July 1484: 144 to 67, 100 to 46, and 90 to 23 respectively for the councils of the People and the Commune and the *Cento*.

[6] Libri Fabarum, 70, fol. 183^{r}: 84 to 42. See above, pp. 184 and 194, n. 6. The council of the People passed it with 164 votes against 76, having first rejected it on the 14th; the council of the Commune with 116 to 45 (ibid., fols. 183^{v}-184^{v}; 14-17 Feb.). In 1476 the *Cento* had renewed the law of 23 July 1471 by a large majority.

interests of the *ottimati*, especially after the restrictions on its composition that were imposed in 1471 had been lifted;[1] and at least some of the nays may have been due to the conviction among this group that the concentration of power had by now gone too far, and that it was not desirable to render it permanent. The behaviour of the *Cento* was doubtless one of the reasons why a lengthy memorandum of 1484, on the question of extending the recent reforms, suggests that the electorate and the membership of the *Cento* should once more be restricted, as they had been between 1471 and 1480, on the ground that 'così facilmente si farebbero, o doverebbero fare, le deliberationi nel Cento, et meglio le electioni'.[2] Only 60 Gonfaloniers of Justice—as against 80 after 1471—to be selected by the Signoria and the Seventy, were to act for one year as electors and, together with the Seventy, as additional members of the *Cento*. The author of the memorandum points out that this would reduce actual attendance from between 125 and 130 to not more than 90, a number which he evidently considered to be more manageable. The right of the Seventy to attend would serve the same purpose of reducing opposition, and of 'improving' the *Cento*. However, although this proposal was in keeping with the present conciliar policy of the régime, it was not embodied in the law of 17 September 1484, perhaps because it was feared that it would meet with too much resistance on the part of that council.[3] As we shall see, it was resuscitated with more success five years later.[4]

Another proposal of the memorandum was, however, accepted. By co-ordinating the various constitutional reforms since 1466, the law of September 1484 simplified the future procedure for renewing them.[5] The law on the Seventy expired in 1485; so did the powers of the *Cento* concerning the *Monte*, while the authority vested in the *Cento* in July 1471 remained in force until the end of 1486, in which year elections *a mano* would, unless renewed, come to an end.[6] The validity of these laws was now extended jointly for five years as from May 1485, elections *a mano* of the

[1] See above, p. 202.
[2] Ed. G. Pampaloni, 'Progetto di riforma alla Costituzione compilato da un seguace di Lorenzo il Magnifico', *Arch. Stor. Ital.*, cxiii (1955), p. 265: 'Vorrei che questi soli che squittinassino il Cento per [poi *ed.*] uno anno potessino venire al Cento et non gli altri veduti Gonfalonieri, come si faceva al tempo de' 47.'
[3] Provv., 175, fols. 114ᵛ–118ʳ (15–17 Sept.); ed. Ricchioni, pp. 180–7.
[4] See below, p. 209.
[5] '. . . verrebbono quasi ragguagliati i tempi' (memorandum, op. cit., p. 264).
[6] See above, pp. 194, 199, 206.

Signoria and elections of the *Otto di Guardia* being henceforth
considered part of the *ordine del Settanta*. At the same time the
Cento was empowered to renew this 'order of the Seventy', as
well as its own powers as acquired in 1471 and after, for another
five years without the assent of the councils of the People and
Commune. The *Balìa* of 1480 had not provided any machinery for
the renewal of its constitutional reforms. As the memorandum
had stated in concluding its suggestions, 'queste cose non si
possono ben fare solo pel Cento, ma bisogna tutti i consigli'.
This remark is illuminating: despite its vast new powers, the
Cento was still not competent to pass all constitutional legislation
by its sole authority. If the other two councils could be persuaded
(as in 1471 and 1480) to create a *Balìa*, one would be able to get
round this difficulty; for to try to have the extension law itself
passed by all three councils 'durerebbe troppa faticha'. But this
suggestion was not accepted: the leading citizens evidently felt
strong enough to dispense with a *Balìa*, and in the end the councils of the People and Commune passed the law with comfortable
majorities,[1] despite the limitations of their powers it continued
to impose on them. One of the reasons for this was doubtless the
promise of a scrutiny that was to begin in November, the city
being 'tutta sollevata per uno desiderio molto giusto di squittinio
generale': no scrutiny had been held for over twelve years, the
Balìa of 1480 having failed to carry one out.[2] Another reason was
probably that no attempt was made to extend the various reforms
beyond the quinquennial terms that had now become normal
Medicean practice, in contrast to the twenty-year period for
which elections *a mano* had been restored in 1466.[3]

The law of 17 September 1484 filled the gap in the reform of
1480 by laying down regulations for its next renewal, which was
entrusted to the *Cento* acting alone, without the assent of the
ancient councils. The *Cento*, on 12 February 1489, duly extended
the 'order of the Seventy' and the laws concerning the *Cento* until
1495, but in doing so it amended the regulations governing the
election *a mano* of the Signoria.[4] This was once more vested in
five *Accoppiatori* instead of the thirty-five who had been in charge
after 1480. However, instead of being appointed by the method
in force between 1471 and 1480, they were now to be chosen each

---

[1] Council of the People: 154 to 41; council of the Commune: 108 to 38. The *Cento* passed
it by 103 votes to 17. See above, p. 206.

[2] See above, p. 199.   [3] See above, pp. 168–9.

[4] Cento, 2, fols. 146ʳ–147ʳ (ed. Ricchioni, pp. 191–4).

year by the Signoria, or by others 'per loro ordine o commissione deputati et nominati', from among the Seventy. The principal criticism put forward of the present arrangement was the lack of secrecy in a committee consisting of thirty-five members—that is of half the council of Seventy—which was evidently not proving an exception to the rule that it was extremely difficult in Florence to keep proceedings of councils and large committees secret.[1]

While the extension law was presented, on 12 February, to the *Cento* only, all three councils were asked to pass a bill which in a modified form followed one of the proposals of the memorandum of 1484 by giving the Seventy full powers to decide annually on the method of electing the *Cento*, as well as the right to attend its meetings.[2] The *Cento* reacted strongly against this further subordination to the Seventy, and passed the law with a majority of only three votes,[3] while the councils of the People and Commune not surprisingly put up considerably less opposition.

The constitutional law had still well over a year to run when it was renewed in February 1489.[4] The next extension, on 21 September 1493,[5] took place over one year and seven months before the 'order of the Seventy' was due to expire. Does this reflect the apprehension that one day the councils, on whose votes it still depended, could create difficulties which might make it advisable to plan well ahead of time? Since the *Cento* had in September 1484 been given authority to make only one quinquennial extension of the constitutional law, its renewed extension had again to be passed by all three councils. This was evidently not considered satisfactory, for it was now decided to entrust the next extension once more to the *Cento*. Perhaps to make this more palatable, the express proviso was added that the extension must not exceed the customary five years.[6] But despite this increase in its authority, the *Cento*, as well as the council of

---

[1] 'Et perchè questo modo consueto è molto tedioso et per quello le cose sono in poca reputatione, maxime pel difecto del secreto, intendendosi parecchi dì innanzi per tutta la città quali habbino a essere e nuovi Signori. . . .'

[2] Provv., 179, fols. 98ʳ–99ʳ (12–14 Feb. 1489); ed. Ricchioni, pp. 188–90. The Seventy was also given full powers to provide for the filling of vacancies, 'per havere sempre lo intero numero di decti septanta'.

[3] 95 to 43 votes. The council of the People passed it with 151 to 65, that of the Commune with 120 to 40 votes. Since this was a constitutional reform, the vote of all three councils was required: see above, p. 208.

[4] It had been valid for five years as from 1 May 1485; see above, p. 207.

[5] Provv., 184, fols. 65ʳ–68ᵛ (19–21 Sept. 1493).

[6] '. . . purchè in tutto . . . non passi il termine di anni cinque'; Provv., 184, fol. 67ʳ.

the People, passed the law with majorities of only one and four
votes respectively.[1]

Was this resistance due to the conviction that the Seventy was
now well on the way to becoming a permanent institution, and
thus, since its personnel too was permanent, a senate with life
membership? On any account, the size of the opposition, over
thirteen years after its creation in 1480, is impressive enough, and
may help us to understand the success of the revolution of 9
November 1494. It offers a peculiar contrast to the self-confidence
and optimism which pervade the preamble of this last extension
law of the régime. Written at a time when the project of a French
expedition to Italy was gathering force, and when Florence's
diplomatic position was rapidly deteriorating, the preamble reads
like a panegyric on the Medicean régime as perfected under
Lorenzo. The Signoria having tried, it says, to find out

> which have been the measures that, besides the grace of omnipotent
> God, have guided our city from unrest, adversities, and mighty wars
> to so great a peace and tranquillity combined with so high an honour
> and reputation, and which have allayed, nay entirely extinguished, the
> perils of imminent troubles and the great dangers of a new and terrible
> war, the answer is clear to anyone who does not want to deceive
> himself: the first cause of this has been the wisdom, the constant
> endeavour, the care, and the great patriotism of a certain citizen who
> died not so long ago, as well as of those who are now alive, and [their]
> solid unity. The second cause has been the ease with which decisions in
> public matters are taken, and the authority of the Signoria, the *Otto di
> Pratica*, and the *Otto di Balìa*, thanks to the election to these offices of
> wise and prudent men. . . .[2]

The constitutional law of September 1484 had laid down that
a general electoral scrutiny was to be held in November of that

---

[1] *Cento*: 82 to 40; council of the People: 132 to 62; council of the Commune: 112 to 40.
The law also streamlined procedure in the Seventy by relieving it of business of minor
importance, which was now delegated entirely to its committees: 'che da insino da hora e
Septanta habbino a deliberare solo quelle [provvisioni] le quali contenessino casi publici
o privati e quali appartenessino allo stato; quelle che parlassino de' casi del Monte, Camera
del Comune, o delle gabelle o loro membri, diminuendo cosa alcuna; quelle che tocchas-
sino casi di graveze o sciemare salarii a' rectori; et non altre in alcuno modo . . . .'

[2] 'Ricerco . . . quali sieno state quelle provisioni, le quali, dopo la gratia dello omni-
potente Dio, habbino la città nostra [da] inquietudine, adversità et potentissime guerre a
tanta pace et quiete con tanto honore et reputatione ridocto, et gli imminenti casi adversi,
le grandi suspitioni di nuova et potente guerra sedato, anzi al tucto extincto, si truova, non
si volendo ingannare, che il senno, la diligentia, sollecitudine et grande amore verso la
patria di qualche cittadino da non molto tempo in qua morto, et de' presenti vivi, et la
buona unione, esserne suta la prima . . . cagione. La seconda, la facilità delle deliberationi ne'
publici bisogni, l'auctorità de' magistrati Signori, Octo di Pratica et Octo di Balìa, per
eleggersi a tali magistrati persone alcune di . . . senno et prudentia. . . .' (Provv., cit.).

year.[1] Despite the dislike of the Mediceans for scrutinies, which was reflected in their repeated postponements, they still remained an essential part of the Florentine system of government and administration, since the vast majority of offices continued to be filled by lot and even the elections *a mano* of the Signoria presupposed the existence of previous electoral qualifications.

It might have been expected that the *Balìa* of April 1480, having failed to carry out the scrutiny that had been one of its tasks, would be reconvened for this purpose, or that the regulations introduced in December 1466 would now be observed.[2] These had provided for scrutiny councils to be composed in future of the Signoria and the Colleges, the *veduti* Gonfaloniers of Justice and 100 elected members, to be chosen, together with a number of artisans, by the *Cento*. After the creation of the Seventy these regulations, with their pronounced oligarchical slant, were evidently considered inappropriate, for they were not now applied. Instead, the law of 17 September 1484 made the Seventy the nucleus of the scrutiny council, but left the decision on how to appoint the elective members and the *Accoppiatori* to the *Cento*.[3] Was this due to the belief that the *Cento* would be more amenable than the ancient councils to further strengthening of the position of the Seventy? In fact, the law passed by that council a fortnight later also put the Seventy and the Signoria in charge of appointing the elective members of the scrutiny council, and two months later the *Cento* reserved for itself the election of the *Accoppiatori*.[4]

In co-opting the *arroti*, the Seventy followed the traditional policy of continuity; of the 231 citizens they elected, 135 had previously been members of *Balìe*, while of the remaining 96 no less than 73 were sons or brothers of *Balìa* members.[5] What distinguishes this election from earlier proceedings of this kind

---

[1] See above, p. 208.

[2] See above, pp. 171, 197, 198, and 199.

[3] Provv., cit., fol. 117^{r-v}. Each *quartiere* was to provide 84 members, including the *ex officio* members, the difference being made up by the elected councillors. The Signoria and the Colleges of Sept.–Oct. 1484, and those who were in office at the time, were to be, like the Seventy, members *ex officio*; all other officials were expressly excluded. All members had to be *veduti ai Tre Maggiori*, and, as usual, a quarter of them were to belong to the Lesser Guilds.

[4] Cento, 2, fols. 93^v–94^v (28 Sept.), 97^v–98^r (20 Nov.). The *Cento* had, on 6 Nov., postponed the beginning of the scrutiny until later that month (ibid., fol. 97^{r-v}). The elective members had already been chosen on 29 Sept.: see register of the *Accoppiatori* of the scrutiny, Tratte, 20, fol. 3^v: their names are listed on fols. 5^v–10^v.

[5] Nine of these were also members of the Seventy.

is that nearly all of these 135 men had belonged to the last *Balìa*, that of 1480.[1] As a result, the personnel of that *Balìa* was now, to a large extent, reconvened[2] to carry out the scrutiny together with additional elected members, much along the lines of the regulations for the scrutiny which it had failed to hold in 1480,[3] and without having to go to the trouble of persuading the councils to agree to a new *Balìa*. At the same time, the *ottimati* did less well than they considered their due; they might indeed have done better if the regulations of December 1466 had been observed. According to Piero Guicciardini, who was one of them, less than one half of the council's membership belonged to that class. For this he blames the leading citizens, who bestowed their favour on new men at the expense of the ancient families, and also chancery officials who helped them carry out this policy. Lorenzo was understood to have drawn up, together with Ser Giovanni Guidi, the first list of candidates for the scrutiny council, all of whom were duly elected by the Seventy.[4]

Even if this story, and it is confirmed by other evidence, is only partly correct, it offers a striking contrast to the outward show of legality in qualifying citizens for membership. The *Cento* had laid down for the elected members of the council the usual family maximum of two, with the proviso that the Signoria could exempt up to nine families, 'perchè ci è pure alcune case che anno più lati et assai huomini degni'.[5] Accordingly, no less than four Ridolfi and five Medici were elected, but two of the Medici, Piero di Messer Orlando and Lorenzo di Pierfrancesco, were disqualified because of tax debts; and of the two substitutes only one belonged to that family. In fact, Piero and Lorenzo were the only two council members to be disqualified on this account,[6] for a

---

[1] 113 of the *arroti*.

[2] Of the official members of the scrutiny council 4 members of the Signoria of Sept.–Oct., 3 of the Colleges, and 65 of the Seventy had been in the *Balìa* of 1480. As one of these is entered twice, as Signore and as one of the Seventy, their total amounts to 71, and the total of members of the *Balìa* of 1480 to 184, that is *c.* 55 per cent. of the entire personnel of the scrutiny council as constituted in Sept.

[3] See above, p. 198.

[4] See below, pp. 213, 215–16.

[5] Provv. of 28 Sept., cit. In 1480 the Signoria had been able to exempt only two families: see above, p. 198, n. 4.

[6] Tratte, 20, fol. 10ᵛ (1 Oct. 1484). The *Accoppiatori* elected Giuliano di Giovenco de' Medici and Puccio d'Antonio Pucci in the place of Piero di Orlando and Lorenzo di Pierfrancesco. According to the law of 28 Sept. the elected members of the council had to be *netti di specchio*. The exclusion was probably not aimed against Lorenzo di Pierfrancesco personally, for on 17 Dec. the *Accoppiatori* especially exempted him and Jacopo Salviati from the age limit for the scrutiny of the highest posts in the administration of the territory, i.e. those of the captain and *Podestà* of Pisa (ibid., fol. 14ᵛ).

third member who was in the same predicament was reinstated after his name had been cancelled from the list of tax debtors. This was Jacopo, son of Agnolo Acciaiuoli,[1] who, like his father, had been exiled in September 1466, and had been subsequently declared a rebel, but whose sentences had been quashed in June.[2] From a different angle, the readmission of Jacopo reflects much the same concern with legality as the election shortly afterwards of Lorenzo de' Medici as one of the ten *Accoppiatori* of the scrutiny.[3]

As for the technicalities of the scrutiny and of the subsequent filling of the bags, the decisions upon them were left to the *Accoppiatori*, the law of 17 September 1484 having granted them 'whatever authority had in the past been bestowed upon the *Signori* and the *Accoppiatori*, or upon the *Accoppiatori* alone'.[4] This is an evident allusion to the extensive powers the *Accoppiatori* of the scrutiny of 1471 had possessed. There can be little doubt that in 1484, as in 1458 and 1472, the *Accoppiatori* decided that the scrutiny should act as an electoral revision, and consequently eliminated, with the exception of special cases, the previous qualifications of citizens who had not been successful in it.[5] This is borne out by the complaints of citizens who had lost their old *polizze* in 1484, reminding us of similar complaints after the scrutiny of 1458.[6]

We are fortunate in possessing a detailed account of the scrutiny of 1484 from the pen of Piero Guicciardini, the historian's father, who was a member of its council.[7] Unlike the registers of the *Accoppiatori*, Piero Guicciardini's account does not confine itself to the technical aspects of the scrutiny and reveals, more

---

[1] Fol. 10ᵛ (1 Oct.).

[2] Otto, periodo repubblicano, 224, fol. 136ʳ. He had been exiled for twenty years on 12 Sept. 1466, and declared a rebel on 29 Jan. 1467. These sentences were cancelled on 2 June 1484.

[3] For their names, see Appendix, no. I. Eight of the ten *Accoppiatori* belonged to the Seventy and had previously served as *Accoppiatori*, but only two, Ruberto Lioni and Lorenzo de' Medici, as *Accoppiatori* for the last scrutiny.

[4] '. . . qualunche auctorità stata insino a quì per simili casi conceduta ai Signori et accopiatori, o accopiatori soli, pe' tempi passati. . . .' (Ricchioni, p. 186; see above, p. 207, n. 3).

[5] See above, pp. 108, 190.

[6] See above, p. 108, and below, p. 224.

[7] Bibl. Naz., XXV. 636, fols. 7ʳ–12ʳ (autograph). (A later copy is in Bibl. Naz., II. IV. 346, fols. 243ʳ–256ᵛ.) Piero Guicciardini became a member of the scrutiny council on 8 Jan. 1485 as one of the new *Sedici Gonfalonieri* (fol. 11ʳ; see above, p. 211, n. 3). By that time the scrutiny of most of the major offices had been completed. Piero's account of this part of the scrutiny is therefore in the nature of a review of the work done by the time he joined the council. See Appendix, no. XI.

clearly than any other contemporary source, the nature and extent of Lorenzo's influence on an important public function.

Piero divides the candidates for electoral qualification—there were about 8,000 of them for the three highest offices, i.e. the Signoria and the Colleges[1]—into five groups, one at either end of the scale and three at the centre. At one extreme he places the ancient families of Magnates, like the Bardi, and some of the ancient *popolani* families, such as the Strozzi, all of which have little or no share in the government (*reggimento*) of Florence; at the opposite extreme those members of the Lesser Guilds who in the past had acquired electoral qualifications for the guild consulate, or had been *veduti* for the Signoria. Of the three 'middle groups' two had affinities with the former: at the top of the scale there were the *popolani antichi nobili*,[2] some of whom, like the Corsini, Soderini, and Albizzi, took part in governing Florence, while others, such as the Peruzzi, were treated on much the same terms as the ancient nobility; at the bottom we find the *artefici più nobili*, and those members of the Greater Guilds who had newly been qualified as such for the *Tre Maggiori*, having previously been counted among the Lesser Guilds.[3] The central group, finally, was represented by families like the Serristori, which while not being *al tutto ignobile*, did not yet belong to the aristocracy, but which had lately acquired all the highest posts in the state, and were well on the way to becoming *popolani nobili* by means of their political influence. On the other hand, most of the ancient aristocracy found their political advancement blocked. This picture of social mobility is completed by the rise through their wealth or personal qualities of families belonging to the *extremo ignobile* into the lowest ranks of the middle groups, to be replaced at the bottom of the scale by even more recent upstarts, *gente più nuova*. 'And thus continuously new men make the grade, and in order to give them a place in the governing class it is necessary to eliminate from it long-established citizens; and that is what is actually done.'[4]

In the voting on the electoral qualifications, the middle group

---

[1] Called briefly the scrutiny of the Priorate.

[2] He includes in this group the Albizzi, Peruzzi, Corsini, Ricci, and Alberti.

[3] Such transfers, for electoral purposes, from the *Minore* to the *Maggiore* were not infrequent, and naturally implied a rise in status.

[4] 'Et così continovamente viene su gente nuova, onde è necessario, che mettendosi ne reggimento tuttavia de' nuovi, a rincontro se ne cacci de' vecchi; et così si fa' (fol. 10ᵛ).

of families, like the Serristori, got the widest support; next came the 'case popolane antiche che hanno el reggimento',[1] such as the Corsini and Soderini and Piero's own family, and although perhaps slightly behind them, those of the middle groups nearest to the *extremo ignobile*: for they were favoured by all the artisans as well as by some of the leading citizens.

But 'new men', *gente nuova*, was a flexible term whose meaning depended, to some extent, on one's own social position. For Piero Guicciardini it embraced, in a wider sense, all the families that had acquired qualifications for the higher offices after 1434, as against the ancient *popolani* families like his own, which had already possessed them before. He calculates that of the *c.* 6,400 citizens of the Greater Guilds who were candidates in the scrutiny of the *Tre Maggiori* which was completed in December 1484, about two-thirds, i.e. *c.* 4,250, belonged to the two top groups.[2] About one-third were *gente nuova*. In this scrutiny these 'new men' received the support of all the members of the Lesser Guilds in the council, of those who were of like status, as well as of upper-class members who were either relatives or friends, or voted for them for political reasons (*per conto di stato*). The candidates from the 'good families', on the other hand, did not stand the same chance of being successful. This could be due to a variety of causes: some of their families belonged to the ancient nobility; others were so numerous that only a fraction of their members would be qualified; others, like the Strozzi, were politically suspect; but the main reason had to be sought in the social composition of the scrutiny council itself. For while this class provided more than one half of all the candidates for qualification for the *Tre Maggiori*, it provided less than one half of the council's membership, which was not enough to make them obtain the required majority. Piero lays the blame for this state of affairs on the great citizens who 'tirono su gente nuova et spacciono e vecchi'—'who pull up new men and undo long-established citizens'—because the former are more amenable to them, and also on the personnel of the chancery who want to humour the great and to favour their own class; 'et a questo modo', he sums up, 'si guasta la civiltà'[3]—'and in this way good government is destroyed'. This is a thinly veiled criticism of Lorenzo de' Medici,

[1] Ibid.
[2] '... di case antiche popolane, et usi avere il regimento dal 1434 indrietro, et di famiglie' (fol. 7ᵛ).
[3] Fol. 7ᵛ.

who, according to reliable information received by Piero Guicciardini, had drawn up the first list of the scrutiny council together with Ser Giovanni Guidi, 'che hora fa il tutto'[1]—'who now manages everything'. Moreover, Ser Giovanni Guidi and some of his colleagues in the chancery successfully lobbied for their relatives in the scrutiny for the minor offices, although this had been expressly forbidden.[2] On the other hand, Lorenzo was, according to Piero Guicciardini, also partly responsible for some members of the Magnate families and of families like the Strozzi being more successful than in any of the scrutinies for the highest offices since 1434, 'parendogli non ci sia pericolo alcuno di loro, tenendosi le borse a mano'—'he thought that they would not be in the least dangerous as long as elections were *a mano*', and would thus be readier to pay their taxes; 'and I believe', Piero adds, 'that Lorenzo is genuinely friendly towards the aristocrats (*uomini da bene*), and I am pleased about this'.[3] Such sentiments were, however, not shared by the *gente nuova* and by most of the lower classes, 'which I believe is entirely due to the fact that their nature prevents them from being friends of the *uomini da bene*'; they believed that by keeping them down they would promote their own advancement.[4] What could be more characteristic than the way in which such people reserved the term *popolani*, for all practical purposes, to themselves, and lumped the genuine *popolani* (like the Guicciardini) together with the ancient nobility? Whatever support they gave to the *case da bene* that were in power was due solely to fear.

It is evident from Piero Guicciardini's observations that, however much Lorenzo influenced the course of the scrutiny, he did not control it. This is borne out by Piero's remarks on the voting in the scrutiny for the offices of Captain and *Podestà* of Pisa. These were the highest of the external offices, and, owing to the exceptional responsibilities attaching to the administration of Pisa, required particularly careful selection. To Piero Guicciardini's satisfaction, Lorenzo was determined that only good citizens who were used to high office, *usi al reggimento*, and particularly to posts of similar importance, should be qualified. The way Lorenzo tried to achieve this is revealing not only for his role in the scrutiny, but also, in a wider sense, for his position in Florence.

---

[1] Fols. 7ʳ, 9ʳ. See also above, p. 212.
[3] Fol. 8ʳ.
[2] Fol. 11ᵛ.
[4] Ibid.

The *Otto di Guardia* had, at the beginning of the scrutiny, issued a ban on unauthorized meetings of members of the scrutiny council, as well as of others of equal social standing,[1] in order to prevent pressure groups (*intelligenze*) from being formed, as was liable to happen on such occasions[2]. Nevertheless Lorenzo, as Piero Guicciardini informs us, organized such an *intelligenza* by requesting about 100 members of the council to vote only for those aristocrats (*uomini da bene*) who deserved these offices. He did so under the pretext of having discovered another *intelligenza* of about 50 members who had promised to vote for one another. This discovery greatly annoyed Lorenzo, not so much because the *intelligenza* was illegal, as because it had been concluded without his knowledge; and he consequently did not include its leaders in his own group.[3] To keep the latter secret, he not only made its members swear an oath, threatening them with his displeasure if they violated it, but also saw to it that they met only in small groups and at different places. To keep his *intelligenza* secret, and to prevent others from lobbying for their own candidates, he moreover made the Gonfalonier of Justice require from the council members an oath that they would observe the secrecy of the ballot and abstain from lobbying for votes; and to avoid being held personally responsible for this ordinance, he took the precaution of having the Augustinian preacher Fra Mariano da Gennazzano warn the Signoria, in the sermon he preached in their Palace the day before the scrutiny for the Pisan offices, that they must not allow the ballot beans to be publicly shown and votes to be requested, as had been happening during the

[1] Fol. 8ᵛ. The ordinance of the Eight of 27 Nov. 1484 is in Otto, periodo repubblicano, 69, fols. 25ᵛ–26ʳ: 'desiderando che lo squittino che lunedì proxime futuro a dì 29 del presente felicemente cominciare si debbe, sia laudabile, et in quello naturalmente et civilmente si proceda, . . . fanno bandire . . . a qualunque persona . . . veduta ad alcuno de' Tre Maggiori ufici . . . che da hoggi durante tutto il tempo di detto squittino non ardischa in alcun modo o sotto alcun colore ragunarsi insieme . . . excepto che nel luogho per ciò ordinato, cioè nel palagio de' nostri Magnifici Signori, oltre al numero di sei . . . sotto pena di fiorini 100 . . . . Notificando a ciaschuno che quando per alcuna legitima cagione di nozze o altro rispecto necessario occorresse che più che ditto numero ad raghunare s'avessi', special application could be made. The *bando*, addressed to the *veduti ai Tre Maggiori*, from whom the scrutiny council was recruited (above, p. 211, n. 3), follows the pattern of earlier prohibitions of *intelligenze*: see above, pp. 118–19.

[2] Ibid.: 'che non si facessi ragunata niuna di squittinanti, nè andassino a cena insieme più di sei squittinanti, acciò che tali intelligentie non si facessino' (fol. 8ᵛ).

[3] '. . . anzi fece dire a buona parte gli sonassino.' They were Francesco d'Orlando Gherardi, Piero di Lorenzo Cappelli, Giuliano di Francesco Salviati, and Niccolò d'Antonio Martelli. Three of these had been members of the 1480 *Balìa*. They all belonged to the younger generation, having been born in 1446, 1437, 1448, and 1444 respectively. Giuliano Salviati was, in 1498, to head the last pro-Savonarola Signoria.

scrutiny of the *Tre Maggiori*—and as was to happen again later on.[1]

· · · · ·

According to Francesco Guicciardini, Lorenzo's position was that of a benevolent despot in a republican constitution who had succeeded in increasing his power to a point where its transformation into a Signoria might appear imminent.[2] Since the first publication of the *Storie fiorentine* in 1859,[3] this view has profoundly influenced the judgements of historians.[4] However, Guicciardini's emphasis on the despotic character of Lorenzo's ascendancy already constitutes a reassessment of judgements current at Florence after the revolution of 1494, when Savonarola set the example in condemning the Medici régime as tyrannical.[5]

Savonarola's condemnation doubtless expressed the feelings of many citizens at the time of the revolution.[6] These in turn had their roots in the opposition to the Medici before 1494. We have not to wait until 1494 to find Lorenzo condemned as 'Florentinum tyrannum'.[7] If Sixtus IV hoped in 1478 that by accusing him of

---

[1] i.e. during the voting on the so-called *Otto Uffici*, which in fact were ten and included the *Ufficiali*, the *Camerario* and the *Provveditore del Monte*, the Sea Consuls, &c.: see fol. 11^{r-v}, and Tratte, 12, fol. 2^v. Piero Guicciardini states that many people felt no longer bound by their oath since in the meantime a new Signoria had taken office. But the chief reason, according to him, was the dislike of the *gente nuova* for the secret ballot, which it rightly considered to be less democratic than the open one. The *Accoppiatori* and the new Gonfalonier of Justice did not enforce it, either because they wished to avoid unpopularity, or because they had some personal axe to grind.

[2] *Storie fiorentine*, p. 80; cf. p. 71. Cf. also *Dialogo del reggimento*, ed. R. Palmarocchi, in *Dialogo e discorsi del reggimento di Firenze* (Bari, 1932), pp. 33–34.

[3] G. Canestrini, *Opere inedite di Francesco Guicciardini*, iii (Florence, 1859).

[4] They have, moreover, been misled by his account of the financial reform of 1490 to consider the temporary commission of Seventeen a new and permanent instrument of Lorenzo's growing autocracy. Cf. e.g. Reumont, ii, pp. 296–7; F.-T. Perrens, *The History of Florence from the Domination of the Medici . . .*, Engl. transl. (London, 1892), i, p. 415; U. Dorini, *Lorenzo il Magnifico* (Florence, 1949), p. 164; E. Bizzarri, *Il Magnifico Lorenzo* ([Milan], 1950), pp. 275–6. For a revision of this interpretation of Guicciardini's account see my article, 'The *Storie fiorentine*', pp. 222–5. See also C. M. Ady, *Lorenzo dei Medici . . .* (London, 1955), pp. 86–87, which corrects the traditional judgement expressed in the same author's article in *Cambridge Medieval History*, viii (Cambridge, 1936), p. 221.

[5] It was hardly a coincidence that his picture of a tyrant in the *Trattato circa il reggimento di Firenze* ii, 2 (ed. A. de Rians (Florence, 1847), pp. 22–31), with its broad hints at Florentine conditions, served Guicciardini in writing his concluding observations on Lorenzo in the *Storie* (pp. 73–82).

[6] Cf. Parenti's sonnet on the liberation of Florence, in J. Schnitzer, *Quellen und Forschungen zur Geschichte Savonarolas*, iv (Leipzig, 1910), p. 11: God, who has 'toltoci da tyrannico furore', 'guarda Firenza / Vissuta in servitù anni sessanta / Da sì crudeli tyranni et rabbia tanta!' Cf. the treaty between Florence and Charles VIII of 25 Nov. 1494 (ed. Capponi in *Arch. Stor. Ital.*, i (1842), p. 364): Charles is to have the title of 'libertatis nostrae conservator ac eius tyrannorum fugator'.

[7] Rinuccini, *De libertate*, in op. cit., p. 302; reform project of the *Dieci*, of Dec. 1494 (Carte Strozz., 2ª ser., 95, no. 12, fol. 35^r): from 1434 onwards, 'siamo suti tiranneggiati. . . . Ma hora che è spenta la tirannide al tutto . . . .'

tyrannically usurping all power in Florence, he would gain the sympathy of the Florentines for his cause, he was not altogether wrong, as is shown by Rinuccini's dialogue *De libertate*, which was completed in April 1479.[1] That this work was not just a *pièce d'occasion* of humanist rhetoric is borne out by Rinuccini's private diary, in which Lorenzo is similarly denounced as 'perniziossimo e crudelissimo tiranno'.[2] Such denunciations, like the eulogies of Lorenzo, give an exaggerated picture of his power. Ugolino Verino's *Caesar* as epithet for Lorenzo is the counterpart to Rinuccini's *tyrannus*; Poliziano calls him Florence's *caput*; according to Landino, he supported 'tam magnae rei publicae molem solus'.[3] Another humanist urged that he should be called *pater patriae*,[4] but this epithet remained reserved to his grandfather, and even so solemn an official document as the law declaring Piero his 'successor', which was passed a few days after his death, did not go beyond calling him *vir primarius nostrae civitatis*.[5]

Like his father and grandfather, and like other leading citizens, Lorenzo held, at one time or another, important posts in the republic; but, unlike Piero and Cosimo, he never belonged to the Signoria, although he became eligible for it in 1479 on reaching the age of thirty;[6] and unlike other *uomini principali*, he never occupied any offices in the administration of the territory. On the other hand, nearly all the offices he held in Florence were of

---

[1] Cf. Sixtus's bull of 1 June 1478, in Fabroni, *Laurentii vita*, ii, p. 125 : 'tyrannide quadam Florentini populi omnem auctoritatem sibi vendicare et usurpare non cessavit.' See also the Florentine reply to Sixtus's accusation of 21 July 1478 (ed. Pignotti, *Storia della Toscana*, iv, p. 117) : you assert that Lorenzo 'tyrannus noster sit'. Rinuccini, loc. cit. : that the war is not 'contra Florentinum populum, sed contra Laurentium Medicem Florentinum tyrannum pro libertate populi susceptum non voces sed publicae litterae in omnes gentes a Rege ac Pontifice missae divulgataeque testantur'. See also above, p. 196, n. 1.

[2] *Ricordi*, p. cxlix. Cf. also Cambi, *Istorie*, in *Delizie*, xxi, p. 65 (1491–2) : Lorenzo 's'era fatto chapo di detta ciptà, et tiranno, più che sse fussi stato signore a bacchetta', i.e. an Italian despot.

[3] A. Lazzari, *Ugolino e Michele Verino* (Turin, 1897), p. 89; Poliziano, *Prose volgari inedite e poesie latine e greche edite e inedite*, ed. I. del Lungo (Florence, 1867), p. 117; *Testi inediti e rari di Cristoforo Landino e Francesco Filelfo*, ed. E. Garin (Florence, 1949), p. 17. Examples of this kind could be easily multiplied. On similar eulogies of Cosimo and Piero di Cosimo, see Alison M. Brown, 'The humanist portrait of Cosimo de' Medici, Pater Patriae', *Journal of the Warburg and Courtauld Institutes*, xxiv (1961), pp. 186–221 (especially pp. 196 ff.).

[4] Aurelio Lippo Brandolini, 'De laudibus Laurentii Medicis', in *Carmina illustrium poetarum italorum*, ii (Florence, 1719), p. 447 : 'Ergo pater patriae communi est voce vocandus.' Cf. Brown, op. cit., pp. 194–5.   [5] Provv., 183, fols. 1ʳ–2ᵛ (13–16 April 1492).

[6] He was qualified for the *Tre Maggiori* in the scrutiny of 1453, and *veduto* (that is drawn, but barred as minor) for the first time in Feb. 1454, and then again in 1457 and 1465 (Tratte, 16, fol. 29ʳ; Tratte, 200, 201 and 202). He was *imborsato* for the Gonfaloniership of Justice in 1463 (Tratte, 17) and again in 1466 and 1472 (Bibl. Naz., II. IV. 346, fol. 140ʳ; Med. av. Pr., LXXXVI, fol. 325ᵛ), and *veduto* for it in Dec. 1482 (Tratte, 203). The minimum age for the Gonfaloniership was forty-five.

special importance for the government of the city.[1] This applies in particular to financial policy: he was one of the five officials of the *Monte* between 1487 and 1490, and belonged to the commissions of the Seventeen *Riformatori* of 1481–2 and 1490–1;[2] and he was five times one of the Twelve *Procuratori*.[3] As a member of the Seventy, he was *Accoppiatore* every other year between 1481 and 1489, in which year membership of that office was once more reduced to five;[4] and he was again appointed to it shortly before his death.[5] He was one of the *Dieci di Balìa* during the first year of the Pazzi war.[6] A few days after the attempt on his life on 26 April 1478 he became, for the first and last time, one of the *Otto di Guardia*, having been elected shortly before that event.[7] The Eight of May–August 1478 had been entrusted, on 16 April, with the task of remedying the disorders from which that office suffered by subjecting it to a thoroughgoing reform, and this was doubtless the reason why Lorenzo had been elected one of them.[8] He resigned, however, after only eighteen days, perhaps in order to counter criticism of being personally involved in the persecution of his enemies after the failure of the conspiracy.[9] Lorenzo was several times a member of the *Cento* after he had reached the required age of thirty-five in 1484;[10] but he had

---

[1] The two principal exceptions are the *Ufficiali dello Studio* and the *Operai del Palagio*, who were concerned with intellectual and artistic activities. Lorenzo belonged to the former continuously between 1472 and 1484 (Tratte, 82, fol. 49ʳ), and to the latter from 1479 to his death (Tratte, 82, fol. 114ᵛ, 83, fol. 109ʳ).

[2] Tratte, 82, fol. 105ʳ; 83, fol. 3ʳ (*Ufficiali del Monte*); Monte Comune, 884 (provisional), fol. 7ᵛ; Tratte, 83, fol. 198ᵛ (XVII *Riformatori*). He first belonged to the XVII of 1490 as one of the *Ufficiali del Monte*; on expiry of his term as *Ufficiale* at the end of Feb. 1491, he was elected one of the 12 additional members.

[3] For six months, from Oct. 1484, 1486, 1487, 1488, and 1489 (Tratte, 82, fol. 68ʳ; fol. 113ʳ⁻ᵛ). He belonged twice to the VIII *di Pratica*, from April 1481, and from July 1491 (ibid., 82, fol. 108ʳ, 83, fol. 110ᵛ).

[4] Register of *Accoppiatori*, Tratte, 21, fol. 1ᵛ: list of the thirty-five members of the Seventy in charge of elections *a mano* for one year from April 1481. See also above, pp. 199, 208.

[5] Tratte, 21, fol. 17ʳ (as from Feb. 1492).

[6] As one of the officials elected by the *Cento* on 13 June 1478 for six months, and re-elected for the same period on 27 Nov. (Tratte, 82, fol. 102ʳ).

[7] For four months, as from 1 May (Tratte, 82, fol. 2ᵛ). The *Balìa* of 1466 had decreed that the new Eight were to be elected at least a fortnight before their predecessors had ended their term of office (Balìe, 30, fol. 13ʳ).

[8] Provv., 169, fols. 6ᵛ–10ʳ (14–16 April 1478); see above, p. 200. Sixtus IV imputed far more sinister motives to Lorenzo's election: in his bull of 1 June 1478 he tried to justify the conspiracy by asserting that, *sicut fertur*, Lorenzo had had himself elected one of the Eight, in order 'multos ex dictis civibus Florentinis primariis partim relegare, partim de medio tollere et occidere' (Fabroni, *Laurentii vita*, ii, pp. 125–6).

[9] Otto, periodo repubblicano, 48, fols. 2ʳ–7ᵛ. Between 1 and 18 May he was absent from twelve out of twenty meetings of the Eight. On the rumours that he intended to use his membership to persecute his enemies, see the preceding note.

[10] For six-monthly sessions in 1485, 1486, 1488, 1489, and 1490 (Tratte, 337).

already been admitted to that council (as well as to the *Balìa*) by special decree in 1466, as substitute for his father,[1] and he had subsequently joined it as one of the forty-seven citizens who formed the permanent nucleus of its electorate between 1471 and 1480.[2] Having belonged to the first forty members of the *Balìa* of 1471,[3] he was also one of the first thirty members of that of 1480, and thus of the Seventy,[4] in which capacities he participated in the election of the additional members of these councils as well as in the electoral scrutinies of 1471 and 1484.[5] But his direct role in these two scrutinies—the only ones to be held between 1469 and 1492—was not confined to this; on both occasions he was elected one of the ten *Accoppiatori* for the scrutiny, and could thus take an active part in the distribution of electoral qualifications among the successful candidates.[6]

Lorenzo's influence on elections to offices and councils was clearly much more extensive than his official functions warranted. We have seen how he was said to have drawn up, together with the faithful Ser Giovanni Guidi, the membership list for the scrutiny council of 1484.[7] Similarly, when it came to creating the *Balìa* of 1471, he nominated the Forty: 'that they will all be on our side', writes the Milanese ambassador to Galeazzo Maria Sforza before their election, 'you will understand from the enclosed list of their names, which has been drawn up by Lorenzo.'[8] 'While previously others besides him were honoured and courted, now everyone flocks to him in order to recommend himself for being included among the elected members, or out of fear, for it is understood that the goods are being sold in his house: let us hope that he knows how to use this opportunity by making *buona ellectione.*'[9] But the outcome showed that Lorenzo's hand was not quite as free as Sacramoro had supposed;[10] and one wonders whether he did not altogether overrate Lorenzo's control of the election, which the *Balìa* law had entrusted to the Signoria and the new *Accoppiatori*, and to the first forty members elected by

[1] Balìe, 30, fol. 73ʳ (4 Dec. 1466); ed. Ricchioni, pp. 145–6.
[2] See above, p. 182.
[3] As in 1466, the regulation concerning the minimum age was suspended for him in 1471; see above, p. 182, n. 3.
[4] See Appendix, nos. VIII–X.   [5] See above, pp. 186, 211.
[6] Tratte, 1148, fol. 26ʳ, and 20, fol. 11ʳ; see above, pp. 182, 187, 199, 211.
[7] Above, p. 212.
[8] Sacramoro to Nicodemo da Pontremoli, 5 July 1471 (ASM, Pot. est., Firenze, 281): 'che se siano tucti…nostri lo comprenderete che ve li mando in lista designati per Lorenzo'. See also above, p. 182.
[9] Sacramoro to Galeazzo Maria Sforza, 5 July (ibid.).   [10] Above, p. 183.

them.[1] Giovanni di Paolo Rucellai, whose son was Lorenzo's brother-in-law, and who was one of the five *Accoppiatori*, gives in his *Zibaldone* a fairly detailed account of the election, without even mentioning Lorenzo's name: the Signoria and *Accoppiatori* did the first part of their job by electing 'de' principali cittadini e fedeli dello stato', and completed it by choosing, together with these, the remaining 200 members.[2] The Milanese ambassadors tended to stress, and sometimes to overstress, Lorenzo's authority in Florence, which their masters would have liked to see developing towards despotic rule,[3] and their reports, though broadly accurate,[4] are consequently liable to give an over-simplified picture of the complex structure of Lorenzo's ascendancy.

In January 1471 the Milanese orator had prophesied that, through the new system of appointing the *Accoppiatori*, Lorenzo would always determine who was going to be in the Signoria— 'venirà sempre ad essere quella Signoria' which Lorenzo will want.[5] Petitions seeking Lorenzo's support for elections to the Signoria indicate that this was taken for granted by citizens who were in a position to know.[6] Yet such confidence in Lorenzo's political patronage could sometimes be exaggerated. Thus, a letter of June 1476[7] shows that in spite of the reform of 1471 the *Accoppiatori* were occasionally capable of acting against Lorenzo's express wishes. Indeed, the fact that it was considered advisable to reform their office once more in 1480 surely meant

---

[1] See above, p. 182.

[2] Florence, Archivio Rucellai, fol. 69ʳ (from the microfilm at the Warburg Institute). On the Zibaldone, see A. Perosa, *Giovanni Rucellai ed il suo Zibaldone*, i, pp. xi–xv.

[3] See Soranzo, 'Lorenzo il Magnifico alla morte del padre', pp. 48 ff. Galeazzo Maria Sforza was greatly pleased about the news from Florence at the beginning of July: 'pare essere optima via . . . et così da nostra parte confortarai Lorenzo nel perseverare in questo modo ad conservarse, accrescere et stabilire la riputatione et auctorità . . .' (to Sacramoro, 9 July 1471; ASM, cit.).

[4] But not always: thus Giovanstefano Castiglione reports a few days after Lorenzo's death (to Giangaleazzo Sforza, 28 April 1492, ASM, Pot. est., Firenze, xlvi (937)) that Lorenzo had been continuously one of the *Accoppiatori* ('et benchè questi acopiatori se mutano omne anno, nondimeno il Magnifico Lorenzo continuamente era confirmato per el consiglio di Cento, et faceva ellegere li compagni a suo modo'), a statement which was patently incorrect, since Lorenzo had not been *Accoppiatore* between 1488 and 1492: see above, p. 220.

[5] Above, p. 181.

[6] Cf. e.g. Donato Acciaiuoli to Lorenzo, Milan, 24 [Jan.] 1475 (Med. av. Pr., XLVIII, 9; quoted by E. Garin, *Medioevo e Rinascimento* (Bari, 1954), p. 276, n. 77): 'Non hebbi tempo quando mi partii di costì raccomandarti uno mio intimo amico et compare el quale ha gran fede in me et desidera una volta, se è possibile, per mia intercessione et tua gratia esser facto de' priori . . . .'

[7] Lorenzo to Jacopo Guicciardini, 29 June 1476 (Med. av. Pr., LXXII, 371): 'Havete intesa la tratta della nuova Signoria, e come Tommaso Ridolfi è Gonfaloniere. Non potetti tanto fare che Benedetto fussi de' Priori . . . .'

that they had proved less reliable than had been anticipated in 1471.[1] In 1476 we find Jacopo Guicciardini asking Lorenzo *che facessi* a certain citizen one of the *Otto di Balìa*, and the man's effective appointment by the *Cento* illustrates Lorenzo's influence on elections that were not entrusted to the *Accoppiatori*.[2] Since after 1466 some of the highest offices, such as the Eight and the *Ufficiali del Monte*, were filled by election in the *Cento*, Lorenzo depended in these cases on the collaboration of that council, which, as we have seen, had left much to be desired,[3] and which, despite its reform in 1471,[4] was in 1480 supplanted as the first Medicean council by the Seventy. The creation of the Seventy, with its extensive electoral powers, doubtless strengthened Lorenzo's hand also in this matter, just as in general the concentration of government in smaller and fewer councils and committees ultimately served to increase his political ascendancy.

It had never been Medicean policy to extend direct controls of appointments to magistracies beyond a small number of key offices. These were, first of all the Signoria, and then, by way of elections in the *Balìe*, in the *Cento*, and finally in the Seventy, such offices as the Eight for criminal jurisdiction, the *Dieci di Balìa* for foreign and military affairs in time of war, and the *Ufficiali del Monte* for financial administration.[5] To get citizens appointed to minor offices comes under the heading of political patronage rather than of political control; at the same time, it might indirectly contribute to the latter by helping to shape Lorenzo's public image. The Milanese ambassador wrote, after his death, that whoever wanted an office would apply to him,[6] and although this was clearly exaggerated, Lorenzo doubtless dispensed a great deal of such patronage through a variety of channels, assisted by the friends and clients he had in all classes.

[1] See above, p. 199.

[2] Jacopo Guicciardini to Lorenzo, Pavia, 17 July 1476 (Med. av. Pr., XXXIII, 541): '. . . tu sai che alla mia partita ti pregai facessi Giuliano Corsellini degli Otto; destimene buona intenzione; e se non fu, stimo fussi a qualche buono fine . . . .' The *Otto di Balìa* were, at that time, nominated by the Signoria and elected by the *Cento* (Balìa, 30, fol. 13ʳ; 5 Sept. 1466); see above, p. 168. For Giuliano Corsellini's election: Tratte, 82, fol. 2ʳ. Similarly on 6 Feb. 1492 Pierfilippo Pandolfini asked Ser Piero da Bibbiena to intercede with Lorenzo in favour of Pierfilippo's son Alessandro being elected one of the next *Otto di Balìa*, 'quando questo non guasti altri disegni di Lorenzo' (Med. av. Pr., CXXIV, 200). Alessandro was in fact elected, as from 1 March: Tratte, 83, fol. 2ʳ.

[3] See above, pp. 176–7, 181.   [4] See above, pp. 183–5.

[5] See above, pp. 49–52, 114, 200, *et passim*.

[6] Giovanstefano Castiglione (see above, p. 222, n. 4), on Piero di Lorenzo: 'Et cuosì chi vole qualche officio si ricommanda a la Sua Magnificentia, come se faceva al Magnifico suo padre.'

There were many offices, for instance in the guilds,[1] which had never been filled by lot; and the chancery personnel was probably not beyond occasionally manipulating the *borse*, for Lorenzo's assistance was sometimes sought for appointments that were still made by lot;[2] but it is unlikely that such manipulations happened frequently. In fact, had it been so easy to meddle with the *borse* of the administrative offices, there would have been little point in making such efforts to control the scrutinies on the basis of which they were filled.

As long as the personnel of most magistracies in Florence's internal and external administration continued to be chosen by lot, qualifications for office through scrutinies remained a matter of great political importance. How far was Lorenzo capable of determining their results? Here again, petitioners might give an exaggerated view of his influence. Thus Leonardo Dati, in a letter written from Rome during the scrutiny of 1471 in support of some relatives, appears to assume that Lorenzo was in control of it.[3] But Piero Guicciardini, who had first-hand information, reveals the difficulties Lorenzo had to face, as late as 1484, in making his influence felt in the scrutiny council.[4] Political enemies could create just as distorted an impression as petitioners for favours. After the revolution of 1494 Lorenzo was accused of having, in 1484, eliminated the names of citizens from the *borse*.[5] In fact, all that had happened was no doubt that, as in 1458 and 1471, failure to qualify in the scrutiny had cost citizens previously acquired qualifications.[6]

Lorenzo's electoral influence forms part of the wider problem of his role in the day-to-day government of Florence. The

---

[1] Cf. the example given by E. H. Gombrich, 'The early Medici as patrons of art', in *Italian Renaissance Studies*, p. 280.

[2] Thus Ser Francesco d'Antonio Dovizi begged Lucrezia Tornabuoni on two occasions to obtain for him, through Lorenzo, posts in the territorial administration (Med. av. Pr., LXXXV, 112 (25 May 1474, for the Vicariate of Vicopisano); ibid., 148 and 152 (12 and 25 May 1475, for the Vicariate of Val di Bagno, or of Certaldo); quoted by Y. Maguire, *The Women of the Medici* (London, 1927), pp. 96–99); but on neither occasion was he successful (see Tratte, 69, 227, 227 *bis*, and 311).

[3] Leonardo Dati to Lorenzo, 16 Nov. 1471 (Med. av. Pr., XXII, 275, partly ed. by F. Flamini, 'Leonardo di Piero Dati', *Giorn. Stor. d. Lett. Ital.*, xvi (1890), p. 100): '. . . Occorre al presente, quanto sono informato, che fate nuova reformatione et scrutinio nella republica vostra . . . . Ho tre nipoti vostri servitori, tucti bottegai et persone bene allevate et contente al buono vivere della terra, obedientissimi chome agnelli innocenti . . . . vi priego che con ogni vostra diligentia et auctorità vi sia di piacere havere l'occhio et ogni diligentia inverso di loro che non siano dimentichati. So la buona volontà vostra, so quanto sapete et potete . . . .'   [4] See above, pp. 216–18.

[5] Piero Parenti, *Storia fiorentina*, Bibl. Naz., II. IV. 169, fol. 209[v]: 'e tratti delle borse nello '84 da Lorenzo de' Medici.'   [6] See above, pp. 108, 190, 213.

absence of minutes of the meetings at the Medici palace, as well
as of those of the Seventy and its committees, makes it extremely
difficult to gain a picture of it.[1] The minutes of the *Pratiche* break
off in 1480,[2] and although this points to the destruction of subsequent records rather than to the absence of meetings, these had
already become much less frequent and lengthy before 1480.[3]
Until 1471 Lorenzo participates fairly frequently in them, but the
minutes usually record only his attendance or his agreement with
other members. When speeches of his are recorded, they mostly
refer to diplomatic business.[4] After 1471, until the minutes break
off in 1480, he appears only four times as a member of a *Pratica*,
his most significant intervention in a debate being on 12 June
1478, after the papal bull against him had been issued.[5]

This dearth of records is, however, not without significance
for the political development of Florence under Lorenzo. Although secrecy of meetings had always been a matter of much
concern for the Florentines, the concentration of conciliar business in fewer citizens and the practically permanent character
of the Seventy made it easier to achieve. Rinuccini's statement,
in 1479, that 'paucissimos ad maximarum rerum consultationem
adhibeant Catones nostri'[6] is a telling criticism of this development, and is even more relevant for the following years. Business
that had previously been debated in *Pratiche* which had been summoned by the Signoria or, in times of war, by the Ten, was now
transacted by the Seventy and its committees and in informal
meetings at Lorenzo's palace. 'No magistrate', says Rinuccini
elsewhere, 'dared, even in the smallest matters, to decide anything
without his consent.'[7] The Milanese ambassador, in a letter
written shortly after Lorenzo's death, probably comes nearer
the truth when he states that whenever Lorenzo notified the
Signoria, the *Otto di Pratica*, the *Otto di Balìa*, or any other officials,

---

[1] There are a few entries of decisions of the Seventy at the end of the register of the *Balìa*
of 1480 (see above, p. 206, n. 3), and in those of the *Cento* (e.g. Cento, 2, fols. 57ʳ–58ʳ). It
is probable that the records of the Seventy were destroyed at the time of the 1494 revolution.

[2] They begin again after the revolution of 9 Nov. 1494.

[3] For the entire period of Lorenzo's ascendancy, there is only one register of the *Consulte e
Pratiche* extant, and its minutes offer, in their scantiness, a striking contrast to the earlier
volumes: as a rule, only a few speeches are entered, and there is usually little or no debate.

[4] Cons. e Prat., 60, fols. 85ᵛ (1469), 94ʳ, 95ᵛ, 98ᵛ, 102ʳ, 103ʳ, 104ʳ, 105ᵛ, 107ʳ, 108ᵛ, 110ᵛ
(1470); 119ʳ, 124ᵛ, 130ᵛ, 133ᵛ (1471).

[5] Fols. 154ᵛ, 155ᵛ, 157ᵛ (1477); 159ʳ⁻ᵛ (1478); 173ʳ (1479: he attends as one of the *Dieci
di Balìa*).

[6] *De libertate*, op. cit., p. 284.

[7] *Ricordi*, p. cxlviii.

of his wishes, these were fulfilled.[1] Yet when it came to making his will felt in a large gathering like the scrutiny council of 1484, he experienced, as we have seen, considerable difficulties in spite of the careful selection of its members, and had to make use of a pressure group[2]—just as, after his father's death, he had used such *intelligenze* in the councils.[3] A remark made much later by his nephew Alessandro de' Pazzi indicates that these were more than occasional expedients; in order to secure his authority Lorenzo had to make use of *sette segrete di compagnie* which did not know of each other.[4] One of the effects of the decline of the old councils and of the establishment of the Seventy was, undoubtedly, to reduce the need for such pressure groups. Recruited from the inner circle of the régime, the Seventy could safely be expected to use its extensive powers according to Lorenzo's wishes. Yet it would be wrong to consider the Seventy merely an instrument in his hands, and incapable of the opposition which the *Cento* had occasionally put up even after its reform. At the beginning of the War of the Neapolitan Barons there was considerable disagreement between Lorenzo and leading citizens of the régime over the policy to be followed.[5] In September 1485 Pierfilippo Pandolfini informs him that the Seventy had failed to hold an election in the way it had been expected. According to Pierfilippo, this was due to Lorenzo's absence in Bagno a Filippo, which was harmful to a number of things, 'nuoce a più cose', and 'emboldens some of the Seventy to try and carry on in their own sweet way, who would not dare to do so when you are present'.[6] He suggests that Lorenzo reform the procedure of the Seventy: no one else could do it.

What was Lorenzo's own view of his position in Florence? According to the famous statement in his *Ricordi*, he had, on his

---

[1] Giovanstefano Castiglione, 28 April 1492 (see above, p. 222, n. 4): 'Et cuosì se'l Magnifico Piero manda a dire cuosa alcuna o ala Signoria o ali octo de la praticha o quilli de la balìa o altri officiali o Podestà, Bariselo o Datiari, cuosì è exequito, como era al tempo del Magnifico Lorenzo.'

[2] See above, p. 217.

[3] See above, p. 177. Cf. Guicciardini, *Storie fiorentine*, p. 79.

[4] 'Discorso', ed. Capponi, *Arch. Stor. Ital.*, i (1842), pp. 422–3. It was probably composed in 1522.

[5] See R. Palmarocchi, *La politica italiana di Lorenzo de' Medici* (Florence, 1933), pp. 59–63.

[6] Med. av. Pr., XXVI, 442 (Florence, 17 Sept. 1485): 'Stamani fu aprovato Jacopo Ventura del numero de' 70. Cimentossi Bernardo del Nero per scambio di M. Tomaso: non giunse . . . chè l'absentia vostra nuoce a più cose, et ci è chi arebbe animo di parlare secondo il gusto suo, chi quando ci siate, non ardiscie fallo. . . . Bisogn[o] era pure che un dì diate quella forma vi parrà sia necessario, perchè le cose si conduchino meglio, chè altri che voi nollo può fare.'

father's death, accepted his new responsibilities as head of the régime only reluctantly;[1] a few months later, when he was planning his first reform, he had affirmed that he intended to follow in the footsteps of Cosimo, 'che era di far tal cose cum più civilità si potesse',[2] and to proceed as much as possible by constitutional methods.[3] He met the Milanese ambassador's arguments in favour of a determined policy to increase his power in Florence by insisting that, while he was seeking the *stabilimento del stato suo*, he did not wish *dare alteratione a la terra* to do so, but by indirect methods, *per una via indirecta*.[4] This remained the guiding principle of the constitutional reforms under Lorenzo, as it had been under Cosimo; if the Duke of Milan thought, in January 1471, that Lorenzo, having 'begun to understand what medicine he needed',[5] might make a bid for despotic government, he was clearly mistaken. His ascendancy in Florence, like that of his father and grandfather, was buttressed by his friendship with foreign princes: during his first difficult years, the support of the Duke of Milan had been of vital importance for him, as it had been for his father; and it was enhanced by the vast prestige he came to enjoy in Italy, and by his diplomatic successes, particularly after the Pazzi war. In virtual control of Florence's foreign policy, he was treated by the Italian princes like one of them; and to foreign observers his authority might well appear to be all but absolute.[6] This ambivalence of Lorenzo's 'public image' at home and abroad reflects the complex nature of his political power. Yet in his dealings with Italian rulers he would sometimes emphasize, as Cosimo had done,[7] the constitutional limitations of his power—and not necessarily for reasons of diplomatic expediency. When, shortly after the creation of the Seventy, the Este ambassador wished to communicate secret information to Lorenzo, he was told to contact the *Otto di Pratica* instead; for Lorenzo refused to violate the new system of

---

[1] See above, p. 175.   [2] See above, p. 178.

[3] Shortly before Piero's death he had told the Milanese ambasssador that he disapproved of the 'molti modi' of his father, which were liable 'a fargli manchare omne dì l'amici dentro . . .' (Sacramoro to Galeazzo Maria Sforza, 17 Sept. 1469, ASM, cit., 278; Soranzo, p. 44).

[4] Sacramoro to Galeazzo Maria Sforza, 9 Jan. 1471 (ASM, cit., 281; Soranzo, p. 70). See above, p. 181.

[5] '. . . che Lorenzo comenzi ad intendere la medicina che gli bisogna'. Galeazzo Maria Sforza to Sacramoro, 4 Jan. 1471 (ASM, cit., 281; Soranzo, p. 70). The Duke was clearly disappointed when Lorenzo did not go beyond the reform of the *Accoppiatori*: to the same, 15 Jan. 1471 (ibid.; Soranzo, p. 73).

[6] See e.g. above, p. 222.   [7] See above, pp. 128-9.

government which had only just been initiated.[1] During peace negotiations at the time of the Ferrara war, he told the Milanese envoys that he had done all he could in trying to persuade the Florentines to accept their master's viewpoint, and that he could not do more, 'considering that he is not Signore of Florence, but a citizen'; and although he had more authority than he deserved, 'in such a case even he had to be patient and to conform to the will of the majority'.[2] Nine years later, a few months before his death, Lorenzo wrote to the Florentine orator in Rome that the 'natural foundation' of his position, as constituted by his popularity in Florence, was much more useful to the Pope than any foundation that was less so—'è molto più utile et commodo questo fondamento naturale che uno accessorio et dependente da fondamento mancho acto'; and in any case, God will provide, 'for these are things which are often acquired without one's merit, and sometimes lost without one's fault'—'perchè sono cose che come spesso se acquistono sanza merito, si smarriscono qualche volta sanza colpa'.[3]

[1] Antonio Montecatino to Ercole d'Este, 24 May 1480 (ASMo, Estero, Firenze, 2): 'dise per parte del prefato Lorencio che io sapeva bene erano ellecti octo cittadini . . . ad udire et intendere et fare queste simile cose: et lui non pigliaria per morte questo arbitrio de scrivere, che s'era rompere lo ordine di questo governo a pena cominciado'. He should not doubt that the Eight would keep the matter secret, 'perchè era ellecto . . . per fare le cose più secrete'.

[2] Antonio di Trivulzio and Malatesta Sacramoro to the Duke, 23 Dec. 1482 (Bibl. Nat., MS. ital. 1592, fol. 170): '. . . non sapere sua Magnificentia che si fare più de quello che l'havea facto, attento che la non è Signore di Firenze, ma citadino; et licet de qualche auctorità più che non gli tocharia per la sorte sua, tamen in simili casi è necessitato anchora ley ad havere pacientia et conformare col volere di più. . . .' On the diplomatic background, see B. Buser, *Lorenzo de' Medici als italienischer Staatsmann* (Leipzig, 1879), pp. 49 ff.

[3] To Piero Alamanni, 17 Sept. 1491 (Medici–Tornaquinci, 3,157).

EPILOGUE

Piero di Lorenzo and the Fall of the Régime

LORENZO died on 8 April 1492. Between 13 and 16 April the councils passed a law granting Piero succession to his father's offices, and making him eligible for all those offices for which Lorenzo had been qualified—'ne inhonorata virtus apud Florentinos sit atque ut . . . ad posteros extet incitamentum reliquis civibus'.[1] Piero consequently replaced his father in the council of Seventy and as one of the *Accoppiatori*.[2] Without special legislation he could not, in fact, have been co-opted by the Seventy and hence elected *Accoppiatore*, since the minimum age for substitutes of deceased members of that council was forty,[3] while Piero was only twenty at the time of Lorenzo's death.[4] Similar exemptions had been granted to Lorenzo in 1466, and again in 1471.[5] The large majorities by which the law was carried in all three councils[6] reflect the smoothness of Piero's 'succession'. In contrast to the situation at the time of Piero di Cosimo's death, there were now no rumours of impending revolution, no gathering of the Medici party in support of its leader: it was the three legislative councils which made the decision in Piero's favour. The mantle of Lorenzo fell on him lightly. 'It is hoped', writes a member of the chancery on the 14th, 'that Piero will be a most worthy heir to all his father's virtues.'[7]

Once established, Piero, like his father and grandfather before him, had to face the problem of how to collaborate with the

---

[1] Provv., 183, fols. 1ʳ–2ᵛ.

[2] See above, p. 220, n. 5. He also replaced Lorenzo as one of the *Operai del Palagio* (see above, p. 220, n. 1). As a member of the Seventy, Piero became eligible for the *Otto di Pratica* and the *Dodici Procuratori*, and could attend the meetings of the *Cento* (see above, p. 209).

[3] Laws of 19 April 1480 (Balìe, 31, fol. 98ᵛ; Ricchioni, *La costituzione politica*, p. 171) and of 17 Sept. 1484 (Provv., 175, fol. 116ʳ; Ricchioni, p. 182).

[4] He was born on 15 Feb. 1472 (Florence, Archivio dell'Opera del Duomo, Libri di battesimo. I am grateful to Dr. Settesoldi for verifying the date for me).

[5] See above, p. 182, n. 3.

[6] It was passed by the *Cento* with 110 votes in favour (the number of votes cast against the bill is not recorded), by the council of the People with 180 votes against 24, and by the council of the Commune with 195 votes against 16 (Provv. cit.).

[7] '. . . e tutti a una s'accordano a farli onore, sperando che lui abbia a essere optimo herede paterno di tutte le sue virtù' (Bartolomeo Dei to Benedetto Dei, ed. L. Frati, 'La morte di Lorenzo de' Medici e il suicidio di Pier Leoni', *Arch. Stor. Ital.*, 5ª ser., iv (1889), p. 260).

leading citizens of the régime. There was no lack of goodwill towards him on their part: indeed, they had for some time been making preparations for his succession. On 24 July 1489 Ser Piero Dovizi wrote to Lorenzo at his villa of Spedaletto[1] that he had been asked by Jacopo Guicciardini and Pierfilippo Pandolfini to sound him on the possibility of giving Piero some political experience and of letting him attend the secret meetings of the régime. If Lorenzo wished, they would discuss the matter with his closest followers. Lorenzo must have given his consent, for a week later Ser Piero reports to him that a meeting of his friends had taken place in Pierfilippo's house, and that they had fully concurred with this plan, although they realized that this would mean taking Piero away from his pleasures.[2] But after Lorenzo's death Piero repaid the confidence of the *cittadini principali* by relying increasingly on the advice of men who were entirely dependent on him, thus intensifying a policy for which Lorenzo had already been criticized. Piero's treatment of the prominent members of his party bears more resemblance to the attitude of Piero di Cosimo after 1464 than to the sophisticated behaviour of Lorenzo after 1469. Francesco Guicciardini, whose grandfather had, as we have seen, played a leading part in bringing Piero into the governing circle, gives a vivid picture of the growing exasperation with Piero among the *ottimati*, and of the resulting division within the régime.[3] His account is confirmed by Ludovico Sforza's analysis of the internal situation in Florence, even though Ludovico, who was then trying to detach the lord of Faenza from Florence, was likely to exaggerate its gravity. The Milanese envoy, writes Puccio Pucci to Piero de' Medici on

---

[1] To Lorenzo de' Medici at Spedaletto (Carte Strozz., 1ª ser., 3, fols. 138–9): '. . . da qualche tempo in qua hanno ragionato insieme . . . con qualchuno di questi amici vostri, che essendo Piero vostro horamai si può dire huomo facto, per havere havere di proximo figliuoli, et di singulare ingegno, parebbe loro sommamente necessario, et utile alla città, a Piero, et a loro medesimi, . . . che voi cominciassi a darli reputatione, et intrometterlo a qualunque bene importante faccienda, dandoli auctorità et credito, et in effecto accompagnarlo con loro nelle consultationi secrete come fanno. . . . Et volendo ne conferiranno con gl'altri più intimi amici. . . .'

[2] To the same, 31 July 1489 (Med. av. Pr., LVI, 38): 'Questi vostri cittadini furono hiermattina insieme in casa di Pierfilippo chiamati da Jacopo et da lui. . . . Et consiglorono, per rechare le molte cose in una, che questa sia una necessaria provisione, non manco fructuosa allo stato loro che al resto, et che si debbe pregarvene.' They want Piero to be admitted 'in ogni loro secreto privato et darli ogni possibile reputatione et auctorità'.

[3] *Storie fiorentine*, pp. 84–86. Guicciardini was doubtless well informed on these events, in which his family took a prominent part. See also Bartolomeo Cerretani, *Storia fiorentina*, extracts in J. Schnitzer, *Quellen und Forschungen zur Geschichte Savonarolas*, iii (Munich, 1904), pp. 39–40.

25 May 1493 from Faenza,[1] had tried to persuade Astorre Manfredi to adhere to Milan on the ground that he could expect no help from Florence; for the régime there was divided. Bernardo Rucellai had aligned himself with Paolantonio Soderini; Bernardo del Nero, Niccolò Ridolfi, and Pierfilippo Pandolfini formed a second group;[2] and, finally, there was Piero with a few young men—and even the Medici family itself was divided. This clearly refers to the antagonism between Piero and the two sons of Pierfrancesco de' Medici, Lorenzo and Giovanni.[3]

But if Piero incurred the displeasure of a number of the *cittadini principali*, he did nothing that would indicate a departure from the system of government which had been perfected under Lorenzo. The 'order of the Seventy' was, as we have seen, renewed once more in September 1493.[4] Piero was *Accoppiatore* twice, first as substitute for his father in 1492, and then again from February 1494;[5] he belonged to the *Otto di Pratica* for six months from July 1492, having previously served as one of the *Dodici Procuratori*.[6] There was no reason to believe that Piero did not intend to adhere to Lorenzo's constitutional system; nor does the strong opposition in the councils to its renewed extension indicate some special resistance to him: there had been opposition to the law on the *Cento* in 1489.[7] There remained throughout the period of Medicean ascendancy an undercurrent of dissatisfaction, which was revealed, time and again, in narrow majorities for Medicean legislation. Exceptional circumstances were required to make it a serious danger to the régime.

[1] Med. av. Pr., LIV, 168 (I owe the reference to this letter to Dr. Lauro Martines): '. . . non dovesse sperare favore o adiuto da Signori fiorentini perchè lo stato della città vostra era diviso. Et allegava che da una parte erano ristrecti Bernardo Rucellai et Pagolantonio Soderini, et da un'altra parte s'intendevano insieme Bernardo del Nero, Niccholò Ridolfi et Pierphilippo Pandolfini; et da altra parte eravate voi con alcuni giovani; et che etiam nella casa vostra de' Medici era dissensione. . . .'

[2] Parenti says that Piero's inner circle, his *stato intrinseco*, included Lorenzo Tornabuoni, Antonio di Bernardo Miniati, Ser Giovanni Guidi, Ser Niccolò Michelozzi, and Ser Simone Grazzini, and that his principal adviser after Lorenzo's death was Antonio Malegonnelle (*Storia fiorentina*, Bib. Naz., II. IV. 169, fol. 195ʳ). Antonio di Bernardo was *Provveditore* of the *Ufficiali del Monte*. Giovanni Guidi was, as notary of the *Riformagioni*, one of the highest officials of the chancery; he had been a close collaborator of Lorenzo (see e.g. above, p. 216). Niccolò Michelozzi had been for many years Lorenzo's chancellor (see M. Del Piazzo, *Protocolli del carteggio di Lorenzo il Magnifico* . . . (Florence, 1956), pp. xiii ff.). Simone Grazzini was notary of the *Tratte* (see Marzi, *La cancelleria fiorentina*, pp. 254-5). Antonio Malegonnelle was *Accoppiatore* in 1491-2 (see Appendix, no. I). See also Guicciardini, *Storie fiorentine*, pp. 85-86, 91.   [3] Ibid., p. 90.   [4] Above, p. 209.

[5] Tratte, 21, fols. 18ʳ, 21ʳ. He had been re-elected in Sept. 1492 (ibid., fol. 18ᵛ).

[6] Tratte, 83, fols. 110ʳ, 114ʳ. He had been elected one of the *Dodici Procuratori* on 27 April, but had to resign this office on being elected, on 23 July, one of the *Otto di Pratica*.

[7] See above, p. 209.

Such circumstances were provided by the rapidly deteriorating diplomatic position of Florence after 1492, and by Piero's handling of the situation at home and abroad. It is not our purpose to investigate the events which culminated, in October 1494, in Piero's capitulation to Charles VIII of France, whose overtures he had been resisting obstinately; but there can be no doubt that his flight from Florence on 9 November was the direct result of the débâcle of his policy of close alignment with the King of Naples against France and Milan. The virtual control of Florence's foreign policy, which had been so important an element in Lorenzo's ascendancy, became the principal cause of Piero's downfall.

When on 26 October 1494 Piero, without an official mandate, went to the French camp, doubtless in the hope of emulating his father's successful mission to the King of Naples,[1] the *Otto di Pratica*, who were in charge of foreign affairs, were torn by dissension.[2] When it became known that he had surrendered important fortresses to the French king, Piero was refused the full powers to negotiate with Charles that he had demanded.[3] He was openly criticized throughout the city, and the Signoria summoned all the *veduti* Gonfaloniers of Justice to a large *Pratica*; and these men, 'who were already greatly dissatisfied with Piero's behaviour, although they had at first been his followers, now began to change colour'.[4] Thus, during the last critical days of the Medici régime, the *veduti* for the Gonfaloniership emerge once more as a political force. Having in the past been, in varying degrees, an asset as well as an embarrassment to the leaders of the régime, these men now began to turn openly against its head.[5] The division within the régime, which had once been so dangerous to his grandfather, proved to be Piero's undoing when it affected the Signoria itself.

That the Signoria might one day use its wide powers against them was a danger from which the Medici had tried to protect themselves from the very beginning by controlling elections;

---

[1] See e.g. my article 'Politics and constitution in Florence at the end of the fifteenth century', in *Italian Renaissance Studies*, cit., p. 149.

[2] Parenti, op. cit., fol. 186[r–v]: he left Empoli in despair over the 'altercatione factasi tralli Octo della Pratica'.

[3] Ibid., fols. 187[v]–188[r].

[4] Ibid., fols. 189[v]–190[r] (ed. Schnitzer, op. cit., iv, p. 8). Cerretani speaks of a joint meeting of the Seventy and these citizens (*Storia fiorentina*, Bibl. Naz., II. III. 74, fol. 180[v]); but since practically all the Seventy were *veduti* Gonfaloniers, this comes to the same thing.

[5] Parenti says, however, that many of the summoned citizens refused to attend the *Pratica*.

and in this they had succeeded by the end of 1466, the republican reaction having shown how very real such a danger could be. The creation of the Seventy had further reduced it by weakening the Signoria's authority. But the Signoria still remained the supreme executive organ; and however perfected and sophisticated the Medicean system of controls had become, it still depended on the loyal collaboration and support of the leading citizens of the régime. This was shown in 1465, when some of the *Accoppiatori* had opposed Piero di Cosimo, and when the Signoria headed by Niccolò Soderini had initiated republican reforms.[1] It was shown again when, at the beginning of November 1494, part of the Signoria turned against Piero and carried the rest with them; and this in spite of the fact that the Signoria had been elected by *Accoppiatori* of whom Piero was one, and that they were considered 'amici grandi ed affezionati del reggimento'.[2] In fact, they nearly all belonged to long-established Medicean families.[3] According to Parenti, they began to desert him when information reached them that Piero had offered a large sum to Charles VIII for maintaining him in power—*exemplo grande di fortuna*.[4] On his return on 8 November Piero indignantly rejected this accusation; but when, on the following day, he tried to enter the Palace of the Signoria with an armed retinue, it was believed that he was planning to seize the Palace and thus reassert his power by the use of force.[5] In a marginal note to his manuscript, Parenti adds the more likely explanation that Piero only wanted to ask the Signoria not to proceed against him immediately;[6] that he intended to seize the Palace was the official explanation given out later in the day.[7] This view was probably

---

[1] See above, pp. 141–2, 144–7.

[2] Guicciardini, *Storie fiorentine*, p. 96; cf. Cerretani, quoted in 'Politics and constitution', op. cit., p. 150, n. 2. The *Accoppiatori* who held, on 26 Oct., the last election *a mano* of the early Medici régime were, besides Piero, Bernardo del Nero, Francesco Valori, Battista Serristori, and Michele di Corso (Tratte, 21, fol. 21ᵛ).

[3] They were Luca di Bertoldo Corsini, Gianfrancesco di Bernardo de' Lippi, Francesco di M. Otto Niccolini, Filippo di Nicol Sacchetti, Giuliano di Nofri Lenzoni, Chimenti di Francesco Angeli, Antonio di Giovanni Lorini, Francesco d'Antonio Taddei, and, as Gonfalonier of Justice, Francesco di Martino dello Scarfa.

[4] Fol. 191ʳ.

[5] Parenti, fol. 192ᵛ ('riassumere per forza lo stato'). On the events of that day, see my 'Politics and constitution', pp. 150–1, and bibliography on p. 151, n. 2.

[6] '... per assicurare la Signoria che provedimento non facessi finchè lui el lunedì ad ordine fussi. La quale openione molto è probabile. Altri dicono' that he intended to seize the Palace.

[7] Letters in Missive, 1ᵃ cancelleria, 50, fols. 1 ff. The letter to the Marquess of Mantua is ed. by A. Portioli, 'Nuovi documenti su Girolamo Savonarola', *Arch. Stor. Lombardo*, i (1874), pp. 334–5; it is of 9 Nov., 'hora noctis sexta'.

decisive in swaying against him the majority in the Signoria,[1] among whom his leading opponent appears to have been Luca di Bertoldo Corsini; like his opposite number among the Colleges, Jacopo di Tanai de' Nerli, he was the son of one of the Seventy. After the Signoria had summoned the people to come armed to the Piazza in front of their palace, Piero realized that, at least for the time being, his cause was lost: in the evening he fled with his two brothers.[2] 'Et in tal modo', comments Parenti, 'per la sua temerità Piero de' Medici lo stato anni 60 durato fino dal suo bisavolo perdè, et libera la città rimase, per opera più di dio che delli huomini.'[3]

Piero's flight created a situation which even his enemies could have hardly foreseen. According to Cerretani,[4] his opponents among the leading Mediceans had wished only to reduce, but not to destroy, his power. Once this had happened, it was unlikely that the Medicean system of government could survive, although some citizens may well have been thinking of Lorenzo di Pierfrancesco de' Medici as a possible successor to Piero.[5] On the day following on Piero's flight the Signoria summoned a large *Pratica* which, in contrast to the previous one, was composed not of the *veduti* Gonfaloniers of Justice, but of the *veduti ai Tre Maggiori*, and was consequently far more representative of the office-holding class of Florence.[6] This *Pratica* advised the abolition of the Seventy, the *Otto di Pratica*, and the *Cento*;[7] and on the 11th the Signoria followed this advice.[8] The next two weeks were overshadowed by Charles VIII's entry into Florence and by the treaty negotiations with him; it was not until the 30th that the debate on the future government of Florence was resumed.[9] On 2 December a *Parlamento* approved a law which ratified the abolition of the Medici councils and decreed the

---

[1] According to Parenti, fol. 196ᵛ, the Signoria remained divided even after Piero's flight, Antonio Lorini, Francesco Taddei, Francesco Niccolini, and Giuliano Lenzoni tending towards the 'tirannide e contro alla libertà populare'.

[2] Parenti, fol. 194ʳ⁻ᵛ; cf. 'Politics and constitution', loc. cit.

[3] Fol. 194ᵛ.

[4] Fol. 191ʳ: 'In questo tempo [i.e. the beginning of Nov.] nella ciptà di Firenze pe' nimici di Piero di nocte in varii luoghi s'era facto raghunati et conventiculi; e quali sua nemici non erano se non huomini de' primi suti amici sempre loro, loro padri et avoli, de chasa sua; ma il loro disegno era non ispiacciare Piero de' Medici afacto, ma abassarlo alquanto. . . .'

[5] Filippo Nerli, *Commentari* (Trieste, 1859), i, p. 106.

[6] Deliberazioni dei Signori, ordinaria autorità, 96, fol. 87ᵛ.

[7] Parenti, fol. 195ᵛ.

[8] Deliberazioni, cit., fol. 88ᵛ.

[9] Parenti, fol. 208ᵛ. On this day a large *Pratica* was summoned for this purpose.

holding of a scrutiny at the end of 1495.[1] In the meantime, twenty *Accoppiatori* were, for one year, to elect the Signoria, having been elected, in their turn, by the Signoria and the Colleges. The explanation which was given for this postponement of the return to election by lot of the Signoria until after the scrutiny seems reasonable enough: had sortition been restored immediately, the purses filled after the scrutiny of 1484 would have had to be used, and this might well have produced a government which would have recalled Piero de' Medici.[2] However, many Florentines believed that leading citizens of the past régime were hoping to safeguard their own position in this way.[3] During the following days the view came to prevail that the restoration of the pre-Medicean constitution was not sufficient, and that a more radical reform was required. On 23 December the Great Council was established, which was to remain the foundation of the republican constitution until 1512.

[1] On this, as well as on the following events, see my articles 'I primi anni del Consiglio Maggiore di Firenze (1494–1499)', *Arch. Stor. Ital.*, cxii (1954), pp. 151 ff., and 'Politics and constitution', pp. 152 ff.

[2] Parenti, fol. 208ᵛ, on the *Pratica* of 30 Nov.: '. . . che a mano le borse si tenessino finchè nuovo squittino si facessi: acciò che non intervenissi come nel 33 . . . la sorte dare potrebbe honori in partigiani di Piero, e quali lo richiamerebbono. . . .' It had been the mistake of Rinaldo degli Albizzi to end electoral controls prematurely, and the mistake was not to be repeated. See above, p. 7.

[3] Parenti, fol. 210ᵛ.

Appendix

NOTE

THE following lists are based on the documents referred to under the titles, but do not constitute editions of their text, having been rearranged for the convenience of the reader. In the registers of the *Balìe* the names are given in Latin: they have been rendered in Italian. In cases where a patronymic becomes a family name between 1434 and 1494 (e.g. Peri for di Pero) the latter is used throughout. The sections of the *Balìa* lists containing the names of the official members are left in their original order, the division into the four *quartieri*, S. Spirito, S. Croce, S. Maria Novella, and S. Giovanni, being wherever possible indicated by a space between the groups. The names in the sections devoted to the elected members (*arroti*) have been rearranged in alphabetical order to allow the reader to follow, at a glance, the development of the elected personnel of the *Balìe*, in regard to both individuals and families. In the original lists, with the exception of that for 1434, *arroti* belonging to the Lesser Guilds (*artigiani*) are entered after those of the Greater Guilds: this procedure has here been adopted throughout. In the lists of the official members of the *Balìe*, as well as of the *Accoppiatori* (Appendix, no. I), citizens belonging to the Lesser Guilds are normally identified by the indication of their craft following their names (in the case of the Consuls of the Guilds, all but the first seven belong to the Lesser Guilds). Finally, the headings within all the lists correspond in content, but not necessarily in form, to those in the original lists.

I

ACCOPPIATORI

(Tratte, 1148, fols. 25ʳ–29ᵛ)[1]

SCRUTINY OF 1434 (1434–9)[2]

Luca di Bonaccorso Pitti
Piero di M. Luigi Guicciardini
Nero di Filippo del Nero *rigattiere*

---

[1] This list is an early sixteenth-century chancery compilation.

[2] The first dates refer to the year of appointment; the dates in brackets to the years during which *Accoppiatori* of scrutinies were in charge also of elections *a mano* of the Signoria. Where there is no reference to scrutinies, the *Accoppiatori* are appointed for electing *a mano* only. In these cases brackets are used to indicate the periods during which the *Accoppiatori* were actually in charge of such elections, having been appointed for periods exceeding one year.

Niccolò di Cocco Donati
Antonio di Salvestro Serristori
Pero di Dino Peri *galigaio*

Simone di Francesco Guiducci
M. Giuliano di Nicolaio Davanzati

Neri di Domenico Bartolini [Scodellari]
Nerone di Nigi Dietisalvi [Neroni]

SCRUTINY OF 1440 (1440–1)

Neri di Gino Capponi
Giovannozzo di Francesco Pitti

Francesco di Francesco Berlinghieri
Paolo di Zanobi da Ghiacceto

Giovanni di Simone Altoviti
Piero di Brancazio Rucellai
Domenico di Tano Petrucci *coltriciaio*

Lorenzo di Giovanni de' Medici
Niccolò di Bartolomeo Valori
Giovanni di Antonio Pucci *maestro*
Cosimo di Giovanni de' Medici—in place of Lorenzo, who had died

1443 (1443–4)

Giovanni di Antonio Canigiani
Bernardo di M. Lorenzo Ridolfi
Francesco di Bonaccorso Corsellini [*ottonaio*]

Andrea di Salvestro Nardi
Bernardo di Filippo Giugni
Giovanni del Zaccaria di Jacopo *coltriciaio*

M. Carlo di Francesco Federighi
Francesco di Jacopo di Francesco Ventura

Antonio di Ser Tommaso Masi
M. Domenico di Niccolò Martelli

SCRUTINY OF 1444 (1444–9; 1452–5; 1458–65)

Tommaso di Lorenzo Soderini
Luca di Bonaccorso Pitti

Alamanno di Jacopo Salviati
Francesco di Cambio Orlandi

Manno di Giovanni Temperani
Domenico di Matteo di Ser Michele [Pescioni]
Guarente di Giovanni di Tommaso Guarenti *maestro*

Dietisalvi di Nerone di Nigi [Dietisalvi Neroni]
Giuliano di Tommaso Martini
Niccolò di Zanobi Bonvanni *beccaio*
Ugolino di Niccolò Martelli—in place of Giuliano Martini, who
   had died

SCRUTINY OF 1448 (1452–5; 1458–65)

Neri di Gino Capponi
Luigi di M. Lorenzo Ridolfi
Bartolomeo di Giovanni Michelozzi *coreggiaio*

Bernardo di Bartolomeo Gherardi
Matteo di Morello Morelli
Giovanni del Zaccaria di Jacopo *coltriciaio*

M. Carlo di Francesco Federighi
Martino di Francesco dello Scarfa

Bernardo di Cristofano Carnesecchi
Piero di Cosimo de' Medici

1452 (1452–5; 1458–65[1])

The same as the *Accoppiatori* of 1444 and 1448, with the exception
of Domenico di Matteo Pescioni, Guarente di Giovanni Guarenti,
M. Carlo Federighi, and Bernardo Carnesecchi, who had died. In their
place, M. Agnolo di Jacopo Acciaiuoli, Antonio di Lenzone Lenzoni,
Lionardo di Bartolomeo Bartolini, and Lorenzo di Andrea della Stufa.[2]

SCRUTINY OF 1458 (1458–65[3])

Piero di Gregorio di Andrea del Benino
Luigi di Piero di M. Luigi Guicciardini
Francesco del Nero di Filippo del Nero *rigattiere*

---

[1] To serve in groups of five and seven respectively; see above, p. 105.
[2] See above, p. 105, n. 2.
[3] To serve in groups of five and seven respectively; see above, p. 105.

M. Otto di Lapo di Giovanni Niccolini
Lodovico di Cece da Verrazzano

Giovanni di Domenico Bartoli
Francesco di Jacopo Ventura

M. Alessandro di Ugo degli Alessandri
Matteo di Marco Palmieri
Bartolomeo di Francesco di Ser Andrea *corazzaio*

SCRUTINY OF 1465

Bernardo di M. Lorenzo Ridolfi
Bernardo del Nero di Filippo del Nero *rigattiere*

M. Bernardo di Filippo Giugni

Bartolomeo di Lorenzo Lenzi

M. Carlo di Agnolo Pandolfini

1466

M. Luca di Bonaccorso Pitti
M. Antonio di M. Lorenzo Ridolfi

Ruberto di Francesco Lioni
Franco di Nicol Sacchetti

Giovanni [di Jacopo] di Francesco Ventura
Andrea di Niccolò Carducci
Ser Niccolò di Michele di Feo Dini [*galigaio*]

M. Domenico di Niccolò Martelli
Giovanni di Antonio Lorini
Romolo di Andrea di Nofri Romoli [*maestro*]

1467

Jacopo di Piero Guicciardini
Giovanni di Antonio Serristori—lost the office on being
    appointed one of the *Dieci di Balìa*
Niccolò di Andrea Giugni—in his place
Paolo di Jacopo Federighi
Andrea di Cresci di Lorenzo di Cresci
Antonio di Pero di Dino Peri [*galigaio*]

1468

Bernardo di Tommaso Corbinelli
Giovanni di Salvatore del Caccia

Piero di Niccolò Malegonnelle
Antonio di Taddeo di Filippo di Taddeo
Bartolomeo di Ser Antonio del Troscia [*albergatore*]

1469

Zanobi di Sandro Biliotti
Jacopo di Niccolò di Cocco [Donati]
Bongianni di Bongianni Gianfigliazzi
Niccolò di Matteo Cerretani
Cherubino di Francesco Galluzzi [*biadaiolo*]

1470

Piero di Lutozo Nasi
Giovanni di Taddeo dell'Antella
Antonio di Lionardo de' Nobili
Pierfrancesco di Lorenzo de' Medici
Lenzone di Antonio Lenzoni [*galigaio*]

1471

Recco di Uguccione Capponi
Lorenzo di Lapo Niccolini
Giovanni di Paolo Rucellai
M. Agnolo di Lorenzo della Stufa
Antonio di Bernardo di Miniato [di Dino] [*coreggiaio*]

SCRUTINY OF 1471

M. Giovanni di Antonio Canigiani
Jacopo di Piero Guicciardini
Piero di Giovanni di Piero di Bartolomeo [Pieri] *scodellaio*

Mariotto di Lorenzo Benvenuti
Ruberto di Francesco Lioni

M. Piero di Giovanni Minerbetti
Piero di Niccolò Malegonnelle
Ser Niccolò di Michele di Feo Dini [*galigaio*]

Antonio di Puccio di Antonio Pucci
Lorenzo di Piero di Cosimo de' Medici

1472

Tommaso di Luigi Ridolfi
Piero di Francesco Mellini
Niccolò di Francesco Tornabuoni
Matteo di Marco Palmieri
Francesco di Paolo Canacci [*maestro*]

1473

M. Tommaso di M. Lorenzo Soderini
Girolamo di Matteo Morelli
Lionardo di Bartolomeo Bartolini
Duti di Antonio Masi
Michele di Corso [di Lorenzo di Covero] delle Colombe [*oliandolo*]

1474

Gino di Neri Capponi
Averardo di Alamanno Salviati
Domenico di Giovanni Bartoli
Antonio di Puccio Pucci
Agnolo di Francesco Miniati [*coreggiaio*]

1475

M. Luigi di Piero Guicciardini
Ruberto di Francesco Lioni
M. Piero di Giovanni Minerbetti
Carlo di Nicola de' Medici
Giovanni di Francesco di Ser Andrea [*corazzaio*]

1476

Bernardo del Nero di Filippo del Nero
Berlinghieri di Francesco Berlinghieri
Donato di Neri Acciaiuoli
Maso di Luca degli Albizzi
Miniato di Bernardo di Miniato [di Dino] [*coreggiaio*]

1477

Bertoldo di Gherardo Corsini
Giovanni di Antonio Serristori
Tommaso di Piero Davanzati
Domenico di M. Carlo Pandolfini
Nofri di Antonio Lenzoni [*galigaio*]

1478

M. Antonio di M. Lorenzo Ridolfi
Francesco di Piero di Giovanni Dini
Bernardo di Piero Rucellai
Antonio di Niccolò Martelli
Piero di Giovanni Pieri [*scodellaio*]

1479

Niccolò di Giovanni Capponi
Ristoro di Antonio Serristori
Cipriano di Chimenti Sernigi

Pierfilippo di M. Giannozzo Pandolfini
Giovanni di Miniato di Dino [*coreggiaio*]—died before entering office
Carlo di Giovanni Carradori [*rigattiere*]—in his place

1480 (–1489)

Annually one-half of the council of Seventy; see Appendix, nos. IX, X.[1]

SCRUTINY OF 1484

Ruggieri di Niccolò Corbinelli
M. Antonio di M. Lorenzo Ridolfi

Giovanni di Antonio Serristori
Ruberto di Francesco Lioni

Lorenzo di Agnolo Carducci
Mariotto di Piero Rucellai

Lorenzo di Piero di Cosimo de' Medici
Francesco di Filippo Valori

Michele di Corso [di Lorenzo di Covero] delle Colombe [*oliandolo*]
Antonio di Bernardo di Miniato [di Dino] [*coreggiaio*]

1489

Jacopo di Piero Guicciardini
Francesco di Piero Dini
Lorenzo di Piero Davanzati
Francesco di Filippo Valori
Michele di Corso [di Lorenzo di Covero] delle Colombe [*oliandolo*]

1490

Niccolò di Luigi Ridolfi
M. Agnolo di M. Otto Niccolini
Antonio di Bernardo di Miniato [di Dino] [*coreggiaio*]
Bernardo di Giovanni Rucellai
Pierfilippo di M. Giannozzo Pandolfini

1491

Bernardo del Nero di Filippo del Nero
Giovanni di Antonio Serristori
M. Antonio di Piero Malegonnelle
Antonio di Taddeo di Filippo di Taddeo
Paolantonio di M. Tommaso Soderini

---

[1] The names of the thirty-five, who function in alternate years, are in Tratte, 82, fol. 229ᵛ. The *Accoppiatori* list includes the names of ten *Accoppiatori* who allegedly served from 1 Sept. 1480 for one year. But at that time the 35 were in office.

1492

M. Piero di Francesco Alamanni
Giuliano di Francesco Salviati
Maso di Francesco Salviati
Maso di Luca degli Albizzi
Piero di Lorenzo de' Medici—in place of his father
Giovanni di Francesco [di Ser Andrea] Puccini [*corazzaio*]

1493

Niccolò di Luigi Ridolfi
M. Agnolo di M. Otto Niccolini
Francesco di Piero Dini
Pierfilippo di M. Giannozzo Pandolfini
Antonio di Bernardo di Miniato [di Dino] [*coreggiaio*]

1494

Bernardo del Nero di Filippo del Nero
Giovanni di Antonio Serristori
Piero di Lorenzo de' Medici
Francesco di Filippo Valori
Michele di Corso [di Lorenzo di Covero] delle Colombe [*oliandolo*]
Battista di Giovanni Serristori—in place of his father, who had
  died

II

BALÌA OF 1434

(Balìe, 25, fols. 2ʳ–6ʳ and 34ʳ–38ᵛ)

Signoria

Giovanni di Mico Capponi
Luca di Bonaccorso di Neri Pitti

Fabiano di Antonio Martini *beccaio*
Pero di Dino Peri *galigaio*

Simone di Francesco Guiducci
Tommaso di Antonio di Ser Tommaso Redditi

Neri di Domenico Bartolini Scodellari
Baldassare di Antonio di Santi [Chiarucci]

Niccolò di Cocco Donati (Gonfalonier of Justice)

Sedici Gonfalonieri

Tura di Francesco di Tura Bonaveri
Francesco di Bonaccorso Corsellini *ottonaio*
Bernardo di Salvestro Belfradelli
Francesco di M. Tommaso Soderini

Donato di Michele di Nofri Arnolfi
Giovanni di Simone di Ser Matteo Biffoli
Lorenzo di Luca Salvucci *coreggiaio*
Lorenzo di Agnolo di Tinaccio Compiobbesi

Antonio di Vieri Altoviti
Cristofano di Matteo di Teghia *linaiolo*
Bartolomeo di Bencivenni dello Scarfa
Niccolò di Tommaso Malegonnelle

Lorenzo di Veri di Andrea Rondinelli
Terrino di Niccolò di Manovellozzo Manovelli
Antonio di Piero Migliorotti *chiavaiolo*
Parente di Michele di Ser Parente

Dodici Buonuomini

Sassolino di Arrigo Sassolini
Antonio di Bartolomeo Ridolfi
Giovanni di Cristofano di Simone *maestro*

Piero di Manetto di Tuccio Scambrilli
Antonio di Piero di Andrea Villani
Andrea di Taddeo di Duccio Mancini

Tommaso di Rinieri Popolani
Francesco di Ser Guasparre Masini
Cambino di Niccolò Cambini *linaiolo*

Bartolomeo di Lorenzo di Cresci
Ghezzo di Agnolo di Ghezzo della Casa
Banco di Sandro di Filippo *coltriciaio*

Capitani di Parte Guelfa

Bernardo di Antonio da Uzzano
Matteo di Morello di Paolo Morelli
Matteo di Niccolò Cerretani
Ormanno di Baldassare Foraboschi
Giovanni di Andrea di Niccolino *calzolaio*
Niccolò di M. Niccolò da Rabatta
Antonio di Marsilio Vecchietti
Lapaccino di Benedetto Lapaccini [del Toso] *linaiolo*
Breusso di Piero de' Pazzi

Arroti

S. SPIRITO

Bernardo di Pegolotto Balducci
Mariotto di Mariotto di Lodovico Banchi
Antonio di Giovanni Barbadori
Tommaso di Bartolomeo Barbadori
Andrea di Lipaccio de' Bardi
Ubertino di Andrea de' Bardi
Antonio di Giovanni Benci
Giovanni di Amerigo Benci
Banco di Niccolò di Bencivenni
Francesco di Niccolò del Benino
Piero di Goro di Andrea del Benino
Antonio di Piero Benizi

Nicolaio di Giovannozzo Biliotti
Sandro di Giovanni Biliotti
Piero di Nofri Bonaccorsi
Raffaello di Bernardo di Ugolino Bonsi
Ruberto di Giovanni di Brancazio Borsi
Antonio di Lotteringo Boverelli
Felice di Michele Brancacci
Buglaffo di Filippo del Buglaffo
Bernardo di Francesco Canigiani
Daniello di Luigi Canigiani
Neri di Gino Capponi
Nicola di Piero di Bartolomeo Capponi
Zanobi di Niccolò di Mico Capponi
Giovanni di Barduccio di Cherichino
Pazzino di Giovanni Cicciaporci
Antonio di Bartolomeo di Tommaso Corbinelli
Giovanni di Tommaso Corbinelli
Bartolomeo di Bertoldo di M. Filippo Corsini
Giovanni di Stefano Corsini
Guido di Tommaso Deti
Niccolò di Fecino di Duccio Dietifeci
Alesso di Gherardo di Matteo Doni
Giovanni di Ser Falcone Falconi
Foresta di Giovanni Foresti
Astorre di Niccolò di Gherardino Gianni
Francesco di Tommaso Giovanni
Lorenzo di Giovanni Grasso
Battista di Niccolò di M. Luigi Guicciardini
Piero di M. Luigi Guicciardini
Francesco di Guidetto Guidetti
Orsino di Lanfredino Lanfredini
Bernardo di Uguccione Lippi *mercante*
Mariotto di Dinozzo di Stefano Lippi
Piero di Chino di Piero Lippi
Antonio di Ridolfo di Paolo Lotti
Giovanni di Boninsegna Machiavelli
Lorenzo di Filippo Machiavelli
Giannozzo di Bernardo Manetti
Piero di Francesco di M. Jacopo Marchi
Agostino di Jacopo di Agostino Martini
Lutozo di Jacopo di Lutozo Nasi
Rinieri di Cristofano del Pace
Giovannozzo di Francesco Pitti
Ruberto di Bonaccorso Pitti

Tommaso di Luigi Pitti
Castello di Piero Quaratesi
Francesco di Andrea Quaratesi
Bartolomeo di Jacopo Ridolfi
Jacopo di Luca Ridolfi
M. Lorenzo di Antonio Ridolfi
Schiatta di Uberto Ridolfi
Giovanni di Guido Rinucci
Domenico di Francesco Sapiti
Antonio di Scarlatto di Nuto [Scarlatti] *ritagliatore*
Amerigo di Matteo dello Scelto
Mariotto di Francesco di Giovanni di Ser Segna
Giorgio di Piero di Alessandro Serragli
Niccolò di Agnolo Serragli
Niccolò di Lorenzo di M. Tommaso Soderini
Giovanni di Bartolo Strada
Luca di Gregorio di Fetto Ubertini
Donato di Michele Velluti
Paolo di Giannozzo Vettori
Giovanni di Lorenzo Zampalocchi

Artigiani

Agnolino di Guglielmo di Agnolino *pezzaio*
Piero di Lorenzo di Piero di Agnolino *pezzaio*
Francesco del Buono [Bramanti] *beccaio*
Simone di Giorgio di Agostino di Lapo Bruni [*coreggiaio*]
Cino di Luca di Cino *coreggiaio*
Giuliano di Agostino di Como *biadaiolo*
Niccolò di Aringo di Corso *calzolaio*
Corso di Lorenzo di Covero *oliandolo*
Antonio di Fantone di Naldo Fantoni *vinattiere*
Giuliano di Cristofano di Lorenzo *legnaiolo*
Bartolomeo di Giovanni Michelozzi *coreggiaio*
Nero di Filippo del Nero *rigattiere*
Niccolò di Jacopo di Niccolò di Nome [*vinattiere*]
Alessandro del Rosso di Piero del Rosso *fornaciaio*

S. CROCE

M. Albizzo di Niccolò di M. Francesco Albergotti
Francesco di Altobianco degli Alberti
Taddeo di Giovanni dell'Antella
Doffo di Giovanni Arnolfi
Francesco di Guerriante Bagnesi
Vieri di Filippo del Bancozzo
Francesco di Cionaccio Baroncelli

Giovanni di Piero di Jacopo Baroncelli
Santi di Giovanni di Francesco di Ser Bartolo *lanaiolo*
Jacopo di Bellaccino di Bellaccio
Lodovico di Lorenzo di Marco Benvenuti
Francesco di Francesco Berlinghieri
Domenico di Tommaso di Domenico Borghini
Zanobi di Giovanni Bucelli
Niccolò di Francesco Busini
Michele di Salvatore del Caccia
Nofri di Giovanni di Bondì del Caccia
Antonio di Niccolò di Michele Castellani
Lodovico di Salvestro Ceffini
Nofri di Salvestro Cennini
Tommaso di Scolaio di Lapo Ciacchi
Tommaso di Niccolò Ciampoleschi
Bartolo di Domenico Corsi
Giovanni di Niccolò di M. Bettino Covoni
Cocco di Niccolò di Cocco Donati
Zanobi di Cocco Donati
Riccardo di Niccolò Fagni
Sinibaldo di Filippo *ritagliatore*
Francesco di Simone di Ser Piero dalla Fioraia
Maestro Galileo di Giovanni Galilei
Attaviano di Piero Gerini
Bernardo di Bartolomeo di Gherardo Gherardi
Paolo di Zanobi da Ghiacceto
Giovanni del Maestro Cristofano di Giorgio
Andrea di Niccolò Giugni
Bernardo di Filippo Giugni
Giovanni di Domenico Giugni
Giovanni di Lionardo Jacopi
Luigi di Francesco di Biagio Lioni
Domenico di Niccolò Magaldi
Guido di Bese Magalotti
Duccino di Taddeo di Duccino Mancini
Bastiano di Matteo di Antonio Martini
Antonio di Francesco di Duccio Mellini
Bernardo di Nofri di Duccio Mellini
Bartolomeo di Giano Morelli
Andrea di Salvestro Nardi
Giovanni di Lapo Niccolini
Francesco di Mariano di Niccolò *setaiolo*
Francesco di Cambio Orlandi
Simone di Mariotto Orlandini

Luca di Matteo di M. Luca da Panzano
Ser Lorenzo di Paolo *proconsole*
Rustico di Giovanni [di Franceschino] Pepi
Ser Giovanni di Dino Peri
Rinieri di Niccolò Peruzzi
Antonio di Lionardo Raffacani
Gualterotto di Jacopo Riccialbani
Francesco di Cino Rinuccini
Salito di Jacopo Risaliti
Andreuolo di Nicol di Franco Sacchetti
M. Tommaso di Ser Jacopo Salvetti
Alamanno di M. Jacopo Salviati
Giovanni di M. Forese Salviati
Antonio di Salvestro di Ser Ristoro [Serristori]
Bonsignore di Niccolò Spinelli
Lorenzo di Antonio Spinelli
Lodovico di Cece da Verrazzano
Giuliano di Amerigo Zati
Bernardo di Zanobi di Ser Zello

Artigiani

Lodovico di Ser Cristofano di Agnolo Cerrini *coltriciaio*
Andrea di Simone di Lorenzo del Corso *calderaio*
Giovanni di Miniato di Dino *coreggiaio*
Mariano di Stefano di Nese [Duranti] *forbiciaio*
Zanobi di Jacopo di Ser Francesco *coreggiaio*
Francesco di Bernardo Galluzzi *biadaiolo*
Antonio di Giovanni di Bartolo Grazia *linaiolo*
Andrea di Lapo Guardi *coreggiaio*
Bartolomeo di Matteo di Meglio *calderaio*
Vanni di Niccolò di Ser Vanni *legnaiolo*
Ambrogio di Giovanni del Verzino *linaiolo*
Giovanni del Zaccaria ⟨di Jacopo⟩ *coltriciaio*

S. MARIA NOVELLA

Zanobi di Michele Acciaiuoli
Giovanni di Simone di M. Tommaso Altoviti
Oddo di Vieri Altoviti
Bernardo di Anselmo Anselmi
Piero di Jacopo Ardinghelli
Daniello di Nofri di Azzo *lanaiolo*
Zanobi di Lodovico della Badessa
Andrea di Segnino Baldesi
Guido di Francesco di M. Niccolò Baldovinetti

Mariotto di M. Niccolò Baldovinetti
Giovanni di Domenico Bartoli
Lionardo di Bartolomeo Bartolini
M. Piero di Lionardo Beccanugi
Matteo di Bonaccorso Berardi
Marco di Bartolomeo Bonavolti
Carlo di Gagliardo Bonciani
Domenico di Lionardo di Domenico Boninsegni
Niccolò di Paolo Bordoni
Luigi di Alessandro di Ser Lamberto [del Nero Cambi]
Niccolò di Andrea Carducci
Niccolò di Giovanni Carducci
Cante di Giovanni Compagni
M. Giuliano di Nicolaio Davanzati
Lottieri di Davanzato Davanzati
Lionardo di Marco di Giotto Fantoni
Federigo di Jacopo di Francesco Federighi
Niccolò di Giuliano di Rinieri del Forese
Giovanni di Ser Luca Franceschi
Francesco di M. Rinaldo Gianfigliazzi
Giuntino di Guido Giuntini *lanaiolo*
Simone di Salvestro [di Simone] Gondi
Jacopo di Dino di M. Guccio di Dino [Gucci]
Nastagio di Simone Guiducci
Filippo di Benedetto Lapaccini del Toso
Luigi di Zanobi Lapaccini del Toso
Antonio di Piero di Lapozzo
Lorenzo di Piero Lenzi
Francesco di Francesco di Pierozzo della Luna
Niccolò di Tommaso Malegonnelle[1]
Ugolino di Jacopo Mazzinghi
Andrea di Tommaso Minerbetti
Giovanni di Andrea Minerbetti
Lorenzo di M. Andrea da Montebuoni
Niccolò di Giovanni di Bartolo di More
Zanobi di Bartolomeo de' Nobili
Domenico di Matteo di Ser Michele [Pescioni]
Niccolò di Ainolfo Popoleschi
Niccolò di Piero di Tommaso Popoleschi
Paolo di Vanni Rucellai
Piero di Brancazio Rucellai
Piero di Cardinale Rucellai
Giovanni di Betto Rustichi

[1] Also listed as one of the *Sedici Gonfalonieri.*

Chimenti di Cipriano di Ser Nigi di Ser Giovanni [Sernigi]
Betto di Signorino di Manno Signorini
Guglielmino di Agnolo Spini
M. Marcello di Strozza Strozzi
M. Palla di Nofri Strozzi
M. Palla di M. Palla Strozzi
Giovanni di Giacomino di Goggio Tebalducci
Manno di Giovanni di Temperano di Manno [Temperani]
Francesco di M. Simone Tornabuoni
Francesco di Jacopo Ventura
Agnolo di Bindo Vernaccia
Giovanni di Simone Vespucci
Bartolomeo di Antonio di Jacopo del Vigna
Lionardo di Ser Viviano di Neri Viviani
Neri di Ser Viviano di Neri Viviani

Artigiani

Brunetto di Domenico [Brunetti] *beccaio*
Antonio di Dino Canacci [*legnaiolo*]
Paolo di Niccolò Ciuti *linaiolo*
Brancazio di Michele di Feo Dini *galigaio*
Giuliano di Particino di Giovanni *albergatore*
Guarente di Giovanni di Tommaso Guarenti *maestro*
Antonio di Domenico Lenzi *armaiuolo*
Pierozzo di Giovanni di Luca *pezzaio*
Antonio di Jacopo Monti *ferravecchio*
Domenico di Tano Petrucci *coltriciaio*
Agnolo di Paolone Puccini *linaiolo*
Giovanni di Puccio *oliandolo*[1]
Francesco di Antonio di Ser Tommaso Redditi [*linaiolo*]
Andrea di Stagio *cofanaio*
Francesco di Tommaso dello Strinato *rigattiere*

S. GIOVANNI

Boccaccio di Salvestro Alamanneschi
Antonio di Tedice degli Albizzi
Luca di M. Maso degli Albizzi
Niccolò di Gentile degli Albizzi
Aldobrandino di Giorgio di Aldobrandino del Nero
Jacopo di Giorgio di Aldobrandino del Nero
Bartolomeo di Ugo degli Alessandri
Battista di Doffo Arnolfi
Giovanni di Filippo di Michele Arrighi [da Empoli]

---

[1] Second list: *pellipario*

Uberto di Jacopo Arrighi
Branca di Domenico Bartolini Scodellari
Bianco di Salvestro del Maestro Benvenuto
Jacopo di Giovanni Bischeri
Bono di Giovanni Boni *cambiatore*
Niccolò di Luca di Giovanni Cambi
Niccolò di Francesco Cambini
Giovanni di Filippo di Barone Cappelli
Berto di Zanobi Carnesecchi
Simone di Paolo di Berto Carnesecchi
Antonio di Ser Lodovico della Casa
Niccolò di Matteo Cerretani
Cosimo di Antonio di Santi [Chiarucci]
Bernardo di Jacopo di Ser Francesco Ciai
Gentile di Ghino Cortigiani
Cresci di Lorenzo di Cresci
Dietisalvi di Nerone di Nigi Dietisalvi [Neroni]
Antonio di Luca di Manetto da Filicaia
Berto di Francesco da Filicaia
Matteo di Neri di Francesco Fioravanti
Bartolomeo di Ser Benedetto di Ser Lando Fortini
Francesco di Taddeo di Giano Gherardini
Jacopo di Guccio Ghiberti
Piero di Francesco di Ser Gino [Ginori]
Niccolò di Francesco Giraldi
Francesco di Vieri Guadagni
M. Zanobi di Jacopo di M. Biagio Guasconi
Antonio di Migliore di Tommaso Guidotti
Antonio di Bernardo di Ligi
Uberto di Giovanni di Andrea di Neri Lippi
Giovanni di Antonio Lorini
Carlo di Niccolò Macinghi
Meglino di Giovanni di Migliorozzo Magaldi
M. Francesco di Ser Benedetto Marchi
Ugolino di Niccolò di Ugolino Martelli
Giuliano di Tommaso di Guccio Martini
Antonio di Ser Tommaso Masi
Bernardo di Antonio de' Medici
Filippo di Migliore di Giunta [Migliori]
Stefano di Nello di Ser Bartolomeo di Ser Nello
M. Bartolomeo di Giovanni Orlandini
Giovanni di Stagio Barducci [Ottavanti]
Matteo di Marco di Antonio Palmieri
Carlo di Agnolo di Filippo di Ser Giovanni [Pandolfini]

Nofri di Giovanni di Michele di Ser Parente
Andrea di Guglielmino de' Pazzi
Piero di Bartolomeo Pecori
Tommaso di Geri della Rena
Piero di Giovanni de' Ricci
Borgo di Borgo Rinaldi
Bartolomeo di Luca di Piero Rinieri
Bono di Jacopo Ristori
Niccolò di Bardo Rittafè
Andrea di Rinaldo Rondinelli
Zanobi di Jacopo del Rosso *vaiaio*
Nuccio di Benintendi Solosmei
Andrea di Sinibaldo da Sommaia
Ruberto del Mancino Sostegni
Lorenzo di Andrea di M. Ugo della Stufa
M. Guglielmino di Francesco Tanaglia
Bartolo di Bartolo Tedaldi
Niccolò di M. Baldo della Tosa
Filippo di Bartolomeo Valori
Niccolò di Bartolomeo di Taldo Valori

Artigiani

Benedetto di Puccino di Ser Andrea *corazzaio*
Banco di Simone di Banco *rigattiere*
Giovanni di Baroncino [Baroncini] *spadaio*
Niccolò di Zanobi Bonvanni *beccaio*
Bartolomeo di Jacopo Casini *bottaio*
Bartolomeo di Giovanni Giani *linaiolo*
Lorenzo di Benino di Guccio *coltriciaio*
Simone di Andrea di Guccio *beccaio*
Salvestro di Michele Lapi *brigliaio*
Benedetto di Piero di More *oliandolo*
Benintendi di Antonio Pucci [*maestro*]
Andrea di Nofri Romoli *lastraiolo*
Bonamico di Lionardo di Teo *corazzaio*

III

BALÌA OF 1438

(Bibl. Naz., XXV. 379, fols. 143ʳ–145ᵛ; Tratte, 132 *bis*, fols. 163ᵛ–165ᵛ; British Museum, MS. Egerton 3764, fols. 166ʳ–167ᵛ)[1]

Signoria

Benedetto di Giovanni Cicciaporci
Tommaso di Lorenzo di M. Tommaso Soderini

Giano di Marchionne di Giano Torrigiani
Michele di Giovanni Galilei

Lionardo di Francesco Ventura
Rinaldo di Lionardo Altoviti

Lorenzo di Niccolò Monti *rigattiere*
Bartolomeo di Jacopo Casini *bottaio*

M. Bartolomeo di Giovanni Orlandini (Gonfalonier of Justice)

Sedici Gonfalonieri

Bernardo di Antonio di Jacopo Paganelli
Stefano di Francesco di Giovanni di Ser Segna [Segni]
Francesco di Antonio di Jacopo Biliotti
Giuliano di Agostino di Como *biadaiolo*

Francesco di Cionaccio di Francesco Baroncelli
Giovanni di Zaccaria di Jacopo *coltriciaio*
Lodovico di Piero Bonaventura Ricoveri
Giovanni di M. Forese di Giovanni Salviati

Carlo di Tommaso Redditi *coltriciaio*
Niccolò di Giuliano di Rinieri del Forese
Niccolò di Giano di Bonaccorso Berardi
Antonio di Marsilio di Vanni Vecchietti

Giovanni di Ser Tommaso di Ser Francesco Masi
Giovanni di Baroncino di Giovanni [Baroncini] *spadaio*
Giovanni di Tedice di Jacopo degli Albizzi
Benintendi di Antonio Pucci

---

[1] No official lists of this *Balìa* appear to be extant. I have used the lists contained in the *Priorista* Giovanni (B.N. XXV, 379) and in the *Priorista* Gaddi (Tratte, 132 *bis*, and B.M., MS. Egerton 3764), and have emended a few evident copying errors.

Dodici Buonuomini

Matteo di Ser Piero di Arrigo Mucini
Filippo di Giacchi di Michele Giacchi
Michele di Arrigo di Gardo *orpellaio*

Antonio di Giano di Bartolomeo Morelli
Antonio di Salvestro di Ser Ristoro di Ser Jacopo [Serristori][1]
Filippo di Lorenzo Nutini *legnaiolo*

Andrea di Tommaso di Andrea Minerbetti
Daniello di Nofri di Azzo
Brancazio di Michele [di Feo] Dini *coreggiaio*

Francesco di Chimenti di Zanobi Guidotti
Bernardo di Alamanno di M. Salvestro de' Medici
Niccolò di Francesco di Antonio Giraldi

Capitani di Parte Guelfa

Lorenzo di Ser Falcone di Giovanni Falconi
Lamberto di Pierozzo di Giovanni Franceschi [dal Vivaio]

Andrea di Taddeo di Duccio Mancini
Lorenzo di Bartolo di Segna [Guidi] *rigattiere*

Zanobi di Testa di Jacopo Girolami
Niccolò di Piero di Bartolo Cini
Nicolaio di Giovanni di Luca [*pezzaio*]

Gentile di Ghino Cortigiani
Piero di M. Marco Marchi *albergatore*

Otto di Guardia

Mariotto di Dinozzo di Stefano Lippi
Bartolomeo di Giovanni Michelozzi *coreggiaio*

Maestro Galileo di Giovanni Galilei
Andrea di Lapo Guardi *coreggiaio*

Lionardo di Marco di Giotto Fantoni
Francesco di Tommaso di Marco Bartoli

Piero di Francesco di Ser Gino Ginori
Giuliano di Tommaso di Guccio Martini

[1] Also listed as *Accoppiatore*.

Otto di Guardia (new)

Piero di Goro di Andrea del Benino
Niccolò di Bartolomeo di Tommaso Corbinelli

Tommaso di Giannozzo di Tommaso degli Alberti
Niccolò di Andrea di Niccolò Giugni

Anfrione di Lorenzo di Piero Lenzi
Antonio di Jacopo Monti *ferravecchio*

Manetto di Zanobi di Berto Carnesecchi
Francesco di Bartolomeo Cambini *linaiolo*

Dieci di Balìa

M. Lorenzo di Antonio di Niccolò Ridolfi
Neri di Gino di Neri Capponi
Nero di Filippo del Nero *rigattiere*[1]

Alamanno di M. Jacopo di Alamanno Salviati
Bernardo di Filippo di Niccolò Giugni

Giovanni di Simone di M. Tommaso Altoviti
M. Piero di Lionardo di Niccolò Beccanugi

Nerone di Nigi di Nerone Dietisalvi [Neroni][1]
Cosimo di Giovanni di Bicci de' Medici
Puccio di Antonio Pucci *maestro*

Accoppiatori

Piero di M. Luigi di M. Piero Guicciardini
Luca di Bonaccorso di Neri Pitti
Nero di Filippo del Nero *rigattiere*

Antonio di Salvestro di Ser Ristoro di Ser Jacopo [Serristori]
Pero di Dino Peri *galigaio*

M. Giuliano di Nicolaio di Ruberto Davanzati
Simone di Francesco di Simone Guiducci

Nerone di Nigi di Nerone Dietisalvi [Neroni]
Neri di Domenico Bartolini Scodellari

[1] Also listed as *Accoppiatore*.

Secretari

Giovannozzo di Francesco di Neri Pitti
Giovanni di Mico di Niccolò Capponi[1]

Niccolò di Cocco di Donato di Cocco [Donati][1]
Taddeo di Giovanni di Masino dell'Antella
Fabiano di Antonio Martini *beccaio*

Tommaso di Antonio di Ser Tommaso Redditi
Niccolò di Andrea di Niccolò Carducci[1]

Baldassare di Arrigo di Simone *agoraio*[1]
Baldassare di Antonio di Santi Chiarucci
Matteo di Niccolò di Giovanni Cerretani[1]

Ufficiali del Monte

Bernardo di Uguccione di Francesco Lippi

Andreuolo di Nicol di Franco Sacchetti

Luigi di Marco di Tommaso Bartoli
Guarente di Giovanni Guarenti *maestro*

Aldobrandino di Giorgio di Aldobrandino [del Nero]

Ufficiali del Banco

Francesco di Filippo de' Nerli
Andrea di Guglielmo de' Pazzi
Lorenzo di Giovanni di Bicci de' Medici
Stagio di Matteo Bonaguisi

Sei di Mercanzia

Bartolo di Bartolo Tedaldi
Francesco di Jacopo Ventura
Cresci di Lorenzo di Cresci
Matteo di Morello Morelli
Giovanni di [Ser] Luca Franceschi
Cambino di Francesco Cambini

[1] *om. Priorista* Gaddi.

Consuls of the Guilds

Ser Francesco di Ser Tommaso Masi
Jacopo di Giovanni Villani
Orlando di Guccio de' Medici
Lorenzo di Gino Capponi
Giovanni di Betto Rustichi
Bernardo di Cristofano Carnesecchi
Bencivenni di Cristofano Bencivenni
Andrea di Francesco del Gaburro
Bartolo di Gherardo Marucelli
Niccolò di Aringo di Corso
Lodovico di Guccio della Badessa
Duccio di Ser Lorenzo Giannini
Giovanni di Antonio Pucci
Cambino di Niccolò Cambini
Francesco di Bernardo Galluzzi
Sandro di Neri di Nuccio
Luca di Donato Michelozzi
Giovanni di Piero di Bartolomeo [Pieri]
Antonio di Domenico Lenzi
Giovanni di Piero di Guido
Paolo di Agostino di Paolo

Arroti

S. SPIRITO

Francesco di Piero di Tommaso Alamanni
Bernardo di Tommaso Antinori
Bernardo di Pegolotto Balducci
Bartolomeo di Lorenzo di Totto de' Bardi
Antonio di Giovanni di Guernieri Benci
Giovanni di Amerigo di Simone Benci
Banco di Niccolò di Bencivenni
Francesco di Niccolò di Andrea del Benino
Sandro di Giovanni di Bartolo Biliotti
Baldassare di Bernardo di Ugolino Bonsi
Ruberto di Giovanni di Brancazio Borsi
Antonio di Lotteringo Boverelli
Filippo di Cristofano del Buglaffo
Giovanni di Antonio di Jacopo Canigiani
Simone di Antonio di Jacopo Canigiani
Uguccione di Mico di Niccolò Capponi
Pazzino di Giovanni di Pazzino Cicciaporci

Antonio di Bartolomeo Corbinelli
Giovanni di Tommaso di Piero Corbinelli
Giovanni di Stefano di Corsino Corsini
Giovanni di Ser Falcone di Giovanni Falconi
Simone di Giorgio di Agostino Formiconi
Francesco di Tommaso di Francesco Giovanni[1]
Luigi di Piero di M. Luigi Guicciardini
Francesco di Guidetto di Jacopo Guidetti
Orsino di Lanfredino Lanfredini
Filippo di Simone di Stefano Lippi
Rinieri di Ridolfo di Paolo Lotti
Guido di Boninsegna Machiavelli
Giannozzo di Bernardo di Giannozzo Manetti
Agostino di Jacopo di Agostino Martini
Lutozo di Jacopo di Lutozo Nasi
Cola di Giuliano di Cola Nerini
Ruberto di Bonaccorso di Neri Pitti
Castello di Piero di Castello Quaratesi
Bernardo di M. Lorenzo di Antonio Ridolfi
Jacopo di Luca di Feo Ridolfi
Antonio di Scarlatto di Nuto [Scarlatti]
Mariotto di Francesco di Giovanni di Ser Segna [Segni]
Giorgio di Piero di Alessandro Serragli
Niccolò di Lorenzo di M. Tommaso Soderini
Gamberino di Andrea del Soldato
Giovanni di Bartolo di Piero Strada
Luca di Gregorio di Fetto Ubertini
Paolo di Giannozzo Vettori[2]

Artigiani

Cino di Luca di Cino *coreggiaio*
Francesco di Bonaccorso Corsellini *ottonaio*
Corso di Lorenzo di Covero *oliandolo*
Antonio di Fantone Fantoni *vinattiere*
Lippo di Giorgio di Giore *calzolaio*
Giuliano di Cristofano [di Lorenzo] *legnaiolo*
Simone del Nero *rigattiere*
Sandro del Rosso di Piero [del Rosso] *fornaciaio*
Sasso di Antonio di Sasso *oliandolo*
Giovanni di Cristofano di Simone *maestro*

S. CROCE

Antonio di Tommaso degli Alberti
Daniello di Piero degli Alberti

[1] *om. Priorista* Gaddi.   [2] *Priorista* Gaddi.

Niccolò di M. Alessandro dell'Antella
Lorenzo di Agnolo di Francesco Baroncelli
Lionardo di Zanobi Bartoli
Santi di Giovanni di Francesco di Ser Bartolo
Lodovico di Lorenzo di Marco Benvenuti
Francesco di Francesco Berlinghieri
Bonifazio di Donato di Bonifazio
M. Lionardo di Francesco Bruni *cancelliere*
Niccolò di Francesco Busini
Michele di Salvatore di Bondì del Caccia
Mainardo di M. Carlo Cavalcanti
Giuliano di Salvestro di Lodovico Ceffini
Nofri di Salvestro di Niccolò Cennini
Bernardo di Jacopo Ciacchi
Tommaso di Scolaio di Lapo Ciacchi
Bartolo di Domenico di Francesco Corsi
Francesco di Piero di Giovanni Dini
Gentile del Maestro Tommaso del Maestro Dino
M. Donato di Niccolò di Cocco Donati
Attaviano di Piero Gerini
Bernardo di Bartolomeo Gherardi
Paolo di Zanobi di Paolo da Ghiacceto
Jacopo di Giovanni di Andrea Giugni
Giovanni di Lionardo Jacopi
Domenico di Niccolò di Migliorozzo Magaldi
Giovanni di Paolo Morelli
Andrea di Salvestro di Michele Nardi
Giovanni di Lapo di Giovanni Niccolini
Antonio di Tommaso Nori
Francesco di Cambio di Orlando Orlandi
Simone di Mariotto Orlandini
Gualterotto di Jacopo Riccialbani
Jacopo di Cino di M. Francesco Rinuccini
Ubertino di Gherardo di Geri Risaliti
Franco di Nicol di Franco Sacchetti
Bernardo di Ser Cambio di Niccolò Salviati
Lorenzo di Antonio di Lorenzo Spinelli
Lodovico di Cece di Frosino da Verrazzano
Giuliano di Amerigo di Bartolo Zati
Bernardo di Zanobi di Ser Zello

Artigiani

Andrea di Simone del Corso *calderaio*
Giovanni di Miniato di Dino *coreggiaio*
Mariano di Stefano di Nese [Duranti] *forbiciaio*

Ghino di Jacopo di Ser Francesco *coreggiaio*
Jacopo di Gallo Galli *legnaiolo*
Antonio di Vanni Mannucci *galigaio*
Bartolomeo del Rosso Pieri *galigaio*
Lorenzo di Luca Salvucci *coltellinaio*
Domenico di Filippo Telli *pianellaio*
Vanni di Niccolò di Ser Vanni *legnaiolo*
Ambrogio di Giovanni del Verzino *linaiolo*

S. MARIA NOVELLA

M. Agnolo di Jacopo Acciaiuoli
Dardano di Michele di Zanobi Acciaiuoli
Bardo di Guglielmo di Bardo Altoviti
Oddo di Vieri di Sandro Altoviti
Giovanni di Domenico di Tommaso Bartoli
Lionardo di Bartolomeo Bartolini
Currado di Berardo di Bonaccorso Berardi
M. Giovanni di Piero del Teghia Bertaldi
Carlo di Gagliardo di Neri Bonciani
Domenico di Lionardo Boninsegni
Luigi di Alessandro di Ser Lamberto [del Nero Cambi]
Antonio di Dino Canacci
Filippo di Giovanni di Filippo Carducci
Francesco di Lorenzo Cigliamochi
Piero di Nicolaio di Ruberto Davanzati
Giovanni di Gherardo Davizi
M. Carlo di Francesco Federighi
Rinieri di Giuliano di Rinieri del Forese
Antonio di Guido Giuntini
Nastagio di Simone di Francesco Guiducci
Filippo di Benedetto Lapaccini del Toso
Lorenzo di Piero Lenzi
Niccolò di Tommaso Malegonnelle
Ugolino di Jacopo Mazzinghi
Giovanni di Andrea di Niccolò Minerbetti
Lorenzo di M. Andrea [da] Bondelmonti [Montebuoni]
Ruberto di Antonio di Francesco de' Nobili
Giannotto di Domenico di Bartolo Ottavanti
Domenico di Matteo di Ser Michele [Pescioni]
Niccolò di Ainolfo di Niccolò Popoleschi
Niccolò di Piero di Tommaso Popoleschi
Piero di Brancazio Rucellai
Piero di Cardinale di Piero Rucellai
Antonio di M. Francesco Salutati

Andrea di Signorino di Manno Signorini
Guglielmo di Ridolfo da Sommaia
M. Marcello di Strozza di Carlo Strozzi
Ugo di Niccolò Vecchietti
Bernardo di Jacopo di Francesco Ventura
Agnolo di Bindo di Agnolo Vernaccia

Artigiani

Manetto di Andrea *ferravecchio*
Simone di Ser Simone Berti *linaiolo*
Brunetto di Domenico Brunetti *beccaio*
Paolo di Niccolò Ciuti *linaiolo*
Francesco di Michele [di Feo] Dini *galigaio*
Giuliano di Particino [di Giovanni] *albergatore*
Piero di Gualberto *oliandolo*
Antonio di Lenzone [Lenzoni] *galigaio*
Domenico di Tano Petrucci *coltriciaio*
Agnolo di Paolo di Lorenzo [Puccini] *linaiolo*
Salvestro di Agostino di Salvestro *linaiolo*

S. GIOVANNI

Boccaccio di Salvestro di M. Filippo Adimari
Lorenzo di Alberto di Bonaccorso Alberti
Luca di M. Maso di Luca degli Albizzi
Niccolò di Gentile di Vanni degli Albizzi
Jacopo di Giorgio di Aldobrandino del Nero
Alessandro di Ugo di Bartolomeo degli Alessandri
Battista di Doffo Arnolfi
Uberto di Jacopo di Francesco Arrighi
Giovanni di Nettolo Becchi
Bianco di Salvestro del Maestro Benvenuto
Bartolomeo di Matteo Bonaguisi
Niccolò di Francesco Cambini
Giovanni di Filippo di Barone Cappelli
Simone di Paolo di Berto Carnesecchi
Niccolò di Matteo di Niccolò Cerretani
Bernardo di Jacopo di Ser Francesco Ciai
Lorenzo di Cresci di Lorenzo di Cresci
Dietisalvi di Nerone di Nigi Dietisalvi [Neroni]
Berto di Francesco di Berto da Filicaia
Andrea di Ser Lando Fortini
Francesco di Taddeo di Giano Gherardini
Jacopo di Guccio di Geri Ghiberti
Antonio di Giuliano di Francesco Ginori

Antonio di Migliorino di Tommaso Guidotti
Giovanni di Baldino di Gianni Inghirami
Giovanni di Tommaso di Bartolo Lapi
Salvestro di Michele di Salvestro Lapi
Giovanni di Antonio di Filippo Lorini
Giovachino di Niccolò Macinghi
M. Francesco di Ser Benedetto Marchi
M. Domenico di Niccolò Martelli
Antonio di Ser Tommaso di Ser Francesco Masi
Nicola di M. Vieri di Cambio de' Medici
Filippo di Migliore di Giunta Migliori
Orlandino di Giovanni Orlandini
Giovanni di Stagio Barducci [Ottavanti]
Matteo di Marco di Antonio Palmieri
Agnolo di Filippo di Ser Giovanni Pandolfini
Carlo di Agnolo di Filippo di Ser Giovanni [Pandolfini]
Parente di Michele di Ser Parente
Bartolomeo di Guidaccio Pecori
Tommaso di Geri della Rena
Antonio di Matteo di Gucciozzo de' Ricci
Borgo di Borgo di Talento Rinaldi
Zanobi di Jacopo del Rosso *vaiaio*
Ruberto del Mancino Sostegni
Lorenzo di Andrea della Stufa
M. Guglielmino di Francesco di Antonio Tanaglia
Niccolò di Bartolomeo di Niccolò Valori

Artigiani
Puccino di Ser Andrea *armaiolo*
Paolo di Niccolò Benci *vinattiere*
Niccolò di Zanobi Bonvanni *beccaio*[1]
Giovanni di Bartolomeo di Geri *staderaio*
Bartolomeo di Giovanni Giani *linaiolo*
Lorenzo di Benino di Guccio *linaiolo*
Berto di Marchionne *rigattiere*
Antonio di Piero Migliorotti *chiavaiolo*
Niccolò di Biagio di Monte *rigattiere*
Niccolò di Jacopo di Panuzio *rigattiere*
Salvestro di Lionardo di Puccio *vinattiere*
Andrea di Nofri Romoli *lastraiolo*
Domenico di Matteo dello Scroffa *beccaio*
Bonamico di Lionardo di Teo *corazzaio*
Lorenzo di Andrea Tosi *coreggiaio*
Niccolò di Baldino del Troscia *albergatore*[1]

[1] *Priorista* Gaddi.

IV

BALÌA OF 1444

(Balìe, 26, fols. 30ᵛ–33ᵛ)

Signoria

Francesco di Donato di Ugolino Bonsi
Tuccio di Lionardo di Francesco Ferrucci

Simone di Amerigo di Bartolo Zati
Giovanni di Salvatore di Tommaso del Caccia

Giovanni di Ser Luca Franceschi
Antonio di Marsilio di Vanni Vecchietti

Tommaso di Antonio di Niccolò Bucherelli *linaiolo*
Niccolò di Benintendi di Andrea Benintendi *rigattiere*

Giuliano di Tommaso di Guccio Martini (Gonfalonier of Justice)

Sedici Gonfalonieri

Luigi di Bartolomeo de' Scali
Corso di Lorenzo di Covero *oliandolo*
Giovanni di Luca di Gregorio di Fetto Ubertini
Zanobi di Niccolò di Mico Capponi

Michele di M. Piero Benini
Gentile del Maestro Tommaso del Garbo
Niccolò di Francesco Busini
Piero di Ser Ricciardo Pieri *rigattiere*

Giovanni di Ser Viviano di Neri Viviani
Antonio di Guido Giuntini *lanaiolo*
Guarente di Giovanni Guarenti *maestro*
Benedetto di Michele di Benedetto di Ser Michele [Pescioni]

Lorenzo di Andrea di M. Ugo della Stufa
Stagio di Matteo Bonaguisi
Francesco di Chiarissimo di Bernardo di Chiarissimo
Domenico di Lorenzo di Francesco *maliscalco*

Dodici Buonuomini

Antonio di Scarlatto di Nuto [Scarlatti] *ritagliatore*
Lotto di Piero di Paolo Lotti
Paolo di Antonio di Piero di Parigi

Niccolò di Domenico di Niccolò Magaldi
Matteo di Morello di Paolo Morelli
Francesco di Giovanni dello Sciocco *biadaiolo*

Benvenuto di Giovanni di Uberto Benvenuti
Filippo di Antonio del Bon Ricchi *cambiatore*
Giovanni di Mattio di Pier Cini *ferraiolo*

Bernardo di M. Baldo della Tosa
Zanobi di Jacopo del Rosso *vaiaio*
Bernardo di Antonio di Giovenco de' Medici

Capitani di Parte Guelfa

Francesco di Andrea Quaratesi
Antonio di Giovanni di Guernieri Benci

Ghino di Jacopo di Ser Francesco [*coreggiaio*]

Boccaccio di Niccolò di Boccaccio

Antonio di Giuliano Ginori
Lorenzo di Bartolomeo Cambini *linaiolo*

Otto di Guardia

Francesco del Buono Bramanti *beccaio*
Antonio di Filippo Giugni
Dardano di Michele Acciaiuoli
Giovanni di Antonio di Filippo Lorini

Gamberino di Andrea del Soldato
Mariano di Stefano di Nese Duranti [*forbiciaio*]
Agnolo di Bindo Vernaccia
M. Bartolomeo di Giovanni Orlandini

Ufficiali del Monte

Bernardo di Tommaso Antinori

Doffo di Giovanni di Nofri Arnolfi
Giovanni di Miniato di Dino *coreggiaio*

Bartolomeo di Lorenzo di Piero Lenzi

Bernardo di Jacopo di Ser Francesco Ciai

Sei di Mercanzia

Bartolomeo di Ugo degli Alessandri
M. Giuliano di Nicolaio Davanzati
Giovanni di Salvestro Popoleschi
Bardo di Guglielmo di Bardo Altoviti
Giorgio di Piero di Alessandro Serragli
Antonio di Bartolomeo del Rosso Pieri *galigaio*

Accoppiatori and Secretari of the Parte Guelfa of 1434

Giovanni di Paolo Morelli
Francesco di Cionaccio Baroncelli

Idem, of 1439[1]

Niccolò di Lorenzo Soderini
Nero di Filippo del Nero *rigattiere*
Simone di Francesco Guiducci
Ser Alberto di Ser Tommaso di Ser Francesco Masi

Secretari of the Ufficiali del Monte

Lorenzo di Antonio Spinelli
Carlo di Agnolo Pandolfini

Secretario of the Sei di Mercanzia and of the Mercanzia of 1434

Puccio di Antonio Pucci

Idem, of 1439[1]

Piero di Gregorio di Andrea del Benino
Andrea di Salvestro di Michele Nardi
Salvestro di Lionardo di Puccio [*vinattiere*]
Nerone di Nigi di Nerone Dietisalvi [Neroni]

Accoppiatori of 1434, and substitutes for deceased Accoppiatori

Luca di Bonaccorso Pitti
Luigi di Piero di M. Luigi Guicciardini
M. Donato di Niccolò di Cocco Donati
Antonio di Salvestro Serristori
Neri di Domenico Bartolini Scodellari
Pero di Dino Peri *galigaio*

[1] Florentine style.

Secretari of 1434 and 1440, Accoppiatori of 1440, and substitutes

Fabiano di Antonio Martini [*beccaio*]
Tommaso di Antonio di Ser Tommaso Redditi
Baldassare di Antonio di Santi [Chiarucci]
M. Giovannozzo di Francesco Pitti
Uguccione di Mico Capponi
Andrea di Niccolò di Andrea Carducci
Niccolò di Matteo Cerretani
Francesco di Marco di Tommaso Bartoli
Simone di Giovanni di Simone di M. Tommaso Altoviti
Neri di Gino Capponi
Francesco di Francesco Berlinghieri
Paolo di Zanobi da Ghiacceto
Niccolò di Brancazio Rucellai
Cosimo di Giovanni de' Medici
Giano di Marchionne Torrigiani
Domenico di Tano Petrucci [*coltriciaio*]
Giovanni di Antonio Pucci [*maestro*]
Filippo di Cristofano del Buglaffo
Tommaso di Lorenzo di M. Tommaso Soderini
Ubertino di Gherardo Risaliti
Franco di Nicol di Franco Sacchetti
Giovanni di Domenico Bartoli
Martino di Francesco dello Scarfa
Simone di Paolo di Berto Carnesecchi
Alessandro di Ugo degli Alessandri
Niccolò di Zanobi Bonvanni [*beccaio*]

Accoppiatori a mano of 1443

Giovanni di Antonio di Jacopo Canigiani
Bernardo di M. Lorenzo di Antonio Ridolfi
Bernardo di Filippo Giugni
M. Carlo di Francesco Federighi
Francesco di Jacopo Ventura
M. Domenico di Niccolò di Ugolino Martelli
Antonio di Ser Tommaso Masi
Francesco di Bonaccorso Corsellini
Giovanni del Zaccaria di Jacopo *coltriciaio*

Secretari of 1443

Antonio di Bartolomeo Corbinelli
Giovanni di Lapo Niccolini

Domenico di Matteo di Ser Michele [Pescioni]
Lionardo di Bartolomeo Bartolini
Pierozzo di Giovanni di Luca *pezzaio*
Manetto di Zanobi Carnesecchi
Benedetto di Puccino di Ser Andrea [*corazzaio*]

Secretari of the Parte Guelfa of 1443

Sandro di Giovanni Biliotti
Giovanni di Stefano Corsini

Bartolomeo di Bonsignore Spinelli
Francesco di Cambio Orlandi

Manno di Giovanni di Temperano di Manno [Temperani]
Matteo di Marco di Tommaso Bartoli
Giuliano di Particino di Giovanni [*albergatore*]

Simone di Francesco di Ser Gino [Ginori]
Bernardo di Cristofano Carnesecchi

Secretari of the Mercanzia of 1443

Simone di Antonio Canigiani
Bernardo di Jacopo Ventura
Alamanno di M. Jacopo Salviati
Bernardo di Bartolomeo di Gherardo Gherardi
Giovanni di Stagio Barducci [Ottavanti]

Consuls of the Guilds

M. Otto di Lapo di Giovanni Niccolini
Francesco di Filippo de' Nerli
Matteo di Giovanni di Matteo Corsini
Francesco di Piero di Francesco Gherucci
Matteo di Borgo di Rinaldo Rinaldi
Francesco di Baldino di Gianni Inghirami
Jacopo di Bartolo di Lapo Ciacchi
Andrea di Francesco di Cecco del Gaburro
Corso di Niccolò di Arrigo Corsi
Mariotto di Salvi [di Stefano] *coltellinaio*
Simone del Nero *rigattiere*
Guido di Piero del Rosso *fornaciaio*
Noso di Giovanni di Noso Fantoni

Niccolò di Baldino del Troscia
Andrea di Matteo Benivieni
Santi di Simone Ambrogi
Neri di Antonio di Segna [Guidi]
Coppo di Guido Cafferelli
Jacopo di Michele dalla Volta
Piero di Jacopo di Berto Canacci
Miniato di Salvestro *fornaio*

Arroti

S. SPIRITO

Bernardo di Pegolotto di Francesco Balducci
Giovanni di Amerigo di Simone Benci
Banco di Niccolò di Bencivenni
Francesco di Niccolò di Andrea del Benino
Baldassare di Bernardo Bonsi
Antonio di Lotteringo Boverelli
Pazzino di Giovanni Cicciaporci
Tommaso di Bartolomeo Corbinelli
Antonio di Lionardo Ferrucci
Orsino di Lanfredino Lanfredini
Mariotto di Dinozzo di Stefano Lippi
Piero di Chino di Piero Lippi
Giannozzo di Bernardo Manetti
Lutozo di Jacopo Nasi
Castello di Piero di Castello Quaratesi
Luigi di M. Lorenzo Ridolfi
Mariotto di Francesco di Giovanni Segni

Artigiani
Cino di Luca di Cino *coreggiaio*
Giuliano di Agostino di Como *biadaiolo*
Bartolomeo di Giovanni Michelozzi *coreggiaio*

S. CROCE

Tommaso di Giannozzo degli Alberti
Mariotto di Lorenzo di Marco Benvenuti
Giuliano di Salvatore di Tommaso del Caccia
Niccolò di Giovanni di M. Amerigo Cavalcanti
Bernardo di Jacopo di Matteo Ciacchi
Piero di Domenico Corsi
Francesco di Piero di Giovanni Dini
Antonio di Fronte di Piero di Fronte

Bernardo del Maestro Galileo di Giovanni Galilei
Bernardo di Giovanni di Lionardo Jacopi
Lotto di Duccino di Lotto Mancini
Piero di Francesco di Duccio Mellini
Piero di Simone di Mariotto Orlandini
Gualterotto di Jacopo Riccialbani
M. Tommaso di Ser Jacopo Salvetti
Lodovico di Cece da Verrazzano
Giuliano di Amerigo di Bartolo Zati

Artigiani

Salvestro di Zanobi del Cica *vinattiere*
Jacopo di Gallo di Antonio Galli [*legnaiolo*]
Francesco di Bernardo Galluzzi *biadaiolo*

S. MARIA NOVELLA

M. Agnolo di Jacopo Acciaiuoli
Oddo di Vieri Altoviti
Piero di Mariotto [di Piero] di Cenni dell'Amorotto
M. Piero di Lionardo Beccanugi
Niccolò di Giano di Bonaccorso Berardi
Carlo di Gagliardo Bonciani
Domenico di Lionardo Boninsegni
Filippo di Giovanni Carducci
Francesco di Lorenzo Cigliamochi
Lionardo di Marco di Giotto Fantoni
Zanobi di Testa Girolami
Alesso di Benedetto Lapaccini del Toso
Niccolò di Tommaso Malegonnelle
Jacopo di Ugolino di Jacopo Mazzinghi
Andrea di Tommaso Minerbetti
Piero di Cardinale Rucellai
Giuliano di Lapo Vespucci

Artigiani

Simone di Ser Simone Berti [*linaiolo*]
Francesco di Michele di Feo Dini [*galigaio*]
Bernardo di Jacopo Monti *ferravecchio*

S. GIOVANNI

Luca di Maso degli Albizzi
Aldobrandino di Giorgio di Aldobrandino del Nero
Bono di Giovanni Boni *cambiatore*
Piero di Lorenzo di Piero Borsi

Giovanni di Filippo di Barone Cappelli
Cresci di Lorenzo di Cresci
Dietisalvi di Nerone di Nigi Dietisalvi [Neroni]
Francesco di Berto di Francesco da Filicaia
Francesco di Chimenti Guidotti
Salvestro di Michele di Salvestro Lapi
Ugolino di Niccolò di Ugolino Martelli
Tommaso di Antonio di Tommaso di Guccio Martini
Piero di Cosimo di Giovanni de' Medici
Filippo di Migliore di Giunta Migliori
Matteo di Marco di Antonio Palmieri
Maso di Geri della Rena
Francesco di Taddeo di Giano Gherardini della Rosa

Artigiani

Paolo di Niccolò di Paolo Benci [*vinattiere*]
Cambino di Francesco Cambini *linaiolo*
Andrea di Nofri Romoli *lastraiolo*

V

BALÌA OF 1452

(Balìe, 27, fols. 16ᵛ–19ᵛ)

Signoria

Giovanni di Biagio di Agnolo *bicchieraio*
Benincasa di Manno di Benincasa Mannucci *legnaiolo*

Duccio di Nofri di Duccio Mellini
Miniato di Tommaso di Francesco Busini

Alessandro di Luigi di Alessandro di Ser Lamberto [del Nero Cambi][1]
Francesco di Lorenzo di Piero Lenzi

Zanobi di Tommaso di Zanobi Ginori
Salvestro di Bartolomeo di Salvestro del Maestro Benvenuto

M. Giovannozzo di Francesco Pitti (Gonfalonier of Justice)

Sedici Gonfalonieri

Bernardo di Uguccione Lippi *mercante*
Benedetto di Baldo di Benedetto *linaiolo*
Mariotto di Dinozzo di Stefano Lippi
Lorenzo di Giovanni di Lorenzo Zampalocchi

Niccolò di Piero di Bonaccorso di Vanni
Benedetto del Maestro Galileo di Giovanni Galilei
Francesco di Lorenzo di Antonio Spinelli
Giovanni di Miniato di Dino *coreggiaio*

Michele di Zanobi di Michele Acciaiuoli
Giovanni di Cante di Giovanni Compagni
Carlo di Giovanni di Salvestro Carradori *rigattiere*
Jacopo di Ugolino di Jacopo Mazzinghi

Lorenzo di Giovanni di Lorenzo della Stufa
Lorenzo di Filippo di Barone Cappelli
Geri di Maso di Geri della Rena
Domenico di Lorenzo di Francesco *maliscalco*

---

[1] Also under *Ufficiali del Monte*.

Dodici Buonuomini

Filippo di M. Francesco Machiavelli
Salimbene di Lanfredino Lanfredini
Niccolò di Schiatta di Uberto Ridolfi

Niccolò di Domenico di Niccolò Magaldi
M. Tommaso di Ser Jacopo Salvetti
Francesco di Simone di Lorenzo *calderaio*

Gherardo di Bongianni di Giovanni Gianfigliazzi
Filippo di Filippo di M. Simone Tornabuoni
Antonio di Lenzone di Simone [Lenzoni] *galigaio*

Federigo di Niccolò di Federigo Gori
Battista di Berto di Francesco da Filicaia
Apollonio di Biagio di Niccolò Monti *rigattiere*

Capitani di Parte Guelfa

Agostino di Jacopo di Agostino Martini
Lorenzo di Vanni di Benedetto *linaiolo*

Mainardo di M. Carlo Cavalcanti
Bernardo di Nofri di Duccio Mellini

Jacopo di Lorenzo di M. Jacopo del Biada
Ser Niccolò di Michele di Feo Dini [*galigaio*]

Francesco di Berto di Francesco da Filicaia
Papi di Tedaldo Tedaldi
Giovanni di Donato Adimari

Dieci di Balìa

Castello di Piero di Castello Quaratesi
Neri di Gino Capponi

M. Otto di Lapo di Giovanni Niccolini
Francesco di Cambio Orlandi

M. Agnolo di Jacopo Acciaiuoli
Domenico di Lionardo di Domenico Boninsegni
Giuliano di Particino di Giovanni *albergatore*

Cosimo di Giovanni de' Medici
Luca di M. Maso degli Albizzi
Bartolomeo di Francesco di Ser Andrea *corazzaio*

Otto di Guardia (*new*)

Antonio di Bernardo di Antonio Ridolfi
Giovanni di Stefano Corsini

Giovanni di Alamanno di M. Jacopo Salviati
Bartolomeo di Bonsignore Spinelli

Lionardo di Francesco Ventura
Francesco di Jacopo Monti *ferravecchio*

Nigi di Nerone di Nigi Dietisalvi [Neroni]
Salvestro di Lionardo di Puccio *vinattiere*

Luca di Salvi di Stefano *coltellinaio*—in place of Francesco di
Jacopo Monti, elected *Ufficiale delle gravezze*

Otto di Guardia (*old*)

Francesco di Piero di Paolo Lotti

Maso di Lorenzo di Ceffo Masini

Niccolò di Tommaso [di Niccolò] Malegonnelle
Bernardo di Piero di Cardinale Rucellai

Orlandino di Giovanni Orlandini
Salvestro di Michele di Salvestro Lapi

Giuliano di Agostino di Como [*biadaiolo*]
Andrea di Lapo Guardi *coreggiaio*

Ufficiali del Monte

Lorenzo di Neri di Agnolo Vettori
Nofri di Giovanni di Bondì del Caccia
Niccolò di Matteo di Niccolò Cerretani
Andrea di Nofri Romoli *lastraiolo*
Alessandro di Luigi [di Alessandro] di Ser Lamberto [del Nero
Cambi][1]

Ufficiali of the old debt of the Monte

Lorenzo di Francesco di Giovanni Segni
Nicolaio di Ugo degli Alessandri

Sei di Mercanzia

Piero di Cosimo di Giovanni de' Medici
Filippo di Migliore di Giunta Migliori
Lorenzo di Parigi di Tommaso Corbinelli

[1] Also under *Signoria*.

Lodovico di Cece da Verrazzano
Agnolo di Zanobi di Taddeo Gaddi
Bartolomeo di Giovanni Giani *linaiolo*

Accoppiatori of 1444

Tommaso di Lorenzo di M. Tommaso Soderini
Luca di Bonaccorso di Neri Pitti

Alamanno di M. Jacopo Salviati

Manno di Giovanni di Temperano di Manno [Temperani]

Dietisalvi di Nerone di Nigi Dietisalvi [Neroni]
Ugolino di Niccolò di Ugolino Martelli
Niccolò di Zanobi Bonvanni [*beccaio*]

Accoppiatori of 1448

Luigi di M. Lorenzo Ridolfi
Bartolomeo di Giovanni Michelozzi *coreggiaio*

Bernardo di Bartolomeo di Gherardo Gherardi
Matteo di Morello di Paolo Morelli
Giovanni del Zaccaria di Jacopo *coltriciao*

Martino di Francesco dello Scarfa

Substitutes for deceased Accoppiatori

Lionardo di Bartolomeo Bartolini
Lorenzo di Andrea di M. Ugo della Stufa

Accoppiatori of 1434

Simone di Francesco Guiducci
Neri di Domenico Bartolini [Scodellari]
Nerone di Nigi di Nerone Dietisalvi [Neroni]
Pero di Dino Peri [*galigaio*]

Accoppiatore of 1440

Domenico di Tano Petrucci [*coltriciaio*]

Accoppiatori of 1443

Giovanni di Antonio di Jacopo Canigiani
Bernardo di M. Lorenzo Ridolfi
Francesco di Bonaccorso Corsellini [*ottonaio*]

Andrea di Salvestro di Michele Nardi
M. Bernardo di Filippo Giugni

Francesco di Jacopo di Francesco Ventura

Antonio di Ser Tommaso Masi
M. Domenico di Niccolò Martelli

Secretari of 1434

Tommaso di Antonio di Ser Tommaso Redditi
Baldassare di Antonio di Santi [Chiarucci]

Secretari of 1440

Giovanni di Domenico Bartoli
Simone di Paolo Carnesecchi
M. Alessandro di Ugo degli Alessandri

Secretari of 1443

Luigi di Piero di M. Luigi Guicciardini
Giovanni di Lapo Niccolini
M. Donato di Niccolò di Cocco Donati
Manetto di Zanobi Carnesecchi
Benedetto di Puccino di Ser Andrea *corazzaio*
Niccolò di Andrea Giugni
Francesco di Piero di Francesco Ginori

Secretari of the Monte of 1441

M. Carlo di Agnolo Pandolfini
Lorenzo di Antonio Spinelli

Secretari of 1444

Giovanni di Salvatore [di Tommaso] del Caccia
Matteo di Marco di Antonio Palmieri

Secretari of 1448

Ruberto di Bonaccorso di Neri Pitti
Piero di Chino Lippi
Lorenzo di Lapo Niccolini
Piero di Simone di Mariotto Orlandini
Francesco di Lorenzo Cigliamochi

Niccolò di Bartolomeo Bartolini
Giovanni di Antonio Lorini
Andrea di Lotteringo della Stufa
Antonio di Puccio di Antonio Pucci
Stefano di Francesco Segni
Antonio di Scarlatto di Nuto [Scarlatti]

Knights

M. Giannozzo di Bernardo Manetti
M. Palla di M. Palla Strozzi
M. Guglielmino di Francesco Tanaglia
M. Orlando di Guccio de' Medici
M. Giannozzo di Agnolo Pandolfini

Proconsul of the Guild of Judges and Notaries

Ser Piero di Antonio Migliorotti

Consuls of the Guilds

Ser Baldese di Ambrogio Baldesi
Alberto di Antonio di Nicola di Lippo Alberti
Jacopo di Giovanni Carducci
Antonio di Taddeo di Filippo di Taddeo
Ridolfo di Guglielmo di Bardo Altoviti
Francesco di Donato Bonsi
Antonio di Antonio degli Erri
Antonio di Cristofano di Romolo Cecchi
Frosino di Guerrieri di Francesco
Andrea di Antonio del Reddito
Cambino di Francesco Cambini
Bernardo di Banco Berardi
Antonio di Biagio Torrigiani
Battista di Taccino di Bizzino
Lionardo di Bartolomeo di Francesco Sali
Domenico di Simone di Bartolo Cambini
Francesco di Michele di Jacopo di Vanni Cittadini
Andrea di Giovanni di Ser Niccolò del Cappa
Lionardo di Sandro di Jacopo *calderaio*
Jacopo di Giovanni Torsellini
Giovanni di Lionardo di Giovanni

Nominated by the Signoria

Jacopo di Giovanni di Gherardo Davizi
Alessandro di Andrea di Lipaccio Ilarioni

Niccolò di Benintendi Falemagini
Piero di Francesco di Duccio Mellini
Francesco di Tommaso di Francesco Busini
Nero di Stefano di Alessandro del Nero Cambi
Antonio di Lorenzo di Piero Lenzi
Francesco di Bartolomeo Baldovini
Antonio di Benedetto di Caroccio Strozzi

Arroti

S. SPIRITO

Francesco di Piero di Tommaso Alamanni
Andrea di Francesco Banchi
Francesco di Niccolò di Andrea del Benino
Giovannozzo di Betto di Giovannozzo Biliotti
Antonio di Lotteringo Boverelli
Cristofano di Filippo di Cristofano del Buglaffo
Gino di Neri di Gino Capponi
Pazzino di Giovanni di Pazzino Cicciaporci
Bernardo di Tommaso di Bartolomeo Corbinelli
Gherardo di M. Filippo Corsini
M. Tommaso di Guido Deti
Antonio di Lionardo di Francesco Ferrucci
Pierozzo di Bartolomeo Franceschi dal Vivaio
Jacopo di Piero di M. Luigi Guicciardini
M. Girolamo di Agnolo Machiavelli
Bernardo di Sala [di Filippo] Marsili
Lutozo di Jacopo di Lutozo Nasi
Bernardo di Antonio Paganelli
Luigi di Giovanni di Ligi Quaratesi
Niccolò di Lorenzo di M. Tommaso Soderini
Francesco di Donato di Michele Velluti

Artigiani

Antonio di Fantone di Naldo Fantoni [*vinattiere*]
Francesco del Nero di Filippo del Nero [*rigattiere*]
Paolo di Antonio di Piero Parigi *galigaio*
Giovanni di Piero di Bartolomeo [Pieri] *scodellaio*

S. CROCE

Giovanni di Taddeo di Giovanni dell'Antella
Francesco di Rinieri di Bardo Bagnesi
Lorenzo di Agnolo [di Francesco] Baroncelli
Mariotto di Lorenzo di Marco Benvenuti

Giovanni di Tommaso di Domenico Borghini
Francesco di Domenico di Matteo Caccini
Giuliano di Salvestro Ceffini
Tommaso di Scolaio di Lapo Ciacchi
Piero di Domenico Corsi
Francesco di Piero di Giovanni Dini
Attaviano di Piero Gerini
Carlo di Zanobi [di Paolo] da Ghiacceto
Luigi di Francesco di Biagio Lioni
Lotto di Duccino di Lotto Mancini
Antonio di Antonio di Stefano di Piero del Papa
Gualterotto di Jacopo Riccialbani
Gherardo di Geri di Gherardo Risaliti
Franco di Nicol di Franco Sacchetti
Lotto di Giovanni di M. Forese Salviati
Giovanni di Antonio di Salvestro Serristori
Andrea di Francesco di M. Giovanni Zati

Artigiani

Lionardo di Zanobi di Niccolò del Cica [*vinattiere*]
Mariano di Stefano di Nese Duranti [*forbiciaio*]
Lorenzo di Bartolo di Segna [Guidi] [*corazzaio*]
Antonio di Bartolomeo del Rosso Pieri [*galigaio*]

S. MARIA NOVELLA

Piero di Mariotto [di Piero] di Cenni dell'Amorotto
Matteo di Marco di Tommaso Bartoli
Guido di Carlo di Gagliardo Bonciani
Andrea di Niccolò di Andrea Carducci
Piero di Nicolaio Davanzati
Federigo di Jacopo di Francesco Federighi
Alesso di Benedetto Lapaccini [del Toso]
Piero di Giovanni di Andrea Minerbetti
Lorenzo di M. Andrea da Montebuoni
Niccolò di Giovanni di Bartolo di More
Guccio di Niccolò di M. Guccio de' Nobili
Giovanni di Salvestro di Tommaso Popoleschi
Niccolò di Brancazio Rucellai
Piero di Cardinale Rucellai
Giovanni di Betto [di Giovanni] Rustichi
Rustico di Giovanni di Ser Nigi [Sernigi]
Andrea di Signorino di Manno Signorini
Guglielmo di Ridolfo da Sommaia
Marsilio di Bernardo di Vanni Vecchietti

Giuliano di Lapo Vespucci
Alessandro di Antonio di Jacopo del Vigna

Artigiani

Simone di Ser Simone Berti [*linaiolo*]
Simone di Mattio di Pier Cini *ferraiolo*
Salvestro di Agostino di Salvestro [*linaiolo*]
Francesco di Tommaso dello Strinato [*vinattiere*]

S. GIOVANNI

Aldobrandino di Giorgio di Aldobrandino del Nero
Arrigo di Filippo di Arrigo Arrigucci
Niccolò di Bartolino di Niccolò Bartolini
Piero di Lorenzo di Piero Borsi
Gentile di Ghino di M. Ruberto Cortigiani
Lorenzo di Cresci di Lorenzo di Cresci
Francesco di Piero di Francesco Gherucci
Simone di Francesco di Ser Gino Ginori
Francesco di Antonio di Francesco Giraldi
Antonio di Migliore di Tommaso Guidotti
Francesco di Baldino di Gianni Inghirami
Zanobi di Piero [di Zanobi] Marignolli
Piero di M. Andrea de' Pazzi
Adouardo di Giovanni Portinari
Benintendi di Antonio Pucci
Antonio di Matteo di Gucciozzo de' Ricci
Matteo di Borgo di Rinaldo Rinaldi
Bono di Jacopo di Benincasa Ristori
Domenico di Jacopo del Rosso *vaiaio*
Ruberto del Mancino Sostegni
Jacopo di Giovanni di Matteo Villani

Artigiani

Benci di Niccolò di Paolo Benci [*vinattiere*]
Zanobi di Jacopo di Niccolò Bucherelli [*linaiolo*]
Domenico di Zanobi del Giocondo *bottaio*
Francesco di Taddeo di Piero di Pero [*calderaio*]

VI

BALÌA OF 1458

(Balìe, 29, fols. 13^r–17^r)

Signoria

Cosimo di Antonio di Andrea Tazzi *coreggiaio*
Giuliano di Agostino di Como *biadaiolo*

Bartolomeo di Lodovico di Cece da Verrazzano
Jacopo di Bernardo di M. Jacopo Salviati

Guglielmo di Ridolfo da Sommaia
Rosso di M. Andrea da Montebuoni

Antonio di Taddeo di Filippo di Taddeo
Giovanni di Jacopo di Giovanni Villani

Luca di Bonaccorso di Neri Pitti (Gonfalonier of Justice)

Sedici Gonfalonieri

Bartolomeo di Lorenzo di Totto Gualterotti
Filippo di Guidetto di Jacopo Guidetti
Battista di Giovanni di Matteo Corsini
Francesco di Niccolò Tucci *albergatore*

Amerigo di Giovanni di M. Amerigo Cavalcanti
Giovanpaolo di Ser Zanobi di Ser Mino *linaiolo*
Bernardo di Bartolo di Domenico Corsi
Ruberto di Francesco di Biagio Lioni

Luca di Salvi di Stefano *coltellinaio*
Giovanni di Cante di Giovanni Compagni
Andrea di Tommaso di Andrea Minerbetti
Benedetto di Giovanni di Benedetto Benvenuti

Niccolò di Francesco Inghirami
Piero di Andrea di Lodovico Lapini *beccaio*
Antonio di M. Alessandro di Ugo degli Alessandri
Berto di Michele di Salvestro Lapi

Dodici Buonuomini

Giuliano di Nicola di Giuliano Nerini
Nicola di Piero di Bartolomeo Capponi
Pazzino di Giovanni di Pazzino Cicciaporci

Niccolò di Michele di Giovanni Riccialbani
Benedetto del Maestro Galileo di Giovanni Galilei
Francesco di Ambrogio del Verzino *linaiolo*

Guido di Carlo di Gagliardo Bonciani
Andrea di Guido Giuntini *lanaiolo*
Niccolò di Brunetto di Domenico Brunetti *beccaio*

Andrea di Andrea di Chimenti di Stefano
Brunetto di Aldobrandino di Giorgio di Aldobrandino [del Nero]
Niccolò di Jacopo di Panuzio *rigattiere*

Capitani di Parte Guelfa

Bernardo di Agnolo di Isaia Martellini
Braccio di Giovanni di Braccio *lanaiolo*
Francesco di Piero di Paolo Lotti

Giovanni di Zanobi del Cica *vinattiere*
Ricciardo di Giachinotto Cavalcanti

Filippo di Paolo di M. Paolo Rucellai
Ridolfo di Uguccione di Dante Giandonati

Giovanni di Pellegrino di Ubaldo Cattani
Stagio di Lionardo di Nicola [*linaiolo*]

Otto di Guardia

Bertoldo di Gherardo di M. Filippo Corsini
Paolo di Antonio Parigi *galigaio*

Tommaso di Lorenzo di Ceffo di Masino Ceffi
Giovanni di Miniato di Dino *coreggiaio*

Federigo di Jacopo di Francesco Federighi
Filippo di Lionardo Bartoli

Nicolaio di Ugo degli Alessandri
Bernardo di Antonio de' Medici

Ufficiali del Monte

Giovanni di Stefano Corsini
Bernardo di Jacopo di Bartolo Ciacchi
Giovanni di Betto di Giovanni Rustichi
Antonio di Niccolò di Ugolino Martelli
Giovanni del Zaccaria di Jacopo *coltriciaio*

Massai di Camera

Giuliano di Niccolò di Antonio Ridolfi
Francesco di Giovanni di Piero Dini
Francesco di Jacopo di Francesco Ventura
Bartolo di Tedaldo Tedaldi
Salvestro di Zanobi di Niccolò del Cica *vinattiere*

Sei di Mercanzia

Francesco di Giannozzo degli Alberti
Filippo di Stoldo di Luca Rinieri
Lorenzo di Gino Capponi
Matteo di Morello di Paolo Morelli
Francesco di Baldino di Gianni Inghirami
Giovanni di Andrea Petrini *albergatore*

Ufficiali del Catasto

Bernardo di M. Lorenzo Ridolfi
Lorenzo di Parigi di Tommaso Corbinelli
Francesco del Nero di Filippo del Nero *rigattiere*

Giano di Marchionne di Giano Torrigiani
Bernardo del Maestro Galileo di Giovanni Galilei
Domenico di Lionardo Boninsegni

Simone di Mattio di Pier Cini *ferraiolo*
Andrea di Filippo di Giovanni Carducci

Gentile di Ghino di M. Ruberto Cortigiani
Andrea di Cresci di Lorenzo di Cresci

Accoppiatori from 1434 onwards

1434

Pero di Dino Peri *galigaio*
Neri di Domenico Bartolini [Scodellari]
Nerone di Nigi di Nerone Dietisalvi [Neroni]

1440

M. Giovannozzo di Francesco Pitti
Cosimo di Giovanni de' Medici

1443

Giovanni di Antonio di Jacopo Canigiani
Francesco di Bonaccorso Corsellini *ottonaio*
M. Bernardo di Filippo Giugni
Antonio di Ser Tommaso Masi
M. Domenico di Niccolò di Ugolino Martelli

1444

Tommaso di Lorenzo Soderini
Francesco di Cambio Orlandi
M. Manno di Giovanni Temperani
Dietisalvi di Nerone di Nigi Dietisalvi [Neroni]
Ugolino di Niccolò di Ugolino Martelli
Niccolò di Zanobi Bonvanni *beccaio*

1448

Luigi di M. Lorenzo Ridolfi
Bernardo di Bartolomeo di Gherardo Gherardi
Martino di Francesco dello Scarfa
Piero di Cosimo di Giovanni de' Medici
M. Agnolo di Jacopo Acciaiuoli
Antonio di Lenzone di Simone [Lenzoni] *galigaio*
Lionardo di Bartolomeo Bartolini
Agnolo di Lorenzo di Andrea di M. Ugo della Stufa—in place
   of his father

Accoppiatori of the scrutiny of 1458

Luigi di Piero di M. Luigi Guicciardini
Piero di Gregorio di Andrea del Benino

M. Otto di Lapo di Giovanni Niccolini
Lodovico di Cece da Verrazzano

Giovanni di Domenico Bartoli

M. Alessandro di Ugo degli Alessandri
Matteo di Marco di Antonio Palmieri
Bartolomeo di Francesco di Ser Andrea *corazzaio*

Secretari from 1434 onwards

1434

Tommaso di Antonio di Ser Tommaso Redditi

1440

Simone di Paolo di Berto Carnesecchi

1443

Giovanni di Lapo Niccolini
M. Donato di Niccolò di Cocco Donati
Manetto di Zanobi Carnesecchi
Benedetto di Puccino di Ser Andrea *armaiolo*

Collegi acting as Secretari, 1443

Niccolò di Andrea di Niccolò Giugni
Francesco di Piero di Francesco Ginori

1444

Giovanni di Salvatore di Tommaso del Caccia

1448

Ruberto di Bonaccorso di Neri Pitti
Lorenzo di Lapo Niccolini
Piero di Simone di Mariotto Orlandini
Francesco di Lorenzo Cigliamocchi
Niccolò di Bartolomeo Bartolini
Giuliano di Particino di Giovanni *albergatore*
Giovanni di Antonio Lorini
Andrea di Lotteringo di Andrea di M. Ugo della Stufa

Collegi acting as Secretari, 1448

Antonio di Puccio di Antonio Pucci
Stefano di Francesco di Giovanni Segni

1454

Gino di Neri di Gino Capponi
Alessandro di Filippo Machiavelli

Carlo di Zanobi da Ghiacceto
Nofri di Giovanni di Bondì del Caccia

Alessandro di Antonio di Jacopo del Vigna

Giovanni di Cosimo de' Medici

Salvestro di Michele Lapi
Benci di Niccolò di Paolo Benci *vinattiere*

Collegi acting as Secretari, 1454

Niccolò di Bartolino di Niccolò Bartolini
Niccolò di Giovanni di Jacopo Nasi
Niccolò di Giano Berardi

Secretari of the scrutiny of 1458

Bonaccorso di Luca di Bonaccorso Pitti
Giovannozzo di Betto di Giovannozzo Biliotti

Franco di Nicol di Franco Sacchetti
Giovanni di Antonio di Salvestro Serristori

Bartolomeo di Lorenzo di Piero Lenzi
Guglielmo di Cardinale Rucellai

Francesco di Jacopo Monti *ferravecchio*
M. Carlo di Agnolo di Filippo Pandolfini

Proconsul of the Guild of Judges and Notaries

Ser Giovanni di Ser Andrea Mini

Previous Proconsul

Ser Niccolò di Michele di Feo Dini

Arroti

S. SPIRITO

Francesco di Piero [di Tommaso] Alamanni
Alberto di Antonio di Nicola di Lippo Alberti
Bernardo di Tommaso [di Francesco] Antinori
Piero di Niccolò di Andrea del Benino
Zanobi di Sandro di Giovanni Biliotti
Niccolò di Giovanni di Jacopo Bini
Simone di Nofri Bonaccorsi
Francesco di Donato di Ugolino Bonsi
Antonio di Lotteringo Boverelli
Cristofano di Filippo del Buglaffo
Niccolò di Giovanni di Mico Capponi
Filippo di Giovanni Corbinelli

M. Tommaso di Guido di Tommaso Deti
Ridolfo di Giovanni di Ser Falcone Falconi
Jacopo di Piero di M. Luigi Guicciardini
Giovanni di Jacopo [di Filippo] Guidetti
Jacopo di Orsino [di Lanfredino] Lanfredini
Benedetto di Bernardo di Uguccione Lippi
Mariotto di Dinozzo di Stefano Lippi
Antonio di Ridolfo di Paolo Lotti
Piero di M. Francesco Machiavelli
Bernardo di Sala di Filippo Marsili
Zanobi di Piero di M. Zanobi da Mezzola
Lutozo di Jacopo di Lutozo Nasi
Tanai di Francesco [di Filippo] de' Nerli
Nerozzo di Piero di Filippo del Nero
Bernardo di Antonio di Jacopo Paganelli
Luigi di Bonaccorso di Neri Pitti
Castello di Piero [di Castello] Quaratesi
Luigi di Giovanni di Ligi Quaratesi
Jacopo di Pagnozzo Ridolfi
Niccolò di Schiatta [di Uberto] Ridolfi
Bernardo di Antonio di Scarlatto di Nuto [Scarlatti]
Niccolò di Lorenzo [di M. Tommaso] Soderini
Gregorio di Antonio di Ubaldo di Fetto Ubertini
Giorgio di Niccolò di Luca di Feo Ugolini
Agnolo di Neri di M. Andrea Vettori
Paolo di Giannozzo Vettori

Artigiani

Agnolino di Guglielmo di Agnolino *pezzaio*
Benedetto di Baldo di Benedetto *linaiolo*
Spinello di Francesco del Buono Bramanti *beccaio*
Como di Giuliano di Agostino di Como *biadaiolo*
Bartolomeo di Agostino Coppini *linaiolo*
Francesco di Aringo di Corso *calzolaio*
Andrea di Francesco del Gaburro *beccaio*
Giovanni di Piero di Bartolomeo [Pieri] *scodellaio*
Giovanni del Rosso di Piero del Rosso *fornaciaio*
Taddeo di Antonio di Martino di Sasso *brigliaio*
Bartolomeo di Antonio di Andrea Tazzi *coreggiaio*
Giunta di Antonio Torrigiani *vinattiere*

S. CROCE

Matteo di Antonio [di Tommaso] degli Alberti
Giovanni di Taddeo [di Giovanni] dell'Antella

Francesco di Rinieri [di Bardo] Bagnesi
Lorenzo di Agnolo [di Francesco] Baroncelli
Michele di M. Piero Benini
Mariotto di Lorenzo di Marco Benvenuti
Berlinghieri di Francesco [di Francesco] Berlinghieri
Girolamo di Francesco di Taddeo Bischeri
Zanobi di Riccardo [di Zanobi] Borgognoni
Francesco di Tommaso di Francesco Busini
Pierantonio di Nofri di Salvestro Cennini
Jacopo di Bernardo di Jacopo Ciacchi
Jacopo di Matteo [di Domenico] Corsi
Jacopo di Niccolò di Cocco Donati
Attaviano di Piero Gerini
Orlando di Bartolomeo di Gherardo Gherardi
Zanobi di Paolo di Zanobi da Ghiacceto
Paolo di Giorgio del Maestro Cristofano di Giorgio
Bernardo di Giovanni [di Lionardo] Jacopi
Luigi di Francesco di Biagio Lioni
Lotto di Duccino [di Lotto] Mancini
Bastiano di Matteo di Antonio Martini
Piero di Francesco [di Duccio] Mellini
Morello di Paolo [di Morello] Morelli
Piero di Salvestro di Michele Nardi
Chirico di Giovanni di Franceschino Pepi
Gerozzo di Jacopo di Latino de' Pilli
Gherardo di Geri [di Gherardo] Risaliti
Tommaso di Ubertino [di Gherardo] Risaliti
Jacopo di Nicol di Franco Sacchetti
M. Tommaso di Ser Jacopo Salvetti
Francesco di Alamanno Salviati
Lotto di Giovanni di M. Forese Salviati
Niccolò di Antonio di Salvestro Serristori
Cristofano di Bartolomeo di Bonsignore Spinelli
Francesco di Lorenzo [di Antonio] Spinelli
Cece di Frosino di Cece da Verrazzano
Andrea di Francesco di M. Giovanni Zati

Artigiani

Francesco di Michele Becchi *fibbiaio*
Matteo di Andrea di Bonsi *vinattiere*
Coppo di Guido Cafferelli *coreggiaio*
Andrea di Giovanni di Ser Niccolò del Cappa *coreggiaio*
Antonio di Bernardo di Miniato di Dino *coreggiaio*
Cherubino di Francesco Galluzzi *biadaiolo*
Andrea di Lapo Guardi *coreggiaio*

Bastiano di Domenico Lulli *corazzaio*
Antonio di Pero di Dino [Peri] *coreggiaio*
Niccolò di Francesco Salvetti *borsaio*
Luca di Lorenzo di Luca Salvucci [*coreggiaio*]
Bartolomeo di Jacopo del Zaccaria *coltriciaio*

S. MARIA NOVELLA

Lodovico di Adouardo Acciaiuoli
Piero di Neri di M. Donato Acciaiuoli
Bardo di Guglielmo [di Bardo] Altoviti
Simone di Giovanni di Simone di M. Tommaso Altoviti
Piero di Mariotto [di Piero] di Cenni dell'Amorotto
Francesco di Marco di Tommaso Bartoli
Marco di Tommaso di Marco Bartoli
Boccaccio di Niccolò di Boccaccio
Alessandro di Luigi [di Alessandro] del Nero Cambi
Andrea di Niccolò di Andrea Carducci
Tommaso di Piero di Nicolaio Davanzati
Domenico di Jacopo di Francesco Federighi
Gherardo di Bongianni Gianfigliazzi
Carlo di Salvestro [di Simone] Gondi
Francesco di Zanobi Lapaccini [del Toso]
Francesco di Lorenzo di Piero Lenzi
Piero di Niccolò di Tommaso Malegonnelle
Jacopo di Ugolino di Jacopo Mazzinghi
Piero di Giovanni di Andrea Minerbetti
Lorenzo di M. Andrea da Montebuoni
Niccolò di Giovanni di Bartolo di More
Cesare di Domenico di Tano Petrucci
Giovanni di Salvestro [di Tommaso] Popoleschi
Bernardo di Piero di Cardinale Rucellai
Niccolò di Brancazio Rucellai
Giovanni di Martino di Bencivenni dello Scarfa
Cipriano di Chimenti di Cipriano Sernigi
Giovanni di Guccio di Andrea da Sommaia
Giovanni di Antonio di Pecorella Spini
Benedetto di Francesco di Benedetto Strozzi
Giacomino di Tommaso di Giacomino di Goggio [Tebalducci]
Filippo di Filippo di M. Simone Tornabuoni
Niccolò di Francesco [di M. Simone] Tornabuoni
Marsilio di Bernardo [di Vanni] Vecchietti
Giovanni di Jacopo di Francesco Ventura
Bernardo di Piero [di Simone] Vespucci
Giuliano di Lapo Vespucci
Bartolomeo di Antonio di Jacopo del Vigna

Artigiani

Giovanni di Antonio di Jacopo di Agnolo *oliandolo*
Santi di Simone Ambrogi *pezzaio*
Francesco di Paolo Canacci *legnaiolo*
Carlo di Giovanni [di Salvestro] Carradori *rigattiere*
Giovanni di Guarente di Giovanni Guarenti *maestro*
Antonio di Domenico Lenzi *armaiolo*
Manetto di Andrea di Manetto *ferravecchio*
Monte di Jacopo Monti *ferravecchio*
Piero di Jacopo di Francesco Neretti *linaiolo*
Paolo di Pasquino di Francesco Pasquini *ferraiolo*
Jacopo di Giovanni Torsellini *bottaio*
Niccolò di Cenni di Vanni *ferraiolo*

S. GIOVANNI

Antonio di Luca di M. Maso degli Albizzi
Lucantonio di Niccolò di Luca degli Albizzi
Maso di Luca di M. Maso degli Albizzi
Giovanni di Aldobrandino di Giorgio di Aldobrandino [del
   Nero]
Jacopo di Uberto di Jacopo Arrighi
Arrigo di Filippo [di Arrigo] Arrigucci
Francesco di Bartolomeo [di Tommaso] Baldovini
Amerigo di Giovanni di Amerigo Benci
Salvestro di Bartolomeo del Maestro Benvenuto
Giovanni di Bono di Giovanni [Boni] *banchiere*
Antonio di Cambino Cambini
Niccolò di Matteo di Niccolò Cerretani
Lorenzo di Cresci di Lorenzo di Cresci
Francesco di Nerone di Nigi Dietisalvi [Neroni]
Battista di Berto da Filicaia
Francesco di Piero di Francesco Gherucci
Jacopo di Guccio Ghiberti
Zanobi di Tommaso di Zanobi Ginori
Francesco di Antonio [di Francesco] Giraldi
Antonio di Migliore [di Tommaso] Guidotti
Tommaso di Giovanni di Tommaso Lapi
Bernardo di Taddeo [di Bartolomeo[1]] Lorini
Zanobi di Piero di Zanobi Marignolli
Duti di Antonio di Ser Tommaso Masi
Pierfrancesco di Lorenzo [di Giovanni] de' Medici
Filippo di Migliore di Giunta Migliori
Giovanni di M. Bartolomeo di Giovanni Orlandini

---

[1] MS.: di Filippo.

Francesco di Andrea di Frosino [da Panzano] *lanaiolo*
Piero di M. Andrea de' Pazzi
Bartolomeo di Guidaccio [di Jacopo] Pecori
Saracino di Antonio Pucci
Antonio di Michele [di Niccolò] da Rabatta
Maso di Geri [di Maso] della Rena
Antonio di Matteo di Gucciozzo de' Ricci
Matteo di Borgo di Rinaldo Rinaldi
Ruberto del Mancino Sostegni
Giovenco di Lorenzo di Andrea della Stufa
Matteo di Jacopo di Giovanni Villani

Artigiani

Andrea di Francesco di Ser Andrea *corazzaio*
Niccolò di Benintendi di Andrea Benintendi *rigattiere*
Zanobi di Jacopo [di Niccolò] Bucherelli *linaiolo*
Cambino di Francesco Cambini *linaiolo*
Lorenzo di Giovanni di Ser Piero Centellini *corazzaio*
Bartolomeo di Cinozzo di Giovanni Cini *linaiolo*
Domenico di Zanobi del Giocondo *bottaio*
Giovanni di Ser Lapo Mazzei *corazzaio*
Apollonio di Biagio di Niccolò Monti *albergatore*
Salvestro di Lionardo di Puccio *vinattiere*
Romolo di Andrea di Nofri Romoli *lastraiolo*
Bartolomeo di Ser Antonio di Baldino del Troscia *albergatore*

VII

BALÌA OF 1466

(Balìe, 30, fols. 8ʳ–12ʳ)

Signoria

Mattio di Filippo di Giovanni Ciari
Bernardo di Francesco di Bernardo Paganelli

Salvestro di Zanobi di Niccolò del Cica *vinattiere*
Zanobi di Jacopo di Benintendi Falemagini *oliandolo*

Giovanni di Cardinale di Piero Rucellai
Bencivenni di Piero di Bencivenni Grazzini

Bartolomeo di Niccolò di Ugolino Martelli
Filippo di Ser Jacopo di Ser Filippo da Lutiano

Ruberto di Francesco di Biagio Lioni (Gonfalonier of Justice)

Sedici Gonfalonieri[1] (*until 7 September*)

Lorenzo di Bartolomeo di Lorenzo Gualterotti
Tommaso di Filippo di Giacchi di Michele Giacchi
Piero di Niccolò di Lodovico del Bon Rinucci
Bernardo di Giovanni di Noso Fantoni *vinattiere*

(*from 8 September to 31 December*)

Niccolò di Stefano Corsellini *ottonaio*
Vieri di Ugolino di Vieri
Bartolomeo di Donato di Ugolino Bonsi

Antonio di Federigo di Niccolò Gori
Alberto di Bernardo di Zanobi di Ser Zello
Gabriele di Michele Becchi *fibbiaio*
Giovanni di Filippo di Niccolò Giugni

Ser Niccolò di Michele di Feo Dini *galigaio*
Ruggieri di Tommaso di Andrea Minerbetti
Marsilio di Bernardo di Vanni Vecchietti

---

[1] The remaining members of the *Sedici* are listed among the *veduti* Gonfaloniers of Justice.

Piero di Simone di Paolo di Berto Carnesecchi
Filippo di Francesco di Giovanni Calandri *corazzaio*
Giovanni di Borromeo Borromei

Dodici Buonuomini[1] (*until 14 September*)

Nicol di Andreuolo di Nicol Sacchetti
Giano di Marchionne di Giano Torrigiani
Zanobi di Pasquino di Francesco Pasquini *ferraiolo*
Rinaldo di Berto di Francesco da Filicaia

(*from 15 September until 14 December*)

Salvestro di Ruberto di Bonaccorso Pitti
Giovanni di Corsino di Jacopo Corsini
Cristofano di Giuliano di Cristofano [di Lorenzo] *legnaiolo*

M. Biagio di Lapo di Giovanni Niccolini
Giovanni di Tommaso di Francesco Busini

Lorenzo di Piero di Nicolaio Davanzati
Bartolomeo di Tommaso Sassetti
Ardito di Ardito di Francesco Arditi *fabbro*

Antonio di Bono di Giovanni Boni
Lorenzo di Giovanni di Ser Piero Centellini *corazzaio*

Arroti

S. SPIRITO

*Andrea di Francesco di Piero Alamanni
*Bernardo di Tommaso di Francesco Antinori
 Pegolotto di Bernardo di Pegolotto Balducci
*Francesco di Niccolò di Andrea del Benino
*Piero di Niccolò di Andrea del Benino
 Tommaso di Tommaso di Gualtieri Biliotti
*Zanobi di Sandro di Giovanni Biliotti
 Piero di Giovanni di Jacopo di Piero Bini
 Bernardo di Baldassare di Bernardo Bonsi
*Antonio di Lotteringo Boverelli
*Cristofano di Filippo di Cristofano del Buglaffo
*Daniello di Luigi di Piero Canigiani
*Giovanni di Antonio di Jacopo Canigiani
*Agostino di Gino Capponi
*Gino di Neri di Gino Capponi

[1]The remaining members of the *Dodici* are listed among the *veduti* Gonfaloniers of Justice.
* Member of the *Balìa* as *veduto* Gonfalonier of Justice.

  *Lorenzo di Gino di Neri Capponi
  *Niccolò di Giovanni di Mico Capponi
  *Nicola di Piero di Bartolomeo Capponi
   Recco di Uguccione di Mico Capponi
  *Bernardo di Tommaso di Bartolomeo Corbinelli
  *Lorenzo di Parigi di Tommaso Corbinelli
  *M. Tommaso di Guido Deti
  *Ridolfo di Giovanni di Ser Falcone Falconi
   Antonio di Lionardo di Francesco Ferrucci
   Giacchi di Filippo Giacchi
   Tommaso di Francesco di Tommaso Giovanni
   Francesco di Lorenzo di Giovanni Grasso
   Piero di Bartolomeo di Lorenzo di Totto Gualterotti
  *Jacopo di Piero di M. Luigi Guicciardini
  *M. Luigi di Piero di M. Luigi Guicciardini
   Jacopo di Orsino di Lanfredino Lanfredini
  *Mariotto di Dinozzo di Stefano Lippi
   Uguccione di Bernardo di Uguccione Lippi
 *†Bernardo di Paolo di Ridolfo Lotti
  *Alessandro di Filippo di Lorenzo Machiavelli
   Paolo di Giovanni di Lorenzo Machiavelli
   Filippo di Piero di Bernardo Magli
   Lionardo di Niccolò Mannelli
   Bernardo di Sala di Filippo Marsili
   Lorenzo di Lutozo di Jacopo Nasi
  *Tanai di Francesco di Filippo de' Nerli
   Bernardo di Antonio di Bernardo Paganelli
  *Bonaccorso di M. Luca di Bonaccorso Pitti
  *M. Giovannozzo di Francesco Pitti
  *M. Luca di Bonaccorso di Neri Pitti
  *Luigi di Bonaccorso di Neri Pitti
  *Ruberto di Bonaccorso di Neri Pitti
   Filippo di Francesco di Jacopo del Puglese
  *Luigi di Giovanni di Ligi Quaratesi
  *M. Antonio di M. Lorenzo di Antonio Ridolfi
  *Bernardo di M. Lorenzo di Antonio Ridolfi
  *Giovanni di M. Lorenzo di Antonio Ridolfi
  *Jacopo di Pagnozzo Ridolfi
   Jacopo di Paolo di Bartolo di Schiatta Ridolfi
   Bono di Niccolò di Lodovico di Bono Rinucci
  *Lorenzo di M. Tommaso di Lorenzo Soderini
 *†Niccolò di Lorenzo di M. Tommaso Soderini

        * Member of the *Balìa* as *veduto* Gonfalonier of Justice.
        † Cancelled, with marginal note: *privatus*.

*M. Tommaso di Lorenzo di M. Tommaso Soderini
*Giorgio di Niccolò di Luca di Feo Ugolini
*Agnolo di Neri di M. Andrea Vettori
*Lorenzo di Neri di Agnolo Vettori

Artigiani

Giovanni di Biagio di Agnolo *bicchieraio*
Nicola di Antonio di Antonio *galigaio*
Simone di Antonio di Simone Benozzi *vinattiere*
Bartolomeo di Francesco del Buono Bramanti *beccaio*
Giuliano di Agostino di Como *biadaiolo*
Francesco di Bonaccorso Corsellini *ottonaio*
Corso di Niccolò di Aringo di Corso *calzolaio*
Michele di Corso di Lorenzo [di Covero] delle Colombe *oliandolo*
Francesco di Simone di Noso Fantoni *vinattiere*
Lorenzo di Marco di Lorenzo ⟨Bruciolo⟩ *legnaiolo*
Michelozzo di Bartolomeo di Giovanni Michelozzi *coreggiaio*
Bernardo del Nero di Filippo del Nero *rigattiere*
Bartolomeo di Ser Piero Nuti *oliandolo*
Giovanni di Andrea Petrini *albergatore*
Piero di Giovanni di Piero di Bartolomeo Pieri *scodellaio*
Rosso di Piero di Antonio del Rosso *fornaciaio*
Taddeo di Antonio di Martino di Sasso *brigliaio*
Soldo di Antonio di Andrea del Soldato *coreggiaio*
Luca di Antonio di Biagio Torrigiani *vinattiere*

S. CROCE

Matteo di Antonio di Tommaso degli Alberti
*Giovanni di Taddeo dell'Antella
Lodovico di Taddeo di Giovanni dell'Antella
*Francesco di Rinieri di Bardo Bagnesi
Lorenzo di Agnolo di Francesco Baroncelli
*Mariotto di Lorenzo di Marco Benvenuti
*Berlinghieri di Francesco di Francesco Berlinghieri
Zanobi di Riccardo di Zanobi Borgognoni
Francesco di Tommaso di Francesco Busini
*Giovanni di Salvatore di Tommaso del Caccia
Zanobi di Francesco di Zanobi Cafferelli
Donato di M. Carlo Cavallereschi
Piero di Lorenzo di Ceffo di Masino Ceffi
Mauro di Salvestro di Lodovico Ceffini
Pierantonio di Nofri di Salvestro Cennini
Bernardo di Jacopo di Bartolo Ciacchi

* Member of the *Balìa* as *veduto* Gonfalonier of Justice.

*Bardo di Bartolo di Domenico Corsi
*Francesco di Piero di Giovanni Dini
*Francesco di Niccolò di Cocco Donati
*Jacopo di Niccolò di Cocco Donati
  Benedetto del Maestro Galileo di Giovanni Galilei
*Bartolomeo di Gherardo di Bartolomeo Gherardi
*Orlando di Bartolomeo di Gherardo Gherardi
*Carlo di Zanobi di Paolo da Ghiacceto
*Zanobi di Paolo di Zanobi da Ghiacceto
  Domenico di Giovanni di Domenico Giugni
  Niccolò di Andrea di Niccolò Giugni
  Zanobi di Giovanni di Lionardo Jacopi
  Lionardo di Domenico di Niccolò Magaldi
*Lotto di Duccino di Lotto Mancini
*Piero di Francesco di Duccio Mellini
*Girolamo di Matteo di Morello di Paolo Morelli
*Matteo di Morello di Paolo Morelli
*Morello di Paolo di Morello di Paolo Morelli
*Salvestro di Andrea di Salvestro Nardi
*Lorenzo di Lapo di Giovanni Niccolini
*M. Otto di Lapo di Giovanni Niccolini
*Paolo di Lapo di Giovanni Niccolini
  Giovanni di Simone di Mariotto Orlandini
*Chirico di Giovanni di Franceschino Pepi
  Alamanno di Filippo di Cino Rinuccini
*Tommaso di Ubertino di Gherardo Risaliti
*Franco di Nicol di Franco Sacchetti
*Jacopo di Nicol di Franco Sacchetti
  Giovanni di Alamanno di M. Jacopo Salviati
*Lotto di Giovanni di M. Forese Salviati
*Giovanni di Antonio di Salvestro Serristori
*Niccolò di Antonio di Salvestro Serristori
*Ristoro di Antonio di Salvestro Serristori
  Bernardo di Bonaccorso di Niccolò Soldani
*Cristofano di Bartolomeo di Bonsignore Spinelli
*Francesco di Lorenzo di Antonio Spinelli
  Giovanni di Marchionne di Giano Torrigiani
*Bartolomeo di Lodovico di Cece da Verrazzano
*Cece di Frosino di Cece da Verrazzano

Artigiani

Francesco di Michele Becchi *fibbiaio*
Benintendi di Jacopo di Benintendi Falemagini *oliandolo*

    * Member of the *Balìa* as *veduto* Gonfalonier of Justice.

Giovanni di Betto di Giovanni [Betti] *vinattiere*
Matteo di Andrea di Bonsi *linaiolo*
Mariotto di Lodovico di Cristofano Cerrini *coltriciaio*
Zanobi di Zanobi di Niccolò del Cica *vinattiere*
Bernardo di Bucello di Bucello del Corso *vinattiere*
Antonio di Bernardo di Miniato di Dino *coreggiaio*
Cherubino di Francesco di Bernardo Galluzzi *coltriciaio*
Antonio di Giovanni di Bartolo Grazia *linaiolo*
Neri di Antonio di Segna Guidi *corazzaio*
Guido di Ser Giovanni di Guido Guiducci *oliandolo*
Agnolo di Francesco di Lorenzo [Miniati] *coreggiaio*
Antonio di Pero di Dino Peri *galigaio*
Ser Ricciardo di Piero di Ser Ricciardo Pieri *rigattiere*
Andrea di Niccolò di Francesco Salvetti *coreggiaio*
Luca di Lorenzo di Luca Salvucci *coreggiaio*
Bartolomeo di Domenico di Filippo Telli *pianellaio*
Bartolomeo di Jacopo di Jacopo del Zaccaria *coltriciaio*

S. MARIA NOVELLA

*†M. Agnolo di Jacopo Acciaiuoli
*†Jacopo di M. Agnolo di Jacopo Acciaiuoli
 *Piero di Neri di M. Donato Acciaiuoli
 *Bardo di Guglielmo di Bardo Altoviti
*†Ruberto di Giovanni di Simone di M. Tommaso Altoviti
 *Simone di Giovanni di Simone di M. Tommaso Altoviti
 *Domenico di Giovanni di Domenico Bartoli
 *Filippo di Lionardo di Marco Bartoli
 *Lionardo di Bartolomeo di Lionardo Bartolini
 *Niccolò di Berardo di Bonaccorso Berardi
  Piero di Berardo di Bonaccorso Berardi
  Bartolomeo di Federigo di Boccaccio
*†Guido di Carlo di Gagliardo Bonciani
 *Simone di Gagliardo di Carlo Bonciani
  Bernardo di Giovanni di Domenico Cambi
 *Andrea di Niccolò di Andrea Carducci
  Carlo di Niccolò di Andrea Carducci
 *Francesco di Lorenzo Cigliamocchi
  Giovanni di Cante di Giovanni Compagni
 *Tommaso di Piero di Nicolaio Davanzati
  Tommaso di Domenico di Tommaso Faggiuoli
 *Federigo di Jacopo di Francesco Federighi
 *Francesco di M. Carlo di Francesco Federighi

* Member of the *Balìa* as *veduto* Gonfalonier of Justice.
† Cancelled, with marginal note: *privatus*.

*Paolo di Jacopo di Francesco Federighi
 Tommaso di Giovanni di Ser Luca Franceschi
 Bongianni di Bongianni di Giovanni Gianfigliazzi
*†Carlo di Salvestro di Simone Gondi
 Benedetto di Benedetto Lapaccini [del Toso]
*Bartolomeo di Lorenzo di Piero Lenzi
*Piero di Niccolò di Tommaso Malegonnelle
*Jacopo di Ugolino di Jacopo Mazzinghi
*Andrea di Tommaso di Andrea Minerbetti
*Piero di Giovanni di Andrea Minerbetti
 Lorenzo di M. Andrea da Montebuoni
 Antonio di Lionardo di Antonio de' Nobili
*Guccio di Niccolò di M. Guccio de' Nobili
 Antonio di Michele di Benedetto [di Ser Michele] Pescioni
 Cesare di Domenico di Tano Petrucci
*Giovanni di Paolo di M. Paolo Rucellai
*Guglielmo di Cardinale di Piero Rucellai
*Niccolò di Brancazio Rucellai
*Giovanni di Martino di Francesco dello Scarfa
*Martino di Francesco di Bencivenni dello Scarfa
 Cipriano di Chimenti di Cipriano Sernigi
 Agnolo di M. Palla di M. Palla Strozzi
*†Giacomino di Tommaso di Giacomino di Goggio [Tebalducci]
 Piero di Giovanni di Giacomino di Goggio [Tebalducci]
*Giovanni di M. Manno di Temperano di Manno [Temperani]
*M. Manno di Giovanni di Temperano di Manno [Temperani]
*Filippo di Filippo di M. Simone Tornabuoni
*Niccolò di Francesco di M. Simone Tornabuoni
 Salvatore di Vanni di Niccolò Vecchietti
*Giovanni di Jacopo di Francesco Ventura
 Bindo di Agnolo di Bindo Vernaccia
*Bernardo di Piero di Simone Vespucci
 Piero di Giuliano di Lapo Vespucci
*Bartolomeo di Antonio di Jacopo del Vigna

Artigiani

Francesco di Niccolò di Agnolo *pezzaio*
Giovanni di Antonio di Jacopo di Agnolo *oliandolo*
Santi di Simone Ambrogi *pezzaio*
Andrea di Manetto di Andrea *ferravecchio*
Antonio di Guasparre di Giovanni dal Borgo *coreggiaio*
Francesco di Paolo Canacci *maestro*
Simone di Mattio di Pier Cini *ferraiolo*

> * Member of the *Balìa* as *veduto* Gonfalonier of Justice.
> † Cancelled, with marginal note: *privatus*.

Bartolomeo di Brancazio di Michele di Feo Dini *galigaio*
Giuliano di Particino di Giovanni *albergatore*
Giovanni di Guarente di Giovanni Guarenti *maestro*
Sandro di Antonio di Domenico Lenzi *corazzaio*
Antonio di Lenzone di Simone Lenzoni *galigaio*
Monte di Jacopo Monti *ferravecchio*
Piero di Jacopo di Francesco Neretti *linaiolo*
Giovanni di Stagio di Lionardo di Nicola *linaiolo*
Domenico di Giovanni di Cristofano di Ser Gianni Pannilini
  linaiolo
Paolo di Pasquino di Francesco Pasquini *ferraiolo*
Niccolò di Cenni di Vanni *ferraiolo*
Filippo di Jacopo di Michele dalla Volta *ferraiolo*

S. GIOVANNI

*Antonio di Luca di M. Maso degli Albizzi
*Maso di Luca di M. Maso degli Albizzi
*Giovanni di Aldobrandino di Giorgio [di Aldobrandino] del
  Nero di Madonna
*Maso di Nicolaio di Ugo degli Alessandri
Jacopo di Uberto di Jacopo Arrighi
*Domenico di Neri di Domenico Bartolini Scodellari
*Neri di Domenico Bartolini Scodellari
*Amerigo di Giovanni di Amerigo Benci
Bono di Giovanni Boni *cambiatore*
Bartolomeo di Lorenzo di Bartolomeo di Ser Santi Bruni
Francesco di Niccolò di Francesco Cambini
*Antonio di Paolo di Berto Carnesecchi
Francesco di Berto di Zanobi Carnesecchi
Agnolo di Pigello Cavicciuli
*Niccolò di Matteo di Niccolò Cerretani
Ridolfo di Jacopo di Ser Francesco Ciai
Francesco di Gentile di Ghino Cortigiani
*Andrea di Cresci di Lorenzo di Cresci
*Lorenzo di Cresci di Lorenzo di Cresci
*†M. Dietisalvi di Nerone di Nigi Dietisalvi [Neroni]
*†Francesco di Nerone di Nigi Dietisalvi [Neroni]
*†Nigi di Nerone di Nigi Dietisalvi [Neroni]
Battista di Berto di Francesco da Filicaia
*Francesco di Piero di Francesco Ginori
*Zanobi di Tommaso di Zanobi Ginori
*Francesco di Baldino di Gianni Inghirami

* Member of the *Balìa* as *veduto* Gonfalonier of Justice.
† Cancelled, with marginal note: *privatus*.

*Salvestro di Michele di Salvestro Lapi
 Tommaso di Giovanni di Tommaso Lapi
 Bernardo di Taddeo di Bartolomeo Lorini
*Giovanni di Antonio di Filippo Lorini
*Antonio di Niccolò di Ugolino Martelli
*M. Domenico di Niccolò di Ugolino Martelli
*Ugolino di Niccolò di Ugolino Martelli
 Tommaso di Antonio di Tommaso di Guccio Martini
*Antonio di Ser Tommaso Masi
 Duti di Antonio di Ser Tommaso Masi
*Alamanno di Bernardo di Alamanno de' Medici
*Carlo di Nicola di M. Vieri de' Medici
*Lorenzo di Piero di Cosimo di Giovanni de' Medici
*Pierfrancesco di Lorenzo di Giovanni de' Medici
*Giovanni di M. Bartolomeo di Giovanni Orlandini
*Matteo di Marco di Antonio Palmieri
*M. Carlo di Agnolo di Filippo Pandolfini
 Domenico di M. Carlo di Agnolo Pandolfini
 Guglielmo di Antonio di M. Andrea de' Pazzi
*Jacopo di M. Andrea di Guglielmino de' Pazzi
*Antonio di Puccio di Antonio Pucci
 Antonio di Michele di Niccolò da Rabatta
*Maso di Geri di Maso della Rena
 Girolamo di Gentile di Michele Ristori
*Agnolo di Lorenzo di Andrea di M. Ugo della Stufa
*Andrea di Lotteringo di Andrea di M. Ugo della Stufa
*Giovenco di Lorenzo di Andrea di M. Ugo della Stufa
*Antonio di Taddeo di Filippo di Taddeo
 Bartolomeo di Filippo di Bartolomeo Valori
 Giovanni di Jacopo di Giovanni Villani

Artigiani

Benedetto di Puccino di Ser Andrea *corazzaio*
Niccolò di Giovanni di Sandro Barbigia *fabbro*
Bartolomeo di Giovanni Baroncini *spadaio*
Benci di Niccolò di Paolo Benci *vinattiere*
Niccolò di Benintendi di Andrea [Benintendi] *rigattiere*
Giuliano di Ser Bonaccorso di Piero di Bonaccorso *corazzaio*
Niccolò di Zanobi Bonvanni *beccaio*
Zanobi di Jacopo di Niccolò Bucherelli *linaiolo*
Francesco di Michele di Jacopo [di Vanni] Cittadini *corazzaio*
Domenico di Zanobi del Giocondo *bottaio*
Zanobi di Ser Jacopo di Bonaiuto Landi *cassettaio*
Giovanni di Andrea di Lodovico Lapini *beccaio*

* Member of the *Balìa* as *veduto* Gonfalonier of Justice.

Pero di Bartolo di Pero di Ligi *calderaio*
Giovanni di Bartolomeo di Gherardo Marucelli *maliscalco*
Mazzeo di Giovanni di Ser Lapo Mazzei *corazzaio*
Niccolò di Jacopo di Panuzio *rigattiere*
Francesco di Ramondo di Piero *albergatore*
Romolo di Andrea di Nofri Romoli *maestro*
Bartolomeo di Ser Antonio di Baldino del Troscia *albergatore*

VIII

BALÌA OF 1471

(Balìe, 31, fols. 9ʳ–12ᵛ)¹

Signoria

Niccolò di Schiatta di Uberto Ridolfi
Bono di Niccolò di Lodovico di Bono Rinucci

Giovanni di Salvatore di Tommaso del Caccia
Paolo di Michele di Giovanni Riccialbani

Antonio di Taddeo Ambrogi *pezzaio*
Ardito di Ardito di Francesco Arditi *ferraiolo*

Duti di Antonio di Ser Tommaso Masi
Tommaso di Antonio di Tommaso di Guccio Martini

Piero di Niccolò di Tommaso Malegonnelle (Gonfalonier of Justice)

Accoppiatori

Recco di Uguccione di Mico Capponi
Lorenzo di Lapo di Giovanni Niccolini
Giovanni di Paolo di M. Paolo Rucellai
M. Agnolo di Lorenzo di Andrea di M. Ugo della Stufa
Antonio di Bernardo di Miniato di Dino *coreggiaio*

The first 40 members

S. SPIRITO

Zanobi di Sandro di Giovanni Biliotti
M. Giovanni di Antonio di Jacopo Canigiani
Bernardo di Tommaso di Bartolomeo Corbinelli
Jacopo di Piero di M. Luigi Guicciardini
M. Luigi di Piero di M. Luigi Guicciardini
M. Luca di Bonaccorso di Neri Pitti
M. Antonio di M. Lorenzo di Antonio Ridolfi
M. Tommaso di Lorenzo di M. Tommaso Soderini

Artigiani

Michele di Corso di Lorenzo [di Covero] delle Colombe *oliandolo*
Bernardo del Nero di Filippo del Nero *rigattiere*

¹ The names of the *Collegi* are not included in the list.

S. CROCE

Giovanni di Taddeo di Giovanni dell'Antella
Mariotto di Lorenzo di Marco Benvenuti
Jacopo di Niccolò di Cocco Donati
Ruberto di Francesco di Biagio Lioni
Piero di Francesco di Duccio Mellini
Girolamo di Matteo di Morello Morelli
Franco di Nicol di Franco Sacchetti
Giovanni di Antonio di Salvestro Serristori

Artigiani

Cherubino di Francesco Galluzzi *biadaiolo*
Antonio di Pero di Dino Peri *galigaio*

S. MARIA NOVELLA

Domenico di Giovanni di Domenico Bartoli
Lionardo di Bartolomeo di Lionardo Bartolini
Piero di Berardo di Bonaccorso Berardi
Tommaso di Piero di Nicolaio Davanzati
M. Bongianni di Bongianni di Giovanni Gianfigliazzi
Antonio di Lionardo di Antonio de' Nobili
Cipriano di Chimenti di Cipriano Sernigi
Niccolò di Francesco di M. Simone Tornabuoni

Artigiani

Ser Niccolò di Michele di Feo Dini *galigaio*
Lenzone di Antonio di Lenzone Lenzoni *galigaio*

S. GIOVANNI

M. Bernardo di M. Giovanni Bongirolami *dottore*
Andrea di Cresci di Lorenzo di Cresci
Giovanni di Antonio di Filippo Lorini
Ugolino di Niccolò di Ugolino Martelli
Lorenzo di Piero di Cosimo de' Medici
Pierfrancesco di Lorenzo di Giovanni de' Medici
Matteo di Marco di Antonio Palmieri
Antonio di Taddeo di Filippo di Taddeo

Artigiani

Romolo di Andrea di Nofri Romoli *maestro*
Bartolomeo di Ser Antonio di Baldino del Troscia *albergatore*

Arroti

S. SPIRITO

Piero di Francesco di Piero Alamanni
Alberto di Antonio di Nicola di Lippo Alberti
Francesco di Lorenzo di Giovanni Amadori
Tommaso di Bernardo di Tommaso Antinori
Pegolotto di Bernardo di Pegolotto Balducci
Piero di Giovanni di Jacopo Bini
M. Domenico di Baldassare di Bernardo Bonsi
Giovanni di Raffaello di Bernardo Bonsi
Gino di Neri di Gino Capponi
Niccolò di Giovanni di Mico Capponi
Mattio di Filippo di Giovanni Ciari
Bartolomeo di Niccolò di Bartolomeo Corbinelli
Giuliano di Francesco di Bonaccorso Corsellini
Bertoldo di Gherardo di M. Filippo Corsini
Falcone di Nicola di Lapo Falconi
Antonio di Lionardo di Francesco Ferrucci
Tommaso di Francesco di Tommaso Giovanni
Lorenzo di Bartolomeo di Lorenzo Gualterotti
Jacopo di Orsino di Lanfredino Lanfredini
Mariotto di Dinozzo di Stefano Lippi
Gianpaolo di Paolo di Ridolfo Lotti
Paolo di Giovanni di Lorenzo Machiavelli
Antonio di Tuccio di Marabottino Manetti
Piero di Lutozo di Jacopo Nasi
Tanai di Francesco di Filippo de' Nerli
Antonio del Nero di Filippo del Nero
Antonio di Bernardo di Antonio Paganelli
Bernardo di Francesco di Bernardo Paganelli
M. Giovannozzo di Francesco Pitti
Luigi di Giovanni di Ligi Quaratesi
Giovanni di M. Lorenzo di Antonio Ridolfi
Jacopo di Paolo di Bartolo di Schiatta Ridolfi
Tommaso di Luigi di M. Lorenzo Ridolfi
Ulivieri di Domenico di Francesco Sapiti
Lorenzo di Francesco di Giovanni Segni
Piero di Giorgio di Piero di Alessandro Serragli
Ubaldo di Antonio di Ubaldo di Fetto Ubertini
Piero di Andrea di Michele Velluti
Amerigo di Niccolò di Amerigo da Verrazzano
Agnolo di Neri di M. Andrea Vettori

Artigiani

Giovanni di Biagio di Agnolo *bicchieraio*
Simone di Antonio di Simone Benozzi *vinattiere*
Francesco di Aringo di Corso *calzolaio*
Bernardo di Antonio di Fantone di Naldo Fantoni *vinattiere*
Lorenzo di Jacopo di Benincasa Mannucci *rigattiere*
Piero di Giovanni di Piero di Bartolomeo [Pieri] *scodellaio*
Rosso di Piero di Antonio del Rosso *fornaciaio*
Sasso di Antonio di Martino di Sasso *chiavaiolo*
Soldo di Antonio di Andrea del Soldato *chiavaiolo*
Torrigiano di Antonio di Biagio Torrigiani *vinattiere*

S. CROCE

Benedetto di Francesco di Giannozzo degli Alberti
Lodovico di Taddeo di Giovanni dell'Antella
Francesco di Rinieri di Bardo Bagnesi
Marco di Agnolo di Cionaccio Baroncelli
Pandolfo di Benvenuto di Niccolò di Marco Benvenuti
Benedetto di Niccolò di Giorgio di Betto Berlinghieri
Berlinghieri di Francesco di Francesco Berlinghieri
Zanobi di Riccardo di Zanobi Borgognoni
Giovanni di Tommaso di Francesco Busini
Galeotto di Michele di Salvatore del Caccia
Giovanni di Nofri di Giovanni del Caccia
Donato di M. Carlo Cavallereschi
Pierantonio di Nofri di Salvestro Cennini
Scolaio di Tommaso di Scolaio Ciacchi
Francesco di Piero di Giovanni Dini
Francesco di Niccolò di Cocco Donati
Bartolomeo di Gherardo di Bartolomeo Gherardi
Orlando di Bartolomeo di Gherardo Gherardi
Zanobi di Paolo di Zanobi da Ghiacceto
Filippo di Antonio di Filippo Giugni
Niccolò di Andrea di Niccolò Giugni
Gherardo di Andrea di Lapo Guardi
Niccolò di Domenico di Niccolò Magaldi
Morello di Paolo di Morello Morelli
Francesco di Piero di Salvestro Nardi
Paolo di Lapo di Giovanni Niccolini
Francesco di Antonio di Tommaso Nori
Giovanni di Simone di Mariotto Orlandini
Chirico di Giovanni di Franceschino Pepi
Giovanni di Latino di Primerano dei Pilli
Gualterotto di Jacopo Riccialbani

Alamanno di Filippo di Cino Rinuccini
Nicol di Andreuolo di Nicol Sacchetti
Salvetto di M. Tommaso Salvetti
Giovanni di Alamanno di M. Jacopo Salviati
Lotto di Giovanni di M. Forese Salviati
Niccolò di Antonio di Salvestro Serristori
Bernardo di Bonaccorso di Niccolò Soldani
Bartolomeo di Lodovico di Cece da Verrazzano
Simone di Amerigo di Bartolo Zati

Artigiani

Francesco di Michele Becchi *fibbiaio*
Zanobi di Jacopo di Benintendi Falemagini *oliandolo*
Giovanni di Betto di Giovanni [Betti] *vinattiere*
Coppo di Guido Cafferelli *coreggiaio*
Benedetto di Ser Francesco Guardi *coreggiaio*
Neri di Antonio di Segna Guidi *corazzaio*
Guido di Ser Giovanni di Guido Guiducci *oliandolo*
Agnolo di Francesco di Lorenzo [Miniati] *coreggiaio*
Luca di Lorenzo di Luca Salvucci *coreggiaio*
Bartolomeo di Jacopo di Jacopo del Zaccaria *coltriciaio*

S. MARIA NOVELLA

Donato di Neri di M. Donato Acciaiuoli
Nofri di Zanobi di Michele Acciaiuoli
Attaviano di Oddo di Vieri Altoviti
Piero di Giovanni di Guglielmo di Bardo Altoviti
Piero di Carlo di Tommaso Bartoli
Zanobi di Zanobi di Lionardo Bartolini
Piero di Domenico di Lionardo Boninsegni
Nero di Stefano di Alessandro del Nero Cambi
Andrea di Niccolò di Andrea Carducci
Carlo di Niccolò di Andrea Carducci
Lorenzo di Agnolo di Bartolomeo Carducci
Giovanni di Cante di Giovanni Compagni
Lorenzo di Piero di Nicolaio Davanzati
Francesco di M. Carlo di Francesco Federighi
Tommaso di Giovanni di Ser Luca Franceschi
Benedetto di Piero di Bencivenni Grazzini
Ricciardo di Tommaso di Simone Guiducci
Tommaso di Simone di Francesco Guiducci
Benedetto di Benedetto Lapaccini [del Toso]
Bartolomeo di Niccolò di Jacopo Malegonnelle
Bernardo di Domenico di Jacopo Mazzinghi
Piero di Giovanni di Andrea Minerbetti

Antonio di Lorenzo di M. Andrea da Montebuoni
Antonio di Michele di Benedetto Pescioni
Cesare di Domenico di Tano Petrucci
Salvestro di Giovanni di Salvestro Popoleschi
Bernardo di Piero di Cardinale Rucellai
Mariotto di Piero di Brancazio Rucellai
Betto di Giovanni di Betto Rustichi
Francesco di Tommaso Sassetti
Francesco di Piero di Bencivenni dello Scarfa
Manno di Signorino di Manno Signorini
Antonio di Giovanni di Antonio Spini
Agnolo di M. Palla di M. Palla Strozzi
Filippo di Francesco di M. Simone Tornabuoni
Giovanfrancesco di Filippo di Filippo Tornabuoni
Jacopo di Francesco di Jacopo Ventura
M. Guidantonio di Giovanni Vespucci *dottore*
M. Piero di Giuliano di Lapo Vespucci
Bartolomeo di Antonio di Jacopo del Vigna

Artigiani

Antonio di Guasparre di Giovanni di Jacopo dal Borgo *coreggiaio*
Francesco di Paolo di Francesco Canacci *maestro*
Bartolomeo di Brancazio di Michele di Feo Dini *galigaio*
Sandro di Antonio di Domenico Lenzi *corazzaio*
Nofri di Antonio Lenzoni *galigaio*
Zanobi di Giovanni del Maestro Luca *galigaio*
Piero di Jacopo Neretti *linaiolo*
Paolo di Pasquino di Francesco Pasquini *ferraiolo*
Niccolò di Cenni di Vanni *ferraiolo*
Guasparre di Simone di Michele dalla Volta *ferraiolo*

S. GIOVANNI

Jacopo di Antonio di Tedice degli Albizzi
Maso di Luca di M. Maso degli Albizzi
Giovanni di Aldobrandino di Giorgio di Aldobrandino del Nero
  di Madonna
Antonio di M. Alessandro di Ugo degli Alessandri
Domenico di Neri di Domenico Bartolini Scodellari
Francesco di Niccolò di Francesco Cambini
Filippo di Giovanni di Filippo di Barone Cappelli
Antonio di Paolo di Berto Carnesecchi
Francesco di Berto di Zanobi Carnesecchi
Agnolo di Pigello Cavicciuli
Niccolò di Matteo di Niccolò Cerretani

Jacopo di Bernardo di Jacopo Ciai
Francesco di Gentile di Ghino Cortigiani
Paolo di Francesco di Paolo Falconieri
Alessandro di Antonio di Luca di Manetto da Filicaia
Francesco di Piero di Francesco Ginori
Gino di Giuliano di Francesco Ginori
Francesco di Antonio di Francesco Giraldi
Antonio di Migliore di Tommaso Guidotti
Tommaso di Giovanni di Tommaso Lapi
M. Domenico di Niccolò di Ugolino Martelli
Niccolò di Antonio di Ser Tommaso Masi
Alamanno di Bernardo di Alamanno de' Medici
Averardo di Bernardo di Antonio di Giovenco de' Medici
Carlo di Nicola di M. Vieri de' Medici
Giovanni di M. Bartolomeo di Giovanni Orlandini
Domenico di M. Carlo di Agnolo Pandolfini
Frosino di Andrea di Frosino da Panzano
Guglielmo di Antonio di M. Andrea de' Pazzi
M. Jacopo di M. Andrea de' Pazzi
Antonio di Puccio di Antonio Pucci
Antonio di Matteo di Gucciozzo de' Ricci
Girolamo di Gentile di Michele Ristori
Mancino di Ruberto del Mancino Sostegni
Andrea di Lotteringo di Andrea di M. Ugo della Stufa
Giovenco di Lorenzo di Andrea di M. Ugo della Stufa
Francesco di M. Guglielmino di Francesco Tanaglia
Bartolo di Piero di Maffeo Tedaldi
Bartolomeo di Filippo di Bartolomeo Valori
Giovanni di Jacopo di Giovanni Villani

Artigiani

Giovanni di Francesco di Ser Andrea *corazzaio*
Benci di Niccolò di Paolo Benci *vinattiere*
Giuliano di Ser Bonaccorso di Piero di Bonaccorso *corazzaio*
Zanobi di Jacopo di Niccolò Bucherelli *linaiolo*
Francesco di Michele di Jacopo Cittadini *corazzaio*
Domenico di Zanobi del Giocondo *bottaio*
Zanobi di Ser Jacopo di Bonaiuto Landi *cassettaio*
Giovanni di Andrea di Lodovico Lapini *beccaio*
Mazzeo di Giovanni di Ser Lapo Mazzei *corazzaio*
Jacopo di Salvestro di Lionardo di Puccio *vinattiere*

IX

BALÌA OF 1480

(Balìe, 31, fols. 92ᵛ–95ᵛ)[1]

Signoria

Ridolfo di Pagnozzo Ridolfi
Lionardo di Stoldo di Lionardo Frescobaldi

Ruberto di Francesco di Biagio Lioni[2]
Lorenzo di Mariotto di Lorenzo Benvenuti

Antonio di Guasparre di Giovanni dal Borgo [*coreggiaio*]
Giovanni di Francesco di Jacopo Neretti [*linaiolo*]

Piero di Lorenzo di Filippo Cappelli
Tommaso di Bartolomeo di Ser Benedetto Fortini

Bernardo di Pazzino di Luca Alberti (Gonfalonier of Justice)

The first 30 members

S. SPIRITO

Niccolò di Giovanni di Mico Capponi
Bernardo di Tommaso di Bartolomeo Corbinelli
Jacopo di Piero di M. Luigi Guicciardini
M. Luigi di Piero di M. Luigi Guicciardini
Bernardo del Nero di Filippo del Nero
M. Antonio di M. Lorenzo di Antonio Ridolfi
Tommaso di Luigi di M. Lorenzo Ridolfi
M. Tommaso di Lorenzo di M. Tommaso Soderini

Artigiano
Michele di Corso di Lorenzo [di Covero] delle Colombe

S. CROCE

Giovanni di Taddeo di Giovanni dell'Antella
Ruberto di Francesco di Biagio Lioni
Piero di Francesco di Duccio Mellini
Girolamo di Matteo Morelli
Giovanni di Antonio di Salvestro Serristori

---

[1] The names of the *Collegi* are not included in the list.
[2] Also one of the first 30 members.

Artigiano

Antonio di Bernardo di Miniato di Dino

S. MARIA NOVELLA

Tommaso di Piero di Nicolaio Davanzati
M. Bongianni di Bongianni Gianfigliazzi
Piero di Niccolò di Tommaso Malegonnelle
M. Piero di Giovanni di Andrea Minerbetti
Filippo di Francesco di M. Simone Tornabuoni

Artigiano

Ser Niccolò di Michele di Feo Dini

S. GIOVANNI

M. Bernardo di M. Giovanni Bongirolami
Andrea di Cresci di Lorenzo di Cresci
Giovanni di Antonio di Filippo Lorini
Ugolino di Niccolò di Ugolino Martelli
Lorenzo di Piero di Cosimo de' Medici
Domenico di M. Carlo Pandolfini
Antonio di Puccio di Antonio Pucci
M. Agnolo di Lorenzo di M. Ugo della Stufa
Antonio di Taddeo di Filippo di Taddeo

Arroti

S. SPIRITO

Luigi di Francesco Alamanni
Piero di Francesco di Piero Alamanni
Francesco di Lorenzo di Giovanni Amadori
Francesco di Antonio di Tommaso Antinori
Tommaso di Bernardo di Tommaso Antinori
Francesco di Antonio di Giovanni Benci
Carlo di Lionardo di Piero del Benino
Piero di Niccolò di Andrea del Benino
Zanobi di Sandro di Giovanni Biliotti
Piero di Giovanni di Jacopo di Piero Bini
M. Domenico di Baldassare di Bernardo Bonsi
Giovanni di Raffaello di Bernardo Bonsi
Antonio di M. Giovanni di Antonio Canigiani
Gino di Neri di Gino Capponi
Recco di Uguccione di Mico Capponi
Mattio di Filippo Ciari
Ruggieri di Niccolò di Bartolomeo Corbinelli
Giuliano di Francesco di Bonaccorso Corsellini

Bertoldo di Gherardo di M. Filippo Corsini
Piero di Bertoldo di Gherardo Corsini
M. Tommaso di Guido Deti
Piero di Bartolomeo Gualterotti
Oddo di Niccolò di Piero Guicciardini
Antonio di Francesco Guidetti
Jacopo di Orsino Lanfredini
Paolo di Giovanni di Lorenzo Machiavelli
Bernardo di M. Giannozzo Manetti
Lorenzo di Lutozo [di Jacopo] Nasi
Piero di Lutozo di Jacopo Nasi
Tanai di Francesco di Filippo de' Nerli
Nerozzo di Piero di Filippo del Nero
Antonio di Bernardo di Antonio Paganelli
Bonaccorso di M. Luca Pitti
Bernardo di Inghilese di Schiatta Ridolfi
Lorenzo di Bernardo di M. Lorenzo Ridolfi
Paolantonio di M. Tommaso di Lorenzo Soderini
Ubaldo di Antonio di Ubaldo di Fetto Ubertini
Niccolò di Giorgio di Niccolò di Luca Ugolini
Agnolo di Neri di M. Andrea Vettori
Piero di Francesco di Paolo Vettori

Artigiani

Francesco di Baldo di Nofri di Baldo
Simone di Antonio di Simone Benozzi
Francesco di Cino di Luca di Cino
Giovanni di Giuliano di Agostino di Como
Stefano di Niccolò Corsellini
Francesco di Aringo di Corso
Antonio di Paolo di Antonio Parigi
Piero di Giovanni di Piero [di Bartolomeo] Pieri
Rosso di Piero di Antonio del Rosso
Antonio di Sasso di Antonio di Martino di Sasso
Torrigiano di Antonio di Biagio Torrigiani

S. CROCE

Benedetto di Francesco di Giannozzo degli Alberti
Piero di Daniello di Piero degli Alberti
Giovanni di Agnolo di Cionaccio Baroncelli
Berlinghieri di Francesco Berlinghieri
Giovanni di Tommaso di Domenico Borghini
Zanobi di Riccardo di Zanobi Borgognoni
Antonio di Francesco di Tommaso Busini

Galeotto di Michele di Salvatore del Caccia
Giovanni di Nofri di Giovanni del Caccia
Giovanni di Niccolò di Giovanni Cavalcanti
Antonio di Tommaso di Scolaio Ciacchi
Jacopo di Bernardo di Jacopo Ciacchi
Francesco di Piero di Giovanni Dini
Niccolò di M. Donato di Niccolò di Cocco [Donati]
Francesco di Gherardo di Bartolomeo Gherardi
Francesco di Orlando di Bartolomeo Gherardi
Carlo di Zanobi di Paolo da Ghiacceto
Zanobi di Paolo di Zanobi da Ghiacceto
Francesco di Zanobi di Bernardo Girolami
Filippo di Antonio di Filippo Giugni
Niccolò di Andrea di Niccolò Giugni
Giuliano di Lionardo Gondi
Gherardo di Andrea di Lapo Guardi
Bernardo di Giovanni di Lionardo Jacopi
Lionardo di Niccolò Magaldi
Lotto di Duccino di Lotto Mancini
Giovanni di Jacopo di Giovanni Morelli
Tommaso di Paolo Morelli
Francesco di Piero di Salvestro Nardi
M. Agnolo di M. Otto di Lapo Niccolini
Lapo di Lorenzo di Lapo Niccolini
Giovanni di Simone di Mariotto Orlandini
Paolo di Michele di Giovanni Riccialbani
Alamanno di Filippo di Cino Rinuccini
Nicol di Andreuolo di Nicol Sacchetti
Salvetto di M. Tommaso Salvetti
Averardo di Alamanno di M. Jacopo Salviati
Lotto di Giovanni di M. Forese Salviati
Averardo di Antonio di Salvestro Serristori
Ristoro di Antonio di Salvestro Serristori[1]
Bernardo di Bonaccorso di Niccolò Soldani
Cristofano di Bartolomeo di Bonsignore Spinelli
Simone di Amerigo Zati

Artigiani
Orsino di Niccolò di Benintendi Falemagini
Giovanni di Betto di Giovanni Betti
Miniato di Bernardo di Miniato di Dino
Cherubino di Francesco di Bernardo Galluzzi
Benedetto di Ser Francesco Guardi
Guido di Ser Giovanni di Guido Guiducci

---

[1] MS.: Ristoro di Salvestro di Antonio Serristori. Tratte, 336 *corr.*

Agnolo di Francesco di Lorenzo Miniati
Francesco di Ser Giovanni di Dino Peri
Alessandro di Piero del Rosso Pieri
Luca di Lorenzo di Luca Salvucci
Bartolomeo di Jacopo del Zaccaria

S. MARIA NOVELLA

Guglielmo di Bardo di Guglielmo Altoviti
Cosimo di Matteo di Marco Bartoli
Domenico di Giovanni Bartoli
Bernardo di Lionardo di Bartolomeo Bartolini
Piero di Berardo di Bonaccorso Berardi
Simone di Gagliardo di Carlo Bonciani
Piero di Domenico di Lionardo Boninsegni
Ruberto di Domenico di Lionardo Boninsegni
Nero di Stefano Cambi
Lorenzo di Agnolo di Bartolomeo Carducci
Cante di Giovanni di Cante Compagni
Lorenzo di Piero di Nicolaio Davanzati
Francesco di M. Carlo di Francesco Federighi
Giovanni di Paolo di Jacopo Federighi
Tommaso di Giovanni di Ser Luca Franceschi
Piero di Giannozzo di Stoldo Gianfigliazzi
Francesco di Andrea di Guido Giuntini
Tommaso di Simone Guiducci
Francesco di Zanobi di Luigi Lapaccini [del Toso]
Lorenzo di Anfrione di Lorenzo Lenzi
M. Antonio di Piero di Niccolò Malegonnelle
Jacopo di Ugolino di Jacopo Mazzinghi
Ruggieri di Tommaso di Andrea Minerbetti
Antonio di Lorenzo di M. Andrea da Montebuoni
Antonio di Lionardo di Antonio de' Nobili
Cesare di Domenico di Tano Petrucci
Bartolomeo di Niccolò di Piero Popoleschi
Bernardo di Piero di Cardinale Rucellai
Mariotto di Piero di Brancazio Rucellai
Betto di Giovanni di Betto Rustichi
Benedetto di Antonio di M. Francesco Salutati
Francesco di Tommaso Sassetti
Cipriano di Chimenti di Cipriano Sernigi
Piero di Antonio Signorini
Giovanni di Guccio di Andrea da Sommaia
Antonio di Giovanni di Antonio Spini
Strozza di M. Marcello Strozzi

Piero di Tommaso di Giacomino [di Goggio Tebalducci]
Francesco di M. Manno di Giovanni Temperani
Gianfrancesco di Filippo di Filippo Tornabuoni
Jacopo di Francesco di Jacopo Ventura
M. Guidantonio di Giovanni di Simone Vespucci
Bernardo di Alessandro di Antonio del Vigna

Artigiani

Giovanni di Simone di Ser Simone Berti
Piero di Brunetto di Domenico Brunetti
Paolo di Francesco di Paolo Canacci
Simone di Mattio di Pier Cini
Bartolomeo di Brancazio di Michele di Feo Dini
Ghino di Cristofano di Azzino Ghinucci
Nofri di Antonio Lenzoni
Zanobi di Giovanni del Maestro Luca
Giovanni di Stagio di Lionardo di Nicola
Strinato di Francesco di Tommaso dello Strinato
Guasparre di Simone di Michele dalla Volta

S. GIOVANNI

Maso di Luca di M. Maso degli Albizzi
Piero di Lucantonio di Niccolò degli Albizzi
Giovanni di Aldobrandino di Giorgio di Madonna [Aldobrandini
   del Nero]
Jacopo di M. Alessandro di Ugo degli Alessandri
Maso di Nicolaio di Ugo degli Alessandri
Zanobi di Niccolò di Zanobi Bonvanni
Carlo di M. Antonio Borromei
Francesco di Niccolò di Francesco Cambini
Filippo di Giovanni di Filippo Cappelli
Andrea di Bernardo di Cristofano Carnesecchi
Paolo di Simone Carnesecchi
Paolo di Niccolò di Matteo Cerretani
Jacopo di Bernardo di Jacopo Ciai
Paolo di Francesco di Paolo Falconieri
Alessandro di Antonio di Luca da Filicaia
Francesco di Piero Ginori
Francesco di Antonio di Francesco Giraldi
Ser Giovanni di Ser Bartolomeo Guidi
Migliore di Antonio di Migliore Guidotti
Piero di Salvestro di Michele Lapi
Tommaso di Giovanni Lapi
Antonio di Giovanni di Antonio Lorini

Niccolò di Antonio di Niccolò Martelli
Duti di Antonio di Ser Tommaso Masi
Attilio di Nicola di M. Vieri de' Medici
Averardo di Bernardo di Antonio de' Medici
Lorenzo di Pierfrancesco di Lorenzo de' Medici
Piero di M. Orlando de' Medici
Pierfilippo di M. Giannozzo Pandolfini
Frosino di Andrea di Frosino [da Panzano] *lanaiolo*
Alessandro di Piero di Bartolomeo Pecori
Dionigi di Puccio di Antonio Pucci
Francesco di Giovanni di Antonio Pucci
Michele di Antonio di Michele da Rabatta
Geri di Maso di Geri della Rena
M. Bartolomeo di Giovanni Scala
Giovenco di Lorenzo di Andrea della Stufa
Gismondo di M. Agnolo di Lorenzo della Stufa
Francesco di Filippo di Bartolomeo Valori

Artigiani

Giovanni di Francesco di Ser Andrea
Girolamo di Benci di Niccolò Benci
Lorenzo di Niccolò Benintendi
Francesco di Michele di Jacopo Cittadini
Lorenzo di Domenico di Lorenzo [di Francesco]
Zanobi di Ser Jacopo di Bonaiuto Landi
Gherardo di Giovanni di Bartolomeo Marucelli
Mazzeo di Giovanni di Ser Lapo Mazzei
Biagio di Lorenzo di Niccolò Monti
Jacopo di Salvestro di Lionardo di Puccio
Niccolò di Giovanni di Sandro di Ser Ricovero
Francesco di Andrea di Nofri Romoli

COUNCIL OF SEVENTY OF 1480

(Balìe, 31, fols. 92ᵛ, 100ᵛ–101ʳ)

The first 30 members

(see above, pp. 309–10)

The 40 members

S. SPIRITO

Piero di Niccolò di Andrea del Benino
Zanobi di Sandro di Giovanni Biliotti
Giovanni di Raffaello di Bernardo Bonsi
Gino di Neri di Gino Capponi
Bertoldo di Gherardo di M. Filippo Corsini
Jacopo di Orsino Lanfredini
Piero di Lutozo di Jacopo Nasi
Bonaccorso di M. Luca di Bonaccorso Pitti
Agnolo di Neri di M. Andrea Vettori

Artigiano

Piero di Giovanni di Piero [di Bartolomeo] Pieri

S. CROCE

Berlinghieri di Francesco Berlinghieri
Francesco di Piero Dini
Orlando di Bartolomeo Gherardi
Niccolò di Andrea di Niccolò Giugni
Lapo di Lorenzo di Lapo Niccolini
Giovanni di Simone di Mariotto Orlandini
Nicol di Andreuolo Sacchetti
Averardo di Alamanno di M. Jacopo Salviati
Ristoro di Antonio di Salvestro Serristori
Cristofano di Bartolomeo di Bonsignore Spinelli

Artigiani

Cherubino di Francesco di Bernardo Galluzzi
Agnolo di Francesco di Lorenzo Miniati

S. MARIA NOVELLA

Domenico di Giovanni di Domenico Bartoli
Piero di Berardo di Bonaccorso Berardi

Lorenzo di Agnolo di Bartolomeo Carducci
Francesco di M. Carlo di Francesco Federighi
Antonio di Lionardo di Antonio de' Nobili
Giovanni di Paolo di M. Paolo Rucellai
Cipriano di Chimenti di Cipriano Sernigi

Artigiani

Carlo di Giovanni di Salvestro Carradori
Nofri di Antonio Lenzoni

S. GIOVANNI

Maso di Luca di M. Maso degli Albizzi
Giovanni di Aldobrandino di Giorgio [di Aldobrandino] del
  Nero di Madonna
Jacopo di M. Alessandro di Ugo degli Alessandri
Francesco di Piero Ginori
Duti di Antonio di Ser Tommaso Masi
Pierfilippo di M. Giannozzo Pandolfini
Francesco di Filippo di Bartolomeo Valori

Artigiani

Giovanni di Francesco di Ser Andrea ⟨Puccini⟩
Francesco di Michele di Jacopo Cittadini

PIERO GUICCIARDINI ON THE SCRUTINY
OF 1484

(Bibl. Naz., XXV. 636, fols. 7^r–12^r)

[fol. 7^r] Ricordo come addì 30 di novembre 1484 et a hore XVII si
cominciò a squittinare el priorato per gl'infrascripti cittadini, e quali
furno eletti d'ottobre credo passato pe' Settanta, ma con ordine in modo
non furno se none quegli erono disegnati per chi governa, chè per
quanto ritrassi di buon luogo, la prima bozza fu fatta da Lorenzo et Ser
Giovanni soli. L'ordine del vincere fu ch'e primi che andorono a partito rimasono, et non credo che ne scattasi uno.

Gli uomini sono questi etc. et la Signoria et e Collegi.

L'ordine dello squittinare el priorato fu questo, che prima si trassono
e gonfaloni a sorte quali dovevano andare prima a partito, che fu el
primo Lione rosso, et l'ultimo fu el Nicchio. Et prima andavano a partito
e veduti, cominciando da quegli del cerchio, che era la prima borsa;
dipoi la 2^a borsa de' beneficiati, cioè quegli che havevano el padre, o'l zio,
o 'l fratello, o l'avolo veduti dal 34 in qua; dipoi la 3^a de' non veduti.
Et finita la Magiore, si faceva el medesimo della Minore. Vero è che gli
Accoppiatori, che furno questi etc., fecieno che de' non veduti non
andassi a partito più che 75 della Magiore et 25 della Minore per gonfalone, et non havessino meno d'anni 20, excepto quegli che havessino
la boce di qualchuno de' Signori o degli Accoppiatori, che ne potevono
dare 2 per ciascheduno in ogni gonfalone.

Andorno prima a partito, come di sopra è detto, e veduti dal 34 in
qua, et nel numero de' veduti per la Magiore andorno a partito e veduti
nella Minore che volevono andare per la Magiore, chè ne ferno di questo
el partito gli Accoppiatori, benchè non sia ragionevole che uno che sia
veduto per la Minore vadi a partito per la Magiore come gli altri veduti;
et è una delle cose fatte in questo squittino in favore de' nuovi.

Andorno dipoi e beneficiati dal 34 in qua, et quelli che nella Minore
havevono el beneficio et vollono andare per la Magiore andorno come
gli altri beneficiati sanza farne alcuna distintione pel medesimo partito.

Gli ultimi furno e non veduti, come di sopra è detto.

[fol. 7^v] In questo partito del priorato è ito a partito circa a cinque-
cento per gonfalone, raguagliando l'uno per l'altro, de' quali il quinto
incirca sono quegli della Minore, et degli altri 4/5 che vanno per la
Magiore circa a dua terzi sono di case antiche popolane, et usi avere il
regimento dal 1434 indrietro, et di famiglie. L'altro terzo è di gente

nuova, et dal quel tempo in qua. In modo che io credo che di tutto il numero che è ito a partito pel priorato, ne sia più che la metà huomini di buone case, che hanno meno favore, perchè quel terzo di gente più nuova che vanno per la Magiore hanno in favore tutti gli artefici, che sono il quarto, di poi tutti quegli de la Magiore simili a loro, et buona parte degli altri, o per parentado, o per amicitia, o per conto di stato. Gli altri dua terzi della Magiore huomini di buone case hanno meno favore, o per essere di famiglia, o per essere gran numero in una casa, come Altoviti etc., chè di 120 che di loro ne va a partito, non credo ne rimanga nel priorato il quarto, o per essere sospecti allo stato, come Strozzi et simili; ma la maxima è perchè nel numero degli squittinanti n'è meno che la metà di simili case, chè non sono tanti che bastino a fargli vincere. La qual cosa procede dagli omini grandi, che tirono su gente nuova et spaccino e vecchi, perchè meglio si vagliono di simili, et non n'anno paura di loro come degli uomini dabene. Procede ancora da questi notai et ministri di palagio, che sempre favorischono e simili a loro et mostrono a' grandi che tal cosa si fa per loro. Et a questo modo si guasta la civilità.

Sarebbe meglio che la Magiore squittinassi la Magiore et la Minore la Minore, perchè squittinando insieme ne segue che la Magiore si guasta, perchè la Minore sempre caccia gente adosso ala Magiore, et la Minore si guasta perchè la Magiore fa il simile a la Minore, parendo a molti della Magiore che non tocchi a loro tirare nella Minore gente nuova che non la intendono. Ma questo modo dello squittinare insieme credo sia suto trovato in favore de' nuovi, benchè non sia trovato nuovo.

[fol. 8^r] Nondimeno per quanto ho potuto per hora ritrarre, in questo partito del priorato n'a vinto più della terza borsa, cioè di famiglie, come Giovanni de' Bardi, et di case del 34, come Strozzi et simili, che non hanno vinto in niuno altro squittino dal 34 in qua. Et questo credo in parte sia proceduto da Lorenzo, che n'a favoriti qualcuno et ha voluto dare questo beneficio del priorato a qualcuna di queste case, parendogli non ci sia pericolo alcuno di loro, tenendosi le borse a mano, et che sia da fargli più volentieri paganti; et credo che Lorenzo realmente sia amico degli uomini dabene, il che a me è piaciuto, giudicando sia bene aiutare gli uomini dabene, et che il ritirare qualcuno di quegli del 34 sia el modo a dissolvere quello homore; perchè se mille anni si tenessi adrieto una casa, mille anni sarebbe nimica dello stato; et ho veduto che di quegli che nel 66 furno per essere confinati, essendo suti poi carezzati dallo stato, sono stati de' fedelissimi; et così stimo interverrebbe di questi del 34, se col tempo et per ogni squittino se ne dimesticassi qualcuno.

Questo ritirare huomini dabene rimasti indrieto non piace a questi nuovi venuti nel reggimento dal 34 in qua, ne alla maggior parte degli artefici, di che non credo ne sia altra cagione, se none che naturalmente

non sono amici degli uomini dabene, parendo loro che 'l tenere bassi
gli uomini dabene sia la via a inalzare loro. Et che questo sia vero lo
dimostra che simil gente nuova fanno peggio alle famiglie et a quegli
che nel 34 perderno lo stato, che non fanno e popolani antichi che si
trovorno a spacciare le famiglie, et dipoi a spacciare quegli del 34.
Oltra di questo lo dimostra che simil gente nuova non chiama popolani
se non simili a loro et qualche spicciolatello, et noi altri veri popolani
spacciano per famiglie, et tutto quello favore che danno hora alle case
dabene che hanno el reggimento in mano fanno per paura.

[fol. 8ᵛ] Finì el partito del Priorato adì 18 di dicembre, che se n'è
fatto uno gonfalone el dì, cioè la sera e veduti et beneficiati della Magiore,
et poi la mattina el resto, acciò che e non veduti andassino a partito di dì,
che serviva loro assai, perchè si vedevono le fave l'uno a l'altro, chè la
magior parte l'a date scoperte in questo partito.

Addì 18 di dicenbre si cominciò a squittinare el Capitano et Podestà
di Pisa, che va in uno partito medesimo, et fassi di chi vince dua polize per
uno. Et perchè questo partito è d'importanzia grande, parendo a Lorenzo
che fussi bene non lo vincessino se none gli uomini usi al reggimento et
usi havere simil dignità, et oltra questo buoni, di che non si può se
none grandemente commendare, ordinò una intelligentia di circa a 100
persone del numero degli squittinanti, e quali fieno scripti dappiè, a'
quali fece dire dessino favore agli uomini dabene et che lo meritavano,
et agli altri stringessino el capo; et acciò che tale intelligentia fussi segreta,
ordinò che la sera medesima si ragunassino in più luoghi, come 8 in casa
Piero Corsini et 8 in casa Ruggieri Corbinelli etc.; et che questi la sera
facessino le parole a quel numero che in casa loro si ragunassi; et oltra
a dire loro che se alcuno lo dicessi a altri che di questo numero, mostre-
rebbe d'averlo per male, fece ancora dar loro il giuramento, chè insino
a hora è ito segreto, e così credo andrà. Et fece dire a tutti come egli
aveva scoperta una intelligentia di circa a 50 che era in effetto di favorire
l'uno l'altro, della quale n'era capo Francesco d'Orlando Grardi, Piero
Cappelli, Giuliano Salviati et Niccolò d'Antonio Martelli; et questo
credo facessi per scoprirla e dissolverla, usando di loro male parole, chè
si vede gli dispiacque assai come cosa triste et non a proposito a lo stato
suo che simile intelligentie si facessino sanza sua saputa. Et credo ch'egli
avessi qualche voglia di segnarne qualcuno che lo poteva fare giuridi-
camente, perchè havevono fatto contro al bando s'era mandato nel
principio dello squittino per parte degli Otto, che non si facessi ragunata
niuna di squittinanti, nè andassino a cena insieme più di sei squittinanti,
acciò che tali intelligentie non si facessino; [fol. 9ʳ] nella quale intelligentia Lorenzo non misse niuno di quegli 4 capi sopradetti, anzi fece dire
a buona parte gli sonassino, et maxime Francesco Grardi et Piero
Capelli; etiam dimostranza ve n'è in sulla torna che di Giuliano Salviati
et Niccolò Martelli non fece dire nulla come o meno incolpati, o persone

da essere riguardati. Non vi messe ancora niuno de' Pucci, nè Messer Puccio, nè Dionigi, chè si vede vuole tirare gli orechi a Dionigi, et la cagione non so; neanche niuno de' Martelli, nè Filippo Valori, nè molti altri de' quali credo ne metterà poi in un'altra intelligentia fata a qualche suo proposito, et lascerà di quegli ha messa in questa, come tutto dì si fa. Questa intelligentia credo si trovassi a compilare Lorenzo et Ser Giovanni, che hora fa il tutto, et forse ancora Gismondo della Stufa et Piero Corsini, che ancora loro in questo squittino hanno corso la cavallina, et Piero Filippo et Antonio di Bernardo.

Et perchè questa intelligentia non si scoprissi, rendendo le fave coperte loro et non gli altri, et ancora perchè questa medicina sola non era abastante a tenere questo partito del Capitano di Pisa stretto, et che non si favorisse se none gli uomini dabene, come di sopra è detto, ordinò che la mattina si cominciò a squittinare questo partito inanzi si cominciassino a rendere le fave, che il Gonfaloniere parlò monstrando di quanta importanza era questo partito, et confortassi a rendere le fave coperte, et nolle chiedere l'uno a l'altro, et dare favore a chi lo meritava; et chi altrimenti facessi, gli sarebbe dimostro l'errore suo. Et fece dare a ciascheduno el giuramento in su el libro de' vangeli che darebbono le fave coperte, che nolle chiederebbono l'uno a l'altro, et che e non renderebbono fave nere a quegli che sapessino che negli altri uficii si fussino portati male; le quali tre cose non potrebbono essere più utile a volere bene squittinare. Et acciò che questo ordine non paressi a la brigata fussi nato da Lorenzo, s'era ordinato destramente con fra Mariano predicatore, che predicando el dì dinanzi in palagio entrassi nello squittino et ricordassi alla Signoria ch'egli era male lasciare rendere le fave scoperte et chiederle l'uno a l'altro, come s'era fatto nel priorato, etc.

El modo dello squittinare questo partito fu che si trassono e gonfaloni a sorte, et gli Accoppiatori il dì dinanzi ferno che e Gonfalonieri non potessino mandare a partito se none il terzo de' veduti di ciaschuno gonfalone, e quali havessino anni ventiquattro o più; et ferno che non si dessi boce a niuno, se none a uno che fu Lorenzo di Pierfrancesco de' Medici.

[fol. 9ᵛ] Questo modo di mandare el terzo de' veduti di ciascheduno gonfalone, benchè non si sia usato per gli altri squittini, chè ne solevano mandare tanti equalmente per gonfalone, nondimeno è molto più giusto et miglior modo, perchè non è ragionevole che in uno gonfalone piccolo ne vadi tanti a partito quanti in un grande, et mandandone il terzo o la metà de' veduti, ciascheduno gonfalone ha la rata sua.

Cominciossi, come deto è disopra, adì 18 a squittinare questo partito del Capitano di Pisa, et ogni dì se n'è fatti quattro gonfaloni, dua per mattina et dua per sera; et per quanto ho potuto ritrarre, questo partito è ito stretto et non ha vinto se none huomini di qualità; et la cagione principale è suta l'avere inteso la volontà di Lorenzo, et oltra di questo il rendere le fave coperte et non le chiedere l'uno a l'altro.

Finito questo partito del Capitano di Pisa, si cominciò adì 22 di deto a squittinare il partito de' quattordici ufici, benchè oggi sieno 18, come disotto si vedrà, di che sene fa tante borse come disotto si dice. Del quale partito gli Accopiatori ordinorno che si traessino gonfaloni, et che ciascheduno Gonfaloniere mandassi a partito la metà de' veduti del suo gonfalone, e quali havessino anni venti o più, et ferno che Signori et Accopiatori potessino dare dua boci per uno a chi paressi loro. Dipoi facendone romore e Collegi, agiunsono che ancora e Collegi ne potessino dare dua per uno, ma solamente a' veduti. Ma per quanto ho potuto ritrarre, chi hebbe le boce ne fecie poco frutto, perchè oltre a l'essere fanciulli quegli che hebbono le boce et d'età da non potere sapere che pruova habbino a fare, credo dessi ancora loro disfavore el non potere dare boce quegli del cerchio alle cose loro.

Andò a partito dua gonfaloni per volta si ragunavono, et squittinossi questo partito con la medesima severità di rendere le fave coperte et di nolle chieder eche nel partito disopra; et per quanto ho potuto ritrarre, è ito stretto, et molti che nel 1471 vinsono questo partito, hora noll'anno raffermo; perchè quanto hora la cosa è ita stretta, et bene, tanto andò allora larga, et male. Perchè è minor male il non dare queste dignità [fol. 10ʳ] a chi le merita che darle acchi non le merita, perchè ogni volta si può dare a chi le merita; ma ritorle acchi nollo merita, havendogliene una volta date, non si può sanza scandalo.

Agl'uomini nuovi, et quegli che sanza bucherare e per l'ordinario non si rinchuorono d'obtenere questo partito, non è piaciuto il dare le fave coperte, et nolle potere chiedere; et benchè nollo dicessino, si vedeva havevono per male quando el Gonfaloniere, faccendosi punto di romore, si rizzava et ricordava lo stare cheti, et osservare el giuramento. Et hieri, essendo ito già a partito la metà de' gonfaloni, et dicendosi per qualcuno in mentre che uno andava a partito: 'questo è uno huomo dabene, mio parente', et simile parole, el Gonfaloniere si rizzò et disse che questo era uno chiedere le fave, et che alla Signoria non piaceva che il giuramento per verso alcuno non s'osservassi; in modo che ognuno si racchetò. Le quali parole dispiacquono assai a' simili detti di sopra. Et invero secondo el mio giuditio el dare le fave coperte dà noia agli uomini nuovi et ancora a' troppo nobili, che hanno bisogno di far forza per ottenere, et la ragione è questa. Nel numero degli squittinanti, et così in Firenze, sono cinque sorte d'huomini, dua extreme et opposite l'una a l'altra, et tre medie; delle quali sono dua più simile agl'estremi et una nel mezzo. La prima sono gli uomini di famiglie come Bardi et Rossi etc.; l'ultima, che è l'opposita, sono gl'ignobili che nell'arte minori hanno vinto el consolato, et ancora quella parte degli artefici più infima che è veduta del priorato. Sopra costoro sono gli artefici più nobili, et quegli della Maggiore che di nuovo hanno vinto el priorato per la Magiore, come Particini, Romoli, Salvetti et simili, e quali, benchè sieno nel mezzo, nondimeno sono propinqui a quello infimo extremo, perchè di poco ne sono usciti et sono loro simili. L'altro mezzo appresso all'estremo nobile sono e popolani antichi nobili come Albizi, Peruzzi, Corsini, Ricci, Alberti et simili. Nel mezzo di questi dua mezzi sono certe case, le quali, benchè non sieno ancora nobile, nondimeno non sono al tutto ignobile, et le quali, benchè di fresco, nondimeno hanno havute tutte le dignità, come Serristori, Lioni, Taddei, Berardi et simile.

[fol. 10ᵛ] Di tutte queste sorti quegli del mezzo come Serristori etc. hanno negli squittini più favore che gli altri, perchè da tutti sono più favoriti; et così nello stato sono più adoperati.

Apresso a costoro hanno favore quegli del mezzo propinqui al-l'extremo nobile, come Corsini, Soderini, Albizi etc., cioè quelle case popolane antiche che hanno el reggimento. L'altre, come Peruzzi, Strozzi et Ricci et simile, sono tractate come di famiglia, perchè dagli uomini vili non sono riguardate per conto del reggimento et dagli uomini da-bene grandi dello stato sono tenute adrietro.

El medesimo favore o poco meno hanno quegli del mezzo propinquo all'extremo ignobile, come Particini, Bonvanni et simili, perchè da tutta la Minore sono favoriti et da qualcuno de' grandi, o per parentado o per conto di stato o per amicitia, in modo che dal vincere el Capitano di Pisa in fuora, vincono tutti gli altri partiti; et quello qualcuno di loro ancora vince. Et in effeto costoro vengono su et fannosi nobili col mezzo dello stato, et in poco tempo vincono ogni cosa.

Restono e dua extremi, de' quali el nobile, cioè di famiglia, da parecchi case in fuora che hanno pure un poco di reggimento, come Tornabuoni, Nerli, et qualcuno altro, tutti gli altri, come Bardi, Rossi, Manelli etc., non vincono nulla; et se pure qualcuno vince el priorato, non va più su, nè per questo dà principio alla casa. L'altro extremo ignobile, benchè ancora lui non vinca se none qualcuno el priorato, o al più el Mazzocchio, nondimeno tutta via si fa inanzi, in modo che chi a questo squittino acquista el priorato, a un altro acquisterà qualche migliore partito, secondo la qualità sua, o le ricchezze, et in poco tempo faccendosi col mezzo de l'arte et della 'ndustria et con poca gravezza ricchi, escono di questo extremo ignobile et vanno a quello più su sempre sagliendo, et nel luogo loro succede gente più nuova et riempiono quello extremo ignobile, et così continovamente viene su gente nuova, onde è necessario, che mettendosi nel reggimento tutta via de' nuovi, a rincontro se ne cacci de' vecchi; et così si fa.

[fol. 11ʳ] Finito el partito de' 14 uficii, che finì adì 29 di dicenbre 1484, si cominciò a squittinare el partito degli otto uficii, che sono X, et cominciossi a squittinare alla Signoria entrata di nuovo, che n'era Gon-faloniere Averardo de' Medici; et cominciossi dico el primo dì doppo desinare di gennaio 1484, et addì 8 di detto fu finito decto partito, inanzi ch'e Gonfalonieri nuovi entrassono in uficio, che fra gli altri ne fu io.

El modo a squittinare questo partito fu che tracti a sorte e gonfaloni, gli Accoppiatori ordinorno che ciascheduno Gonfalonier mandassi a partito la metà de' veduti del suo gonfalone che havessino anni XVIII o più, et ferno che il Gonfaloniere et gli Accoppiatori potessino dare tre boci per uno, et Signori et Collegi dua, et gli altri del cerchio una per uno, a chi paressi loro, o di minore età, o non veduti.

Questo partito degli otto si squittina dinanzi agli undici uficii, non perchè gli undici non sieno di maggior importanza, perchè è poca differentia dal partito de' XIIII a quello degli XI, ma per dar parte alla Minore che hanno el quarto della maggior parte degli uficii di questo partito, benchè d'alcuni vanno insieme colla Maggiore a sorte, come el Camarlingo del Monte et Cassiere di Camera. Nella qual cosa la Minore ha gran vantaggio dalla Maggiore in quelli uficii che la Minore ha el quarto; perchè io non credo che l'ottavo degli artefici vinchino questo partito degli otto all'avenante di quelli che della Maggiore lo vincono; cioè che se 80 della Maggiore lo vincono, non credo che X della Minore lo vinchino; et la ragione è questa, perchè gli artefici prima non sono il sexto di quelli che vanno a partito in questo partito degli otto; la seconda perchè molto ne sono più stretti di noi, et per esser questo partito degli otto el primo lor partito, e perchè naturalmente sono più stretti di noi.

Squittinossi questo partito degli otto con manco severità ch'e passati, perchè si cominciò per molti a chiedere le fave et scoprirle, parendo a molti esser liberi dal giuramento, essendo entrata la Signoria nuova. Ma la cagione principale fu perchè gli uomini nuovi al reggimento havevono per male che le fave si dessino coperte, parendo loro che il dare le fave coperte non voglia dire altro se none che si squittini stretto, come credo sia il vero. [fol. 11ᵛ] Il che gli Accoppiatori lasciorno seguire, o per ottenere qualche loro spetialtà più facilmente, o per non havere carico col popolo che hanno per male che gli squittini vadino stretti. Il medesimo fece ancora il Gonfaloniere che, da una volta o dua in fuora, non volle mai parlare nè confortargli a rendere le fave coperte, benchè qualche volta gli fussi ricordato dagli Accopiatori, secondo che poi ho ritratto, parendo forse loro che in qualcuno la cosa andassi troppo largha. Ma la ragione vorrebbe et l'utile publico che si squittinassi colle fave coperte et cheti, acciò che ciascheduno fusse libero di sè, et non andassi preso dalle voglie et grida di chi gli è allato.

Bucherossi assai in questo partito nella Maggiore et per le case prime et use al reggimento, et ancora per molti nuovi al reggimento ignobili et troppo nobili et di quelli che rimasono adrietro nel 34. Ma sopra tutto si bucherò assai per gli artefici.

Bucherorno gli Accoppiatori et Ser Giovanni in questo partito, et ancora nel passato de' XIIII, et per le cose loro et per alcuna altra loro spetialtà, chè ve n'era qualcuna non molto ragionevole, come Antonio di Bernardo per 4 sua figliuoli che di nuovo mette nella Maggiore, et Ser Giovanni per figliuli sua et per il fratello et nipoti, chè in vero non mi pare si convengha che chi è al segreto bucheri sì scopertamente, et maxime per le cose sua proprie; et maxime e notai come Ser Giovanni che in questo squittino ha havute più spetialtà che tutto il resto, et più credo n'abbi optenute, perchè mi pare habbi governato tutto a suo modo, et tutti e modi dello squittinare sono usciti et suti trovati da llui.

Andò in questo partito degli otto et prima de' XIIII per la Maggior parechi de' figliuli della Minore, cioè e figliuli di Antonio di Bernardo che ne mandò prima ne' XIIII dua, e poi in questo 4, che credo optenessino, poichè tanti ne mandava. Andòvi de' Pieri, Romoli, Lenzoni et uno figliuolo di Corso delle Colombe, et alcuni altri.

[fol. 12ʳ] Addì 9 di gennaio 1484 si cominciò a squittinare el partito degli undici uficii, che sono hora XII, et l'ordine fu che tratti e gonfaloni a sorte, gli Accopiatori ordinorono che ciaschuno Gonfaloniere mandassi a partito tutti e veduti del suo gonfalone, et oltra questo detono al Gonfaloniere et loro cinque boce per uno, a' Signori [e] Collegi 4, e agli altri del cerchio dua per uno a chi paressi loro o veduti o non veduti o minori.

Questo partito è di grande importanza, et è poco differente dal partito de' XIIII, perchè sono uficii di fuora et di simile importanza; nondimeno credo andassi più largo che il partito passato degli otto uficii, che porta assai meno; et la cagione fu perchè e più cominciorno a rendere le fave e darle scoperte; et cominciossi a gridare et levare il romore quasi come al priorato. Sparsesi ancora certe boce d'alcuni dello squittino, come di Zanobi Frasca et Guido Guiducci, che non rendevono se non fave bianche a ognuno, et maxime agli uomini dabene; la qual cosa si sparse per tutta la terra, et fu buona parte ragione perchè molti, per non esser tenuti male, fave [*sic*] rendessino le fave scoperte, e dessinle nere a molti contra la voglia loro.

Oltra questo fu ragione che questo partito fussi più largo el mandare tanti fanciulli et nuovi a partito per l'assai boce che s'erono date, chè fu gonfalone che ne mandò a partito 250 et più. Il che mi pare sia al tutto contrario a volere che si squittini bene, chè non si vorrebbe andassino a partito se none d'età fussino cognosciuti, e che e non veduti non andassino alla mescolata co' veduti, benchè forse questo non nuoce agl'uomini di buone case che non sono veduti.

Sarebbe più ragionevole che come nel priorato e veduti vanno prima, dipoi e beneficiati et ultimo e non veduti, così in ciascuno partito di questi che portono più andassino a partito prima et di per se e veduti di tal partito, dipoi e benificiati, cioè figluoli o al più fratelli de' veduti di tal partito, et ultimo e non veduti; et se queste distintione si facessino et non si mandassi e fanciulli a partito, ma persone che passassino anni 20, si farebbe meno errori et in meno tempo assai si finirebbe uno squittino.

INDEX